FOUNDATIONS
of BUSINESS
ANALYTICS

FOUNDATIONS *of* BUSINESS ANALYTICS

An Applied Approach

YULIA KOSARENKO

CS BUSINESS PRESS

Toronto | Vancouver

Foundations of Business Analytics: An Applied Approach
Yulia Kosarenko

First published in 2025 by
CS Business Press, an imprint of CSP Books Inc.
180 Bloor Street West, Suite 1401
Toronto, Ontario
M5S 2V6

www.csbusinesspress.ca

EU Authorized Representative: Mare Nostrum Group B.V., Mauritskade 21D, 1091 GC Amsterdam, The Netherlands, gpsr@mare-nostrum.co.uk.

Library and Archives Canada Cataloguing in Publication

Title: Foundations of business analytics : an applied approach / Yulia Kosarenko.
Names: Kosarenko, Yulia, author.
Description: Includes bibliographical references and index.
Identifiers: Canadiana (print) 20250128888 | Canadiana (ebook) 20250128942 |
     ISBN 9781773384795 (softcover) | ISBN 9781773384818 (EPUB) |
     ISBN 9781773384801 (PDF)
Subjects: LCSH: Industrial management—Decision making—Textbooks. |
     LCSH: Quantitative research—Textbooks. | LCGFT: Textbooks.
Classification: LCC HD30.23 .K67 2025 | DDC 658.4/03—dc23

Cover design by Troy Cunningham
Page layout by S4Carlisle Publishing Services

25   26   27   28   29   5   4   3   2   1

Printed and bound in Ontario, Canada

We acknowledge the support of the Government of Canada.
Nous reconnaissons l'appui du gouvernement du Canada. | Canadä

Dedication

To Roman, my tireless critic and supporter: you always believed in me and made the completion of this project possible. And to my family for making the world so much more interesting and worth writing about.

Brief Table of Contents

Detailed Table of Contents

Preface

As I taught dozens of cohorts in a postgraduate business analytics program, I observed a pattern in how people approach business analytics: we all want to make use of magic without learning the science behind the magic.

Students want to start writing sophisticated machine learning algorithms before understanding how to prepare the data. Analysts are itching to create impressive visualizations, forgetting to analyze their datasets for bias. Managers want access to dashboards loaded with charts and tables—while still making most of their decisions on gut feel. Companies spend millions on big data projects, sometimes not even attempting to first benefit from their smaller, more easily accessible data.

Too many businesspeople think that "data storytelling" is the answer to all their problems. But data does not tell us stories. Data answers our questions—if we know how to ask the right questions and weave the answers into a story.

Statistics, surveys, and news articles show again and again that organizations are often not getting value from their data. Some struggle with data quality, some complain they don't have enough data, and some say that they spend too much money on collecting big data without getting a return on their investment.

In business, as in life, there is no magic bullet. Successful business analytics requires quality data, consistent processes, and enterprise investment in both technology and qualified resources. Most importantly, it requires that everyone involved understands the capabilities and limitations of analytics, what methods work best in different situations, and how to ask smart questions.

This is why this book is dedicated to making businesspeople, as well as aspiring data analysts and business intelligence professionals, comfortable with business analytics as a discipline.

To generate useful insights from data, we must begin with the fundamentals: understanding data, different types of analytics, and methods and tools suitable for different analytical purposes, and how to approach developing analytics solutions.

We need to practice asking analytics questions, which starts with an understanding of business problems and goals.

We must understand the logic behind using analytics insights to support business decisions, as well as factors that may hinder this process.

We should learn to watch out for typical challenges and pitfalls when using various sources of big and small data so that the resulting insights are trustworthy and effective.

The goal of this book is to provide foundational knowledge to those involved in developing and using insights from enterprise data: developers of analytics solutions, business decision-makers, and anyone who analyzes data as part of their job. It is meant to fill the gap between texts that are too simplistic, cheerfully promoting the value of data without providing the reader with sufficient conceptual knowledge, and heavy texts that dive right into statistics and algorithm design without taking the time to build a foundation for learners new to analytics.

As business analytics maturity in many organizations is still emerging, foundational knowledge is essential for both the upskilling of professionals who want to get into the field of analytics and for the managerial cohort who need to gain a better understanding of the value, benefits, and success factors of analytics.

This book will explain:

- The foundational concepts of data, types and sources of data, and the data life cycle
- Types and uses of analytics for solving a variety of business problems
- Stages of the analytics life cycle
- The analytics architecture of an enterprise and classification of analytics solutions
- How analytics solutions are developed and the challenges enterprises face in the process

As we move through the chapters, we will outline the steps required to build analytics solutions that allow businesspeople to harness the power of insights and make better business decisions. You will explore the fundamentals of data management: what is needed to build data pipelines that feed clean and prepared data into analytics solutions and the main principles of building different types of analytics solutions. You will learn to recognize different types of analytics: descriptive, diagnostic, predictive, and prescriptive, and what methods and techniques they require. We will define the analytics life cycle—the sequence of stages in the development of analytics solutions and what activities support each stage. We will also address the main principles of managing analytics projects, key components of data pipelines, and the roles responsible for tasks in the analytics life cycle.

Regardless of what programming languages are used to develop the data transformation programs, or what platforms are used to design and support the analytical models, the principles behind designing better analytics solutions are the same. Once you understand the purpose and the expected outcomes of each phase of the business analytics life cycle, you can utilize the tools available in your company to implement the right solution for the right problem.

The book does not delve deeply into specific statistics, data mining, or predictive modelling methods. It is a visually rich introduction into the field with a focus on practical applications, examples, and case studies, and thus will be complementary to existing texts.

Now dive in, explore, and as you learn new concepts, relate them to your work and life experiences. When you read a news article, consider what insights it provides and what data would have been required to make the conclusions presented therein. When you encounter an interesting metric, imagine how you would calculate it, and how you could use it to make decisions. When you read about failed projects, grossly underestimated numbers, or disappointing performance by artificial intelligence, consider what could have gone wrong, what mistakes might have led to such results, and whether the failure could have been prevented.

Use the ideas you learn from this book to become a sophisticated consumer of analytics, a curious data analyst, or an aspiring data scientist. Any book is just a collection of knowledge, ideas, structures, and visuals that help you learn, think, and ask new questions. The rest is up to you.

How to Use This Book

TERMINOLOGY

The purpose of this book is to introduce the reader to a wide range of concepts and perspectives required to build a successful business analytics practice. Defined terms are highlighted in **bold** throughout the text, with *Tips on Terms* inserts explaining synonyms and frequently confused terms. At the end of each chapter, you will find a recap of key terms and definitions.

As data science and analytics fields continue to develop at a fast pace, the proliferation of terms and synonyms from different sources may be confusing to a newcomer. Wordy and lengthy definitions and the interchangeable use of terms only adds to the confusion. It is critical to get familiar with various terms and their synonyms used in the field. Remember that different organizations and industries may develop preferences for certain terms where synonyms exist. Always confirm the terms and their meaning when working with a particular organization.

METHODS OVERVIEW

The book will mention a variety of analytics methods and algorithms, focusing on their purpose and applications without providing full technical instructions. Refer to the recommended readings and other resources for in-depth studies of the methods.

CASE STUDY

Learning works best when we apply what we learn using practical examples. Throughout this text, we will use a case study to relate new concepts to real-life examples.

The case study is based on a fictional landscaping and snow removal business, YardExperts, which has a presence across most of the provinces and territories in Canada. Landscaping and snow removal services represent the most significant parts of the company's business, with some revenue coming from retail. The company has retail gardening supplies stores in various locations, which also serve as kiosks for signing up for contracts and answering questions about YardExperts' custom services.

As you read about various analytics methods and approaches, consider how YardExperts might use its data to achieve business goals. Think about any challenges this company might have to overcome to make use of analytical insights and what you would propose to do if you worked there.

TABLES AND VISUALS

Each chapter offers a variety of elements for summarizing and illustrating the concepts presented. Comparison tables help to clarify and differentiate related terms. Numerous visuals were designed not only to illustrate the materials but also to highlight the power of visualization when conveying information to an audience. Simplified architecture diagrams in Chapter 8 were created with the goal to make you more comfortable with using architecture models in real organizations. Even if you don't have to create such diagrams, being able to read and interpret them is a valuable competency.

Diagrams presented in the book are not limited to any specific modelling notation. Instead, simple elements like rectangles, circles, and lines are used as much as possible. While different organizations or professional groups may favour a specific notation that you may be required to follow, I encourage you to see the beauty of a simple model as a communication tool and practice it whenever you have an opportunity.

CHECKLISTS AND SAMPLE QUESTIONS

Checklists are practical tools for planning and executing activities. When a task seems overwhelming, and possible avenues to explore too numerous, a checklist can help you stay on track and tackle the job at hand in a logical sequence. This book, particularly the second half, includes multiple checklists to guide you through various tasks of the business analytics life cycle.

Numerous examples of analytics questions are provided to help make your questions more specific. Many of the sample questions contain placeholders that you will substitute with the parameters specific to your scenario; these placeholders are identified by angle brackets, such as in this question: "What is the probability that <observation> belongs to <category>?"

CHAPTER SUMMARY

Each chapter ends with a summary to help the reader validate their understanding of the concepts.

Key Points to Remember reinforce the main takeaways and summarize the ideas presented in each chapter.

Next, you will find a recap of each chapter's *Key Terms* with definitions.

While *Test Your Knowledge* questions, with answers provided at the end of the book, serve as a quick way to validate your understanding, *Questions for Critical Thought* are more open-ended. They encourage the reader to consider the concepts learned in each chapter in various contexts, including the complexities of real organizations. For these questions, there isn't always one precise correct answer. Rather, they may lead to conversations, further explorations, and even debates. In a classroom setting, use these questions to start discussions. As an independent learner, consider how you would answer these questions to explain various aspects of business analytics to someone else. Explaining difficult concepts to others helps us gain a more in-depth understanding of the same in the process.

Each chapter concludes with suggested *Recommended Readings* and resources for further exploration of each topic.

Chapter 1

Understanding Data

It all starts with data: we collect it, sort it, examine it, and make connections and conclusions. This chapter will define different types of data, their characteristics, and their uses. It will highlight:

- The distinction between data, information, and knowledge
- Characteristics of structured data, unstructured data, and semi-structured data
- Types of quantitative and qualitative data
- Properties and usage of big and small data

1.1 DATA, INFORMATION, AND KNOWLEDGE

What do we mean when we say *data*? This concept can have more than one interpretation depending on the perspective.

For a computer programmer, data is information stored in a digital form on electronic devices.

For a scientist, data may mean measurements collected from observing a phenomenon.

For a statistician, data refers to facts and statistics gathered for the purpose of summarization and statistical analysis.

An engineer might define data as outputs recorded using sensing devices, some accurate and some erroneous.

A philosopher might more broadly associate data with things we can reasonably believe to exist.

And a businessperson may use the word *data* to refer loosely to all the information that they believe their company generates and should be using better.

So what do we mean when we refer to data in the context of business analytics?

Such is the nature of human language that sometimes it is easier to define something by comparing it to another concept. For the purposes of this book, we will clarify the definition of *data* in comparison to *information*.

For anyone who works in the field of analytics and data science, these terms are not interchangeable. We can forgive businesspeople for loosely referring to their favourite dashboard as "my trusted data source." After all, the customer is always right.

For analytics professionals, the distinction between data and information is essential. Let's use a story to illustrate it.

⚙️ EXAMPLE

Imagine you are looking for a rental place not too far from your college. There are two comparable places with the same rent nearby; the first place is three kilometres away from the college campus, and the second place is one kilometre away. Which one would you pick?

Assuming that the apartments are identical in size and amenities, is the second place always preferable? Did you hesitate before answering, suspecting a trick?

What if I tell you that the closer apartment is one kilometre away at the top of a steep hill at the end of a gravel road that is closed most of the time in winter due to poor road conditions? You would have to walk uphill and downhill every day, slippery or not.

Or what if the second place is located across a canal, and while the direct distance is one kilometre, the nearest bridge is five kilometres away, and there is no public transportation to the other side?

While I've provided you with some data—two measurements of three kilometres and one kilometre that reflect direct distances from the two places to your target—I did not provide you with enough information to make a decision.

Let's go back to your goal here. When you are choosing an apartment, what do you really want?

A place that is closest when looking at the map? Or a place that will allow you to get to your destination the fastest? Or should it be the fastest and the cheapest if you don't want to pay for taxi rides?

The additional details I've just mentioned—the steep hill, the road conditions, the obstacle in the form of the canal, and the lack of transportation options—provided you with essential context. You need this context in addition to the cold facts, the measurements of the distance between two points.

The context turned data into meaningful information.

Data by itself is not useful by default. It could be erroneous. There could be too much of it or too little. It may be disorganized or classified in a way that is not helpful to the problem you are solving. Relevant data can be mixed up with irrelevant details that create noise and distract you. Data may be confusing or distorted. Using incomplete or fragmented data may be misleading.

To make decisions, it's not enough to have data, or even a lot of data. We have to interpret data using additional knowledge about the context in which the data was collected and captured. When we process data and prepare it for consumption, we transform it into information. Data by itself may not be meaningful, but information must have a meaning.

The juxtaposition of the following two dictionary definitions reflects this point.

Data refers to factual information (such as measurements or statistics) used as a basis for reasoning, discussion, or calculation.[1]

Information refers to the communication or reception of knowledge or intelligence.[2]

As we collect and interpret data, we create information that can be further analyzed. We analyze information to infer something from it, to generalize, to see the patterns, notice the correlations, and discover dependencies. This is the process of generating insights and creating new knowledge.

Insight is the act of seeing something new, unexpected, or previously unknown.

Knowledge is the understanding of the collected information and a potential to apply this understanding in action.

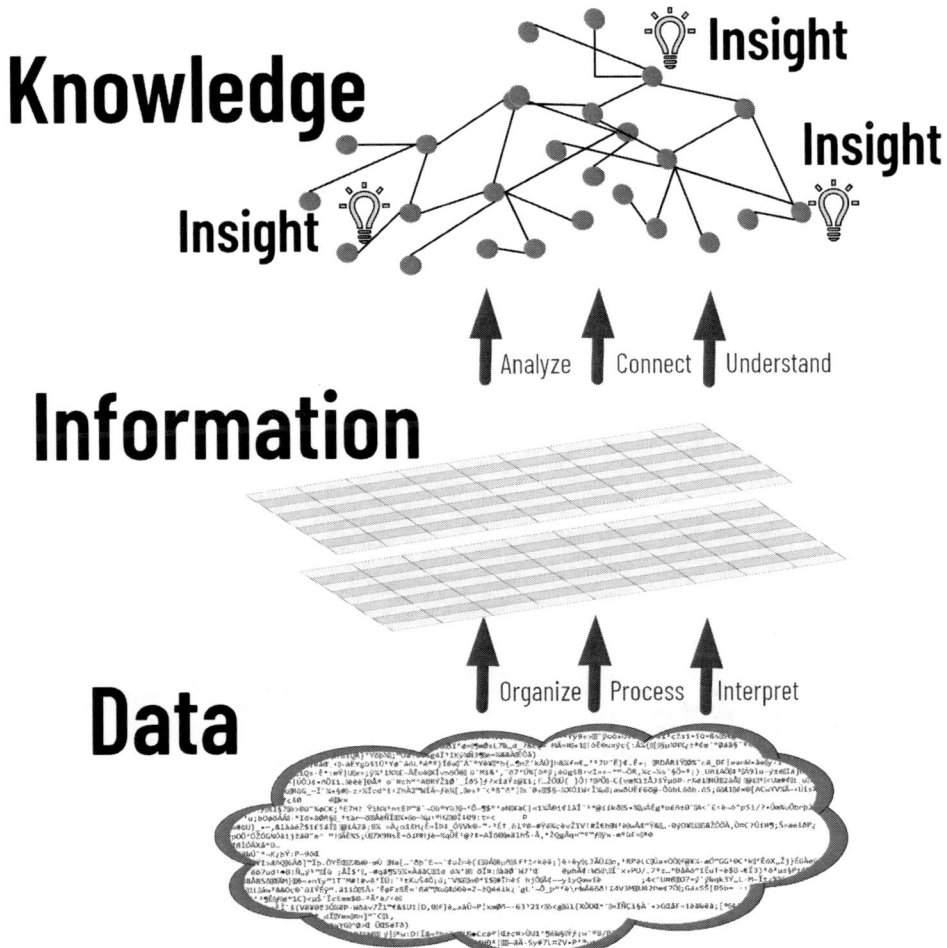

Figure 1.1   Data, Information, and Knowledge

⚙ EXAMPLE

Imagine sending a message via radio transmission. The message must be transmitted as a sequence of signals travelling over the radio waves and captured by the intended recipient. The transmission may not be perfect: some signals might get lost, be received incorrectly, or be affected by atmospheric noise from weather conditions at the time of transmission.

When the radio transmission is received, it may have gaps or inconsistencies. The receiver may infer the missing bits based on the rest of the message. To interpret the meaning of the message, the receiver might rely on what they expected to receive as well as prior communications.

If the radio transmission is data, then the meaning that the receiver infers from the transmission is the information received.

As the message, or the data, is understood by its receiver, data is transformed into information.

Notice how in this example, the receiver's previous knowledge helps them to interpret and better understand the transmission. This is why knowledge of the business domain is one of the pillars of data science: understanding the industry and the business context is important for interpretating data and finding ways to use it effectively.

On the one hand, the interpretation of data helps to build knowledge. On the other hand, we use the knowledge that we already have to make interpretation of data easier. Sometimes, this feedback loop can create problems. If we rely on our current knowledge so much that we start to miss new emerging signals from data, or if we start seeking confirmation for what we already believe to be true, our interpretation of data may become biased.

Bias is a preference for a specific argument or outcome that may not be based on the totality of facts or fair judgment.

We'll discuss bias again in later chapters.

📖 TIPS ON TERMS

Sometimes, the popular buzzword *insight* is used loosely to refer to numbers and statistics. This is what happens with buzzwords—it's tempting to use them frequently. However, anyone who studies business analytics should be more deliberate when using these terms. *Insight* refers to new ideas or knowledge—for example, a relationship, correlation, or dependency that was previously unknown to us and that we discovered through analysis.

"We are selling on average one hundred lawn mowers per month every summer" is not an insight. It's a number that can be calculated from sales data. This sentence implies that this number is stable and not a surprise.

"This summer, we saw a 50% increase of lawn mower sales in suburban markets at-tributed to the new super-quiet model, while rural market sales remained very similar to previous years." This statement describes an analytical finding where the sales volumes were segmented by the type of market to validate whether the new super-quiet model would be preferred by certain customers. This is new piece of knowledge—an insight.

Table 1.1 summarizes the key distinctions between data, information, and know-ledge. The rest of this book will outline different types of data, the data life cycle, how it's interpreted and transformed into useful information, and how businesses can derive useful insights from data through business analytics.

Table 1.1 Comparison of Data, Information, and Knowledge

Data	Information	Knowledge
Objective facts that exist whether we observe them or not; observations without interpretation	Data interpreted within a particular context; created by humans that observe and collect data with a purpose	Insights gained from the analysis of information to understand phenomena, make connections, generalize experience, predict future outcomes, and make decisions
Can be perceived with our senses or measurement instruments	Stored and shared via human-created media (clay, paper, silicon chips)	Captured in the human brain, written artifacts, or electronic format
Exists regardless of whether we ask questions	Answers the questions What? When? Where? and Which?	Answers the questions How? Why? and What If?

CASE STUDY

YardExperts Conducts a Customer Survey

YardExperts decided to conduct a field data collection in early spring to identify poten-tial customers. The company hired students to conduct walkabouts in various neigh-bourhoods and collect information about landscaping needs. The data collection methods will be a combination of observations and resident surveys.

Students were given paper forms with a list of suggested questions and observations. The survey consists of a mix of multiple-choice, checkbox, and free-form questions. The observation part of data collection includes questions about the state of the front yard, trees, and decorative bushes on the property, as well as whether the house has a "For Sale" or "Sold" sign on the lawn. Students were also asked to observe lawn signs that indicate landscaping work done by a competitor and to note the name and contact information of the competitors, as well as any other information that they think may be relevant to determining potential customers. During the survey, students could offer the homeowners leaflets with landscaping services discounts.

Now, imagine receiving the results of this field survey: paper forms completed by hand, with quick notes and comments. This is raw data: captured observations and responses. The forms will vary in quality and completeness.

Some responses may be hard to read, inaccurate, or missing. The free-form text cannot be analyzed as is—someone will have to read and extract relevant points from the comments.

Think of survey results collected on paper as raw data.

To convert this data into organized information, all collected responses will be processed by a team of YardExperts administrators. They will enter the responses in a spreadsheet prepared by a data analyst, Tori. Tori will use her experience to format the spreadsheet and create drop-down lists for various attributes to keep the data consistent. Each administrator will interpret the survey responses to fit them into the spreadsheet.

Sometimes, the responses will not make much sense, and a few surveys get discarded.

Sometimes, Tori's drop-down lists need to be expanded to add new values.

For missing answers, the team was instructed to enter a text value "NA" instead of leaving the field blank.

Responses that contain long comments or requests for services get sent to a sales representative so they can give prospective customers a call.

This is a process of **digitization**: converting raw data into digital format—that is, into information that can be processed and interpreted further.

The result of this digitization effort is a spreadsheet populated with all the survey results. The spreadsheet includes column names to support the interpretation of the content. It includes important housekeeping details such as the survey date, the name of the person who collected the data, and, if available, the name and contact information of the potential customer. Each survey record is given a unique identifier. This spreadsheet contains information: the interpretation of the raw data collected from the survey.

Table 1.2 YardExperts Digitized Survey Results Sample

Survey ID	Date	Conducted by	Street number	Street name	Yard signage	Front yard landscaping	Needs	Wants a quote
101	06/01/24	Sonny T.	15	Main St.	For sale	Lawn, old bushes	NA	No
102	06/01/24	Sonny T.	25	Main St.	NA	Lawn, neglected	Replace lawn	Yes
103	06/03/24	Lydia M.	1310	Clubhouse Dr.	NA	Flower beds	Irrigation	Yes
104	06/04/24	Nigel A.	340	Rose Cres.	NA	Gravel, fountain	NA	No
105	06/04/24	Nigel A.	360	Rose Cres.	Competitor	Rock garden	Thinking	Maybe
106	06/04/24	Nigel A.	363	Rose Cres.	NA	Lawn, Japanese maples	Lawn care	Yes

This information will be further analyzed by Tori and regional sales managers, as the goal of this market research is to identify potential customers. The following insights may emerge:

- Locations that have a strong competitor presence
- Locations with many houses for sale where new owners might be interested in a new landscaping contract
- Specific patterns in survey responses such as strong interest in starting a butterfly garden or a native plants lawn

These insights represent knowledge extracted by analyzing the information collected through market research.

1.2 STRUCTURED, UNSTRUCTURED, AND SEMI-STRUCTURED DATA

Most broadly, data is categorized as structured or unstructured. Here, again, the term *data* has another flavour. When data professionals talk about structured and unstructured data, they refer to datasets—collections of related pieces of data.

A **dataset** is a collection of data points stored and managed together.

Structured data refers to datasets that can be stored in a table format, organized in rows and columns.

As humans we are very familiar with structured data—we collect, manage, and use it daily. It can be stored in human-readable repositories such as lists and matrices. We keep track of our expenses in spreadsheets, fill in forms, and manage our tasks via to-do lists with categories and due dates.

Before computers were invented, humans kept structured records on paper, in accounting books and ledgers, for millennia. These ledgers usually had rows of information representing records or observations, with similar pieces of information captured about each observation. Whether on paper or in electronic format, we tend to structure data into tables, or rectangular datasets.

A **rectangular dataset** is a collection of observations organized in rows of data representing a sequence of each observation's characteristics as columns.

There are numerous synonyms used to refer to the elements of a rectangular dataset. These are presented in Figure 1.2.

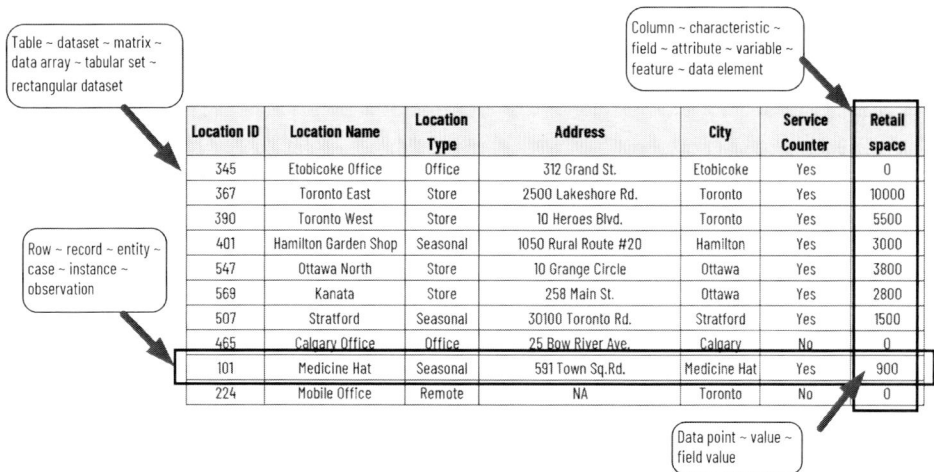

Table ~ dataset ~ matrix ~ data array ~ tabular set ~ rectangular dataset

Column ~ characteristic ~ field ~ attribute ~ variable ~ feature ~ data element

Row ~ record ~ entity ~ case ~ instance ~ observation

Location ID	Location Name	Location Type	Address	City	Service Counter	Retail space
345	Etobicoke Office	Office	312 Grand St.	Etobicoke	Yes	0
367	Toronto East	Store	2500 Lakeshore Rd.	Toronto	Yes	10000
390	Toronto West	Store	10 Heroes Blvd.	Toronto	Yes	5500
401	Hamilton Garden Shop	Seasonal	1050 Rural Route #20	Hamilton	Yes	3000
547	Ottawa North	Store	10 Grange Circle	Ottawa	Yes	3800
569	Kanata	Store	258 Main St.	Ottawa	Yes	2800
507	Stratford	Seasonal	30100 Toronto Rd.	Stratford	Yes	1500
465	Calgary Office	Office	25 Bow River Ave.	Calgary	No	0
101	Medicine Hat	Seasonal	591 Town Sq.Rd.	Medicine Hat	Yes	900
224	Mobile Office	Remote	NA	Toronto	No	0

Data point ~ value ~ field value

Figure 1.2 Elements of a Rectangular Dataset

Structured data is typically stored in rectangular datasets. Consider a file created using a spreadsheet tool. It may contain one or more tabs, each one organized as a table of rows and columns. Each tab may contain records of a different nature, connected to other tabs through relationships between data.

The format of each tab is straightforward—rows and columns. The column format within each tab is consistent. Column names are often included to describe the content of each column. The rows have identifiers to distinguish one observation from another.

Data stored within such datasets can be understood by human users through visual inspection and typically contains numbers, dates, and strings (sequences of characters—snippets of text).

Each tab of a spreadsheet file is an example of a rectangular dataset. Spreadsheet tabs are examples of structured data.

CASE STUDY

Storing Structured Datasets

In this example, a spreadsheet file contains two tabs with records of different nature, each one being a rectangular dataset.

Service code	Service name	Hours	Frequency	Contract type	Price
L1	Lawn mowing	1	Weekly	Yard	100
L2	Lawn seeding	1	On demand	Yard	150
L3	Grub treatment	1.5	Annual	Yard	200
L4	Weed treatment	1	Monthly	Yard	125
S1	Snow removal	2	Weather-based	Snow	200
S2	Snow removal - roof	4	Weather-based	Snow	560

Figure 1.3.a YardExperts Order Tracking Spreadsheet: Services Tab

Order Number	Customer ID	Order date	Location ID	Service	Order total	Status	Comments
123	504895	05/25/2024	569	Lawn mowing	100	In progress	First-time customer
124	456012	05/25/2024	507	Lawn seeding	150	In progress	Large dog
125	465221	05/25/2024	465	Grub treatment	200	In progress	Weekdays only
126	404899	05/26/2024	101	Weed treatment	125	New	New
127	404578	02/02/2024	224	Snow removal	200	Completed	Difficult customer

Figure 1.3.b YardExperts Order Tracking Spreadsheet: Orders Tab

A traditional database is another example of structured data. While it may contain many more tables than a spreadsheet (hundreds or thousands), and some database tables may contain millions of records, they are still highly structured. Each database table has a fixed, well-defined format, with each column of each table conforming to a definition declared when the database was created (called a schema). Most database management tools are designed to store structured data.

A **database** is a collection of related tables of structured data stored in electronic format.

Databases are usually created and managed using specially designed software tools called database management systems.

A **database management system (DBMS)** is software designed to store, retrieve, and manage data in databases (see Appendix B for examples).

Businesses manage a large variety of structured data every day, including:

- Records of business transactions
- Characteristics of people and objects
- Accounting entries

EXAMPLE

Transactions are regular events recorded by businesses. These records consist of well-defined attributes that must be captured for each event—the same details are recorded for each purchase, subscription payment, or contractual agreement. A table containing the attributes of YardExperts orders in the previous figure is an example of transactional data.

Every business must manage data about people, objects, and locations. This data usually includes standard attributes such as names, addresses, and categories. These attributes are standardized to make the management of this important business data easier. Data with well-defined attributes can be stored and managed as structured.

Accounts were probably the first group of data that humans started to track in writing. Nowadays, accounting standards dictate how all financial information must be tracked and what attributes are required, making accounts data structured.

In the next chapter, we discuss different types of structured enterprise data in more detail.

TIPS ON TERMS

Datasets, Tables, Spreadsheets, and Databases

Data is a general concept representing facts, measurements, and statistics, while a *dataset* is a collection of related data values stored and managed together.

A *table* is a rectangular dataset where data values are organized in rows and columns. A *spreadsheet* is a computer application that allows for the storage and management of data as cells in electronic documents formatted as tables. A spreadsheet file may contain multiple tables.

What is the difference between a database and a dataset? A *dataset* usually refers to one or a few tables. Datasets often represent data already selected for a specific purpose—for example, as a result of a query from a database.

A *database* is much larger in scope and detail. Think of a database as a place to keep all records of a software application and a dataset as an extract of data used for a specific purpose such as for analysis.

What about unstructured data? Humans encounter it every day, but we cannot view and interpret it in its raw format. Usually, we see it after it's been translated into something we can comprehend.

For example, digital image data stored in various electronic formats (e.g., JPG, PNG, or TIFF) is unstructured. A human will not be able to view an image file in its raw format and see the picture encoded within. This is where we need imaging software to present it to us as a picture on the computer screen. The software helps us visualize it—that is, it translates the data into a picture our brain understands.

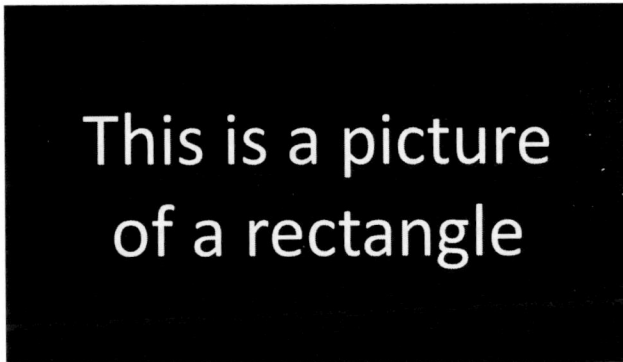

Figure 1.4 Graphic Image as Seen through Imaging Software

This simple image was created using an office productivity tool and stored in a raster-format PNG (Portable Network Graphic). As humans, we can see it as the image above by using software tools such as image viewers or editors. When you click on an electronic image, the computer device you are using does not open it to you in raw format. Your device is likely set up to automatically translate the electronic data into a picture using appropriate software.

However, if you attempt to view the raw data stored in the same PNG file pictured in Figure 1.4, you will see something like Figure 1.5—unstructured data.

Other examples of unstructured data are video and audio files, word processing documents, and website content.

Unstructured data is data in a variable or very complex format that cannot be organized into the traditional structure of rows and columns to reflect observations and their attributes.

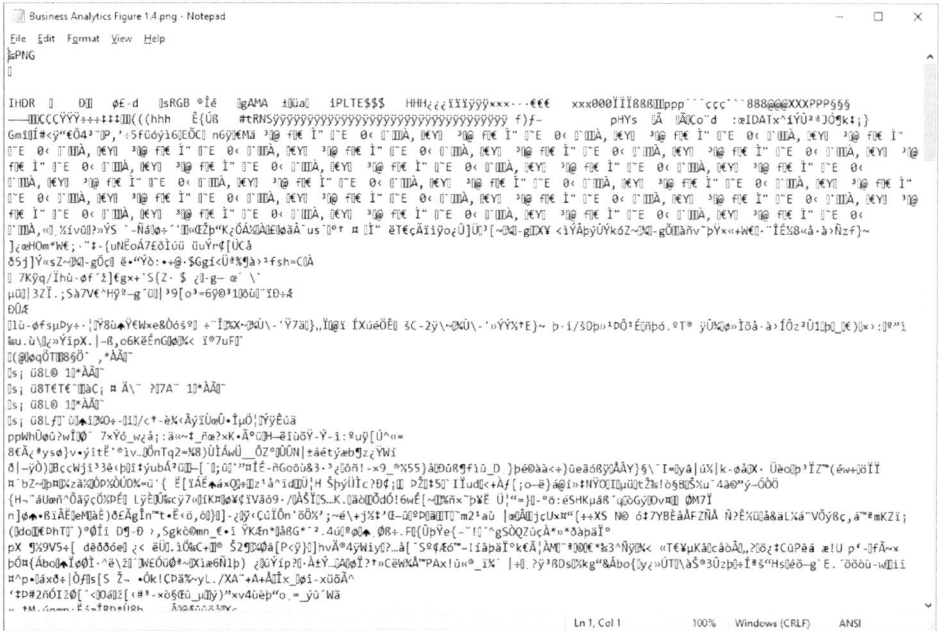

Figure 1.5 Graphic Image in Raw Format as Seen Using a Text Viewer (Segment)

For example, we cannot predictably organize the content of a Microsoft Word or a PDF document into rows and columns. The author of the document can include any number of headings, sections, and subsections, paragraphs of varied length, embedded images, tables, and external links in any random place. Word processing files exemplify unstructured data.

Table 1.3 Comparison of Structured Data and Unstructured Data

Structured data	Unstructured data
Can be stored in table format (rows and columns)	Cannot be stored in table format
Well-defined structure	Lack of structure or very complex structure
Stored in organized lists, spreadsheets, or databases	Stored in data lakes or NoSQL (not only SQL) solutions
Can be managed and processed using Structured Query Language (SQL)	Cannot be processed using SQL; requires machine learning and artificial intelligence tools for processing
Easier to organize and search	Difficult to organize and search with traditional solutions
Requires less storage	Requires more storage
Comprises about 20% of enterprise data (Gartner)	Comprises about 80% of enterprise data (Gartner)
Data from enterprise applications, transaction logs, customer profiles, inventory, accounting records captured as numbers, strings, dates, and categories	Images, video, audio, word processing files, scanned forms, website and social media content and comments, internet of things (IoT) streaming data
Also called traditional, quantitative, transactional	Also called non-traditional, qualitative

Other examples of unstructured data include:

- Imaging data collected by the Hubble Space Telescope
- Browsing history
- Purchasing habits
- Fitness activity
- Vehicular traffic, GPS tracking information
- Social media activity such as views, clicks, likes, shares, location check-ins, hashtags used, duration spent watching videos, time spent on a page
- Patterns of consuming digital media such as music, movies, e-books

When we talk about structured and unstructured data, we refer to datasets: collections of related data. The structuredness of datasets is not binary (yes or no)—it is a spectrum. Depending on the purpose of the dataset and the technology and methods that generated it, the dataset may be comprised of highly structured, less structured, and unstructured data in different proportions.

To accommodate this spectrum, we define **semi-structured data**, referring to datasets made up of both structured and unstructured data. A semi-structured dataset will include segments formatted like the attributes and fields we find in structured datasets, combined with some unstructured data.

A good example of semi-structured dataset is an email message. Email messages are transmitted as packets of data, including structured segments that we call fields or tags, such as the date, time, sender, recipient, subject, and an importance indicator.

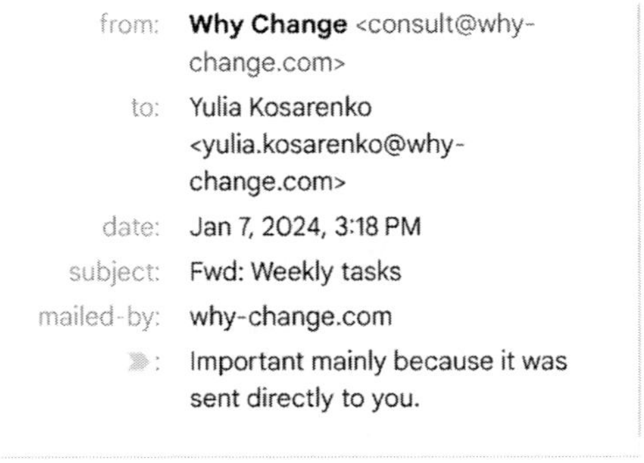

from:	**Why Change** <consult@why-change.com>
to:	Yulia Kosarenko <yulia.kosarenko@why-change.com>
date:	Jan 7, 2024, 3:18 PM
subject:	Fwd: Weekly tasks
mailed-by:	why-change.com
≫ :	Important mainly because it was sent directly to you.

Figure 1.6 Email Tags Example

These fields are attached to the body of the email, which may contain:

- The text of the message, including formatting (bold, italic, different font sizes and colours)
- Special characters, emojis
- Images and videos embedded in the message
- Hyperlinked text or images

- One or more attached files in a multitude of formats
- Additional tags such as the importance or whether a proof of delivery was requested
- Malware, ransomware, or other unexpected hidden data

The combination of all these varied elements in an unpredictable sequence is unstructured data. The combination is a semi-structured packet of the email content accompanied by pre-defined fields such as those shown in Figure 1.6.

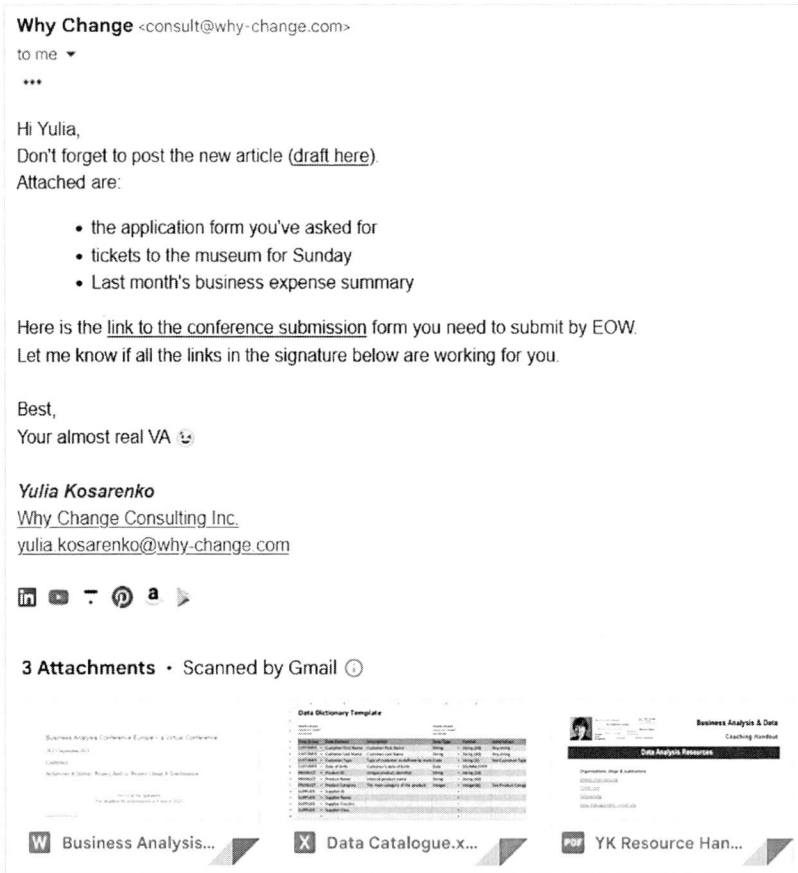

Figure 1.7 Email with Attachments, Emojis, and Embedded Links

Other examples of semi-structured data are:

- Digital photos that store image metadata—additional data about the digital image such as camera model, settings, or location details
- Accessible PDF files that include tags, headings, and other attributes specified by the accessibility requirements
- Files in XML and JSON format (see Recommended Readings to learn more about these formats)

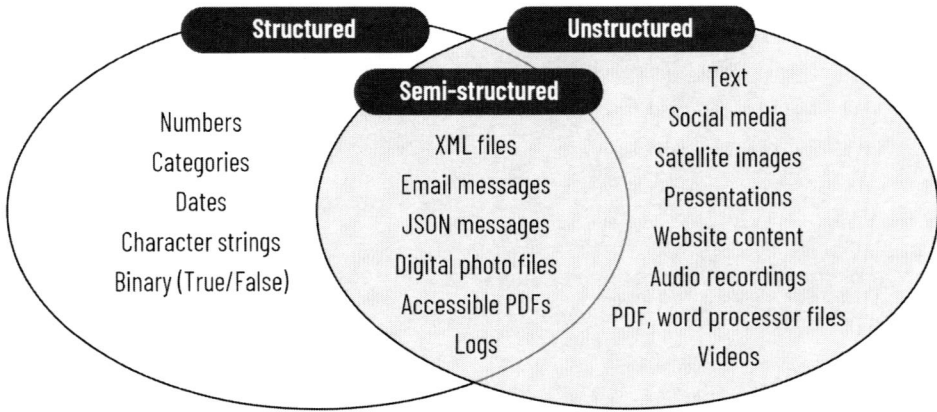

Figure 1.8 Structured, Semi-Structured, and Unstructured Data

1.3 QUANTITATIVE AND QUALITATIVE DATA

Now we will look further into the observations captured in structured datasets. These are characteristics that can be observed and take on different values, referred to as **variables**. For example, the type of property, the size of the lot, and the acidity of soil may be variables of interest for the analysis of the homeowners' landscaping needs conducted by YardExperts.

We can categorize variables based on the level of measurement that can be applied to the observations. The level of measurement determines how the data can be analyzed and what statistics, metrics, and visualizations can be applied to each type of data.

Some observations can be measured or counted using numbers and represent quantitative (numeric) data. Those that cannot be measured or counted are referred to as qualitative data.

Qualitative or categorical data represents observations that cannot be measured but can be described using language or sorted into categories.

When data is sorted into groups (categories), the groups should be mutually exclusive—meaning they should not overlap. The groups are given distinct labels, which in turn become categorical values. All observations that fall into the same category will share the same categorical value.

For example, garden plants can be sorted into categories such as trees, shrubs, perennials, and annuals. Thus, we just created a categorical variable, Garden Plant Category, with four distinct categorical values: Tree, Shrub, Perennial, and Annual.

We can think of category labels as names, hence the term *nominal data*. Nominal data corresponds to the lowest level of measurement where data is named, and the named categories have no inherent order.

Nominal data represents observations that can be sorted into categories without a meaningful order or ranking.

Examples of nominal data include:

- Colours: white, blue, yellow
- Languages: English, French, Spanish, Mandarin
- Provinces: Ontario, Quebec, Nova Scotia, Alberta

A special case of nominal data sorted into two groups is called Boolean (or binary) data: True/False, Yes/No, Pass/Fail, Present/Absent.

Boolean data represents observations sorted into two mutually exclusive categories.

When categories have an inherent, meaningful order, this categorical data becomes ordinal.

Ordinal data represents observations that can be sorted into categories with a meaningful order or ranking.

Examples of ordinal data include:

- Sizes: small, medium, large
- Letter grades: A, B, C, D
- Satisfaction levels: satisfied, somewhat satisfied, neutral, somewhat dissatisfied, very dissatisfied

Quantitative or numerical data represents observations that can be measured and expressed as numbers.

Based on the variable measured, quantitative data can be interval data or ratio data.

Interval data refers to observations that allow the identification of evenly spaced intervals but not a true zero.

Examples of interval data include:

- Dates: while the individual dates are spaced at even intervals, there is no true zero
- pH levels from 0 to 14: on this scale, 0 is not an absence of measure as it corresponds to a certain concentration of hydrogen ions
- Test scores: ranges of values of many scoring systems do not include zero (e.g., the SAT score range is from 400 to 1600)

Ratio data refers to observations where we can identify evenly spaced intervals and a true zero.

True zero in this case means a complete absence of measure.

Examples of ratio data are:

- Counts of objects, e.g., the number of customers
- Weight, height, volume measurements

Ratio metrics such as the number of applicants per job vacancy, customer retention rate, and accidents per million miles driven are other examples of ratio data.

Quantitative data can also be categorized as discrete or continuous, depending on the possible values.

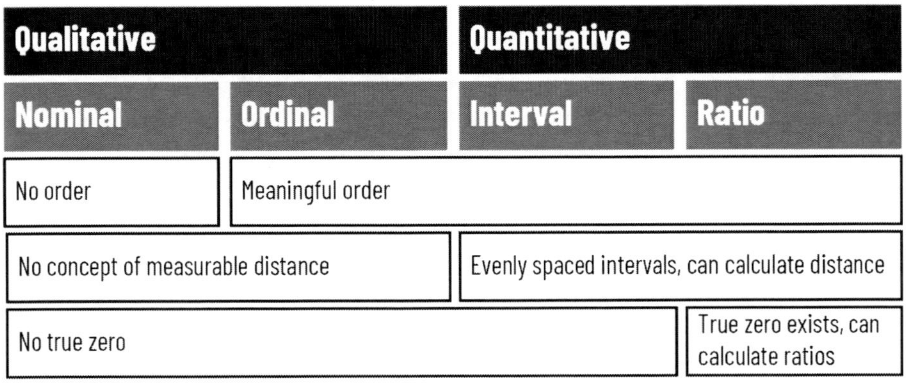

Qualitative		Quantitative	
Nominal	**Ordinal**	**Interval**	**Ratio**
No order	Meaningful order		
No concept of measurable distance		Evenly spaced intervals, can calculate distance	
No true zero			True zero exists, can calculate ratios

Figure 1.9 Levels of Measurement

Discrete data refers to observations that can be counted where possible values are non-divisible and can be listed.

Most frequently, discrete data is presented as whole numbers (e.g., 0, 1, 2, 3), such as when we refer to counts of real-life objects: the number of customers, orders, or complaints.

From a data perspective, a discrete value does not have to be a whole number but must be indivisible. For example, if you agree that certain variables can be expressed as 1.0, 1.5, 2.5, 2.5, 3.0, 3.5, and so on, with a 0.5 interval, this is also discrete data. Each of these values is non-divisible, and there are no values in between those that we can list.

Continuous data captures observations that can be measured on a scale.

Continuous data can be any value within a range of values on a scale. For example, there will be infinite continuous values in any interval. Another term used for this is *analog data*.

Continuous data is used to capture measurements such as length, weight, and volume. It is captured using real numbers: 0.0001, 124.569, −190.00001.

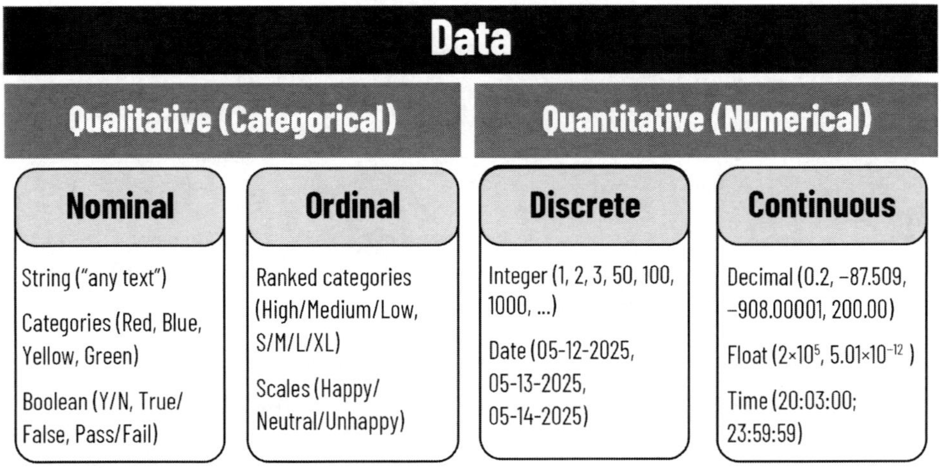

Data			
Qualitative (Categorical)		**Quantitative (Numerical)**	
Nominal	**Ordinal**	**Discrete**	**Continuous**
String ("any text")	Ranked categories (High/Medium/Low, S/M/L/XL)	Integer (1, 2, 3, 50, 100, 1000, ...)	Decimal (0.2, −87.509, −908.00001, 200.00)
Categories (Red, Blue, Yellow, Green)	Scales (Happy/ Neutral/Unhappy)	Date (05-12-2025, 05-13-2025, 05-14-2025)	Float (2×10^5, 5.01×10^{-12})
Boolean (Y/N, True/ False, Pass/Fail)			Time (20:03:00; 23:59:59)

Figure 1.10 Quantitative and Qualitative Data Examples

Both interval and ratio data can be either discrete or continuous. The following figure shows examples.

	Interval	Ratio
Discrete	Year SAT score	Numbers of countable objects
Continuous	Temperature in Celsius or Fahrenheit pH levels	Temperature in Kelvin Length, weight, volume Ratio metrics

Figure 1.11 Interval and Ratio Quantitative Data Examples

The interval versus ratio distinction can depend on the measurement scale used, such as with temperature measurement scales, where only the Kelvin scale has an absolute scientific zero.[3]

A good way to verify your understanding of the data type is by considering what operations are meaningful for this data, as demonstrated in Figure 1.12.

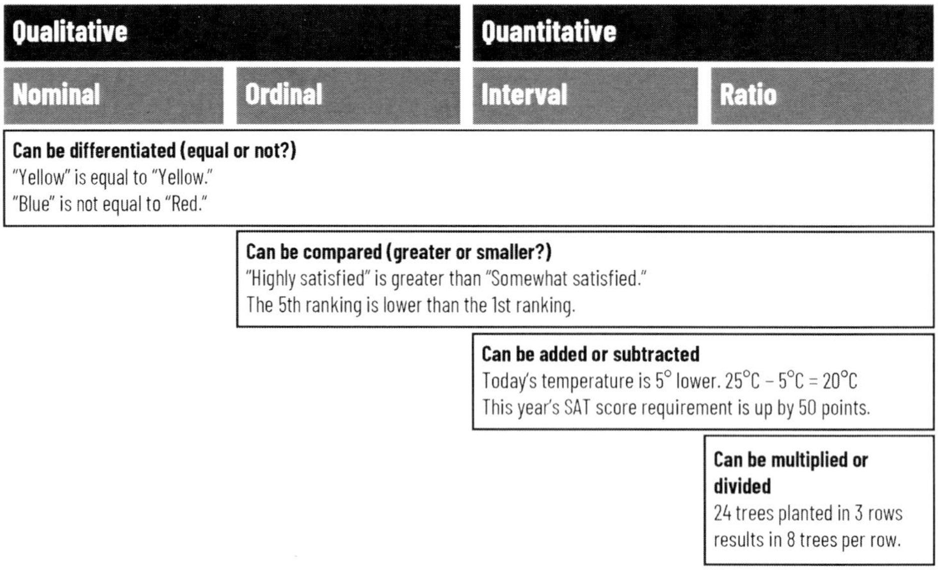

Qualitative		Quantitative	
Nominal	**Ordinal**	**Interval**	**Ratio**

Can be differentiated (equal or not?) "Yellow" is equal to "Yellow." "Blue" is not equal to "Red."

Can be compared (greater or smaller?) "Highly satisfied" is greater than "Somewhat satisfied." The 5th ranking is lower than the 1st ranking.

Can be added or subtracted Today's temperature is 5° lower. 25°C – 5°C = 20°C This year's SAT score requirement is up by 50 points.

Can be multiplied or divided 24 trees planted in 3 rows results in 8 trees per row.

Figure 1.12 Meaningful Operations by Measurement Level

It is important to distinguish the theoretical data type (the nature of observation) from digital formats of storing the data. For example, a continuous value can theoretically have unlimited precision (the numbers to the right of the decimal point). For practical purposes and for storage in a digital format, continuous values will be limited to a certain precision, as defined by the programming language or DBMS limitations. Continuous values are stored digitally as a decimal of limited length.

Each DBMS and programming language supports specific data types. The most common are in Table 1.4.

Table 1.4 Common Digital Storage Data Types

Data type	Description	Examples
Integer	Whole numbers	1; 10; 20,000; −345; 0
Float	Decimal numbers with a "floating point," e.g., the position of the decimal point may float while the total length of the field is limited	0.1234; −908.00001; 2,000.9; 0.03
Date	Calendar dates including year, month, and day of the month	Mar/05/2020; 2019-01-31
Time	Time of the day, including hours, minutes, and seconds This may be combined with the date and time zone information to create a timestamp	20:03:00; 23:59:59
Boolean	Data type with two possible values, stored as one bit of information (0 or 1)	True/False
Character	Single character	A, x, N, b
String	Sequence of characters May be of limited or unlimited length	"This is a string"

For various data analysis purposes, we may convert data from one type to another. For example, rounding allows data to be converted from continuous to discrete. Binning allows assignment of quantitative values to ranges (bins), thus converting numerical data to categorical data (further covered in Chapter 7).

Categorical values may be stored as strings, characters, or integers depending on the permissible values used to label the categories. It is important to consider the nature of the observations captured (data type) versus the format in which these observations are captured.

Data format refers to the notation used to store the value of a variable.

EXAMPLE

Example 1

Software versions are often labelled using number sequences. For example, as of writing this chapter, the latest Minecraft releases listed on Minecraft.net included 1.20.30, 1.20.15, 1.20.14, 1.20.13, 1.20.12, 1.20.10, 1.20.1.[4]

While the format of these values uses numeric characters, it does not make it quantitative data.

These version numbers represent labels of the game versions, making this categorical (qualitative) data.

Example 2

Consider phone numbers. Are they numeric data?

Can you compare phone numbers 1002002233 and 2004004466? Is the second number twice as big as the first one? Can you determine the distance between two phone numbers? Does it make sense? What would be the measurement unit?

It's an existing convention to use digits for phone numbers. A phone number written out using numbers can be translated into another format. For example, 1-800-GOT-JUNK is a *phoneword* that represents the number 1-800-468-5865, written out in an easier-to-remember mnemonic format. Phone numbers represent qualitative nominal data.

Figure 1.13 Telephone Keypad Layout with Letters

Example 3

Hexadecimal numbers use a base of 16 instead of the base 10 system we are used to and can represent large numbers with fewer digits. They are frequently used in computing as each hexadecimal number can be represented as a sequence of four bits (0s or 1s). They use characters from 0 to 9 and from A to F (where A represents 10, B represents 11, and so on, up to F, which represents 15). A hexadecimal number 10 is equal to 16 in decimal system.

A hexadecimal number 1F5D can be translated to 8,029 in the base 10 system. You can apply all arithmetic operations to hexadecimal numbers—for example, 1F5D × B7 = 166B7B, which in decimal values is equivalent to 8,029 × 183 = 1,469,307.[5]

Hexadecimal numbers can be prefixed by identifiers to avoid confusion with other types of data, such as 0x. For example, 0x10 can represent a hexadecimal number 10 equal to the number 16 in decimal system.

Example 4

Categorical data can be represented using numbers, such as the pain levels from 0 to 5. The numbers in this case represent category labels, not measurements—for example, 0 = no pain, 1 = very little pain, up to 5 = unbearable pain.

We will not be able to determine a meaningful interval between different levels of pain, assume that the difference between 3 and 2 is the same as between 2 and 1, or say that the pain level of 4 is twice as bad as the pain level of 2.

Some observations can be captured as different data types depending on how they are measured.

⚙ EXAMPLE

Example 5

Depending on the grading system, school grades can be:

- Quantitative (from 0% to 100%)
- Qualitative ordinal (letter grades from A to F)
- Boolean (Pass/Fail)

Example 6

While dates are interval data without an absolute zero, a *time interval* is ratio data. It may be:

- Discrete if measured in the number of days between two dates
- Continuous if measuring the duration between two points in time in seconds, milliseconds, etc.

Example 7

When it comes to monetary measures such as a person's income, it may be expressed as:

- Qualitative value (when identifying an income range that a particular person's income falls into, e.g., $0–$49,999, $50,000–$100,000, > $100,000)
- Quantitative value (when determining the exact amount on a tax return, e.g., $99,500.24)

What about a product price? Would we consider the quantitative value discrete or continuous?

- When we identify prices in dollars and cents, this data has limited precision of two decimals after the decimal point. This makes it discrete since we can recount each possible value between two price points.
- If we were to calculate a 13% sales tax on the order total of $99.99, the exact tax amount would be $12.9987.

When we make calculations with money, we operate with continuous data. Then, for practical purposes, we round it to two decimal places, discretizing it.

CASE STUDY

Identifying Types of Data

Consider this dataset containing YardExperts' order details. What is the data type of each attribute? Are the answers always straightforward?

Table 1.5 YardExperts Order Details Data

Order number	Customer ID	Order date	Location ID	Service	Order amount	Status	Comments
123	504895	05/25/2024	569	Lawn mowing	100	In progress	First-time customer
124	456012	05/25/2024	507	Lawn seeding	150	In progress	Large dog
125	465221	05/25/2024	465	Grub treatment	200	In progress	Weekdays only
126	404899	05/26/2024	101	Weed treatment	125	New	New
127	404578	02/02/2024	224	Snow removal	200	Completed	Difficult customer

Order number is formatted using numbers.

Is it quantitative? Does it represent a quantity or a measurement? Can you perform meaningful arithmetic operations with it? No, you can't. The company chose to use only digits when assigning order numbers, but it could have been an alphanumeric sequence such as "Order123-2025."

This is qualitative nominal data. An order number is a label assigned to each order. Whether it will be stored as an integer or a string in a database will depend on the design.

Customer ID is formatted as string (sequences of characters). This is qualitative nominal data—labels that identify individual customers.

Order date refers to date in MM/DD/YYYY format—numeric discrete data.

Location ID, while formatted as numbers, is nominal data—labels assigned to each location.

Service refers to string. This is nominal data: these service types do not indicate a natural order.

Do you think this can be any text, or does this column contain a pre-determined list of values? To make data more consistent, it would be a good practice to use a list of values to track services sold to customers.

Order total is a numeric value. In this table, it looks like a whole number. However, we cannot assume this is always true, especially if sales taxes must be calculated. Monetary values are considered decimal values.

Status is formatted as a string and represents categorical (qualitative) data. Whether it is ordinal or nominal will depend on how this category is defined: what all possible values are and whether they can be ordered.

For example, a sequence of values "New"/"In progress"/"Completed" is ordinal.

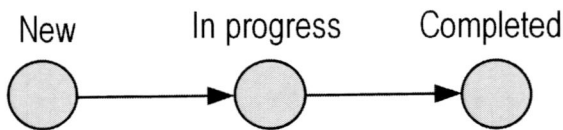

Figure 1.14 A Linear Order Life Cycle

If the order life cycle has more stages and complex loops and branches, there may be no strict order. For example, this enumeration of order status does not indicate an ordered sequence of values:

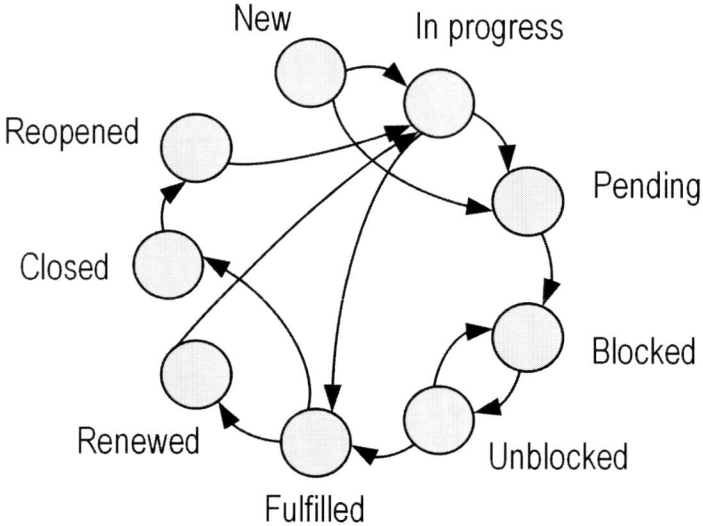

Figure 1.15 Order Life Cycle Where Stages Do Not Have a Linear Order

Comments are string, qualitative nominal data. A comment field usually allows any text, although the length of the field may be limited by the software used to store the data.

As demonstrated in this case study and previous examples, data types required for storing data variables will depend on systems of measurements, agreements, and standards. It is therefore important to capture data definitions, rules, and constraints, which is the purpose of data dictionaries and data catalogues, defined in the next chapter.

TIPS ON TERMS

Whole numbers are *discrete*.

Integer variables are *discrete*.

Decimal numbers can be considered discrete as long as the values can be enumerated, and the intervals between values cannot be further divided—for example: 0.0, 0.1, 0.2, 0.3, 0.4, etc., with a 0.1 interval. It will depend on what is being measured.

Categorical variables can be called discrete since we can enumerate them. However, this does not make it numeric data.

Analog data is a synonym for continuous data.

Calculated values such as ratios and averages are continuous; however, if there is an agreement to round them, they become discrete, such as when rounding a high school grade point average (GPA) to a whole number.

Nominal data can be called named data.

Boolean data can be called binary or dichotomous data.

Strings can be referred to as text or varchar (variable character) data.

1.4 BIG AND SMALL DATA

The term **big data** refers to the massive accumulation of data from a variety of sources that is too complex to be processed by traditional database management tools.

The advance of computing and information technologies makes big data ubiquitous due to the ease with which data can be created by various tools and devices, as well as the diminishing cost of data storage.

Figure 1.16 captures some of the many sources of big data.

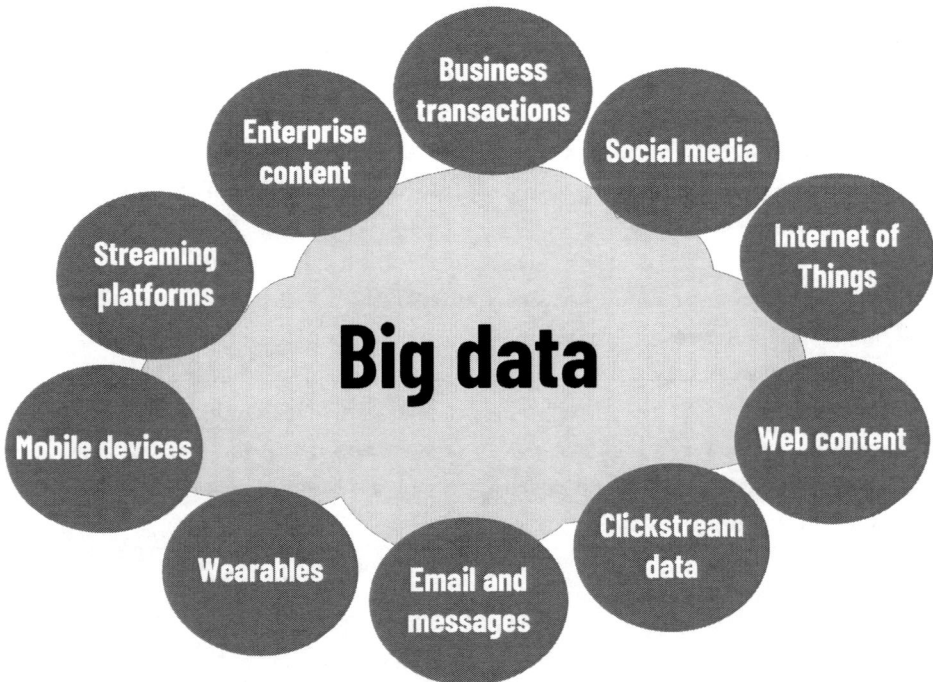

Figure 1.16 Sources of Big Data

We can recognize big data by its characteristics, called the *five V's of big data*.

Table 1.6 Five V's of Big Data

V of big data	Description
Volume	Data is generated in enormous volumes, in particular, by IoT devices
Velocity	Data is generated, moved, and accumulated at high speed, with ever-increasing expectations for real-time data and analytics
Variety	Data is generated in many different formats, in particular, semi- and unstructured data that requires new methods of processing
Veracity	Data is generated by a wide range of sources, raising concerns about its accuracy, quality, and trustworthiness
Value	Data has the potential to provide significant value to business

The richness of big data sources and the potential to capture massive amounts of information drives the fifth V of big data—the value of using it to make better decisions. However, the value of big data is a potential, not a given. Realizing this potential requires significant effort to explore, mine, process, and interpret big data according to the needs of business. The rest of this textbook addresses the process of harnessing the power of data to deliver useful enterprise insights.

With so much fascination and hype about big data, we don't often hear the opposite term. Small data is what big data isn't: well-defined, produced in volumes manageable by traditional means, and much easier to process and analyze. Small data is the traditional structured data of enterprises: data in spreadsheets and databases, lists, catalogues, and registers of transactions.

It's the opposite of big data in many senses as it has less variety and lower velocity and veracity as it comes from more trustworthy internal sources.

Small data refers to data that comes in a simple enough format and small enough volumes to be processed by a single computer or understood by a human user.

An enterprise that has not mastered the use of its small data is unlikely to be successful in harnessing the power of big data. For an organization that is just starting to discover the opportunities within data and analytics for solving business problems, small data is the natural start.

This book will consider the potential of both big and small data for solving business problems with analytics.

Table 1.7 Small Data versus Big Data

Characteristic	Small Data	Big Data
Objectives	Specific, pre-defined	Broad or undefined
Structure	Structured	Structured, semi-structured, and unstructured
Volumes	Small to medium (gigabytes to terabytes)	Huge (petabytes and more—see Appendix A)
Storage	One computer or server	Multiple servers, cloud
Sources	Traditional (enterprise systems)	Include non-traditional sources (social media, IoT, web, and streaming data)
Usage	Business intelligence and reporting	Advanced and predictive analytics
Interpretation	Easy to interpret and extract the meaning	Difficult or impossible to grasp the meaning without performing complex processing
Analysis	Easy to analyze and visualize; analysis can be done manually or with traditional tools, e.g., SQL	Difficult to get the information and analyze, requires sophisticated and specialized tools

1.5 CHAPTER SUMMARY

Key Points to Remember

- Raw data can be incomplete, inaccurate, unformatted, unsuitable, outdated, or inconsistent. It requires preparation, cleaning, and interpretation.
- We need context to turn data into meaningful information.
- Most traditional methods of managing data, including spreadsheets and databases, are designed to handle structured data.
- Different methods are required for processing and analysis of structured, semi-structured, and unstructured data.
- Data type defines what operations can be performed with the data.
- Some observations can be captured as different data types depending on how they are measured.

Key Terms

Bias: a preference for a specific argument or outcome that may not be based on the totality of facts or fair judgment.

Big data: massive accumulation of data from a variety of sources that is too complex to be processed by traditional database management tools.

Boolean data: observations sorted into two mutually exclusive categories.

Continuous data: observations that can be measured on a scale.

Data: factual information (such as measurements or statistics) used as a basis for reasoning, discussion, or calculation.

Database: a collection of related tables of structured data stored in electronic format.

Database management system (DBMS): software designed to store, retrieve, and manage data in databases.

Data format: notation used to store the value of a variable.

Dataset: a collection of data points stored and managed together.

Digitization: conversion of raw data into digital format.

Discrete data: observations that can be counted where possible values are non-divisible and can be listed.

Information: the communication or reception of knowledge or intelligence.

Insight: the act of seeing something new, unexpected, or previously unknown.

Interval data: observations that allow identification of evenly spaced intervals but not a true zero.

Knowledge: an understanding of the collected information, and a potential to apply this understanding in action.

Nominal data: observations that can be sorted into categories without a meaningful order or ranking.

Ordinal data: observations that can be sorted into categories with a meaningful order or ranking.

Qualitative (categorical) data: observations that cannot be measured but can be described using language or sorted into categories.

Quantitative (numerical) data: observations that can be measured and expressed as numbers.

Ratio data: observations that allow identification of evenly spaced intervals and a true zero.

Rectangular dataset: a collection of observations organized in rows of data representing a sequence of each observation's characteristics as columns.

Semi-structured data: datasets made up of both structured and unstructured data.

Small data: data that comes in a simple enough format and small enough volumes to be processed by a single computer or understood by a human user.

Structured data: datasets that can be stored in a table format, organized in rows and columns.

Unstructured data: data in a variable or very complex format that cannot be organized into the traditional structure of rows and columns to reflect observations and their attributes.

Variable: a characteristic that can be observed and take on different values.

Questions for Critical Thought

1. What is the difference between data type and data format?
2. What types of data can be collected through surveys: structured, semi-structured, or unstructured?

3. Can any calculated statistic or a metric be considered an insight? Why or why not?
4. What operations can be performed on different types of quantitative and qualitative data?
5. Where does big data come from?
6. Is all big data unstructured?
7. What does the fifth V of big data mean?
8. What is more useful: big or small data?

Test Your Knowledge

1. Which survey question would produce discrete data?
   a. What areas around your home you would like to improve? (A) Front yard, (B) Back yard, (C) Patio, (D) All of the above
   b. Describe your landscaping goals in 3–5 sentences
   c. How many trees do you have on your property?
   d. Do you have a specific budget for landscaping for the next 12 months? (A) No more than $500, (B) $500–$1,000, (C) No limit

2. What type of data would be collected from the following survey question?
   Indicate your preferred landscaping style: (A) Rock garden, (B) Flower beds, (C) Perfect lawn, (D) Don't know
   a. Quantitative—discrete
   b. Quantitative—continuous
   c. Qualitative—ordinal
   d. Qualitative—nominal

3. What type of data would be collected from the following survey question?
   What is the size of your property in square feet?
   a. Quantitative
   b. Qualitative
   c. Semi-structured
   d. Boolean

4. What type of data would be collected from the following survey question?
   Have you experienced any drainage problems in the past?
   a. Quantitative—discrete
   b. Quantitative—continuous
   c. Semi-structured
   d. Boolean

5. Which survey question would produce qualitative ordinal data?
   a. Describe your property's topography and features.
   b. When does your garden receive sunlight? (A) Morning to noon, (B) Noon to 3 p.m., (C) After 3 p.m.
   c. Are there any landscaping features that you would like to keep?
   d. What is the age of your home in years?

Recommended Readings

The Data Administration Newsletter: tdan.com

Dataversity: www.dataversity.net

KD Nuggets: www.kdnuggets.com

Lane, R. (2023, May 17). *What's the Relationship Between XML, JSON, HTML and the Internet?* Retrieved June 27, 2024, from www.deltaxml.com/blog/the-world-of-xml-and-json/whats-the-relationship-between-xml-json-html-and-the-internet/.

Ray, E. (2003, October 28). *Learning XML: Creating Self-Describing Data* (2nd ed.). O'Reilly Media.

Notes

1. Merriam-Webster. (n.d.). *Data*. Retrieved November 20, 2023, from www.merriam-webster.com/dictionary/data.
2. Merriam-Webster. (n.d.). *Information*. Retrieved November 20, 2023, from www.merriam-webster.com/dictionary/information.
3. National Institute of Standards and Technology (NIST). (n.d.). *Kelvin: Introduction*. Retrieved November 20, 2023, from www.nist.gov/si-redefinition/kelvin-introduction.
4. Minecraft Feedback. (n.d.). *Minecraft Release Changelogs*. Retrieved September 8, 2023, from feedback.minecraft.net/hc/en-us/sections/360001186971-Release-Changelogs.
5. Calculator.net. (n.d.). *Hex Calculator*. Retrieved January 2, 2024, from www.calculator.net/hex-calculator.html.

Chapter 2

Data Management in an Enterprise

The success of business analytics depends on how data is created and managed by an organization throughout its life cycle. This chapter focuses on **data management:** processes and practices used to manage an organization's data throughout its life cycle.

You will learn about:

- Data life cycle stages and activities
- Different types of enterprise data and its uses
- Internal and external sources of data

2.1 DATA LIFE CYCLE

As data is used during enterprise activities, it must be stored, processed, protected, analyzed, shared, and eventually destroyed. In other words, data has a life cycle.

The **data life cycle** is a sequence of operations performed with data from its creation to destruction.

CASE STUDY

Tracking the Movement of Purchase Transactions Data

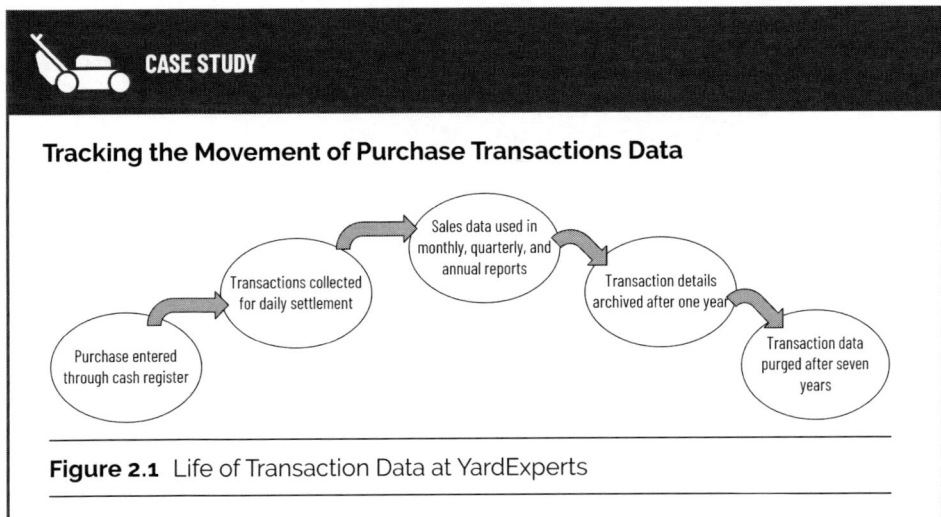

Figure 2.1 Life of Transaction Data at YardExperts

The YardExperts store in Unionville is very busy in spring. Every day, customers come in with their gardening and landscaping needs. Sometimes, they order a full landscaping package, and sometimes, they want to buy gardening tools or supplies.

A service representative listens to the customers, asks clarifying questions, and records new landscaping requests in the system. A store assistant uses a cash register to ring in purchases, and the cash register captures purchase details in digital format.

The data on daily purchases is captured in the register, and it is sent to a system at the central office that stores and consolidates all daily transaction data. This information will be used for daily banking reconciliation that includes settlement with payment card associations.

New landscaping contracts are recorded in a different system. Some contracts will be paid upfront, and the rest will be set up for monthly payments. Each contract payment is also recorded in this system.

Every month, a special program is run to complete the month-end reporting and determine monthly transaction volume, contract volume, retail sales, and other important metrics needed to manage the business.

These metrics are published as a set of monthly reports distributed to the managers of different departments.

At the end of each quarter and fiscal year, additional reports are generated to be shared with market analysts. As a publicly traded company, YardExperts must disclose certain information to investors.

At the end of each year, financial statements are prepared and checked by an external auditor. The auditors receive a specially prepared data extract with all the details required to complete the audit.

Once each annual audit is completed successfully, detailed information about every packet of seeds and every potted plant purchased in every YardExperts store is no longer needed. As it may take up a lot of space, the company has a special procedure to archive all the detailed records of the previous year's operations. Retail sales data is archived after one year, while service contracts data is kept for longer periods of time.

The archived information is moved to special digital storage and deleted from the main systems, thus freeing up space to store new information. Without this periodic archiving, the data accumulation in the company's systems could become an impediment to operations. Storing too much data may impact cost and slow the systems down.

Archived data is stored for a certain time period defined by the company's data retention policies. These policies will depend on regulations specific to each jurisdiction, industry, and type of data.

For example, financial transaction data that can affect income tax must be stored for six years after filing a tax return in Canada as of this book's publication.[1]

After the retention period has passed, the data can be purged. Purging means physical destruction—removal from the electronic media in such a way that it is not possible to restore the data.

The case study example describes a life cycle of data starting from capturing regular daily business activities (store sales) in each YardExperts location and following it through different stages of its use as part of managing the business. Figure 2.2 depicts common stages in the data life cycle of an organization.

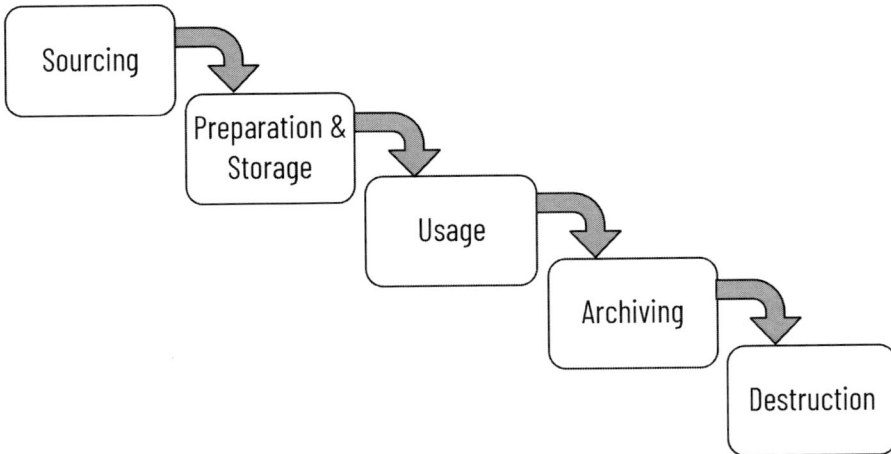

Figure 2.2 Data Life Cycle Stages

The next table describes what is typically done during each stage of the data life cycle. Organizations may use different terms to refer to the data life cycle stages.

The life cycle of data starts with capturing it in operational systems (further explored in Section 2.2).

As data is first captured, it often requires additional processing for integration with other systems or before it can be used for analytical purposes. Chapter 7 will focus on various methods of data preparation, and Chapter 8 will provide an overview of analytics architecture and data pipeline design.

Data usage has many facets—from managing the company's master data and capturing daily transactions (explored in Section 2.3), to summarizing and visualizing it for analytical purposes (Chapter 5), to sharing the insights with stakeholders, providing reports to shareholders, and creating data products for customers.

As data is used throughout the entire data life cycle, it must be secured and protected from unauthorized use. Some analytical insights will be shared publicly, such as weather forecasts and climate statistics. Confidential data and insights will be fiercely protected to maintain competitive advantage or to avoid causing harm. Some aspects of data protection will be explored in Section 11.4.

The requirements for retaining specific business data can be driven by business needs or legislation. Archiving data that is no longer actively used for operational purposes can also be done to improve the performance of operational systems. At the same time, businesses will consider how much historical data they need to retain for record-keeping purposes (consider a pension plan or a family doctor's clinic) and for analytical purposes (such as for long-term macroeconomic analysis).

Table 2.1 Data Life Cycle Activities

Data life cycle stage	Description and activities
Sourcing (data capture, data acquisition)	Collect and capture data values from various sources: • Create or enter data • Receive and capture data signals • Obtain data externally
Preparation and storage (storage and maintenance)	Store, maintain, and prepare data for usage: • Move and store data • Cleanse and enrich data • Transform and synthesize data • Integrate data from multiple sources
Usage (permitted use of data)	Apply data to the tasks of operating and managing the enterprise: • Use data to support operational activities • Protect, monitor, and audit data usage • Search, classify, explore, model, and analyze data • Visualize, share, and publish analytical insights internally and externally • Deliver data products to customers
Archiving (retention)	Store data that is no longer actively used for a defined retention period: • Copy data into archive • Preserve data for future purposes • Remove archived data from active environments
Destruction (purging, permanent deletion)	Remove every copy of data item from enterprise records: • Physically, irretrievably remove data from all forms of storage

At some point, the data will be destroyed. Destruction refers to complete physical deletion that erases data from hardware storage and makes restoring it impossible. This takes more than clicking a "Delete" button and requires special tools for resetting or wiping the hardware storage, often supplemented by overwriting the space with random data.

It is important for enterprises to consider the terms for purging the data they no longer need and are not legally required to retain. Data storage costs money and uses energy and other precious resources like water. The amount of data created and stored by modern technology grows exponentially, while studies show that about 90% of the data stored worldwide represents multiple copies of the same information.[2] The growing capabilities of data storage are not an excuse to store data indefinitely without need.

Another reason for not retaining data beyond reasonable need is the risk of unauthorized access. The more data in possession of an enterprise, the more potential exposure in the case of a data breach or a hacker attack. As enterprises bear legal responsibility for protecting private data, the repercussions of a data breach can be very serious and, for a small- to medium-sized company, even devastating.[3]

2.2 OPERATIONAL AND ANALYTICAL SYSTEMS

Enterprise data is created and managed to support day-to-day business activities, track performance, make decisions, and even govern other data. Enterprises manage their data in a variety of operational and analytical systems.

Operational systems are used to record and manage the day-to-day operations of the enterprise.

The data created from a range of everyday activities—selling goods, interacting with customers, receiving and making payments, and transporting people and objects—is tracked in operational systems. These systems could be software applications, also called enterprise applications, or homegrown solutions built using office productivity tools such as spreadsheets or word processing software.

The main purpose of operational systems is to track and provide quick access to data required to run business activities.

The purpose of **analytical systems** is to aggregate data from a variety of sources for further analysis and to support decision-making. Analytical systems can be used to collect and process data from internal and external systems.

CASE STUDY

YardExperts Operational Systems

To manage its operations, YardExperts employees use several applications.

A Customer Relationship Management (CRM) System is used by employees to manage and look up customer information. This is also where all customer interactions and email communications are stored.

An Inventory Tracking System (ITS) is used to log the movements of all products through the retail side of the business as well as the equipment and supplies used for servicing the contracts.

The YardExperts Order Management System (YOMS) is used to manage all the information about service contracts and service visits.

A Retail Operations System supports all retail activities, from tracking cash registers in all retail locations to collecting and reconciling daily point-of-sale transactions.

A Human Resources (HR) Management System supports HR functions, including tracking employee data, payroll details, and recruitment workflows.

The Contractor Catalogue is a repository of all businesses and contractors that YardExperts regularly engage with to subcontract work.

YardExperts Analytical Systems

Over the years, YardExperts has built several analytical solutions.

> Customer analytics dashboards are a collection of dashboards and reports generated from historical customer and order information. A historical archive of customer and order details is stored in a separate database that feeds the dashboards. This solution is used by marketing, sales, and customer care teams to track sales trends and customer survey results, and to run ad hoc analyses for customer segmentation and customer satisfaction indicators. YardExperts' management team would like to get more systematic and organized in analyzing its customer trends.
>
> The company also has a financial reporting data warehouse. It includes all historical financial data stored both for financial reporting and for audit purposes.

Why are analytical systems needed? Why can't an organization use its operational systems to fulfill analytics needs? There are two main considerations at stake:

1. Difference in purpose and function

    Operational systems are used to enter, retrieve, and update data required to run the business. The design of these systems and underlying data structures must be optimized to support these functions. When data storage is optimized for fast retrieval and updates, the same structures do not perform as well on complex data aggregations and queries. Running complex queries may slow down the underlying database, which in turn would negatively impact operational users of these systems.

2. Specialization of enterprise systems

    Enterprise systems are often designed to support a specific business capability such as customer management, sales, or accounting. This segregation by function means that individual operational systems have limited reporting capabilities relying on data that each system manages. To combine data from several systems for more comprehensive analysis, data from multiple sources needs to be brought together—that is, combined and integrated. This is the function of analytical systems.

The next table compares operational and analytical systems by their purpose, function, and capabilities. Two approaches to data modelling—relational and dimensional—will be further developed in Section 2.6.

Figure 2.3 depicts types of enterprise data managed in operational and analytical systems, further explained in the next section.

Table 2.2 Comparison of Operational and Analytical Systems

Operational systems: Run the business	Analytical systems: Manage the business
Used to run the business: complete daily tasks and keep records	Used to manage the business: generate insights to support decision-making
Create and update business data in real time	Data is read-only and not intended to be modified
Contain current data considered the source of truth	Data is accurate as of the time it was ingested from operational systems
Limited history, may not support storage of large amounts of data	Store large volumes of historical data for extended periods of time
Capture all the details tracked for operational purposes	Store selected data required for analysis, may be aggregated
May be purpose-built to support a specific side of business operations, e.g., marketing, accounting, or logistics	Combine data from different areas of operations for richer analytics capabilities
Data is normalized to avoid redundancy and support frequent updates (relational data models preferred)	Redundancy is accepted to enable rich reporting capabilities and aggregation for different analytical purposes (dimensional data models preferred)
Limited operational reporting capabilities—snapshots of the present	Rich capabilities for reporting, trending, and historical analysis

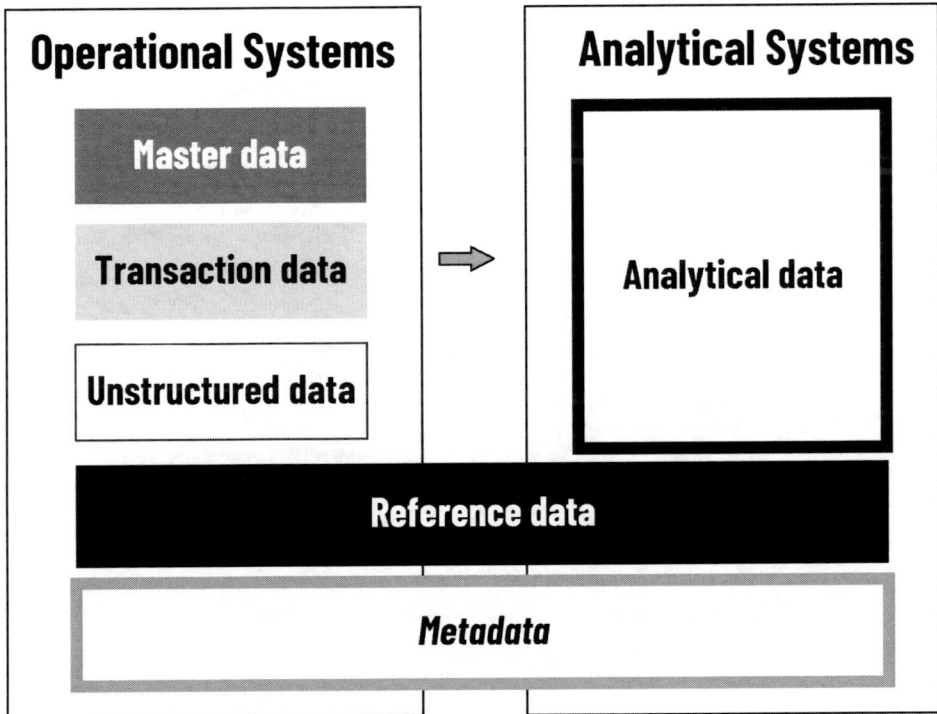

Figure 2.3 Enterprise Data Managed in Operational and Analytical Systems

2.3 TYPES OF ENTERPRISE DATA

Master Data

Every organization has its own important data entities—persons, things, events, or concepts about which the business must keep data:

- People: customers, employees
- Places: locations, warehouses, stores
- Things: products, materials, equipment, fixtures
- Concepts: financial accounts, divisions

Accuracy and responsible management of these data entities are considered mission critical for an organization, as this data is necessary for the execution of essential business processes. As such, this data must be managed in a controlled manner and shared across the enterprise, including its multiple systems and business applications.

Master data refers to key business data entities shared across the enterprise.

To ensure that this data stays current, accurate, and complete, organizations implement special rules and processes.

Master data management refers to a set of rules and processes established to ensure the integrity and consistent use of master data across the enterprise.

In organizations, master data may be referred to as **master lists**, such as the master list of customers, suppliers or products, **catalogues**, such as a service catalogue, the **authoritative source**, or the **golden record of data**.

You may also encounter the term **critical data elements**, referring to the data elements considered critical for successful business operations. For example, the accuracy of a customer's address is critical to the successful delivery of the customer's orders. A complete list of product ingredients is required on product packaging, and any errors or omissions may lead to undesired consequences and even lawsuits.

Master lists are often managed in operational applications such as a Customer Relationship Management (CRM) System. Other applications that require customer data will get the most current details from the CRM.

In the example at the beginning of this chapter, customer data, YardExperts retail locations, and details concerning products sold in the retail locations all represent master data.

Transaction Data

Every organization captures data related to its day-to-day activities, or transactions. **Transactions** are time-bound events that comprise the operations of the business. In a business context, the term *transaction* can also refer to an agreement between two parties to buy or sell something, such as a contract or a subscription payment.

Transactions can be:

- Orders
- Invoices
- Purchases

- Deliveries
- Appointments
- Interactions
- Payments

Since transactions are repeatable business activities, they will have similar well-defined characteristics—attributes that will be captured to support transaction processing. These characteristics include dates, times, parties involved, locations, products and services purchased, and purchase prices and quantities.

Transaction data is data that captures the details of business transactions.

Transactions can have a varied lifespan and velocity: some are generated in high volumes and completed within milliseconds, such as electronic payments, and some will be rare and tracked for days and months, such as orders for custom-made furniture.

In the case study, purchases, contracts, and payments are examples of transaction data. In an organization, transaction data may be referred to as **operational data**, **operating data**, **flow data**, or **time-stamped data**.

Reference Data

To ensure data consistency across all systems and applications, organizations establish reference data.

Reference data is data used to standardize and classify other data and establish permissible values for organizational use.

Reference data can be used to:

- Enumerate permissible values: lists of divisions, countries, regions, languages, or order statuses
- Categorize important entities: product categories and subcategories, customer segments
- Qualify other values: units of measurement

From the previous case study survey example, YardExperts may use standard categories of products, types of landscaping services, and customer groupings to support analysis of company performance.

Reference data is important for:

- Capturing consistent master and transactional data using standard permissible attributes
- Supporting exchange of data between systems using common classification and standard categories
- Using standard categories and groupings for comparability in business analytics

Reference data can be internal to the organization or based on external standards:

- Internal reference data: customer types, order statuses, service categories
- External reference data (domain-specific): vehicle categories, insurance coverage types, payment methods

- Universal reference data (applicable across domains): International Organization for Standardization (ISO) 3166 country codes, ISO 4217 currency codes

Reference data in a company will be relatively stable. Internal reference data will change more frequently than external data. As reference data changes may have repercussions across multiple systems, strict data governance rules are required for approval and application of changes.

Whenever external standards exist, it is a best practice to use them for reference data, as this enables reliable information exchanges with external organizations and supports the use of external data without excessive translation and interpretation efforts.

As part of data governance activities, organizations should seek the appropriate systems of reference and make use of them, including postal addresses, ISO standards, and industry-specific reference data. Using external reference data for analytics makes sharing and visualization more accessible to different audiences. Regulatory and compliance reporting often requires the use of standard nomenclature and reference data, so adopting it is beneficial from both consistency and cost-reduction perspectives.

Table 2.3 Comparison of Master, Transactional, and Reference Data

Master data	Transactional data	Reference data
Represents important data entities relevant to the organization	Represents business activities and events	Represents categories and permissible values for attributes in transactional and master data
Shared across the enterprise	Relevant to specific departments	Shared across enterprise, industry, or multiple industries
Medium velocity: driven by material changes in key business entities	High velocity: new transactions added by day, hour, minute, or in real time	Low velocity: standards are stable and changes infrequent
Changes are controlled via established business processes	Changes are expected as a normal result of business operations	Changes are strictly controlled and cascaded to the affected systems, processes, and documentation
Long life span: reflects the life span of the important business entities, e.g., the life cycle of a product, customer, or location	Short to medium life span: reflects the life cycle of an individual business transaction	Very long life span: reflects the longevity of the relevant industry, country, or international standards

Unstructured Data

Along with well-defined and structured master, transaction, and reference data, organizations will produce unstructured and semi-structured data in the course of daily operations. This data may include communications (messages and emails), forms, documents, spreadsheets, scanned images, photos, and audio and video recordings.

Unstructured data may be simply stored for audit and reference purposes and does not necessarily become a source for analytics. To be used for analytics, unstructured data must first be pre-processed, mined, and transformed. We will explore this more in Chapter 7.

Referring to the case study, YardExperts will produce unstructured data as part of doing business:

- Landscaping contracts: documents and attached images with property plans, "before" and "after" photographs
- Emails, letters, and electronic receipts related to processing transaction chargebacks and customer complaints
- Reports, forms, and notes about inventory replenishment and special orders of plant specimens requested by customers
- PDF copies of all reports and statements sent to the auditors, along with their responses and recommendations

Metadata

Metadata is the data that describes and characterizes other data to support its understanding and interpretation.

Metadata can be translated as "data about data" and provides the context necessary to understand what the data means. It may capture who created the data and for what purpose, describe the fields, their data types, and permissible values, and identify access rights to the data.

There are three main types of metadata.

Business metadata captures the description of the data from a business perspective, such as:

- Business definition
- Meaning
- Source of the data
- Relationships between data elements
- Data owner
- Data quality expectations
- Permissible values

Technical metadata captures the description of the data from the perspective of its storage and processing by software tools, such as:

- Data element name and physical location (e.g., table and column names)
- Data type
- Format (length, size, structure)
- Mapping

Operational metadata captures information about the usage of data, such as:

- Date and time the data was created, updated, or deleted
- Identifier of the user who created, updated, or deleted the data
- Source of data such as another system, user, procedure, business rule, or calculation

Operational metadata allows for tracking and auditing the use of data and monitoring its accuracy and quality. Business and technical metadata captures the information necessary for understanding and correct usage of data for sharing across the organization. This documentation often takes the form of a data dictionary.

A **data dictionary** is a repository of information about data, including its meaning, origin, structure, format, and relationship with other data.

Table 2.4 contains a sample segment from a data dictionary. Each column contains metadata about the respective data elements.

Table 2.4 Data Dictionary Example

Data element	Definition	Data type	Format/permissible values	Master source	Table.column
Product ID	Unique identifier of a product available in company inventory	String (9)	AAnnnnnnn, where AA: department code nnnnnnn: sequential number within each department	Service Catalogue	Products. ProductID
Product name	Name of the product presented to customers	String (150)	Standard product names defined in the product catalogue	Service Catalogue	Products. ProductDesc
Delivery mode code	A standard code that identifies a way for customers to receive purchased products	Integer (1)	Delivery mode codes: 1 = Home delivery 2 = Store pick-up 3 = Installation service	Service Catalogue	DeliveryModes. Code
Delivery date	Date the order was received by customer	Date	MM/DD/YYYY	Order Management System	Order. DeliveryDate

Metadata can be used to define individual data elements, as in the data dictionary example above, or it may apply to a dataset or a complex data type.

For example, let's consider a customer order with all the pieces of data relevant to tracking the order from the moment the customer placed it to its fulfillment.

CASE STUDY

Master, Reference, Transaction, and Metadata

YardExperts tracks many details about customer orders. The information gets updated as the order progresses, gets paid for, and is delivered. At any time, order information showing key data points can be retrieved from the YOMS. These data points represent reference, master, and transaction data, as well as customer order metadata.

YardExperts Order

Customer No: 872750	Order #12345
Customer Name: Leslie Greenthumb	Date: 09/09/2025
Customer Address: 45 Garden St. Greenville	

Product ID	Product	Price	Quantity	Subtotal
450	Cedar mulch	10.00	5	50.00
457	Garden soil	12.00	10	120.00

Payment Mode	Payment Details	Payment Date
Credit Card	*0987	09/15/2025

Delivery Mode	Delivery Date
Home delivery	09/16/2025

Created: 09/03/2025 14:45:01   CreatedBy: 89046664
LastUpdated: 09/04/2025 10:33:23   LastUpdatedBy: 50045765
PriceList: Fall25

Reference data
Master data
Transaction data
Metadata

Figure 2.4 Reference, Master, Transaction, and Metadata in YardExperts Orders

In this example of the YardExperts order, we will find:

- Master data such as the customer details and product attributes
- Reference data such as the mode of payment (where permissible values could be credit card, debit card, and cash), and the delivery mode (where permissible values could be home delivery and store pick-up)
- Transaction data specific to this particular order: order number and date, quantity of items purchased, payment and delivery details

> Metadata, by its nature, is not always in plain sight as it supports the storing and usage of master, reference, and transaction data. The data dictionary of the YOMS would include metadata for each of the fields we see captured in the order. Each order record may include additional operational metadata specific to that order, such as the date the order was created and last updated, the identifier of the users that created and updated the order, as well as which version of the price list was used to determine product prices. These metadata fields apply to the order record rather than its individual attributes.

Metadata can be attached to unstructured data to support its tracking and usage. For example, digital photos stored on an electronic device will contain metadata about each digital image file.

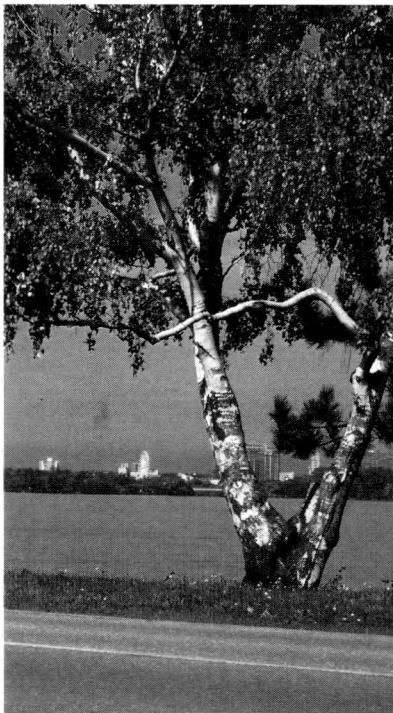

Tree-in-black-and-white.jpg Properties	
Description:	Tree on Niagara river
Type of file:	JPG File (.jpg)
Size:	1.43 MB (1,501,044 bytes)
Created:	November 18, 2023
Dimensions:	1541 x 2689
Width:	1541 pixels
Height:	2689 pixels
Resolution:	350 dpi
Bit depth:	24
F-stop:	f/11
Exposure:	1/320 sec.
Focal length:	42 mm
Flash mode:	No flash

Figure 2.5 Metadata Captured and Stored along with a Digital Photograph

Metadata plays a key role in managing and searching unstructured information such as website content, scanned images, files, and multimedia by capturing details such as:

- Title and descriptions
- Origin of data, authors
- Keywords

- Alternate text for images
- File size
- Content format or encoding

Search engines use metadata to match images and video files to search keywords.

Analytical Data

Analytical data is created and used to generate analytical insights and make business decisions, such as:

- Transaction and master data extracted from various data sources and combined for further analytical processing
- Reference data to help group and aggregate information in ways that are meaningful to business users
- Aggregated data—the same data can be summarized in many ways depending on analytical needs
- Derived, enriched, and calculated attributes
- Historical reports

For example, to analyze purchase trends, a company will use its historical purchase transaction data as well as a pre-defined grouping of customers by segments. This will allow us to see if there are differences or particular trends in various customer demographics. As part of the analysis, the company may change how it defines customer segments, split or merge them, or create a hierarchy of customer segmentation for more granular analysis.

Next, certain benchmarks may be determined for each customer segment, so that future performance can be compared to the benchmarks. These will become analytical data that will be used for comparison and communicating analytics results to business decision-makers. For example, a music streaming service may define different engagement benchmarks for teenage listeners compared with other age groups.

Operational data may require complex transformations to be more usable for analytical purposes—this will be discussed in more detail in Chapter 7. In Chapter 5, we will explore frequently used descriptive metrics that also represent analytical data. In Chapter 9, we will review how analytical data can be organized and presented to the users.

2.4 SOURCES OF DATA FOR ANALYTICS

Analytical insights are discoveries of new knowledge or connections. Discovery of new insights requires analyzing, comparing, and linking information from multiple sources. For example, if we compare the data about declining sales with customer sentiments on social media, we may discover a rise in customer complaints and negative reviews. This might provide an insight into the reason behind the decline in sales.

Such analysis requires combining internal enterprise data created within the organization (sales numbers) with the data received from external sources (complaints and reviews on social media). Understanding the potential of both internal and external sources of data and the different nature of data in these sources is critical for advanced analytical insights.

Internal data is generated from operating the enterprise. Examples are:

- Customer data: captured when onboarding customers, selling them products, and providing services
- Transaction data: collected when performing regular daily activities such as receiving orders, processing complaints, loading and unloading goods, making payments, or taking care of patients
- HR data: collected when hiring, onboarding, and supporting a company's employees

Internal data is usually captured and maintained in the company's operational systems. Its reliability and trustworthiness depend on the maturity of the company's data management practices. For internally sourced data, the organization has control over:[4]

- Data format
- Level of detail captured
- Timeliness, update frequency
- Data quality
- Data security and privacy protection mechanisms

External data is data of interest generated outside the enterprise. It may be generated by any entity that is not part of the enterprise—competitors, regulators, governments, customers, or the general public.

Much of external data is **open-source**—that is, it is data freely available on the internet:

- News, macroeconomic data
- Information shared by governments and international organizations
- Stock market data
- Annual reports of publicly traded companies
- Social media content
- Website content

Third-party data is data obtained (purchased) from companies that sell data products. These companies are known as data aggregators, data poolers, or information conglomerates.

Data from these providers is made accessible through special arrangements—subscription, one-time purchase of a dataset, or as part of a membership.

As the value of data grows, the business of selling data grows with it. In Chapter 11, we will discuss the legal and ethical implications of collecting and selling data. Some examples of third-party data include:

- Market research: consumer trends, purchasing behaviour, and competitor information
- Risk scoring: credit ratings for individuals and businesses

- Scientific research databases: statistics, observations, and research conclusions
- Law enforcement data

When using external data, companies have little or no control over the format, level of detail, and quality of data, unless it's commercial third-party data they purchase, in which case it will come with some guarantees of quality and completeness. External data comes with risks related to:

- Stability: Will it continue to be available? Can the access be shut off?
- Reliability (veracity): Can this data be trusted? Does it reflect the whole population, or could it be biased?
- Quality: How accurate is the data? Does the quality change over time?

⚙️ EXAMPLE

Consider a scenario where an employer is looking to fill a vacancy and is reviewing potential candidates. What information will the employer use?

Internal

- Data the candidate entered into the applicant tracking system while submitting their application (personal details, education, skills, and employment history)
- Data about the candidate's previous job applications, which may include previous résumé details, as well as scores received during earlier application processes and previous outcomes. For example, were they invited for an interview? Offered a job? Did they accept or decline the offer? Was their background search satisfactory the last time?
- Employment history if the candidate used to work for this company or currently works at the company in a different position. This can include all the information from the company's HR management system—positions held, salary history, managers' evaluations, training, injuries, conflicts, awards, and anything else that the employer may track.

External

- Information about job candidates available in the public domain—anything that can be found on the internet. This can include social media profiles, posts and comments, news articles, interviews, and content posted by the person anywhere with open access.
- Reference checks—responses provided by references or HR departments of previous employers. These can be either digital responses to reference check forms or notes captured during an interview or conversation.
- Background check agencies—these services will do a wide range of verifications, from credit history to criminal checks to contacting educational institutions in other countries confirming the candidate's credentials.

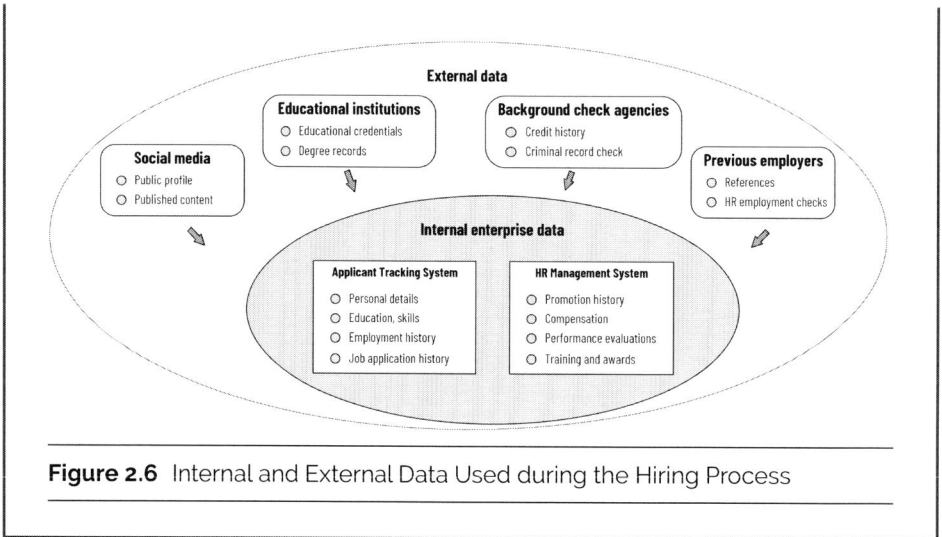

Figure 2.6 Internal and External Data Used during the Hiring Process

Internal and external data can be both human and machine generated.

Human-generated data is created by people using software systems and electronic devices:

- Communication messages such as emails and text messages (SMS)
- Survey responses
- Social media actions, comments, likes, and ratings

Machine-generated data is created by software systems and electronic devices programmed to do so through automation and capturing of events:

- Clickstream data, generated by recording users' clicks on a website
- Spatiotemporal data, tracking the location of objects at a moment in time, such as recording the movement of a delivery truck or a taxicab
- Transaction metadata, such as date, time, and device type used for a digital purchase

It is machine-generated data that contributes most to the big data phenomenon.

The methods of collecting and preparing data, and the expected quality of that data, will vary depending on its nature and the system of origin.

To generate analytical insights, you may use data that already exists, or you may collect additional data. For example, to better understand customer preferences, you may look at the sales statistics to discover popular products. However, if this data is inconclusive or insufficient, or if you want to explore new product features, you may need to collect new data by conducting surveys, focus groups, or interviews.

Data collected for a specific purpose through personal experience or by collecting evidence is called **primary data**.

Data that has been collected and recorded earlier by others for a different purpose is called **secondary data**.

	Internal		External	
	Operational systems	**Analytical systems**	**Open-source**	**Third party**
Human-generated	Emails, messages Lists, catalogues, forms Files, spreadsheets Customer data Survey responses	Manually generated reports, pivots, charts Machine learning labels	Web content Social media activity Reviews & rankings Government data	Subscription services Paywalled websites Law enforcement data
Machine-generated	Transactions Audit logs Metadata Meeting recordings Monitoring data Sensor readings	Pre-processed warehoused data Calculated summaries Metrics & key performance indicators Predictions	Web statistics Clickstream data Stock market data GPS data	Data aggregators Streaming services Shared industry data

Figure 2.7 Internal and External Data Sources

In the example at the beginning of the chapter, sales records were originally recorded to track sales transactions and represent secondary data for this analysis, while any surveys or focus groups designed to ask customers about their desired product features for the purpose of product development will be primary data. If the original research and data collection were done by a third party such as the government or a market research agency, it becomes secondary data for the companies that purchase and make use of this already collected data for their analysis. Therefore, while internal data used for analytics may be primary or secondary, external data is secondary.

Table 2.5 Comparison of Primary and Secondary Data

Primary data	**Secondary data**
Collected for the first time by the person interested in data	Collected earlier by other persons
Raw unprocessed data	Pre-processed and stored in a certain format
More suitable and sufficient if data collection was designed for a specific research purpose	May not fully satisfy data needs as it was originally collected for a different purpose
Data is current as it is collected first-hand for a specific purpose	Recency of data varies, may be out of date
Can be trusted as it is personally observed and collected	Trust in accuracy of data depends on the sources the data comes from; accuracy cannot be verified by the researcher directly
Expensive and time-consuming to collect; resources for organizing observation, data collection, and processing can be expensive	Less expensive as it is already captured and stored; additional costs if data purchased from a third party
Examples: forms, surveys, focus groups, experiments, measurements	Examples: web traffic, government statistics, market research, printed media, open-source databases

2.5 DATA MANAGEMENT PROCESSES AND ACTIVITIES

Effective data life cycle management in an organization requires strong data management capabilities, including:

- Data architecture
- Data governance
- Data storage and operations
- Data analytics
- Data security

Each capability must be supported by established processes, regularly performed activities, policies, and rules governing these activities. Performing these activities will require knowledge, skills, and tools.

While this book is centred around analytics, it is important to understand how the success of analytics depends on an enterprise's other data management activities.

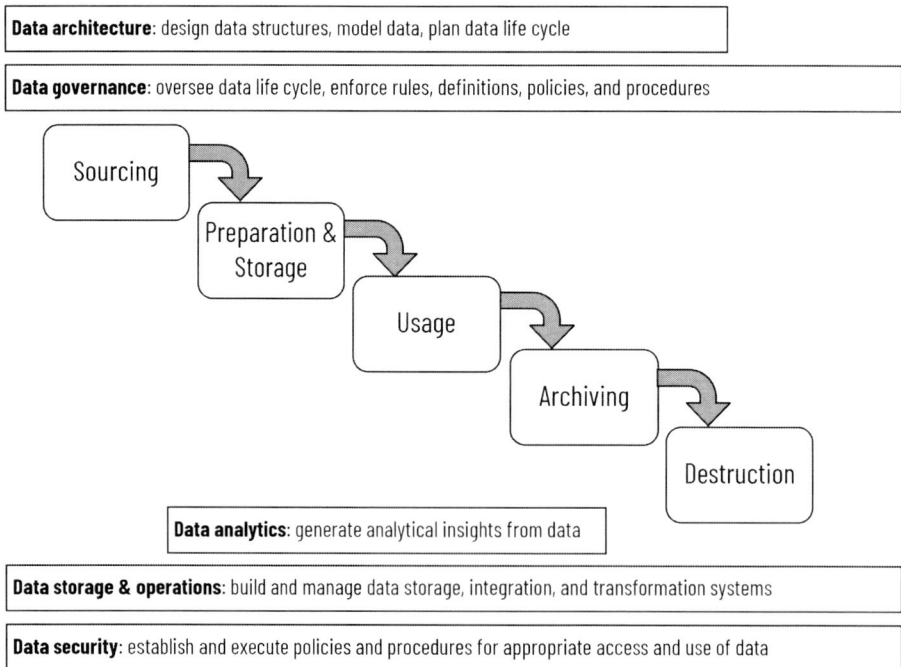

Figure 2.8 Organizational Capabilities for Managing Data Life Cycle

Data Architecture

Data architecture encompasses planning and designing how an organization's data resources should be structured and connected, ensuring that data is available to support business activities.

Data architecture activities include:

- Data modelling

- Designing data structures for operational and analytical systems
- Planning data flows and designing the pipelines for transporting and transforming the data

The business analytics life cycle relies on data architecture for:

- Data architecture documentation to support analysis of data sources and planning data acquisition
- Design of data pipelines for integrating the required data into analytical systems (as explored further in Chapter 8)

To support the design of enterprise data structures and flows, architects create diagrams, models, and documents, which become blueprints for the design and development of systems and pipelines for data management. See Section 2.6 for an introduction to data models.

CASE STUDY

Modelling the Information Flow of YardExperts' Operational Systems

One of the company's objectives this year is to better use its data to generate useful analytical insights. To achieve this, it is necessary to have a clear picture of the flow of information across the enterprise. This can be served by a simple information flow model depicting the movement of information between components of an enterprise. If necessary, such a model may include information flows to and from external entities.

You will learn more about various systems used by the company in subsequent case study examples.

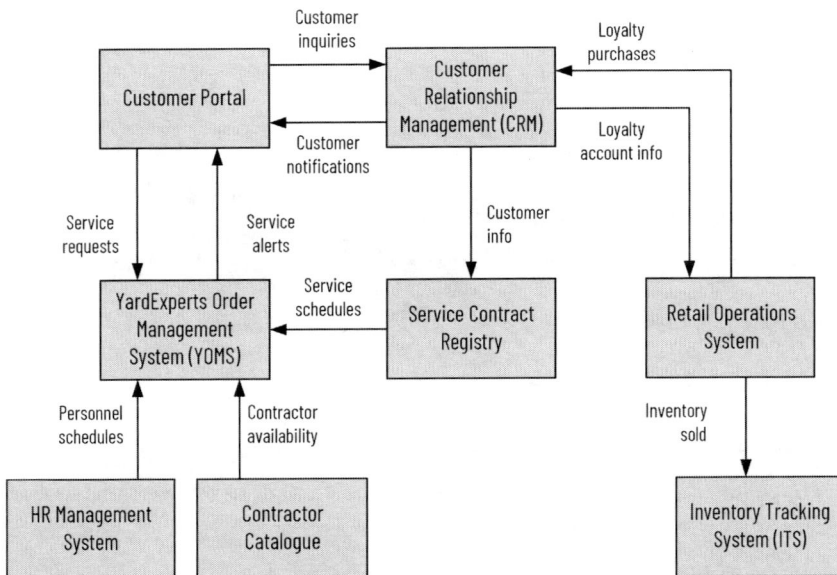

Figure 2.9 YardExperts' Operational Systems Information Flows

Real-life architecture diagrams can be much more complex. However, it's always a good idea to start with simple models that all stakeholders can understand and relate to. Such models can become useful communication tools, especially during the requirements analysis stage of analytics projects, to better understand business problems and data that can be used to solve them.

Data Governance

Data governance encompasses processes and practices used to oversee the management of data to ensure its quality, security, and proper usage.

Data governance activities include:

- Establishing and enforcing consistent definitions of data entities, attributes, and business metrics through data dictionaries and catalogues
- Developing and overseeing policies and procedures for managing data
- Establishing and monitoring data quality standards
- Creating data ownership structures to enforce data quality accountability

From a business analytics perspective, effective data governance is key to improving data quality and correctly interpreting the data being analyzed.

When everyone in the organization uses the same definitions for data entities as well as their attributes and business metrics, reports and analytics that include these metrics will be universally understood and interpreted in the same way. When data quality is supported by rules and policies and regularly monitored, less effort will be required for data cleaning and preparing it for analytics.

As reinforced by the *Data Management Body of Knowledge* (the DAMA-DMBoK) published by the Global Data Management Community, DAMA International, data governance is central to the success of data management in an organization. All aspects of data management, from data architecture and data modelling and design to data warehousing and security, must be based on principles and policies for responsible data management.

CASE STUDY

Sales Metrics Variance

At YardExperts, two different departments create sales reports: the sales department and the accounting department. Unfortunately, to the mutual frustration of the vice-president of sales and the company's chief financial officer, these reports never match.

Upon further investigation, YardExperts' new data analyst discovers that the sales department counts the monthly sales volume based on the date the contract was signed. For example, if a landscaping contract was signed in March, the full contract amount is counted in the March sales volume. The accounting department does not refer to the contract date at all. Instead, their reporting is based on the date when re-curring payments are received from the customers.

Since some customers prepay the whole amount while others choose to pay on a monthly basis, these metrics will never match. This is a type of situation commonly referred to as "comparing apples to oranges."

In the case study, two departments are applying different definitions to the metric they call "sales volume." To resolve this conflict:

- They could agree to use the same definition of the metric.
- They could acknowledge the need for two different metrics—e.g., "contract volume" and "contract payments." "Sales volume" could be reserved to capture Yard-Experts' overall revenue, including both service contract volume and retail sales.

Finding a resolution to this conflict of definitions is a data governance activity.

Definitions of data elements and metrics are captured in a key data governance artifact—a data dictionary.

As depicted in Table 2.4, a data dictionary contains:

- Business metadata: definition and meaning of the data entity or attribute, relationship with other elements, valid values, and related business rules
- Technical metadata: type and format of the data element, its technical purpose such as for attributes that represent unique identifiers or metadata, and tables and column names to represent where the data is stored

While a data dictionary may be created for a system or the scope of one project, a data catalogue is a more comprehensive artifact.

A **data catalogue** is a repository of information about all enterprise data assets.

The scope of a data catalogue includes all systems and data storage of the organization—think of it as an inventory of data in all its shapes and forms managed by the enterprise.

In addition to the business and technical metadata described above, a data catalogue identifies:

- Master source of data: when the same data items are replicated and shared among multiple systems, this indicates which system is considered the authoritative source and the point of reference for all other systems
- **Data lineage:** tracing how data flows through the various systems and undergoes transformations
- **Data security classification:** required levels of protection dependent on the sensitivity of data (see Table 2.6)
- Data retention requirements: the duration of time that data must be retained by an organization to comply with business or regulatory requirements

Table 2.6 Data Security Classification Example

Security classification	Level of protection	Examples
Public	• Can be openly shared with public, e.g., on the company website	Office locations, number of employees
Internal	• Available to staff company-wide • Limited control—minimal impact if exposed	Company policies
Confidential	• Confidentiality is important from business perspective • Negative impact on business and/or brand if exposed	Financial details, sales numbers
Restricted	• Highly sensitive, may be protected by NDAs (non-disclosure agreements) • Exposure may lead to lawsuits, heavy fines, or significant regulatory and reputational impact	Trade secrets, customer personal data

A data catalogue of a large enterprise can be quite complex and may be maintained using specialized tools integrated with other enterprise systems to automate data catalogue updates.

One of the main goals of data governance is to ensure data quality, from defining acceptable quality standards to planning and implementing data quality measures.

Quality data must be clean, consistent, conformed, current, and comprehensive, adding up to *five C's of quality data*.[5]

Table 2.7 Characteristics (Five C's) of Quality Data

Characteristic	Description
Clean	Clean data is accurate and contains no invalid entries
Consistent	Consistent data maintains the same values and interpretation when stored in multiple locations
Conformed	Conformed data uses shared standards and dimensions to reflect the same business meaning
Current	Current data is as recent as required for business purposes
Comprehensive	Comprehensive data is sufficient and complete for its intended purpose

Data quality is essential for successful business analytics. Generating a high-performing predictive model from inaccurate, incomplete, or biased data will result in resources wasted on an unusable or misleading predictive model.

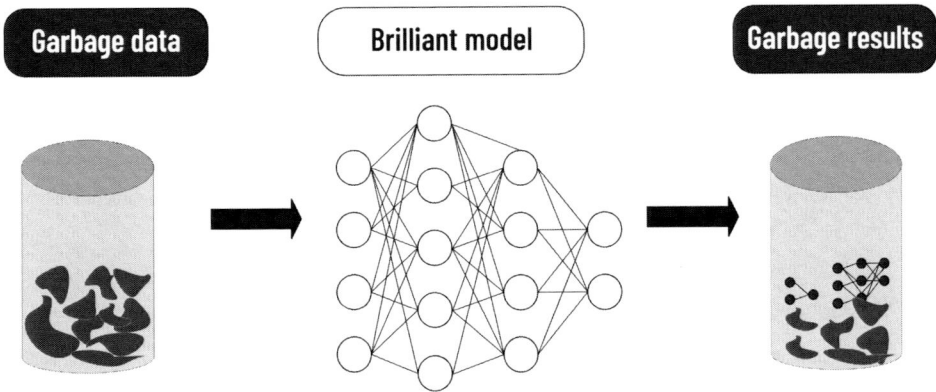

Figure 2.10 The "Garbage in, Garbage out" Principle

Data Storage and Operations

Data storage and operations encompass the management of data assets, including data storage, integration, transformation, and transportation solutions, consisting of such activities as:

- Operating and maintaining data storage solutions
- Creating and maintaining solutions for extracting, transforming, transporting, and integrating data
- Creating, maintaining, and destroying data assets

Data storage and operations encapsulate a broad range of processes required to support all data assets and may differ depending on the types of systems and where they are deployed. This includes the management of structured and unstructured data storage and analytical systems as well as data pipelines, which we will discuss in more detail in Chapter 8.

To ensure data quality across all data operations processes, organizations must follow data policies and procedures established through data governance, as discussed above.

Data Analytics

Data analytics encompasses planning and managing the processing of data for analytical purposes and creating analytics solutions to support business decision-making.

Data analytics activities include:

- Data profiling, preparation, and wrangling for analytical purposes
- Data exploration, querying, and mining
- Designing and developing analytics solutions

These activities will be covered in detail in the rest of the book.

Data Security

Data security encompasses practices for ensuring appropriate access and use of data in accordance with business and regulatory requirements.

Data security activities include:

- Enforcing privacy and security rules, including monitoring compliance and response to security incidents
- Establishing access management policies and procedures
- Defining and implementing data protection protocols such as data encryption

The level of protection required for different groups of data will depend on data security classification such as in the example shown in Table 2.6.

As business analytics solutions rely on enterprise data, we must be aware at all times of how this data must be protected and used responsibly. Some important aspects of this will be covered in Section 11.4.

2.6 MODELLING DATA

To better understand and manage the variety of data across the enterprise, data modelling is used to represent data structures and relationships.

A **data model** is an abstract model that organizes elements of data and standardizes how they relate to one another and the properties of real-world entities.[6]

Data modelling approaches discussed in this chapter are applied to structured data. Data models define and restrict how data will be stored and processed, which makes management of structured data more procedural, more prescriptive, and easier to manage. Unstructured data may not conform to a strict data model or will have a much more complex, varied, and unrestricted structure.

There are three levels of data modelling distinguished by the level of detail and intended usage.

Table 2.8 Levels of Data Modelling

Level of modelling	Conceptual	Logical	Physical
Level of abstraction	High-level business view	Design view	Implementation blueprint
Audience	Business stakeholders, project team	Architect, designer, data modeller	Database administrator, engineer
Goal	Communicate a structured business view of data	Understand the details of the data	Capture a detailed database design
Level of detail	Names business entities Captures business relationships between entities	Entities as data objects Relationships between data objects Primary and foreign keys Entity attributes	Physical object definitions, e.g., tables and columns Referential integrity rules, e.g., foreign keys and constraints Performance and optimization entities, e.g., indexes or partitions
Application dependence	Application-agnostic	Application-agnostic	Application-specific

Conceptual data models are used to:

- Name key business concepts (business entities)
- Name relationships between business entities
- Enforce consistent terminology
- Support business knowledge
- Serve as a communication tool for architects, analysts, and business stakeholders

Conceptual models are **application-agnostic**—that is, they are independent of applications and databases where the data might be managed. They call out business concepts that exist independent of technology implementation. For example, the concepts captured in the following case study example are relevant to YardExperts' business regardless of what systems are used to manage the data and whether the company is using technology to track this information. Concepts such as customer, product, and order are relevant even to a paper-based business that sells products to customers.

CASE STUDY

YardExperts: A Conceptual Data Model

The conceptual model in this example highlights concepts related to customers placing orders for various products based on their preferences. Customers send in payments for orders and may make complaints against orders.

This is the simplest form of a conceptual model that shows only the main concepts.

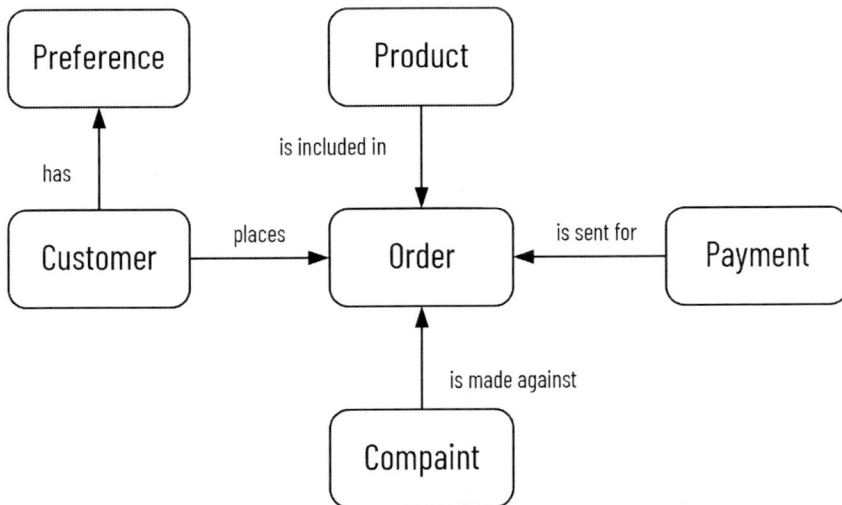

Figure 2.11 Conceptual Data Model Example

Logical models elaborate on conceptual models. They translate business entities into data entities, which sometimes results in defining multiple data entities to represent a business concept. These models will be more specific both in describing the relationships between entities as well as entity characteristics.

Logical data models are used to:

- Establish a detailed description of data entities, including their characteristics
- Optimize the logical organization and structure of data objects
- Fully define relationships between data entities
- Identify additional data entities that may not directly relate to business concepts but are required for optimizing the data structure according to data modelling best practices or specific requirements
- Provide a blueprint for the physical design of data objects to store data captured in the model

There are two main modelling approaches for structured data, each suited for a different purpose:

- **Relational data models** are based on real-world objects represented as tables (relations). They are used for modelling data structures in transactional (operational) systems of an enterprise.
- **Dimensional data models** are based on two types of tables: facts and dimensions. *Facts* represent business events being measured, and *dimensions* provide their attributes. These models are best suited for analytical systems.

Table 2.9 Relational versus Dimensional Data Modelling

Modelling approach	Relational	Dimensional
Used for	Operational systems, transactional data	Analytical systems, aggregated or pre-processed analytical data
Units of storage	Tables (relations)	Cubes
Normalization	Data is normalized: optimized for retrieval and updates	Data is de-normalized: optimized for querying
Numbers of tables	Many tables with relationships between them	Few fact tables connected to many dimensional tables
Elements	Entities, attributes, and *relationships*	Facts and *dimensions*
Models	Entity relationship diagrams (ERDs)	Snowflake schema, star schema[7]

The main building blocks of relational data models are entities and relationships, and the model itself is referred to as an **entity relationship diagram (ERD)**.

Table 2.10 ERD Building Blocks

ERD building block	Examples
Entity: A person, object, event, or concept about which the business keeps data	Customer, product, order, supplier, employee, department, interaction, complaint
Relationship: a logical link between entities that represents how entities relate to each other via business rules or constraints	A product *is supplied by* a supplier An order *contains* products A department *is composed of* employees
Attribute: a distinct characteristic of an entity for which data is maintained	A customer has a *name, address, and cell number* A product has a *price, colour, and size*

Relationships are characterized by **cardinality**, which indicates the number of instances of one entity that can be related to an instance of another entity.

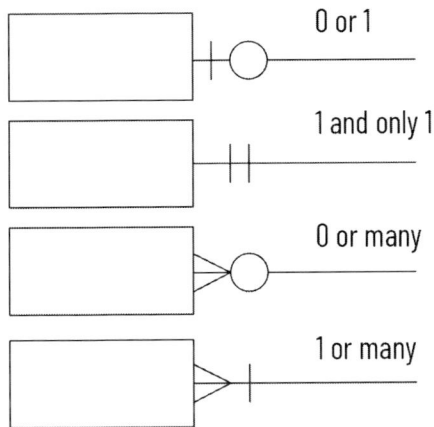

Figure 2.12 Cardinality Symbols in ERDs ("Crow's Foot" Notation)

⚙️ **EXAMPLE**

From Conceptual to Logical Modelling

To illustrate the levels of modelling, let's consider an important business entity—a customer. In a conceptual model, it may be represented by a customer entity highlighting its key relationships, such as that customers place orders.

In a logical model, the data designer may model different groups of customer information. For example, if customers can have multiple addresses, a logical model will define separate customer and address entities with a relationship between them.

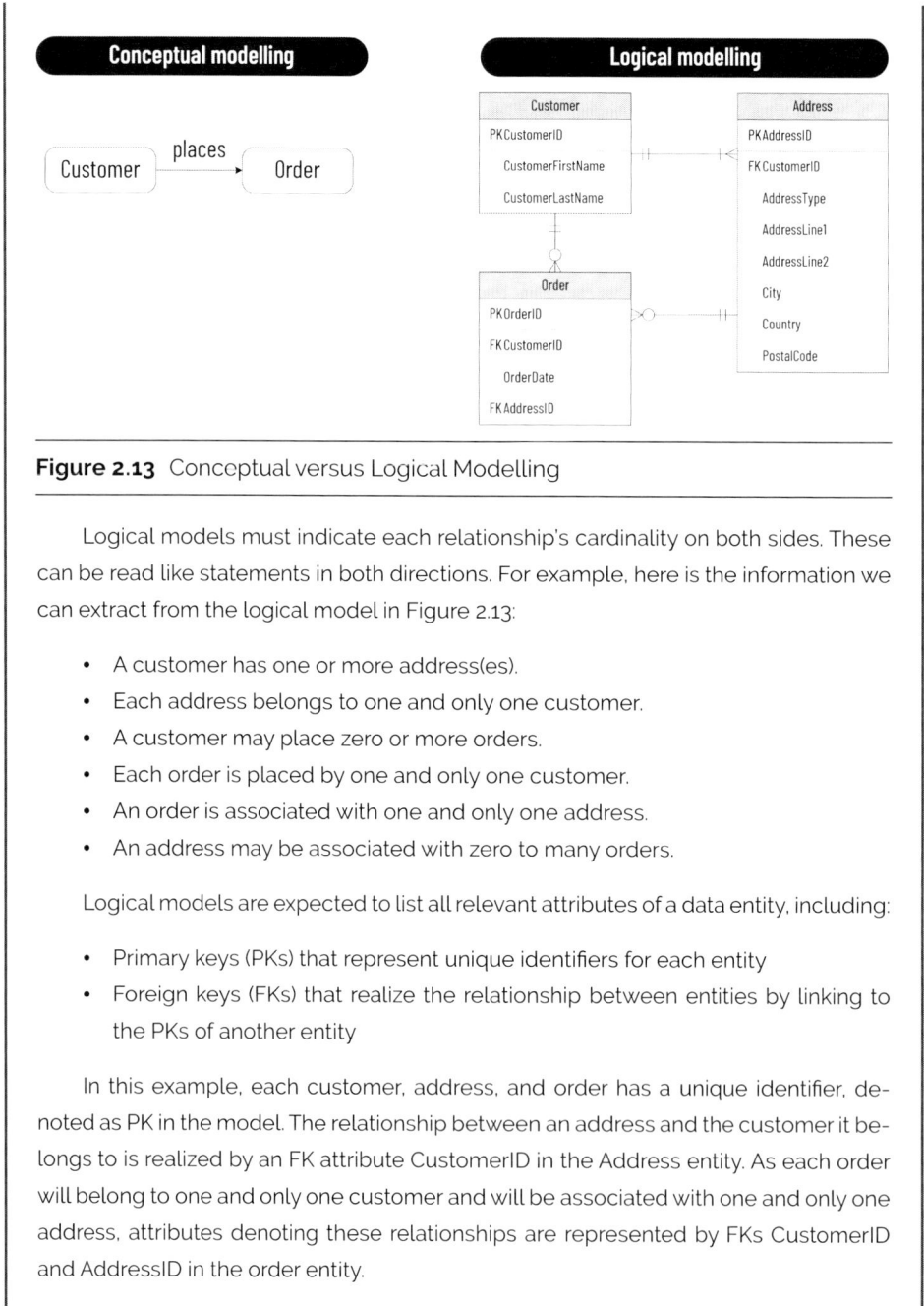

Figure 2.13 Conceptual versus Logical Modelling

Logical models must indicate each relationship's cardinality on both sides. These can be read like statements in both directions. For example, here is the information we can extract from the logical model in Figure 2.13:

- A customer has one or more address(es).
- Each address belongs to one and only one customer.
- A customer may place zero or more orders.
- Each order is placed by one and only one customer.
- An order is associated with one and only one address.
- An address may be associated with zero to many orders.

Logical models are expected to list all relevant attributes of a data entity, including:

- Primary keys (PKs) that represent unique identifiers for each entity
- Foreign keys (FKs) that realize the relationship between entities by linking to the PKs of another entity

In this example, each customer, address, and order has a unique identifier, denoted as PK in the model. The relationship between an address and the customer it belongs to is realized by an FK attribute CustomerID in the Address entity. As each order will belong to one and only one customer and will be associated with one and only one address, attributes denoting these relationships are represented by FKs CustomerID and AddressID in the order entity.

Physical data models serve as specifications for storing data in a particular application—that is, they are **application-specific**. Such models include complete implementation details required for creating and managing databases. Physical data modelling is a tool for database design and management. Conceptual and logical models are used for understanding and analyzing data for analytics purposes.

2.7 CHAPTER SUMMARY

Key Points to Remember

- All data undergoes a life cycle, from the moment it is created, through its usage and transformation and until destruction.
- Understanding the business domain is key to transforming the data into useful information.
- Operational and analytical systems have different purposes that may require different designs and data structures.
- Analytical systems allow the combining and integrating of data from multiple operational systems for more comprehensive analysis.
- While some operational systems support analytical capabilities such as in-database analytics, these capabilities will be limited compared to specialized analytical platforms.
- Every enterprise must define and manage its master, transaction, and reference data.
- Metadata plays an important role in data governance by describing different types of data and defining their valid use.
- Using open-source data carries certain risks related to not having control over how the data is sourced, processed, and presented.
- Machine-generated data contributes significantly to the big data phenomenon.
- The success of analytics in an organization heavily depends on the maturity of data management activities and data quality.
- Modelling data and understanding data models are important skills for data analysis.

Key Terms

Analytical data: data created and used to generate analytical insights and make business decisions.

Analytical systems: systems used to aggregate data from a variety of sources for further analysis and to support decision-making.

Application-agnostic data model: a model created independent of applications and databases where data might be managed.

Application-specific data model: a physical data model created as a specification for storing data in a particular application.

Attribute: a distinct characteristic of an entity for which data is maintained.

Cardinality: a characteristic of a relationship between entities indicating the number of instances of one entity that can be related to an instance of another entity.

Critical data element: a data element deemed critical for successful business operations.

Data analytics: planning and managing the processing of data for analytical purposes and creating analytical solutions to support business decision-making.

Data architecture: planning and designing how an organization's data resources should be structured and connected, ensuring that data is available to support business activities.

Data archiving (retention): storing data that is no longer actively used for a defined retention period.

Data catalogue: a repository of information about all enterprise data assets.

Data destruction (purging, permanent deletion): removal of every copy of a data item from enterprise records.

Data dictionary: a repository of information about data, including its meaning, origin, structure, format, and relationship with other data.

Data governance: processes and practices used to oversee the management of data to ensure its quality, security, and proper usage.

Data life cycle: a sequence of operations performed with data from its creation to destruction.

Data lineage: tracing how data flows through the various systems and undergoes transformations.

Data management: processes and practices used to manage an organization's data throughout its life cycle.

Data model: an abstract model that organizes elements of data and standardizes how they relate to one another and the properties of real-world entities.

Data preparation and storage (storage and maintenance): storing, maintaining, and preparing data for use.

Data security: practices for ensuring appropriate access and use of data in accordance with business and regulatory requirements.

Data security classification: required levels of protection dependent on the sensitivity of data.

Data sourcing (data capture, data acquisition): collecting and capturing data values from various sources.

Data storage and operations: management of data assets including data storage, integration, transformation, and transportation solutions.

Data usage (permitted use of data): application of data to the tasks of operating and managing the enterprise.

Dimensional data model: a model based on two types of tables, facts and dimensions, where facts represent business events being measured and dimensions provide their attributes.

Entity: A person, object, event, or concept about which a business keeps data.

Entity relationship diagram (ERD): a relational data model depicting data entities and relationships between them.

External data: data of interest generated outside the enterprise.

Human-generated data: data created by people using software systems and electronic devices.

Internal data: data generated from operating an enterprise.

Machine-generated data: data created by software systems and electronic devices programmed to do so through automation and capturing of events.

Master data (master lists, catalogues, authoritative source, golden record of data): key business data entities shared across the enterprise.

Master data management: a set of rules and processes established to ensure the integrity and consistent use of master data across the enterprise.

Metadata: data that describes and characterizes other data to support its understanding and interpretation.

Open-source data: data freely available on the internet.

Operational systems (enterprise systems, enterprise applications, transactional systems): systems used to record and manage the day-to-day operations of the enterprise.

Primary data: data collected for a specific purpose through personal experience or by collecting evidence.

Reference data (domain values, code tables, lookup tables, reference codes): data used to standardize and classify other data and establish permissible values for organizational use.

Relational data model: a model based on real-world objects represented as tables of rows and columns (relations).

Relationship: a logical link between entities that represents how entities relate to each other via business rules or constraints.

Secondary data: data that has been collected and recorded by someone else than the user of data.

Third-party data: data obtained (purchased) from companies that sell data products.

Transaction: a time-bound event that happens through the operation of the business.

Transaction data (operational data, operating data, flow data, time-stamped data): data capturing the details of business transactions.

Questions for Critical Thought

1. What are the main types of structured enterprise data?
2. What is the purpose of master data management, and why is it important?
3. How is reference data used in analytics?
4. How does the level of data governance in an organization impact its ability to produce useful business analytics?
5. Why do enterprises destroy data?
6. Consider the examples of internal and external data sources in Figure 2.7. What data quality, variety, or veracity challenges could you expect from different data sources?
7. What is the purpose of data modelling, and how can it be used to support analytics?

Test Your Knowledge

1. What type of enterprise data is described?

   A list of permissible values to describe different customer purchasing intentions such as "Will definitely buy," "Will only buy if on sale," "Might buy as a gift," "Will only consider if other models not available," and "Will never buy."
   a. Reference data
   b. Master data
   c. Transaction data
   d. Analytical data

2. What type of enterprise data is described?

   A list of retail locations that captures each location number, name, address, and square footage.
   a. Reference data
   b. Master data
   c. Transaction data
   d. Analytical data

3. What type of enterprise data is described?

   A tracker for all phone calls received by company's call centre, including date, time, and duration of the call; the name of the customer if provided; the reason for the call; and the resolution of the call.
   a. Reference data
   b. Master data
   c. Transaction data
   d. Analytical data

4. To better track all phone calls received by company's call centre, the following statuses are used to track the resolution of the calls: "Resolved," "Callback required," "Duplicate," and "Not resolved."

   What type of enterprise data is represented by these call resolution statuses?
   a. Reference data
   b. Master data
   c. Transaction data
   d. Analytical data

5. A historical record of all of a company's retail transactions is stored in an enterprise data warehouse. To facilitate faster generation of monthly sales reports, daily sales totals per location and per product are calculated and stored to avoid repeating the

same summarizations every time a new user requests a summary report. What type of enterprise data is represented in these daily sales totals?

a. Reference data
b. Master data
c. Transaction data
d. Analytical data

Recommended Readings

DAMA International: www.dama.org

Howson, C. (2013). *Successful Business Intelligence, Second Edition: Unlock the Value of BI and Big Data*. McGraw-Hill Education.

Kamaly, T. (2022). *The Importance of Data Lifecycle Management (DLM) and Best Practices*. IEEE Computer Society. Retrieved August 25, 2023, from www.computer.org/publications/tech-news/trends/the-importance-of-data-lifecycle-management.

Notes

1. Government of Canada. (2023, July 23). *Where to Keep Your Records, for How Long and How to Request the Permission to Destroy Them Early*. Retrieved November 11, 2023, from www.canada.ca/en/revenue-agency/services/tax/businesses/topics/keeping-records/where-keep-your-records-long-request-permission-destroy-them-early.html.
2. Beckmann, J. (2023, July 12). *30 Impressive Big Data Statistics for 2023*. TechReport. Retrieved February 22, 2024, from techreport.com/statistics/big-data-statistics/.
3. Poremba, S. (2021, November 5). *6 Potential Long-Term Impacts of a Data Breach*. Security Intelligence. Retrieved February 22, 2024, from securityintelligence.com/articles/long-term-impacts-security-breach/.
4. Finlay, S. (2014). *Predictive Analytics, Data Mining and Big Data: Myths, Misconceptions and Methods*. Palgrave Macmillan, p. 75.
5. Sherman, R. (2015). *Business Intelligence Guidebook: From Data Integration to Analytics*. Morgan Kaufmann (Elsevier), pp. 12–13.
6. Wikipedia. (n.d.). *Data model*. Retrieved February 16, 2024, from en.wikipedia.org/wiki/Data_model.
7. Sherman (2015), pp. 208–13.

Chapter 3

Business Analytics and Its Applications

How can we apply analytics in a business context? What do organizations measure and predict using data? What are the practical uses of data insights in managing an enterprise and in running a business? This chapter will highlight:

- How business analytics can support an organization's goals
- Examples of using analytics to manage different aspects of an organization
- Frequently used marketing, customer, financial, and other metrics

3.1 GOALS OF BUSINESS ANALYTICS

Managing business is ultimately about a few fundamental goals:

- Increasing revenue
- Maximizing efficiency
- Minimizing risks
- Staying competitive

Each of these goals requires making decisions: decisions about which materials to use and what suppliers to purchase the materials from; decisions on which products to develop and which to discontinue; decisions about setting the optimal price for a product or service; and decisions on what candidates to hire and how much to pay the best employees to keep them from leaving.

Decisions often require predictions—about economic environment, customers' preferences, competitors' moves, and the company's own affairs. Making better decisions using data and coming up with insights to base these decisions on are enabled by business analytics.

The journey from collecting data to making decisions is not straightforward. Data by itself will not give you all the answers—you will need to ask the right questions first.

For example, knowing that your business is losing 10% of its customer base every quarter is not enough to decide what to do next. Before you can turn this trend around, you need to know why customers are leaving, what they are unhappy about, and what you can change to make them stay. To find answers, you'll need to examine the data from different perspectives, make and test hypotheses, discover important factors, and understand how these factors influence customers' decisions to stay or leave.

Then, you would use these insights to decide what changes to make to entice customers to stay (and attract new ones). Should you change the product, the price, the packaging, or the manufacturing process? Do you need to modify the distribution channels or the service model? Or should the solution involve changes to multiple aspects of your business?

The process of getting the answers from data to help companies make better decisions is what business analytics is about. That's why in this context we use a more specific term: *business analytics* instead of *data analytics* or *analytics*.

Analytics is a broad term that refers to examination of data using statistical and computational methods to uncover patterns and insights. We can perform computational and statistical analysis of meteorological data: data collected from scientific experiments or sociological research. The goal of analysis may be to prove or disprove a scientific hypothesis or predict weather patterns. The goal of business analytics is to provide insights useful for managing a business.

Business analytics is the examination of data to uncover insights that give a businessperson the knowledge to make informed decisions. Figure 3.1 highlights how business analytics can support an enterprise and its goals of increasing revenue (making money), maximizing efficiency (reducing costs), minimizing risks (avoiding problems), and staying competitive (increasing the chances of survival in the market).

Sales & Marketing	Research & Development
⊘ Increase revenue	⊘ Stay competitive
Understand customer needs	Exploit competitive advantage
Find prospective customers	Predict market needs
Make attractive offers	Make better products
Operations	**Risk & Compliance**
⊘ Maximize efficiency	⊘ Minimize risks
Improve business process	Reduce uncertainty
Increase automation	Comply with regulations
Reduce cost	Prevent fraud

Figure 3.1 Business Goals Served by Analytics

3.2 ANALYTICS APPLICATIONS IN AN ENTERPRISE

Achieving the goals depicted in Figure 3.1 will require analytics applied to various aspects of running a business. Analytics insights can be used to address different business challenges, from better understanding potential customers and planning how to satisfy their needs to setting up the production of things that customers would want to buy, while finding the best sources of materials to manufacture these things and determining the prices that would be attractive to customers while still allowing the business to make a profit.

It should not be a surprise if these sound like typical management tasks, as business analytics can be applied to measure and optimize any business function. The next figure provides an overview of *analytics use cases*—uses of analytics for achieving a specific objective. Further down, we will examine these use cases in more detail, exploring how each analytics insight can support a different aspect or managing an enterprise.

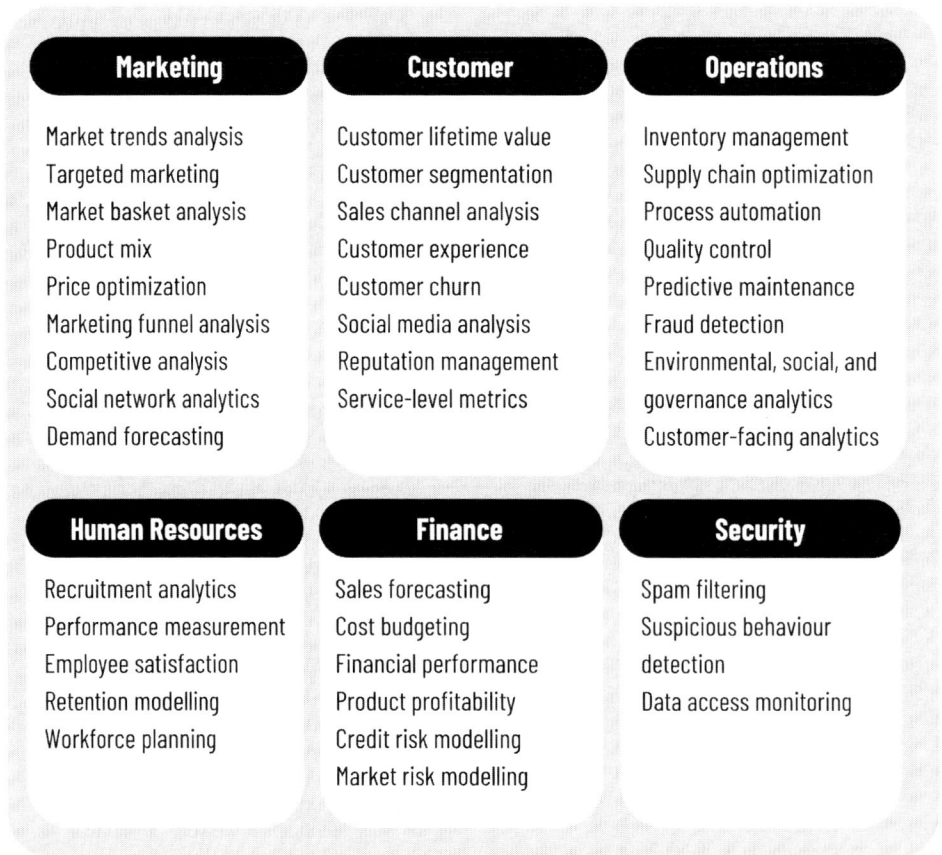

Marketing

Market trends analysis
Targeted marketing
Market basket analysis
Product mix
Price optimization
Marketing funnel analysis
Competitive analysis
Social network analytics
Demand forecasting

Customer

Customer lifetime value
Customer segmentation
Sales channel analysis
Customer experience
Customer churn
Social media analysis
Reputation management
Service-level metrics

Operations

Inventory management
Supply chain optimization
Process automation
Quality control
Predictive maintenance
Fraud detection
Environmental, social, and governance analytics
Customer-facing analytics

Human Resources

Recruitment analytics
Performance measurement
Employee satisfaction
Retention modelling
Workforce planning

Finance

Sales forecasting
Cost budgeting
Financial performance
Product profitability
Credit risk modelling
Market risk modelling

Security

Spam filtering
Suspicious behaviour detection
Data access monitoring

Figure 3.2 Business Analytics Use Cases

CASE STUDY

Use of Analytics in Different Areas of YardExperts' Business

The YardExperts management team is using a variety of analytics solutions to make better business decisions.

In the marketing area, the company conducts regular surveys to identify market trends and the changing needs of the consumers (*market trends analysis*). Understanding changing market trends, especially in the landscaping and gardening sector, is crucial for having the right mix of products in stores for the upcoming gardening season.

As part of its customer service, the company measures the adherence of all snow removal contracts to the established service levels (*service-level metrics*). Timely clearing of snow is an important customer satisfaction factor.

To make its operations more efficient, the company started to use predictive modelling to order spare parts for equipment repairs in advance (*preventative maintenance modelling*). Lengthy waits for the delivery of spare parts during the high season can lead to reduced revenue and loss of customer base.

The company's Research and Development department launched a pilot program of sending customers treatment recommendations using an innovative AI-based disease and pest detection tool (an example of *customer-facing analytics*).

YardExperts is in the service industry, so its success depends on people—its employees and contractors. In the landscaping business, work volume fluctuates significantly with seasons and weather patterns. It is imperative to have a solid process for evaluating and predicting resource needs in order to create a work schedule and engage temporary resources when required. To achieve this, the company uses *workforce planning analytics*.

As with any other business, YardExperts must carefully manage its finances. Due to the seasonality of the business and fluctuations in expenses and revenue between gardening and winter seasons, *cash flow analysis* is critical for the financial health of the company.

Not all analytical capabilities need to be supported internally. Organizations may choose to outsource some of them to external providers. For example, while YardExperts is concerned about security, the company is not large enough to sustain its own security team. Instead, it has a service contract with a cybersecurity service provider that regularly conducts security audits to confirm the company's *security rating* and data protection protocols, and to ensure the company uses appropriate spam filtering and malware protection software. The same agency also provides video security monitoring and perimeter detection analysis for all company premises.

These analytics solutions are the tools that different departments use to manage their respective parts of the business. In addition, a key performance indicator (KPI) dashboard was developed for the YardExperts executives. The purpose of a dashboard is to present multiple analytics insights in one view to make it easier to visualize performance at a glance. From an executive perspective, instead of an in-depth view into every business function, a high-level overview of the overall performance is important. The executive audience does not manage day-to-day details but needs to know the general trend and be alerted to signs of troubles.

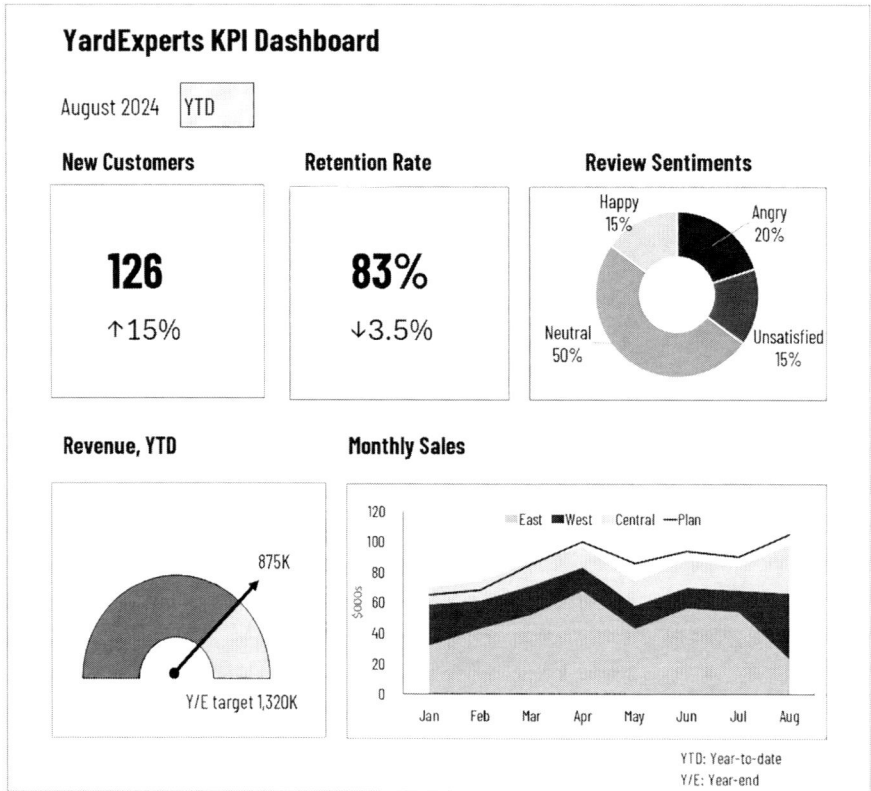

YardExperts KPI Dashboard

August 2024   YTD

New Customers

126

↑15%

Retention Rate

83%

↓3.5%

Review Sentiments

Happy 15%
Angry 20%
Neutral 50%
Unsatisfied 15%

Revenue, YTD

875K

Y/E target 1,320K

Monthly Sales

East West Central Plan

$000s

Jan Feb Mar Apr May Jun Jul Aug

YTD: Year-to-date
Y/E: Year-end

Figure 3.3 Executive Dashboard Example

Further on in the book, we will discuss different types of charts, what makes a good visualization, and how to define different metrics that would be presented on a dashboard like the one in Figure 3.3.

The rest of this chapter will provide an overview of metrics and approaches of applying analytics to various aspects of running a business. In the last chapter, we will review future trends and innovations made possible by the advances of data science.

3.3 MARKETING ANALYTICS

Marketing analytics is used to assess and improve the effectiveness of a company's marketing efforts. It encompasses the analysis of market needs (what to sell), prospective customers (who to sell to), and marketing channels (how to reach/attract customers).

The ultimate goal of marketing analytics is to improve *marketing return on investment* (*ROI*)—the growth of sales and revenue attributed to marketing activities in relation to the money spent on the campaign.

Market Trends Analysis

The analysis of market trends can take many forms. Predicting future customer preferences can provide a company with a competitive advantage, in particular, in the consumer goods industry. Data can be collected through surveys, focus groups, and social media analytics, among other methods. Big data plays a prominent role by providing a rich source of data that the future consumers willingly share on social media and the internet when they search for things they are interested in.

Sources like Google Trends, Mention, and BuzzSumo, to name a few, can provide businesses with analytics on trending keywords and topics. In many industries, there are market research companies specializing in a particular market. Some companies provide market research as a by-product of their main business, thus monetizing their access to large volumes of valuable data. For example, payment processors are in a position to assess purchasing trends by volumes, seasonality, and merchant categories when they have access to detailed payments data for a large share of the market. Of course, the data must be appropriately anonymized and aggregated before being sold to comply with privacy protection laws (refer to Chapter 11 for more on anonymization and other data protection strategies).

Due to the fast-paced growth in data generation and the ubiquity of information on the internet, most enterprises choose to purchase market research from data aggregators rather than replicate the same analysis internally.

Targeted Marketing

The purpose of targeted marketing is to maximize the effectiveness of marketing activities by identifying the most promising targets for advertising and marketing messaging.

This usually involves market segmentation (*audience segmentation*): the analysis of geodemographic and behavioural characteristics of potential customers to group them into segments with similar needs and preferences.

Segmentation allows the marketing teams to tailor the messages to each segment based on predictive modelling of:

- Customer intent: predicting what a particular person is interested in doing, e.g., purchasing a product, going on a trip, or cancelling a subscription
- Propensity to buy: predicting the likelihood of a customer making a purchase

- Uplift (net lift, true lift): predicting the impact of a marketing message on a lead, e.g., whether it will increase or decrease propensity to buy

Another application of this modelling is in designing recommender systems (*recommenders*)—algorithms that optimize individual recommendations for each customer or lead, frequently used on e-commerce websites to suggest similar products or products purchased by other customers with similar interests.

Market Basket Analysis

Market basket analysis refers to the identification of products often bought together to optimize product placement and generate cross-selling recommendations. It is widely used in merchandising for brick-and-mortar retailers as well as for optimizing the placement of products on e-commerce storefronts.

The results of market basket analysis may also feed into a recommendation algorithm.

Product Mix

A *product mix* is the assortment of products and services sold by the company in different markets. *Product mix optimization* involves identifying what products, variations of products, or product bundles to offer in different markets and regions, and in what quantities.

This optimization will involve the analysis of regional market trends, competitive analysis, and market segmentation in different markets. It will also depend on the demand forecasting for particular products and an understanding of the interactions between similar products, such as how the new premium product may impact the sales of a lower-end version of the same product.

Price Optimization

Pricing a product is a crucial decision for a business. Price optimization requires data on market trends and competition prices, on one hand, and, on the other hand, the internal costs of manufacturing, transportation, and support, as well as the current inventory and the expected life cycle of the product. In addition, price elasticity, or the sensitivity of potential customers to price changes, will play a role, and testing of different price points via A/B testing may provide additional insights (for more on A/B testing, see Section 6.1).

Price optimization models can also be used to develop a *dynamic pricing* algorithm— that is, a model that modifies prices in real time based on the market, product availability, and other insights.

Marketing Funnel Analysis

The *marketing funnel* is the journey of a prospective customer from first becoming aware of the product to purchasing it and becoming a loyal customer.

The purpose of marketing funnel analysis is to optimize the effectiveness of marketing channels and activities at each stage of the funnel, with the ultimate goal of converting a lead to a loyal customer. This analysis is used to optimize marketing campaigns and select the best channels for each stage in the marketing funnel. Some metrics used for the funnel analysis include:

- Reach (or the number of leads): potential customers who were reached through a campaign, post, or a newsletter (e.g., received an email or landed on the web page)
- Engagement (or the number of qualified leads): the leads that expressed an interest or engaged with the content, such as by responding to the marketing email, sharing a post, or reading the product description on the e-commerce site
- Lead scoring: the evaluation of leads by their interest and the level of engagement to identify their propensity to buy and customize marketing activities based on the score
- Conversions: the rate of leads converted to customers compared to total leads

Media mix modelling (*MMM*) refers to the analysis of engagement and spending across different marketing channels to evaluate their relative effectiveness at different stages of the marketing funnel and for different market segments.

The assessment of marketing channel effectiveness in its simplest form is based on associating a purchase with the advertisement or marketing message that led to the sale. Often, it is attributed to either the first or the last customer touchpoint. However, this approach does not take the omnichannel perspective into account. For example, a customer may have seen information about a new product on social media, on the company's website, on a movie streaming service, and in a marketing email. Which platform should be given credit for the purchase? Should the credit be distributed between different channels that allowed the marketing message to be reinforced, eventually leading to a sale? *Multi-touch attribution* models allow credit to be given to various marketing touchpoints that influence the conversion.

Competitive Analysis

Competitive analysis is a broad area of analyzing competitors and their offerings, prices, customer mix, marketing activities, and market share. Easier access to more data enables the application of various analytics approaches for this purpose. Competitor analysis also enables businesses to establish performance benchmarks for their own enterprise performance analysis.

Social media analytics can play a significant role in competitive analysis by providing access to large amounts of open-source data about the market and customer sentiments about different brands and products.

Sentiment analysis can be used to assess moods and emotions (positive, negative, or neutral) related to competitors' products, service offerings, and marketing campaigns, or the latest announcements.

Social Network Analysis

Social network analysis refers to the analysis of relationships and interactions within groups of people (networks)—from neighbourhoods to work relationships to social media networks. Understanding how individual members of a network are connected allows for the analysis of how they share information and influence each other.

These insights can be used for applications such as targeted advertising, when selecting particular individuals within the network to target with advertising, and for analysis of information distribution, social trends, or security analytics.

Demand Forecasting

The purpose of *demand forecasting* for particular products in particular markets is to estimate the expected revenue and the resources required to satisfy the demand. Demand forecasting plays a role in inventory management, procurement planning, and human resources allocation. In marketing, predicting potential changes in demand may drive decisions related to marketing campaign planning, promotional messages, and pricing optimization.

⚙ EXAMPLE

Measuring Email Engagement

A number of email marketing solutions on the market offer their customers detailed email engagement metrics,[1] such as:

- Glanced: the percentage of recipients who opened the email and viewed it for less than two seconds
- Skimmed: the percentage of recipients who opened the email and viewed it for two to eight seconds
- Read: the percentage of recipients who opened the email and viewed it for more than eight seconds

These metrics can be used both to assess the effectiveness of an email and to score the leads (the longer the recipient's engagement with an email, the higher the quality of the lead, which ultimately leads to the likelihood of a sale).

3.4 CUSTOMER ANALYTICS

Customer analytics focuses on examining customer motivations, needs, and behaviours to improve customer satisfaction and retention. Customers make inquiries, decide what to purchase and when, receive and use the product, post reviews and file complaints, buy more products (or not), and become the company's main promoters or detractors, depending on their level of satisfaction.

All these activities can be measured with the goal of improving customer experience, increasing the *customer lifetime value* (*CLV*) as a result. CLV is a key metric of customer analytics that captures the total revenue that will be received by a company from the customer over the length of their relationship.

Customer Segmentation

Customer segmentation is a variation of audience segmentation used to group customers by their characteristics, such as geodemographic data; by history, including past purchases and interactions; and by predicted future needs.

The most direct approach to customer segmentation is based on the money spent (such as Silver/Gold/Platinum) or the membership package (Base/Premium). However, this is not based on analytics. Using analytics, customers may be grouped by likely future interests (such as product gamification or educational value), CLV, or loyalty. A popular loyalty classification segments customers into Promoters, Neutrals, and Detractors based on the prevailing sentiment in their customer reviews or the number of referrals.

Sales Channel Analysis

Customer analytics overlap with both sales and service analytics.

This area focuses on the analysis of different distribution channels used to sell the company's products and services. Depending on the distribution model, the company may sell to wholesalers, to retail chains, or directly to the customer via e-commerce, direct mail, warehouses, or brick-and-mortar stores. The effectiveness of these channels can be measured by:

- Total revenue generated by each channel
- Average sales cycle length, which measures how long it takes to convert a lead into a customer
- Average order value, which measures the how much revenue does an average customer's order generate
- Average customer acquisition cost, measuring how much is spent on marketing and sales activities to acquire one customer (make one sale); this may include compensation such as a sales commission

Channel performance can also be measured based on profitability over a period of time, total CLV generated, and the customer experience reported by customers acquired through each channel.

Customer Experience

There are many approaches to measuring customer experience as this is an intangible concept requiring proxy metrics. One such metric is the *net promoter score (NPS)*—the difference between the percentage of customers that are promoters and those that are detractors.

A *customer satisfaction score* can be derived from the analysis of responses to a specially designed customer survey. Companies will craft questions specific to their business and what they consider important to the customers, and then collect, analyze, and assign weights to responses. Methodologies range from simple averages to complicated algorithms.

Many other metrics can serve as proxies for customer satisfaction, including those measuring customer churn, service levels, and social media sentiment, as outlined below.

Customer Churn

Customer churn (also known as *customer attrition*) is a loss of existing customers. *Customer churn rate* is the percentage of customers that leave (cancel contracts, stop buying products) in a given time period. For an individual customer, a *churn score* measures the likelihood that the customer will churn.

Customer churn analysis (also referred to as *customer retention modelling*) focuses on identifying factors that cause customer churn, predicting which customers are likely to churn and when to take what action to retain them.

Social Media Analysis and Reputation Management

Social media analysis can have multiple purposes, from assessing the first reactions to a new product to competitive analysis. The key goal, though, is overall reputation management, referring to monitoring and measuring the social media sentiment about the company. This is achieved by measuring:

- Customer reviews: volume, average rating, and sentiment
- Website performance: page rank, number of visitors, bounce rate, and quality of leads generated
- Social media engagement metrics: shares, mentions, and reactions

Service-Level Metrics

After the first sale, customer loyalty and CLV depend on the customer experience with the product itself and the post-sale service. For products that include a service component, such as customer support, warranty, repairs, and returns, companies must assess the quality of service to:

- Improve customer satisfaction by providing a better service
- Avoid complaints and financial penalties for not fulfilling the obligations outlined in a service-level agreement (SLA)

Service metrics may include:

- First response time: the time it takes to provide the customer with an initial response (also known as time-to-first-response or response SLA)
- First call resolution rate: the percentage of requests resolved on the first call
- Time to resolution (TTR): the elapsed time from receiving the request to fully resolving it (also called average handle time)
- SLA compliance rate: the percentage of service requests with TTR within the established service levels

- Escalation rate: the percentage of service requests that required an escalation to be resolved
- Self-serve resolution rate: the percentage of requests that customers were able to resolve by using self-serve options

---

⚙ **EXAMPLE**

Customer Journey Analytics

A customer journey is the sequence of interactions that a customer has with a company. Depending on the product, it will include touchpoints before and after the purchase, from awareness to expressing an interest, purchase, delivery, and using or returning the product. Customer journey analytics will monitor:[2]

- Journey milestones, e.g., achieving a milestone like a purchase or becoming a promoter
- End-of-journey success, e.g., customer satisfaction score or CLV
- In-journey indicators, which assess customer's sentiments at different steps of the customer journey, e.g., satisfaction with the speed and quality of warranty repairs

Connecting individual customer metrics to a customer journey allows not only the evaluation of the individual steps of the journey but also perspective on how they are connected and might impact each other.

3.5 OPERATIONS ANALYTICS

Operations analytics is used to analyze company operations and process metrics to improve efficiency and reduce the cost of running a business. It covers the analysis of the supply chain, manufacturing, and service delivery, and can be as broad and varied as types of industries and business models. The main objective of operational analytics is to optimize a company's *operating expenses*.

In this category, we also consider *customer-facing analytics*: analytics-based product features. These features are used by customers as they use the products they purchase. For example, fitness tracker users refer to health and fitness analytics indicators on their devices.

While the purpose of internal operational analytics is to manage and reduce operational costs, customer-facing analytics is concerned with making the company's products more competitive and creating new revenue streams.

Inventory Management

Managing inventory is one of the most fundamental operations challenges. The balance between having sufficient inventory to satisfy demand and avoid backorders without over-spending on excessive inventory and its storage is an eternal problem. Monitoring the inventory starts with tracking:

- Inventory volumes—by product type and its fluctuations, with particular attention paid to peak seasons
- Average time to sell—how long each individual item stays on the inventory
- Out-of-stock frequency and duration—such as measuring the percentage of time when a particular item is not available, and the average duration of the unavailability periods

Inventory performance analysis will rely on these metrics as well as demand forecasting to allow for future planning and optimization. The ultimate goal is automating inventory management through prescriptive analytics to determine when and how much stock to order to optimize inventory levels and costs.

Supply Chain Optimization

Optimized inventory management also relies on the performance of the supply chain, with advanced analytics used to:

- Determine appropriate production levels and/or procurement volumes and timelines
- Optimize route planning and logistics
- Measure and analyze supply chain issues such as defects, delivery problems, misdelivery, and goods damage or loss
- Benchmark and compare supplier performance

Process Automation

Operations in an organization rely on processes—standardized sequences of activities performed to achieve specific business goals, such as investigating an insurance claim, conducting a medical test, or completing a quality audit.

Process automation involves using technology to improve the quality and speed of execution of individual tasks. While business processes can be supported by workflow automation technologies, using embedded analytics (further discussed in Section 9.6) can bring additional improvements by reducing the decision and action latency.

Quality Control

Statistical methods are widely used for measuring quality in many industries, especially where rigorous standards exist, such as parts manufacturing, food processing, health care, and pharmaceuticals. Manufacturing standards determine what needs to be measured, and then quality metrics are applied to identify deviations from the standards and whether they are within an acceptable range. Methodologies such as statistical process control and Six Sigma are used in many industries for that purpose, with a heavy emphasis on diagnostics for root cause analysis.

Advanced analytics can provide additional benefits in this area by using machine learning to detect unusual patterns and identify new quality issues or unexpected deviations.

Predictive Maintenance

It usually costs more to fix things after they break than to conduct preventative maintenance. When an organization's resources are limited, its ability to prioritize maintenance activities based on the likelihood of breakage allows it to minimize the losses from equipment or infrastructure breakdown, and potentially even more damaging service outages.

Predictive maintenance can use advanced machine learning methods to identify patterns that lead to breakdowns based on historical data to build predictive models. Depending on the industry, this may involve real-time analytics of sensor data such as measuring physical characteristics of pressure, temperature, vibration, and air or liquid flow.

Fraud Detection

Fraud involves misrepresentation of facts with the intention of deception, with examples including identity theft, credit card fraud, loan and mortgage fraud, falsified insurance claims, and tax fraud. The main purpose of fraud analytics is to identify patterns of fraudulent activities to detect and prevent future fraud.

Data mining methods are used to analyze large volumes of data about fraudulent and legitimate transactions to detect patterns and similarities. The resulting predictive model can then classify new transactions or activities in real time by calculating a *fraud score*— the likelihood that a given transaction is fraudulent. This score can be used with different decision-making approaches, from decision support to full automation, such as when a suspicious credit card payment is blocked, and the card is declined during the payment process.

Environmental, Social, and Governance Analytics

The emerging area of environmental, social, and governance (ESG) analytics measures how an organization handles its social, environmental, and corporate responsibilities. These considerations become important from the perspective of ethical, socially responsible investing and require that companies voluntarily disclose a set of metrics that measure the company's performance in these areas. Some of the metrics could be:

- Carbon footprint or greenhouse emissions (and its reduction)
- Energy and water usage and efficiency metrics
- Waste reduction
- Diversity, equity, and inclusion metrics
- Employee equal opportunity and equal pay

- Community involvement
- Health and safety
- Ethical business practices

Not all of these metrics are quantitative—qualitative metrics are based on proxy measures and data collected through surveys and observations. This is a challenging area of analytics in many organizations due to the scarcity of data, the need for new approaches to data collection, and the potential ambiguity of proxy metrics.

Customer-Facing Analytics

Analytics features built into company products can take many forms:

- Customer dashboards, from fitness trackers to the expense dashboards provided by banking service providers
- Smart devices that take measurements, record data, report, predict, and even make decisions
- Virtual assistants that interpret customer instructions and initiate actions such as making appointments
- Adaptive algorithms such as computer games that change strategy based on how the player is performing

⚙ EXAMPLE

Many Facets of Predictive Maintenance

Identification of potential weak spots in sophisticated equipment, spread-out networks, or hidden infrastructure is a complex undertaking. It may require special sensors to collect measurements such as water pressure, fuel temperature, or vibration levels. These measurements may require real-time processing to provide timely alerts of potential issues. Complex algorithms will be required to analyze large volumes of data received at high velocity, and a breakdown prediction may be based on multiple factors.

At the same time, the benefits can be enormous, especially when expensive or critical infrastructure such as power transmissions, telecommunications, or water supply are involved.[3]

To measure the effectiveness of predictive maintenance, the following metrics can be utilized:

- Planned maintenance percentage—e.g., the percentage of the time spent on planned maintenance versus maintenance overall
- Mean time between failures—measuring the duration of time the equipment was operational on average between maintenance outages
- Unplanned downtime percentage—measuring the unplanned losses of productivity or service due to breakdowns

3.6 PEOPLE ANALYTICS

People (human resources) analytics focuses on the human resources (HR) of the enterprise—employees—from the hiring cycle to the end of the employer-employee relationship. Every company's growth and success depend on hiring qualified workers, supporting them in doing their work efficiently, and being able to retain qualified and productive employees. People analytics may also be referred to as HR analytics, talent analytics, or workforce analytics.

Some of the key outcomes of people analytics are an accurate picture of the *total cost of workforce* and the *employee satisfaction*.

Recruitment Analytics

Recruitment is a costly undertaking, involving fees for agencies, head-hunters, and background checks; time spent by internal employees on candidate assessment and interviews; as well as onboarding and training costs.

Recruitment cost to hire is a metric used to capture the total cost of this process, from the moment the decision to hire is made to having a new employee onboarded and ready to work. *Average time to hire* measures the duration of the recruitment process. The longer the process takes, the greater the impact on productivity from not having the right person on the job while the hiring process is underway. These metrics are often segmented by job type as the supply and demand for different types of professionals can fluctuate with changes in the job market.

Furthermore, measuring relative time and cost to hire allows organizations to conduct *recruitment channel analysis* to determine the best-performing channels. Companies may use these insights to decide whether to do more hiring using internal resources, select preferred recruitment partners, quantify referral bonuses, or negotiate better head-hunting rates.

Performance Measurement

Once a vacancy is filled, a company will determine what aspects of *employee performance* it wants to measure and how. Depending on the job type, it may focus on *productivity measures*, such as the number of customer inquiries processed or the volume of sales, or on *quality metrics*, such as the number of defects per thousand items or customer reviews. Not all jobs lend themselves easily to measurement, especially for knowledge workers, and organizations must consider this carefully based on what behaviour they want to nurture and encourage.

Employee Satisfaction

Once recruited, the employee becomes a valuable resource to the business. To retain employees and support their growth and performance, companies turn to metrics such as an *employee satisfaction index* or an *employee satisfaction score*. These are composite metrics designed to assess employees' relative satisfaction with the employment situation based on answers to employee surveys.

In addition to, or instead of, surveying employees, companies may use such proxy measures as:

- Absenteeism rate: ratio between the number of absent days to total workdays in a given period
- Turnover rate: ratio between the number of employees quitting their jobs to the total number of employees in a given period
- Employee net promoter score: a score that indicates how likely employees are to recommend their organization as a good place to work

Retention Modelling

Measuring employee satisfaction and turnover rate are backward-looking metrics. The next step for employers is to prevent the undesirable turnover of valuable employees. For this, companies turn to predictive analytics, trying to estimate the *flight score* (the likelihood of an employee leaving the job within a certain period) and predict the effectiveness of various retention strategies.

Workforce Planning

As companies plan for their future growth, determining their resource needs, they must include workforce planning. This involves identifying how many workers with particular skills and qualifications will be required in different divisions and locations. This is a variation of an optimization problem that must take into consideration such factors as the expected demand for different products and services in different markets across the seasons, human resources needed to support the predicted business growth, current retention rates, average time to hire, and more.

EXAMPLE

Looking for Predictive Factors in People Analytics

Measuring the behaviour and satisfaction of human beings is not a straightforward task. What may impact employee flight risk? What affects staff performance most? What is the value of training and certification? Which factors contribute to absenteeism?

People analytics can deliver interesting findings by identifying whether there is a relationship between:[4]

- Commute time and flight risk
- Employee engagement and financial performance
- Team size and its productivity
- Use of vacation days and absenteeism

3.7 FINANCIAL ANALYTICS

Financial analytics focuses on all financial aspects of an enterprise. It encompasses financial reporting, budgeting, forecasting, and investment analysis, and is used to analyze a company's profitability, solvency, and liquidity.

Sales Forecasting

An estimate of future sales is a key input to financial planning and budgeting activities. Forecasting can be based on historical trends, market segmentation analysis, and consumer trends. Forecasting can also account for planned product portfolio changes such as retiring old products or introducing new models or types of services.

Cost Budgeting

Budgeting (forecasting future expenses of the company) is based on a model of fixed and variable costs. Cost modelling methods vary from industry to industry. Cost models for utilities, manufacturing, real estate, and service-based businesses will differ because of the differences in the structure of their costs, assets, and liabilities. Even in the same industry, companies may pursue different business strategies such as "rent versus own" for fixed assets. Companies with different corporate structures may have business and regulatory reasons to use different cost models.

Sales forecasting and cost budgeting insights are key inputs into an organization's financial planning cycle. The goal of the financial planning cycle is to define acceptable financial performance targets, defined below.

Financial Performance

Organizations measure their overall financial performance on a regular basis—at least quarterly and annually. This includes measuring:

- Net income (NI) or net profit: revenue remaining after subtracting all costs and taxes
- Net profit margin: percentage of revenue remaining after subtracting all costs and taxes
- Market capitalization (market cap): total market value of all outstanding shares in the hands of shareholders
- Earnings per share (EPS): the portion of the company's net profit allocated to each common share in the hands of shareholders

Some metrics apply specifically to publicly traded companies and either must be reported to the public on a regular basis as a part of required disclosure (EPS) or are routinely required by industry convention (market cap).

Companies that use borrowing for financing their business growth are required to provide other financial metrics in support of their debt covenants or for pricing their new debt offering:

- Debt-to-equity ratio: the ratio of the company's debt compared to the total shareholder equity

- Weighted average cost of capital: calculated as a blend of the average cost of borrowing and the expected return to shareholders for a company in a given industry with a given debt load

Product Profitability

The profitability of an individual product can be much harder to evaluate than the overall profitability of a company. While revenue can usually be easily broken down by product, granular cost analysis and allocation of various enterprise expenses to each product's supply chain are often very difficult. Because profitability is determined as the difference between revenue and cost, companies must establish a cost allocation system that allows them to determine product cost. Choosing the cost allocation model is an important business decision as it may impact business unit and individual employee performance evaluation, incentives, and, as a result, their motivation and productivity. Product profitability analysis is used for the overall portfolio optimization, product and bundle pricing, and competitive analysis.

Credit Risk Modelling

This type of modelling is performed by financial institutions (FIs) that provide lending services: issuing credit cards, giving out loans, and financing mortgages, to name just a few. FIs must assess both the credit risk of an individual transaction or a contract and the overall credit portfolio risk to manage total credit exposure. In addition, financial industry regulators in many countries apply risk-weighted capital requirements to FIs, which necessitates careful risk monitoring by these institutions. Credit risk is a key component of overall risk in banking.

Market Risk Modelling

Market risk models value the risks of a company related to market behaviour and performance. Primary components are usually uncertainty about the prices of resources the company buys (inputs) and uncertainty about the prices of products or services the company sells (outputs). In addition, market risk models may include the effect of market price movements on the company's balance sheet, such as the impact of interest rates on the company's debt. While many methods are used for market risk modelling, a common metric is *value-at-risk*, estimated statistically as the amount of potential financial loss over a certain time period.

⚙ EXAMPLE

Stock Trading Metrics

Both individuals and organizations engage in stock trading as an investment activity. Making decisions to buy, hold, or sell a stock can be based on any number of factors, strategic considerations, and investment goals. Subsequently, a broad range of metrics is available to investors, including:

- Daily trading volume: the number of shares of a stock traded in a day
- Bid/ask spread: can be used as a measure of liquidity, reflecting how easy it would be to convert a stock holding to cash
- Price-to-earnings ratio: calculated as the current share price divided by EPS and may point to whether a stock is overvalued or undervalued

These and many other metrics are widely accessible to both institutional and individual investors as stock trades are executed through centralized stock exchanges. It is important to note that publicly available information is usually provided with a delay (latency). We will discuss the origins and different types of latency in Section 8.5.

3.8 SECURITY ANALYTICS

Security analytics has gained increasing importance with the growing threat of cybercrimes in the world, which relies more and more on information technology. **Security analytics** focuses on both physical security, such as monitoring premises and detecting suspicious activity, as well as on cybersecurity, concerned with the protection of computer systems and business data. Its main objectives are to measure an organization's performance in managing security risks, prevent security events, and respond to cybersecurity threats and incidents.

Metrics for measuring security performance include:

- Mean time to detect: the mean time required by an organization to detect a threat
- Detected intrusion attempts: the number of detected attempts over a period of time
- Security incident impact: can involve measuring the length of downtime or service reduction caused by the incident, the number of data records compromised, or the financial impact of damage control activities

A variety of predictive and prescriptive models are utilized to identify and block potential security incidents.

Spam Filtering

Spam detection models are used to identify typical patterns and features of unsolicited and malicious messages and remove them before they reach their intended recipients. Every time an email is designated as trusted or not, such as when the user moves an unwanted email to the "spam" folder or recovers a wanted email from that folder, the spam filtering model is trained on the new labelled data.

Suspicious Behaviour Detection

The detection of suspicious activity, both physical and electronic, is used to monitor premises and provide protection during political rallies and major sports events, as well as in cybersecurity. The development of computer vision, natural language processing, and deep neural networks allows the deployment of security monitoring technology of ever-increasing complexity. These applications of technology must also consider the legal and ethical frameworks around surveillance versus privacy protection.

Data Access Monitoring

Data access monitoring is the area of cybersecurity concerned with monitoring and detection of potential unauthorized access to data, whether from internal or external agents. Enterprises must protect their data from both external intruders—hackers—and from internal data mining.

EXAMPLE

Measuring Social Engineering Vulnerability

One of the ubiquitous security risks in any organization is social engineering—gaining access to a company's systems or data by manipulation and deception of the employees. It is usually achieved through an electronic communication that pretends to be a legitimate request or a message from a trusted person.

To ensure that employees can recognize phishing or a social engineering attack, many organizations conduct cybersecurity training followed by random phishing simulations. To measure training effectiveness and the risk of social engineering attacks, metrics such as the *phishing simulation click-through rate* can be used. This is the ratio of clicks on a simulated phishing link to the total number of simulated emails sent. Higher click-through rates may indicate insufficient employee vigilance or the need for additional training.

3.9 CHAPTER SUMMARY

Key Points to Remember

- The purpose of business analytics is to support businesspeople in making decisions.
- Every business analytics metric, chart, and predictive model must serve a purpose related to managing the organization or monitoring its performance.
- There are many widely accepted metrics and performance indicators in areas such as marketing, operations, and finance that can be adopted by an organization seeking to make wider use of business analytics.
- There are many ways to measure the performance of an organization beyond traditional financial metrics.
- Different metrics are better suited to organizations in different industries, with different business models and ownership types.

- Some metrics that organizations are required to track are mandated by legislation or regulatory bodies; in such cases, the regulatory bodies may define calculation rules and the required frequency and reporting format.

Key Terms

Analytics: the examination of data using statistical and computational methods to uncover patterns and insights.

Business analytics: the examination of data to uncover insights that give a businessperson the knowledge to make informed decisions.

Customer analytics: the examination of data about customer motivations, needs, and behaviours to improve customer satisfaction and retention.

Financial analytics: generating insights about the financial aspects of running an enterprise.

Marketing analytics: generating insights from data to assess and improve the effectiveness of a company's marketing efforts.

Operations analytics: the analysis of data on company operations and process metrics to improve efficiency and reduce the cost of running a business.

People (human resources) analytics: the examination of human resources data to improve workforce management outcomes.

Security analytics: generating insights to manage an organization's security risks and prevent and respond to security threats and incidents.

Questions for Critical Thought

1. How can the achievement of organizational business goals be supported by business analytics?
2. What approaches can be used to assess how well an organization is serving its customers?
3. What metrics can help an organization stay attuned to the needs and expectations of its employees?
4. How can analytics support an organization in optimizing its processes?
5. How can analytics be used to reduce waste in a manufacturing process?

Test Your Knowledge

1. What can be measured by the marketing return on investment (ROI) indicator?
   a. Profit margin of a marketing services company
   b. Earnings per share of a publicly traded marketing agency
   c. Incremental revenue achieved by running marketing campaigns compared to the money spent
   d. Dividends from investing in an index fund of marketing stocks

2. What aspects of business operations can be measured to support supply chain optimization?
    a. Quality of materials received from different suppliers
    b. Percentage of supplier shipments delivered late
    c. Percentage of customers unhappy with call centre wait times
    d. a and b
    e. a, b, and c

3. What is not a purpose of people (human resources) analytics?
    a. Measuring employee satisfaction
    b. Measuring customer satisfaction
    c. Measuring the effectiveness of an organization's recruitment practices
    d. Measuring staff productivity and the factors that affect it

4. What is true about financial metrics?
    a. All companies must report the same financial metrics to the government
    b. Some financial metrics are only applicable to publicly traded companies
    c. Financial metrics are mostly used by accounting departments to check the accuracy of the general ledger
    d. All of the above

5. Which of the following customer analytics metrics takes into account the predicted revenue that the company may receive from the customer in the future?
    a. Customer acquisition cost
    b. Customer churn score
    c. Customer lifetime value
    d. All of the above

Recommended Readings

American Society for Quality (ASQ). (n.d.). *What Is Six Sigma?* Retrieved June 16, 2024, from asq.org/quality-resources/six-sigma.

Amsden, R., Amsden, D., & Butler, H. E. (1998, January 20). *SPC Simplified: Practical Steps to Quality*. Productivity Press.

Google. (n.d.). *Google Trends: Understanding the data*. Retrieved June 24, 2024, from newsinitiative.withgoogle.com/resources/trainings/fundamentals/google-trends-understanding-the-data/.

Hubbard, D. (2014). *How to Measure Anything: Finding the Value of Intangibles in Business* (3rd ed.). Wiley.

Marr, B. (2016, February 3). *Key Business Analytics: The 60+ Tools Every Manager Needs to Turn Data into Insights*. FT Publishing International.

Notes

1.   Hubspot Knowledge Base. (2024, May 5). *Analyze Your Marketing Email Campaign Performance.* Retrieved June 17, 2024, from knowledge.hubspot.com/marketing-email/analyze-your-marketing-email-campaign-performance.

2.   Felder, I. (2022, May 31). *Everything You Need to Know about Customer Journey Analytics.* Genesys Blog. Retrieved June 17, 2024, from www.genesys.com/blog/post/what-is-customer-journey-analytics.

3.   IBM. (n.d.). *What Is Predictive Maintenance?* Retrieved June 18, 2024, from www.ibm.com/topics/predictive-maintenance.

4.   van Vulpen, E. (n.d.). *15 HR Analytics Case Studies with Business Impact.* Academy to Innovate HR (AIHR). Retrieved June 18, 2024, from www.aihr.com/blog/hr-analytics-case-studies/.

Chapter 4

Types of Analytics

Many organizations already have a lot of data, sometimes more than they can manage. Having an abundance of data does not lead to better business decisions without first investing in developing effective analytics. In this chapter you will learn about:

- Types of analytics (descriptive, diagnostic, predictive, and prescriptive)
- The relationships between different disciplines and their methods used for analytics
- Characteristics of good analytics questions

4.1 TYPES OF ANALYTICS

Have you ever rummaged through your receipts (paper or digital) to try and figure out why your credit card bill seems to be going up month after month?

If you want to get an answer, it won't be enough to just look through your expenses.

If there were an obvious answer—such as that you joined an expensive club with a thousand-dollar-per-month fee—then you would already know where the extra money was going.

Most likely, your rising expenses would be a result of many smaller increases adding up over time. How can you determine what is contributing to the situation? You'd have to search for changes in your spending habits. It would make sense to categorize the expenses—food, personal grooming, clothes, taxi rides, coffee, lunches, and date nights—and if you have a family, also kids' activities, tutors, toys, amusement parks, and birthday parties.

"You should spend less" is not actionable advice. "Try reducing your expenses on eat-out lunches" is much more specific.

When you break down your expenses by categories and total up each category, you are using simple analytics to better understand your spending. You are looking for answers to questions like:

- How was my spending in the last year?
- Is my monthly spending going up or down?

- How much on average do I spend on coffee (or taxis, clothes, parties) every month?
- Which of my expenses have increased compared to the last quarter (year)?

These are descriptive analytics questions.

Descriptive analytics answers the questions "What happened?" or "What is happening?" It provides facts, summaries, and metrics to gain a better understanding of a situation.

Once you have a better idea of where your money went and which expense categories have increased the most, next you would want to know why that happened:

- Was it an unavoidable one-time expense, caused by a specific event (e.g., your car broke down and required expensive repairs)?
- Does it look like a pattern leading to more spending in the future (e.g., if you joined a new club)?
- Are you forming new, expensive habits (e.g., buying premium coffee)?
- Is the increase commensurate with inflation (e.g., you buy the same number of lunches from the same place, but their prices went up)?

These are diagnostic questions you can ask to understand the causes behind the increase in spending.

Once you understand the factors that caused the spike in your expenses, you'll be in a better position to budget for the future. You may ask yourself these questions:

- Based on what you learned while analyzing your expenses, can you estimate your future expenses?
- Will the same pattern continue?
- What is your projected income for the next six months or year? Will you earn enough to cover your expected expenses?

You are now thinking about the future, or trying to *predict* what could happen.

Why do you need answers to these predictive questions? To make a decision about what to do next.

If your predictions indicate that your expenses are manageable or will start coming down, you may not have to do anything beyond ensuring that this actually happens, such as continuing to monitor your expenses to ensure that you stay within budget.

If, conversely, the outlook points to your finances inching into the red zone of insufficient operating funds, you may be forced to make a few tough choices. For example, you might need to ask yourself some questions, such as:

- How much do you need to cut down on each expense category to stay within your budget?
- What is the maximum amount you can borrow and repay within six months?
- How much extra income you do need to earn to be able to cover your rising expenses in the next year?

These are prescriptive analytics questions. You're asking what you should do to achieve a specific future outcome (getting out of debt or spending within your means without having to borrow money).

This example illustrates the path from collecting data about your expenses to making budgeting decisions. Making decisions and determining the best possible course of action requires that you follow a logical path:

1. First, examine what happened and what is going on—know where you are.
2. Then, understand why you are where you are—what led you there.
3. Consider what may happen next—the likely future outcomes.
4. Finally, decide what to do to reach the desired outcome.

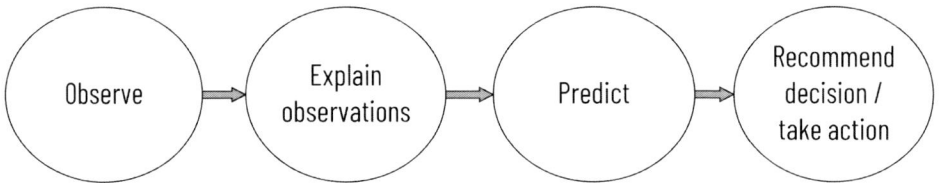

Figure 4.1 The Path from Observation to Decision and Action

This logical path reflects how different types of analytics (descriptive, diagnostic, predictive, and prescriptive) build on one another.

Descriptive analytics is the examination and aggregation of data to understand what happened.

Table 4.1 Descriptive Analytics

Questions	What happened? What is happening?
Goals	Monitor what has occurred Summarize data from multiple sources for human decision-makers Describe the past and present through summarization and visualization
Time horizon	Describes the past and the present
Outcomes	Summaries of historical data, trends, and metrics presented as reports, visualizations, or dashboards

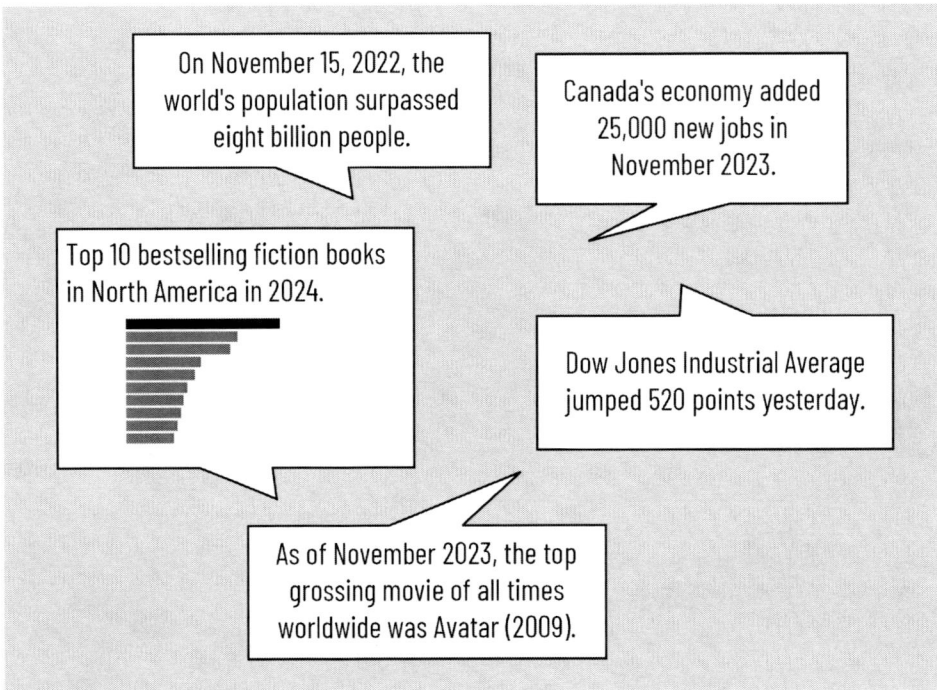

Figure 4.2 Examples of Descriptive Analytics

Diagnostic analytics is the examination of data to understand and explain why something happened and to identify cause-effect relationships.

Table 4.2 Diagnostic Analytics

Questions	Why did it happen? What are the trends? What are the patterns?
Goals	Find patterns, dependencies, and trends to explain why something happened or what caused changes in business outcomes
Time horizon	Provides insights into the past and present: infers why something has happened or is happening
Outcomes	Trends in performance Identified cause-effect relationships of the observed trends Proven or disproven hypotheses

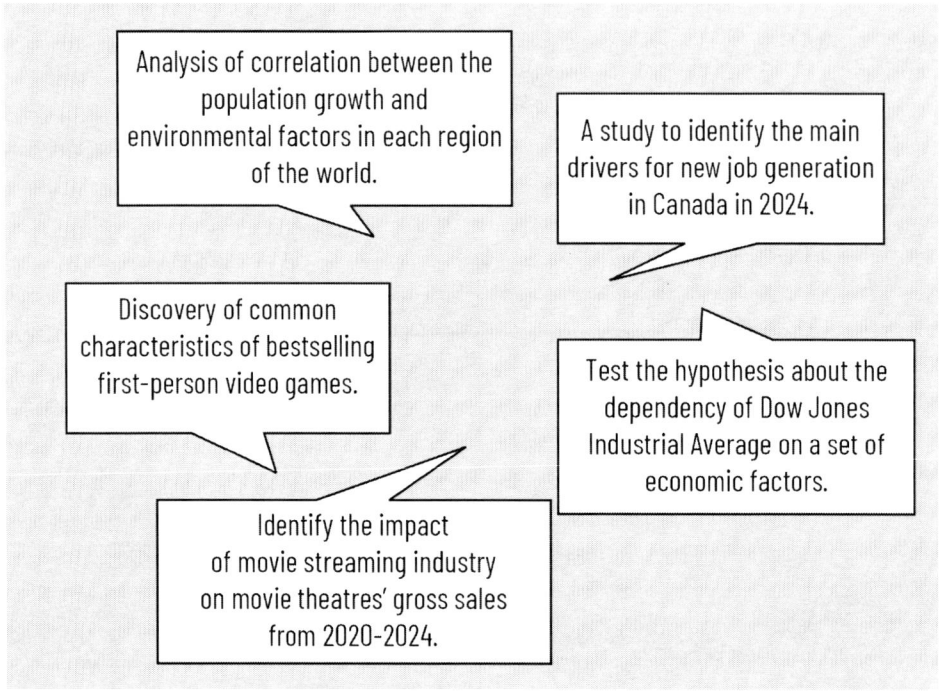

Figure 4.3 Examples of Diagnostic Analytics

Predictive analytics is the examination of data to predict future outcomes.

Table 4.3 Predictive Analytics

Questions	What is likely to happen if ...? What is the probability of ...?
Goals	Determine the likelihood of a future event Estimate likely results to be expected under specific circumstances
Time horizon	Generates predictions about future events or outcomes
Outcomes	Calculated probability of events Estimated future value of variables

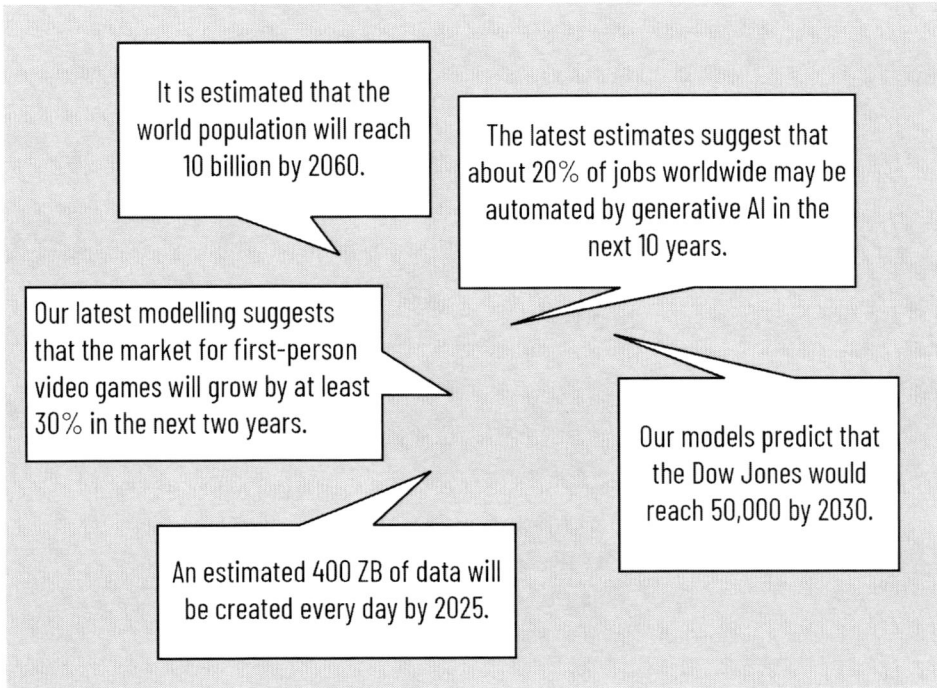

Figure 4.4 Examples of Predictive Analytics

Prescriptive analytics is the examination of patterns in data and predictions to recommend actions for optimizing desired outcomes.

Table 4.4 Prescriptive Analytics

Questions	What should be done to achieve X? What should we do to make Y happen?
Goals	Determine the course of action most likely to achieve desired results
Time horizon	Recommends actions for immediate or future execution
Outcomes	Decisions, action recommendations, or automated actions

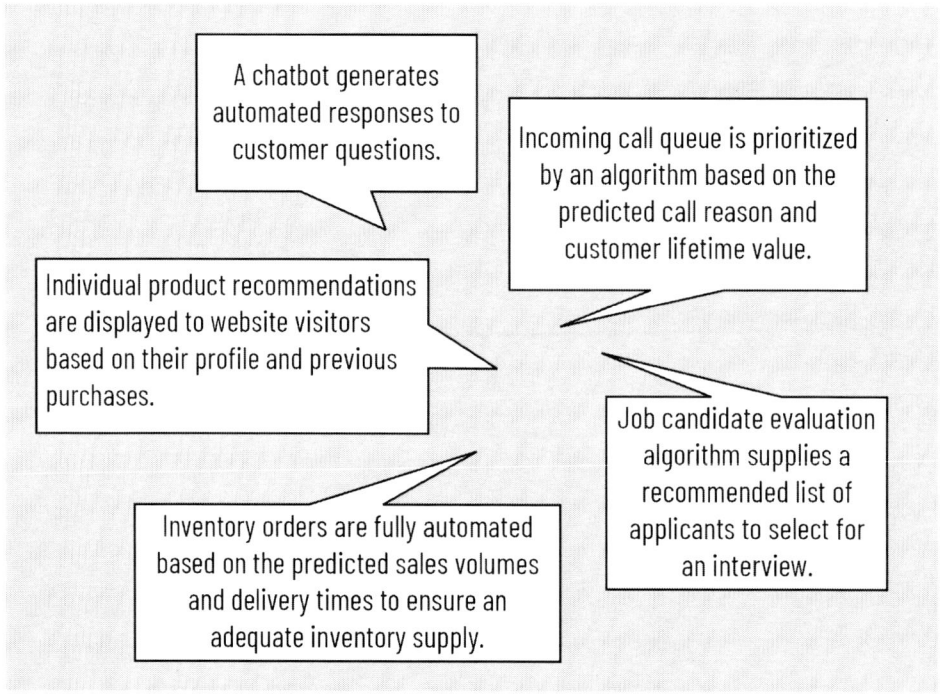

Figure 4.5 Examples of Prescriptive Analytics

This classification of analytics is not just an enumeration of different ways of generating insights. It represents a logical sequence of analysis for making business decisions.

Descriptive analytics provides a baseline and describes the current state of affairs— that is, it summarizes data about the past into informative metrics.

Diagnostic analytics allows us to dig deeper and explain observed trends, as well as to identify factors that influence business performance—discriminating factors.

The discovery of these discriminating factors allows us to look into the future through predictive analytics.

The predictions can then be used to evaluate alternative courses of action to select the most advantageous one. Prescriptive analytics uses predictions to automate decisions or recommend a course of action most likely to bring about the desired result.

In smart organizations, descriptive analytics will be improved and adjusted based on what turns out to be relevant for further diagnostics and predictions, and diagnostic analytics will be revisited as new discriminating factors are discovered. This feedback loop ensures that the organization develops effective descriptive metrics as a foundation for more advanced analytics and optimization tasks.

Further on in this book, we will examine how descriptive, diagnostic, predictive, and prescriptive analytics can be used to analyze different aspects of business, and how analytics solutions can be developed with the right foundations.

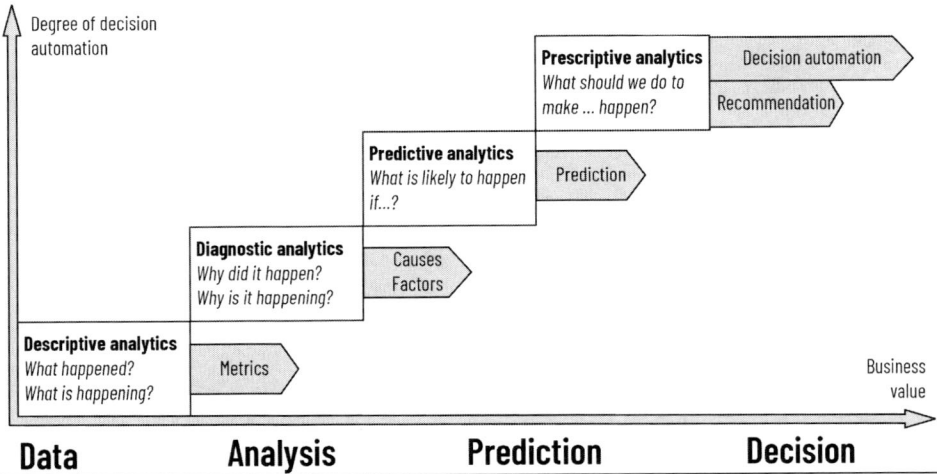

Figure 4.6 Analytics Types and Outcomes

4.2 ANALYTICS VALUE CHAIN

Getting the ultimate value from business analytics comes from optimizing business management through analytics-driven decisions. The path to achieving that starts with observation and collection of data and culminates in making decisions and taking action. This path is the value chain of analytics.

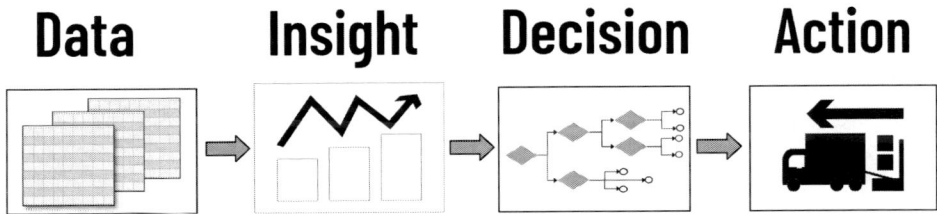

Figure 4.7 The Value Chain of Business Analytics: From Data to Insight to Decision to Action

How can this value chain be implemented through analytics activities? Let's consider a YardExperts' business problem as an example.

CASE STUDY

Analysis of the Customer Churn Problem

YardExperts has a customer churn problem. Customer churn reflects the percentage of existing customers who cancel or decide not to renew their service contracts for landscaping or snow removal.

It costs more to attract new customers than to retain existing ones. Losing customers not only reduces revenue but also leads to higher marketing expenses to return to the same revenue levels. Understanding why customers leave and what can be done to retain them is a key objective for the company. How can data help?

First, the YardExperts customer care team needs to evaluate the current situation with the churn. What is the current churn ratio? What is the trend? Do we know why customers are leaving? What are the main contributing factors?

Is there a correlation between cancellations and the region? The season? Weather pattern changes? The expertise of the local service team? The number of local competitors?

What are customer sentiments? Are they complaining about prices? What are the patterns of complaints?

On the other hand, to entice more customers to stay, it would help to understand what makes customers happy. What are satisfied customers saying? Can this knowledge help retain more customers? Understanding customer needs and what makes them happy or unhappy is imperative for understanding the causes of customer churn.

These questions point to the need for descriptive and diagnostic analytics. Measuring current churn is necessary not only to assess the problem but also to establish a baseline metric. A **baseline** is a minimum or starting point for measuring a variable that will be referenced to identify how the variable changes.

Thus, the value chain of analytics starts with using data to analyze what is happening and why. Figure 4.8 looks at the data YardExperts used for initial analysis, as well as the descriptive and diagnostic analytics they started with.

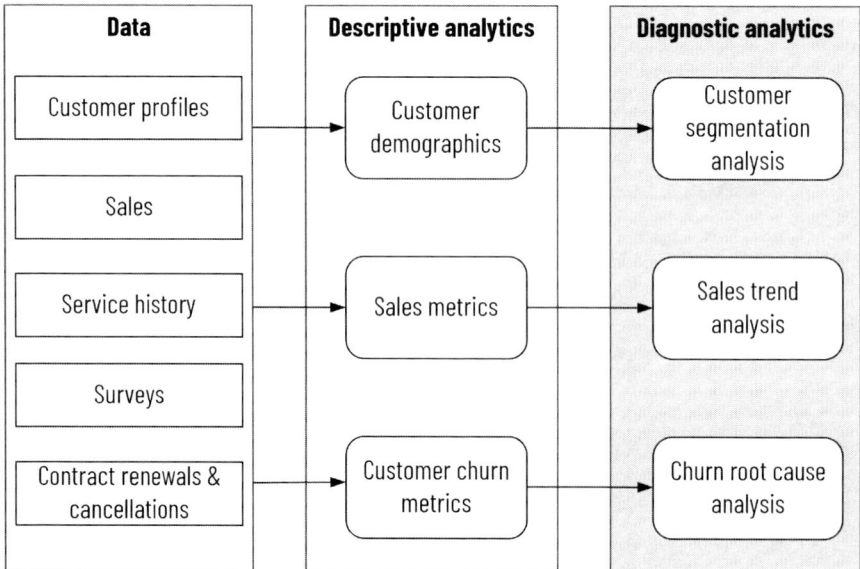

Figure 4.8 The Start of Analytics Value Chain: Measure and Explain Customer Churn

Using the data in Figure 4.8, the YardExperts customer care team will analyze customers' demographic attributes from customer profiles and survey data—for example, whether they live in urban, suburban, or rural areas, their household size, and age groups. This information can be used for further segmentation of customers, which is often necessary for diagnostic analysis. Demographic attributes can help YardExperts understand what customers value more, their purchasing behaviour, and what would make them churn.

Sales data can be analyzed to measure sales volumes as well as trends by season, product, or service. Further diagnostics may reveal what caused changes in purchasing behaviour, what factors affect the volume of sales in different regions, or whether there is a correlation between service history and subsequent sales.

Since customer churn is the main problem to be addressed, the team must also collect current churn metrics, such as the percentage of customers cancelling their contracts every month. Assuming that customers are asked to fill in a brief cancellation survey, the next step involves analyzing the survey results to support churn root cause analysis.

These diagnostic results will now give the team a much better understanding of the business problem. They are learning what is causing customer churn, what factors drive contract cancellations, and which customer segments are the least tolerant of problems and most likely to need extra enticement to stay.

These diagnostic insights can be used for the next step: predictive analytics.

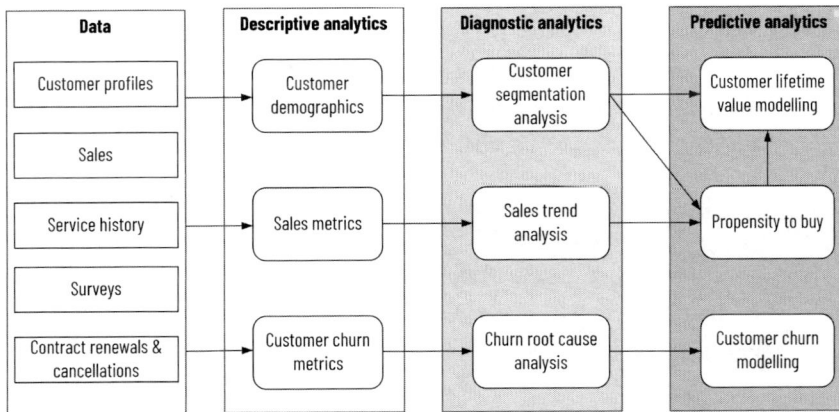

Figure 4.9 Analytics Value Chain: Measure, Explain, Predict

As shown in Figure 4.9, here is how diagnostic analysis can become a foundation for predictive modelling:

- Analysis of sales trends and correlations with service history and customer demographics will become the foundation of propensity to buy modelling.

- Understanding the needs of different customer segments along with propensity to buy modelling will support forecasting of customer lifetime value (CLV).
- Root cause analysis of customer churn will provide significant factors for predicting future customer churn.

What is the value of these predictions?

Let's imagine that through customer churn modelling, the team has identified a group of customers (about 10% of the total) with a 75% or higher churn score (the likelihood of churn at the end of the season). How can this prediction be used to solve the problem?

Does this mean that YardExperts should make the most effort to keep these customers—make calls, offer them significant discounts, and do everything possible to get them to renew a contract? Not necessarily—or rather, this predictive insight alone may not be sufficient for determining the best course of action.

What if some of these customers have a low CLV—that is, the value of their contact is very small? Would it make sense to invest a lot of resources in keeping them when the expected return is minimal?

What if the company does not have sufficient resources to reach out to all customers with high churn scores and will need to prioritize customer retention activities?

What if, among these customers, about 10% are undesirable—they are late on their payments, make a lot of unfounded complaints, or post extremely negative reviews? It may be better for the business to let them go.

What if the model indicates that a particular customer has a 97% churn risk? Would you still invest resources into trying to keep them with such a low chance of success?

All these questions point to the need to optimize strategies for managing churn based on multiple business considerations. All businesses have to do this, because everything has a price, and every business activity carries a cost. YardExperts must evaluate:

- How much effort is justifiable for retaining a customer relative to their CLV
- What a reasonable discount would be to ensure the customer is still profitable
- The churn risk thresholds that justify different levels of action (e.g., sending a retention email, giving a courtesy call, or offering a special discount)

These considerations require more information than the results of the churn model.

As is apparent, prescriptive analytics can be quite complex as business decisions take into account many different factors. To optimize business decisions, the results of multiple predictions may be used as inputs into a prescriptive algorithm.

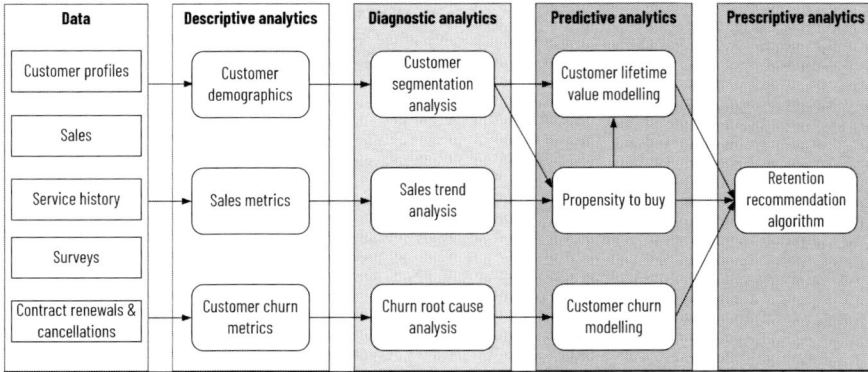

Figure 4.10 Analytics Value Chain: Prescriptive Customer Retention Analytics

In Figure 4.10, the retention recommendations will depend on the modelling of CLV, the customer's propensity to buy additional products and services, and the likelihood of churn.

How should an organization approach solving a business problem as described in the case study example? First, it needs to formulate analytics questions.

4.3 FROM BUSINESS QUESTIONS TO ANALYTICS QUESTIONS

You may have heard a popular saying: "Data has all the answers." Doesn't that sound too good to be true? An analytics professional knows that data by itself cannot provide all the answers.

Imagine starting to analyze available data without having a clear idea of your goals. Yes, you can tease out some facts and relationships, but what will you do with these facts? Will they be relevant to the problem? Smart analytics starts with asking smart questions.

Whether you are a business manager with analytics requirements or a data analyst working on these requirements, the skill of asking good questions is an essential part of your overall business acumen. For a future user of analytics solutions, their requirements must be well understood. For an analytics professional developing the solution, understanding business needs and clarifying what questions must be answered defines whether the solution they design will be utilized or become digital waste.

To get to good analytics questions, we start with business questions. Then, we must translate business questions into analytics questions.

Refer to this checklist as you explore different analytics metrics and questions in Chapter 5 (for descriptive analytics) and Chapter 6 (for diagnostic, predictive, and prescriptive analytics).

✔ **CHECKLIST**

Translating Business Questions into Analytics Questions

1. Ask a business question focusing on the objectives.

    What are you trying to do?

    What key decisions need to be made?

    Who will the answer benefit?

    What do you need to know to solve the problem?

    Example: We need to have a clear picture of our lawnmower sales this year.

2. Consider what type of analytics to use.

    - Descriptive analytics: to summarize what happened
    - Diagnostic analytics: to understand why it happened
    - Predictive analytics: to predict what to expect in the future
    - Prescriptive analytics: to determine the best course of action

    Example: To have a clear picture of our lawnmower sales this year, we need to summarize this year's sales data.

3. Consider what needs to be measured (or predicted).

    What are the important variables?

    Can you measure these variables directly?

    What metrics are appropriate based on the business objectives?

    Can the business question be answered by summarizing the past, or is a prediction required?

    If a prediction is required, what variable, event, or relationship do you need to predict?

    Example: We want to find out the total dollar amount of sales in each province and territory.

4. What are specific circumstances and conditions that should constrain the answer to the question?

    Are you analyzing a specific time frame, geographic area, or selected group?

    How can you define the area of interest clearly to avoid ambiguity and to get a specific answer?

    Example: We are interested in lawnmower sales in Canada, by province and territory, in the year 2024.

    Analytics question: What were the total lawnmower sales in each Canadian province and territory in 2024?

CASE STUDY

Descriptive Analytics Questions

The YardExperts management team is asking descriptive analytics questions. Consider some of the business intelligence questions for which the company's analytics team had to provide analytics.

Marketing Analytics Questions

- How many leads have signed up to receive marketing emails as a result of last month's promotional campaign?
- What was the average click-through rate on our ads placed throughout different channels during the previous quarter?
- What percentage of the detached homes in Municipality X have an active snow removal contract with our company?

Customer Analytics Questions

- What is the breakdown of our active contracts by types of service purchased?
- What is the most frequent reason that our customers cite for contract cancellation?
- What percentage of our customers had to wait for snow removal for more than 12 hours at least once during the last winter? How does this compare with the previous snow season?

People Analytics Questions

- What is our current job offer acceptance rate for landscaping specialists?
- How many vacancies do we have in each region, broken down by job category?
- What is the rate of on-time training completion for new employees in each region?

4.4 GOOD ANALYTICS QUESTIONS

Good analytics questions are:

- Clear: logically constructed and unambiguous, minimizing the risk of misunderstanding the question
- Specific: focused on a specific variable, measure, or direction of analysis
- Constructed in business language: utilizing clear terms that take a business perspective
- Relevant: related to the task of making business decisions
- Feasible: possible to be answered
- Testable: imply the expected result and the way to verify the answer

Asking Better Analytics Questions

1. *A bad example:* "What did we do well last year?"

    Make it more specific: "Determine average customer review score per product line in 2024."

    Make it very specific: "Which of our product lines received the highest average customer reviews in 2024?"

2. *A bad example*: "What was our customer growth?"

    Use clear terms to indicate the metrics that need to be measured: "How did the new contract sign-ups in 2024 compare to the previous year?"

3. *A bad example:* "Are our resources sufficient to deliver on customer requests?"

    There are many problems with this question. It implies a "yes" or "no" answer, which is unlikely to be very informative. It's unclear what *sufficient* means in this context, and what resources would be considered "ours" (who is "we"?). Finally, it is untestable, since we cannot deduce whether it refers to the current or future requests, and whether it refers to our current or future resources.

    Improve the question: "How many technicians will we require by Q2 of 2025 to fulfill all contracts within the SLA (service-level agreement) if the current trend of new contract sign-ups continues?"

4. *A bad example*: "How was the transit ridership over the past five years?"

    Use clear metrics: "How did the average transit ridership in the Toronto Metropolitan Area change month over month in the past five years?"

5. *A bad example:* "What will the quantities of the most popular products be during each quarter of next year?"

    This is another case of unclear metrics since the word *quantities* can be interpreted in many ways: the demand for the most popular products, how many will be manufactured each quarter to fulfill the demand, or how many will be sold. Be explicit: "What is the expected demand for each of our top five most popular products for each quarter of the next year?"

6. *A bad example:* "Was there any difference in how many sales we made last year considering that we have added two new products and including each country that we exited, except for our leading products?"

    There are many problems with this question. It's convoluted and includes multiple questions and conditions. It should be replaced with several separate questions or a set of analytics requirements for a multi-dimensional analysis of last year's sales.

7. *A bad example:* "What is the effectiveness of our strategies and actions?"

> This question is not feasible to answer as it is too broad, poorly defined, and can't even be considered an analytical question. Any answer provided is not likely to be testable. Measuring the effectiveness of a strategy can be a major enterprise challenge as the link between specific business activities and strategy is not always apparent, and significant changes often have multiple causes. In addition, whenever a question is asked about multiple things ("strategies and actions"), it becomes unclear whether they must be looked at separately or together.
>
> Organizations devise whole performance management frameworks to answer such questions (see Section 11.3). A more feasible approach is to ask about a specific metric related to a well-defined activity or campaign. For example: "What was the change in the click-through rate (CTR) on the latest marketing campaign X compared to the average CTR of the previous three campaigns?"

To summarize, a good analytics question can be answered in a meaningful, relevant, and specific manner. This book will provide more examples of good analytics questions as it examines each type of analytics in more depth.

4.5 ANALYTICS METHODS AND APPROACHES

Business analytics solutions rely on a variety of methods and approaches that will be introduced in this book. Understanding the applications and limitations of these methods is useful for all professionals who wish to use analytics to empower their decision-making. Those interested in a career in business analytics or data science will study these methods in depth by taking specialized courses in statistics, machine learning, predictive modelling, big data analytics, and more.

Before we delve into the subject any further, let's address some definitions. Rapid advances in computer science and the development of artificial intelligence in the last decade have led to a proliferation of terms that need to be clarified in order to move forward.

Statistics is a branch of mathematics specializing in collecting, analyzing, and presenting data. In particular, it focuses on analyzing samples of data and making inferences about larger populations. Statistics uses probabilistic methods to describe the world numerically. Statistical methods were used for data analysis long before the invention of computers, with known publications dating back to the 16th and 17th centuries including statistics.[1] Statistical methods are used for generating descriptive, diagnostic, and predictive analytics.

Statistics is one of the pillars of data science, an interdisciplinary field centred around the discovery of knowledge through data analysis. By comparison, data science as a field of study developed with reliance on computing technology and methods of processing large amounts of data using computers.

Data science is the computational science of extracting meaningful insights from raw data.[2]

Data science relies heavily on computational methods, which are necessary when dealing with very large amounts of data, especially when dealing with high variety and velocity of big data. Many of these computational methods fall into the data mining category.

Data mining is the exploration and analysis of large datasets using mathematical methods to discover meaningful patterns and relationships.

Data mining can also be referred to as **knowledge discovery** or **information harvesting**. It explores vast amounts of data to generate and discover hidden insights. Data mining can be used to build machine learning models.

Machine learning is the development of algorithms that can learn patterns from data, apply these patterns to new data, and adapt ("learn") from the new data received by the algorithm.

In other words, machine learning algorithms are designed to handle new situations (new sets of data) through analysis, experience, and adaptation. One fascinating aspect of machine learning is that these algorithms can adapt to new data without being explicitly provided the rules by human engineers, instead relying on drawing inferences from the data itself.

Machine learning falls under the umbrella of one of the branches of computer science—artificial intelligence.

Computer science is the study of computers, computing systems, and their applications.

Computer science is a broad field that encompasses both the theoretical aspects of computing and algorithm design as well as the engineering aspects of building computers and computing systems.

Artificial intelligence (AI) is a discipline concerned with building computer programs that perform tasks requiring intelligence when done by humans.[3]

As such, AI is a branch of computer science. Figure 4.11 depicts various computer science, AI, and data science fields of study and their intersections.

This book explores the application of some of these fields to producing business analytics.

As discussed in Chapter 1, *databases* are used to store structured data in many enterprise applications, as well as in analytical data storage such as data warehouses (explored in more detail in Chapter 8). The quality and integrity of data stored in databases and data warehouses rely on, among other things, data modelling (discussed in Section 2.6). While traditional databases support structured data, different approaches are required for *big data handling*. You will find an overview of the technologies developed for the storage and processing of big data in Section 8.3.

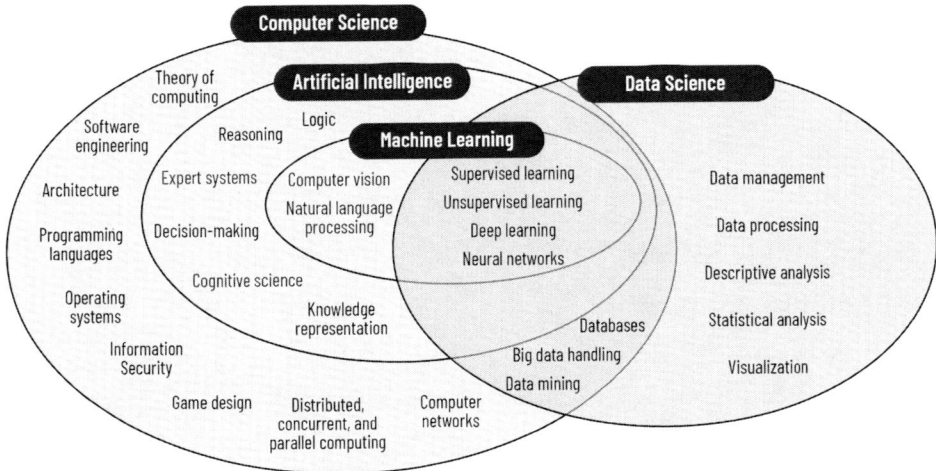

Figure 4.11 Data Science, Artificial Intelligence, and Computer Science Disciplines

Managing data relies on data governance to establish the rules and processes, data architecture to plan and model data structures and movement, along with security, storage, operations, and other *data management* activities discussed in Chapter 2. Data management is foundational to supporting enterprise applications used by organizations to run their business—operational systems (Section 2.2). The various branches of the *computer science* field address planning, designing, and developing hardware and software required to support both operational and analytical systems.

When it comes to analytics, the methods that will be applied will depend on both the objectives and the nature of the data. *Descriptive analysis* methods (reviewed in Chapter 5) are used to deliver traditional business intelligence such as reports, charts, and performance indicators.

Various *statistical analysis* methods can be used for both descriptive and more advanced analysis, such as diagnostic and predictive modelling, which are reviewed in Chapter 6.

Visualization is used broadly in descriptive analysis—in particular, to summarize and present information graphically in reports and dashboards (Section 5.5). Advanced visualization methods can also support tasks such as data exploration, profiling, and *data mining* as part of the analytics life cycle (covered in Chapter 7).

As business analytics goals—including the need for prediction and optimization—become more sophisticated, the task will require more advanced computational methods such as those captured under *machine learning*. These methods can be used for various data science applications including finding patterns and outliers in large volumes of data, as well as for predictive and prescriptive modelling, which we will discuss in Chapter 6. Machine learning is only one of many branches under the broad umbrella of AI. Research and development in the field of AI yield new ideas, products, and solutions not only for managing enterprises but for new technologies and consumer products, such as *computer vision* for robotics and *natural language processing* for the development of large language models and chatbots. We have discussed some of these in Section 3.5 and will continue to explore the development of this field throughout the rest of the book.

Thus, while business analytics encompasses methods and technologies for deriving useful business insights from data, it is enabled by the fields of study depicted in Figure 4.11.

4.6 CHAPTER SUMMARY

Key Points to Remember

- Descriptive, diagnostic, predictive, and prescriptive analytics are the four main types of analytics, with more advanced analytics relying on the insights from previous analysis.
- Descriptive and diagnostic analytics look into the past and the present, while predictive and prescriptive analytics are based on predicting future outcomes.
- Predictive analytics cannot tell us what is going to happen—only what is likely to happen.
- Predictive analytics operates with probabilistic measures, calculating the likelihood of outcomes.
- The four main types of analytics can be applied to all aspects of managing an enterprise, provided that analytics questions are clear and purposeful.
- The foundation for good analytics questions is understanding business objectives.
- To get useful analytics insights, we must translate business questions into analytics questions.
- AI is a subfield of computer science, and machine learning is a subfield of AI.

Key Terms

Artificial intelligence (AI): a discipline concerned with the building of computer programs that perform tasks requiring intelligence when done by humans.

Baseline: a minimum or starting point for measuring a variable that will be referenced to identify how the variable changes.

Computer science: a study of computers, computing systems, and their applications.

Data mining (knowledge discovery, information harvesting): exploration and analysis of large datasets using mathematical methods to discover meaningful patterns and relationships.

Data science: a computational science of extracting meaningful insights from raw data.

Descriptive analytics: the examination and aggregation of data to understand what happened.

Diagnostic analytics: the examination of data to understand and explain why something happened and to identify cause-effect relationships.

Machine learning: the development of algorithms that can learn patterns from data, apply these patterns to new data, and adapt ("learn") from the new data received by the algorithm.

Predictive analytics: the examination of data to predict future outcomes.

Prescriptive analytics: the examination of patterns in data and predictions to recommend actions for optimizing desired outcomes.

Statistics: a branch of mathematics specializing in collecting, analyzing, and presenting data.

Questions for Critical Thought

1. What is the difference between descriptive and diagnostic analytics?
2. What is the difference between predictive and prescriptive analytics?
3. How can predictive analytics use the results of diagnostic analysis?
4. How can analytics questions be made more effective?
5. What are the risks when asking vague analytics questions?

Test Your Knowledge

1. At the end of each month, the company determines the percentage of all customer inquiries that were resolved during the first call.
   What type of analytics is this?
   a. Descriptive
   b. Diagnostic
   c. Predictive
   d. Prescriptive

2. Based on the expected demand for products and suppliers' delivery times, the company's inventory management software identifies when to order more products to ensure sufficient retail inventory is available.
   What type of analytics is this?
   a. Descriptive
   b. Diagnostic
   c. Predictive
   d. Prescriptive

3. A medical clinic is using special software to review patients' current prescription medications and assess the likelihood of adverse affects from new medications that the clinic's doctors consider prescribing.
   What type of analytics is this?
   a. Descriptive
   b. Diagnostic
   c. Predictive
   d. Prescriptive

4. A marketing department is analyzing retail sales data and customer survey data for the last year to identify what demographic attributes made customers more likely to purchase a specific product.

   What type of analytics is this?
   a. Descriptive
   b. Diagnostic
   c. Predictive
   d. Prescriptive

5. A medical clinic reports the total number of patients seen by each doctor to the health authority on a monthly basis.

   What type of analytics is this?
   a. Descriptive
   b. Diagnostic
   c. Predictive
   d. Prescriptive

Recommended Readings

Baesens, B. (2014). *Analytics in a Big Data World: The Essential Guide to Data Science and Its Applications*. Wiley.

Jain, P., & Sharma, P. (2014). *Behind Every Good Decision: How Anyone Can Use Business Analytics to Turn Data into Profitable Insight*. AMACOM.

Notes

1. Wikipedia. (n.d.). *Statistics.* Retrieved December 21, 2023, from en.wikipedia.org/wiki/Statistics.
2. Pierson, L. (2021). *Data Science for Dummies.* Wiley, p. 8.
3. Daintith, J., & Wright, E. (2008). *A Dictionary of Computing.* Oxford University Press.

Chapter 5

Business Intelligence with Descriptive Analytics

The analytics value chain starts with *descriptive analytics*—observing and summarizing what is happening. In this chapter you will learn about:

- Descriptive analytics metrics
- Selecting and summarizing data for business intelligence
- Approaches to presenting descriptive analytics results

5.1 DESCRIPTIVE ANALYTICS APPROACH

Descriptive analytics delivers value to business by:

- Summarizing data from multiple sources for easy consumption by businesspeople
- Making relevant information accessible to allow monitoring of an organization's activities
- Condensing large volumes of operational details into important metrics and key performance indicators for tracking an organization's performance

The outcome of descriptive analytics is quantitative reporting of facts, whether these facts are presented as tables, charts, or single metrics.

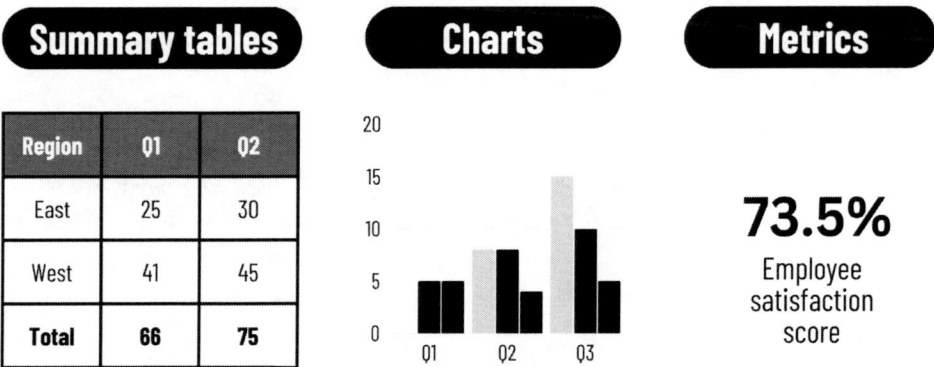

Summary tables

Region	Q1	Q2
East	25	30
West	41	45
Total	66	75

Charts

Metrics

73.5%
Employee satisfaction score

Figure 5.1 Presentation of Descriptive Analytics

To create a convenient summary of metrics for business consumers, descriptive analytics are often combined into reports, dashboards, and scorecards (see more in Chapter 9).

Every company generates descriptive analytics, which encompasses most accounting statements and operational, financial, management, regulatory, and shareholder reporting. Descriptive analytics are often made evident in tables and charts that display sales volumes by products and territories, total numbers of employees, customers, or locations, trends of transaction volume, investment income, or utility spending.

When producing descriptive analytics, we must consider what information we need to convey and what the best way might be to present this information. The methods and presentation of descriptive analytics depend on what is being measured and what kind of summarization is needed. Table 5.1 summarizes a systematic approach to descriptive analytics that will be reviewed further.

Table 5.1 Systematic approach to descriptive analytics

Step	Question addressed
Metrics	What to summarize?
Selection criteria	What is the population?
Method	How to summarize the information?
Presentation format	How to present the results?

TIPS ON TERMS

Business Intelligence versus Descriptive Analytics

The term *business intelligence* is often used interchangeably with *descriptive analytics*.

Some organizations use business intelligence more broadly to include advanced analytics such as diagnostics and data mining, while others equate business intelligence with reporting and dashboards that summarize data about past performance. It is always advisable to clarify how each term is used in an organization.

5.2 DESCRIPTIVE METRICS

Generating descriptive analytics starts with a clear understanding of what information needs to be summarized: sales volumes, time spent on contract administration, customer churn, or customer satisfaction. Summarization through descriptive analysis may involve a single variable (**univariate analysis**), two variables (**bivariate analysis**), or three or more variables (**multivariate analysis**).

What to summarize?	What is the population?	How to summarize?	How to present?
Metrics	**Selection criteria**	**Method**	**Presentation format**

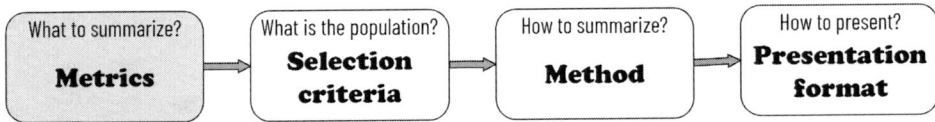

Figure 5.2 Descriptive Analytics Approach: What to Summarize?

Some variables relate to tangible things that can be measured directly:

- When every order is captured, the number of orders can be counted, and the sales volume is measured by summation of order amounts.
- When phone calls are recorded in a system, their duration can be calculated from the time calls are received and ended.
- When a new article is posted on social media, the total number of reposts in the first 24 hours can be tracked by the host platform.

These variables are measured in certain units along one dimension and can be referred to as **measures.**

Other variables describe intangible concepts and are measured using metrics or indicators. They require **indirect (proxy) measurements** or derivations from multiple observations that are believed to correlate with what you want to measure:

- Customer satisfaction may be defined in different ways depending on the products and services sold to the customers. A customer satisfaction index may be derived from several measurements such as the number of complaints, number of referrals, subscription renewals, or customer survey responses.
- A social media post engagement score can be derived from the ratio between the number of reactions, comments, and reposts to the total number of followers in the first 24 hours.

In business analytics, a **metric** is a measure of an operational activity or a business process. Often, metrics are referred to as **operational metrics**, as they measure a company's day-to-day performance in specific areas. Operational metrics can be univariate (measuring one variable), bivariate, or multivariate. Multivariate metrics are also called *composite scores*.

Organizations designate special metrics to track their overall performance compared to established targets—**key performance indicators (KPIs)**. They are referred to as *key* indicators because they are considered important for managing the company and indicative of its overall progress toward strategic goals. Most KPIs are multivariate metrics, sometimes requiring a sequence of calculation and derivation steps.

Every business can establish its own KPIs. However, there are many widely used financial, human resources, marketing, and service metrics, such as:

- Return on investment (ROI)
- Employee retention score
- Advertising ROI
- Average order fulfillment time

Different performance management systems and approaches to defining KPIs are discussed in more detail in Section 11.3.

TIPS ON TERMS

Measures, Metrics, and KPIs

A **measure** applies to tangible things that can be measured directly. *Metrics* are used to measure operational activities or business processes. A metric could also be a measure if applied to something tangible like the number of customer calls received in one day. *Indirect (proxy) metrics* are devised to approximate intangible variables that cannot be measured directly, such as customer satisfaction. *KPIs* are special metrics designed to track the overall performance of the organization compared to important targets.

To clarify the distinction between operational metrics and KPIs, think of the former as tactical measures that relate to specific operational activities, whereas the latter indicate how the company's performance is tracking toward strategic goals.

Operational metrics can be based on direct measures such as the counts of things and events (the number of orders delivered in a day). Calculated operational metrics involving comparisons and ratios are often more useful for managing operations (the percentage of orders delivered on time on a given day).

KPIs usually require comparisons of multiple measures that summarize performance on an enterprise scale, such as comparing the investment to the profit received (ROI), the money spent on advertisement to the new sales attributed to the advertisement (advertising ROI), or the ratio between the employees that stay with the company and the overall number of employees (employee retention score).

Table 5.2 provides sample metrics for various business domains.

Table 5.2 Descriptive Metrics Examples

Domain	Metric	Description
Marketing	Leads captured	Total number of leads captured over a period of time through various marketing channels; capturing a lead usually implies capturing their contact information such as email address and phone number, with permission
Customer	Customer churn rate	Percentage of customers who terminate relationships with a company compared to the number of customers at the beginning of the time period
Operations	On-time delivery rate	Percentage of orders delivered on or before the promised delivery date and time compared to the number of total orders in the same period
Human resources	Time to hire	Number of days between a candidate applying for a job and accepting the job offer
Finance	Gross revenue	Sum of all sales made by the company in a given period, before deducting any expenses
Security	Number of incidents	Total number of detected security incidents in a given period

---

TIPS ON TERMS

Calculated or Derived?

A value is **calculated** if it is a result of performing arithmetic operations. For example:

- Defect rate is calculated by dividing the number of defective parts by the total number of parts manufactured in the given period.
- Net profit is calculated by subtracting total expenses from the total revenue in the same period.

When we refer to descriptive metrics, the term **derived** refers to a value obtained from other values by applying logical reasoning or rules. Some examples are:

- A customer's time zone can be derived from their address postal code.
- Product category can be derived from a product identifier by looking it up in a product catalogue.

Derivation is often applied to qualitative variables, as they cannot be measured numerically.

EXAMPLE

What makes a meaningful metric? It depends not only on what is being measured but who this information is for. Take a real-life example: the size of a book. What book would you consider small, medium, or large? How much can you read in a day? Most readers will think about it in terms of the number of pages. A 400-page book is fairly large, while a 150-page book is small and not enough reading material for a vacation.

Now let's consider the perspective of an author writing a book using word processing software. How can they plan for the size of the book and assess their writing progress? Page breakdown is subject to layout and font size variations, and the number of pages in their manuscript file can be very different from the page count in a finished book. In this case, word count is used as a standard metric of the content volume. Writers often measure their output in terms of thousands of words per day.

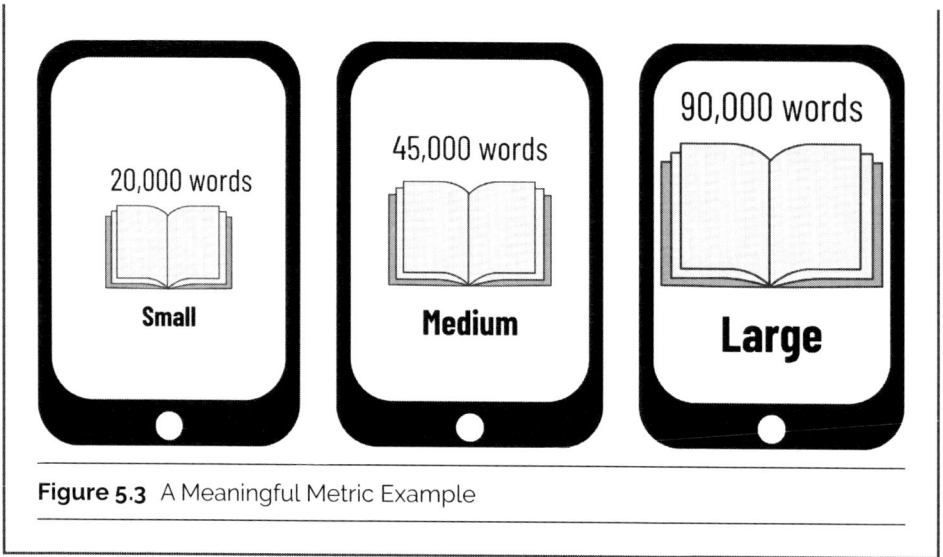

Figure 5.3   A Meaningful Metric Example

5.3 SELECTION CRITERIA

Summarization and analysis of data requires boundaries: how far, how deep, and how wide do you go?

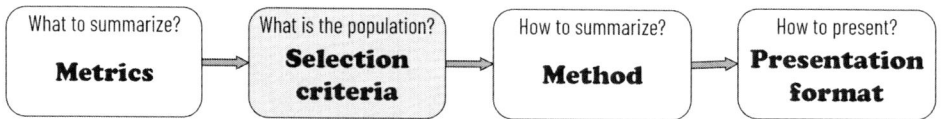

Figure 5.4   Descriptive Analytics Approach: What Is The Population?

Are you interested in sales completed in the last month? In the previous two quarters? In the past five years?

Will you be analyzing all lines of business, or retail sales only?

Is this analysis for regional managers who need to know how their locations are doing, or for the chief executive officer (CEO) of the company who wants to see the big picture?

Data for analytics is collected based on **selection criteria**—specific ranges, limits, or logical conditions that define what data is of interest for analysis. Selection criteria can be based on dimensions.

A **dimension** is an attribute used for organizing, segmenting, and summarizing observations in a dataset. Dimensions must be meaningful from a business perspective—that is, they need to be useful for understanding the data and business information it represents.

Typical dimensions that apply in many contexts are:

- Products (including product groupings and categories)

- Customers (customer categories and segments)
- Organizational structure
- Locations (geographical areas)
- Time

Dimensions are used to define breakdowns and groupings of the observations that will make analysis of data more meaningful. Most dimensions can be hierarchical, as shown in Figure 5.5.

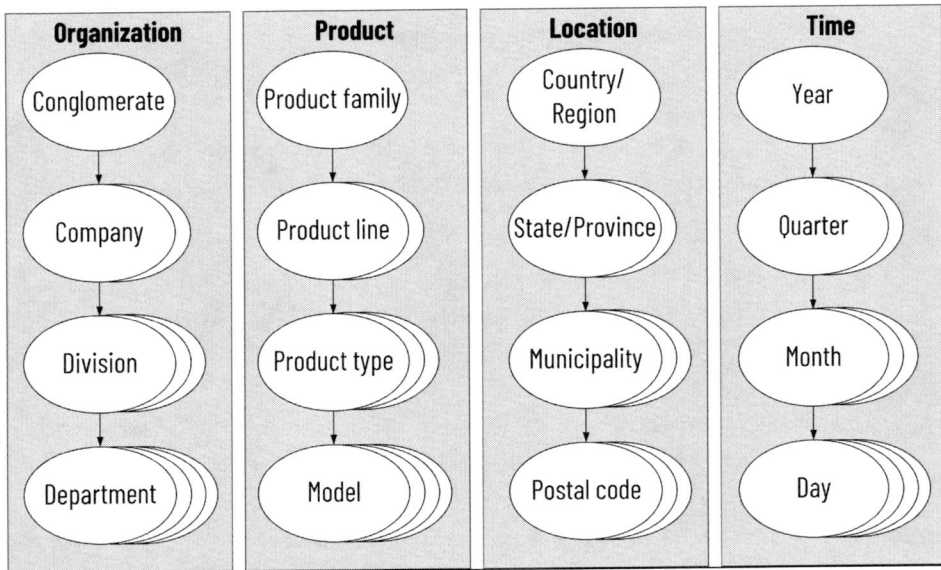

Organization	Product	Location	Time
Conglomerate	Product family	Country/Region	Year
Company	Product line	State/Province	Quarter
Division	Product type	Municipality	Month
Department	Model	Postal code	Day

Figure 5.5 Hierarchy of Dimensions

A hierarchy of dimensions allows us to create multiple levels of aggregations—for example, individual sales can be summarized into daily, monthly, and quarterly totals, or into total sales by product line and family. Aggregations can be done across multiple dimensions, such as when analyzing average time to hire by quarter and department.

In reverse, analytics users often need to drill into details across dimensions, such as breaking down the average time to hire by locations to identify local differences.

Note that useful groupings of observations do not have to be limited to standard dimensions and will also depend on the analytics questions and domain knowledge. For example, a business decision-maker may be interested in grouping sales attributed to different marketing campaigns or experimenting with breaking sales down by different price ranges. At the same time, most selection criteria include at least one of the above dimensions to establish the limits of data analysis.

⚙️ EXAMPLE

Selection Criteria Examples

Example A

Each regional sales manager requires a monthly sales summary for the region they manage. The selection criteria for each regional sales report would require:

- The location where the sale took place must be within the specific region
- The sale date must be within the reporting month

Example B

After a rising number of complaints related to warranties, the warranty services director requested detailed statistics about last quarter's complaints. The selection criteria would require that:

- The date the claim was received must be within the last quarter
- The complaint reason must be warranty-related

Example C

A recall campaign targeting customers who previously purchased Product A of a particular model (Model B) within a particular date range is planned. This product was found to be faulty and now must be replaced. An estimate is required of how many replacements are needed. The selection criteria would require that:

- The item purchased must be Model B of Product A
- The date of the purchase must be within the specified time frame
- The item purchased has not been replaced yet

Note that selection criteria are not the same as report variables. Descriptive analytics may summarize data from different variables, such as when summarizing sales amounts. Selection criteria are used to determine what records will be included in summarization—for example, the region where the purchase happened.

5.4 DESCRIPTIVE METHODS

Appropriate descriptive analytics methods should be selected based on:

- The number of variables being summarized (univariate, bivariate, or multivariate analysis)
- What makes a meaningful summarization
- What presentation approach suits both the data and the intended audience

Applying descriptive analytics methods may produce:

- A single metric
- A smaller dataset created by grouping observations from a larger dataset and aggregating the values in each group
- A visualization of the dataset

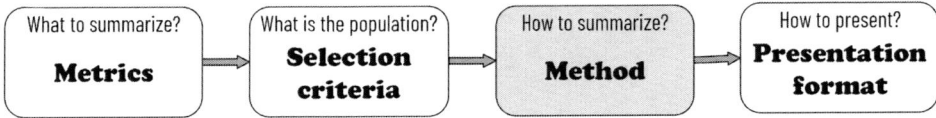

| What to summarize?
Metrics | → | What is the population?
Selection criteria | → | How to summarize?
Method | → | How to present?
Presentation format |

Figure 5.6 Descriptive Analytics Approach: How to Summarize

Summarization via grouping and aggregation results in a set of values for each group, such as the sales volumes over the last year grouped by month or quarters, or the total number of products sold in each category. These aggregated results can be presented in a tabular or graphic format.

Table 5.3 highlights frequently used descriptive summarization and visualization methods for one variable, two variables, and more.

Table 5.3 Descriptive Summarization and Visualization Methods

Summarization and visualization method	Univariate analysis	Bivariate analysis	Multivariate analysis
Single metric	• Mean, mode, median • Range, variance • Cumulative, change, gauge	• Composite score with two variables • Rate of occurrence	• Composite score with multiple variables • KPI
Aggregation into a smaller dataset (tabular presentation)	• Simple frequency table	• Two-dimensional frequency table	• Multi-dimensional data arrays (cubes) stored in data marts (see Section 9.4)
Aggregation into a smaller dataset (visual presentation)	• Pie chart • Bar/column chart • Box plot • Histogram • Waffle chart	• Grouped bar/column chart • Line/area chart • Combination column/line chart • Marimekko chart	• Combined visualizations
Visualization of the whole dataset	• Enumeration of all the values (list) • Dot chart	• Scatterplot	• Bubble chart

Metric Types

What is a meaningful summarization? It depends on what variable is being measured.

Cumulative metrics measure the variables that accumulate value with time, using counters for discrete variables or volume for continuous variables. Examples include number of products sold, number of service requests, revenue, and volume of transported goods.

Cumulative metrics may be measured on a month-to-date (MTD), year-to-date (YTD), 1-month rolling, or 12-month rolling basis, or any other time frame meaningful to the organization.

A **gauge** reflects a variable measured at a moment in time and will decrease or increase to reflect the current measure. Examples include sound volume, number of followers, and employee headcount.

A **rate** measures the occurrence of a variable over a specific interval expressed as a ratio. Examples include defects per million parts manufactured, accidents per million miles driven, and customer complaints per thousand purchases.

A **composite score** is a metric derived from combining multiple variables. It may be measured in absolute numbers (grade point average), by rate (earnings per share), or as a percentage. Many KPIs that are composite scores are expressed as percentages—examples are customer churn rate and employee satisfaction score.

We can also measure the **change** in a variable (also called *delta*) as the difference between values at certain points in time. It can be measured as absolute or relative (percentage) and can be applied to any of the above metrics. In the business world, change is often measured on a month-over-month (MOM), quarter-over-quarter (QOQ), or year-over-year (YOY) basis. Examples are sales volume growth in the first quarter and MOM defect rate reduction.

Descriptive statistics methods such as measures of central tendency, variability, and distribution can also be used for descriptive analysis (see Chapter 6 for using statistical methods for advanced analytics).

Measures of central tendency are summary statistics that characterize the whole dataset by identifying a single value as representative of the whole population. There are several ways to identify central tendency:

- The **mean** is the average value of all the observations in a sample calculated as the total of all values divided by the number of observations.
- The **median** is the middle value in the dataset when all the values are ordered.
- The **mode** is the value that appears the most frequently in the dataset.

When considering these, it is important to understand the advantages and limitations of each.

The mean is only meaningful for numeric data and may not match any single observation in the dataset. When applied to discrete values, it may yield fractional numbers—for example, "the average class enrollment is 25.3 students per class." The mean is less useful in datasets with skewed distributions or significant outliers.

In statistics, an **outlier** is a value that differs significantly from other observations of a variable. Outliers may be an indication of high variability, an unknown factor, or a result of a measurement error.

The median is less affected by extreme values in a dataset. It will match at least one value in a dataset (provided that the dataset contains an odd number of observations). It is useful with ordinal data but less meaningful in small datasets.

The mode is the only central tendency measure that can be used with nominal data—for example, "visual arts is the most frequently chosen elective course." It will always match at least one value in a dataset.

Measures of variability indicate how spread out the observations in a dataset are. Variability can be measured using:

- Range, which corresponds to the distance between the highest and the lowest value in a dataset
- Interquartile range, measuring the middle 50% in a dataset, or the distance between the medians of the upper and lower halves of data (see Figure 5.7)
- Variance and standard deviation, which reflect the average distance from all observations to the mean

Measures of distribution reflect the shape of the dataset:

- Skewness measures the asymmetry in the distribution of data from the mean.
- Kurtosis measures how the distribution of data peaks and flattens compared to the normal distribution bell curve.

A box plot can be a helpful way to visualize a numeric dataset distribution and some of the measures mentioned above. It is based on dividing the dataset into four approximately equal groups of ordered data points (quarters), so that each group contains around 25% of the total number of points. These groups will be separated by quartiles:

- The lower quartile (Q1) corresponds to the lowest 25% of the data points (25th percentile). It is also called lower median—the median of the lower half of the dataset.
- The second quartile (Q2), or the median, corresponds to the 50th percentile—the centre point of the dataset; 50% of the values in the dataset will lie below the median, and the other 50% above the median.
- The upper quartile (Q3) is the 75th percentile, also called the upper median—the median of the upper half of the dataset.
- The interquartile range (IQR) is the distance between Q3 and Q1. It corresponds to the box in the box plot, representing the middle half of the data.
- The whiskers represent the lowest and the highest 25% of the data points. This is why this chart is also called a box and whisker plot.

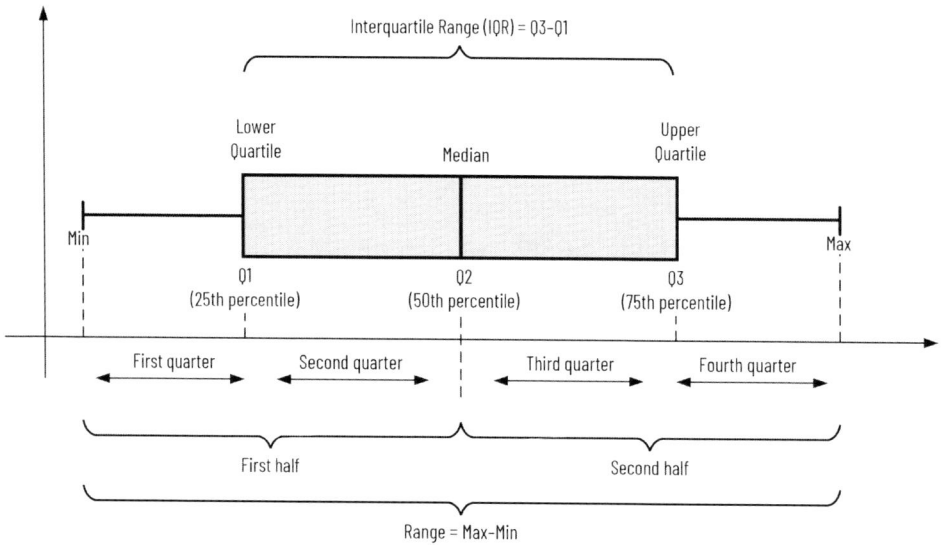

Figure 5.7 Box (Box and Whisker) Plot

TIPS ON TERMS

Quarter versus Quartile

As described above, we can sort a numeric dataset according to its values and divide it into *quarters*, or parts of the dataset containing 25% of all data points each. For example, the first quarter will contain the lowest 25% of the observations, while the fourth quarter will contain the highest 25%.

A *quartile* is a type of percentile, a value separating the quarters, such as Q1 (lower quartile, or 25th percentile) separating the first quarter from the second quarter.

The box plot in Figure 5.7 shows a relatively symmetrical and evenly distributed dataset; when a dataset is skewed, it will be reflected in a boxplot with whiskers of different lengths and an off-centre position of the median.

A box plot can also be used to identify outliers. A popular approach is to allow the whiskers to extend no more than $IQR \times 1.5$ in either direction. Any data point beyond this distance would be considered an outlier and would be plotted as a separate dot as shown in the next figure. Multiple box plots in a chart may represent the distribution of different categories or at different points in time.

Imagine you are visualizing movie ratings using box plots. While a median can be reflective of the overall movie popularity, the shape and length of the whiskers will indicate how uniform or spread out the ratings are. Some movies will be universally liked or not, and other movies may create a division of opinions. A not very successful movie, such as Movie B in Figure 5.8, can still have devoted fans giving it very high ratings, which may be shown as outliers on a box plot.

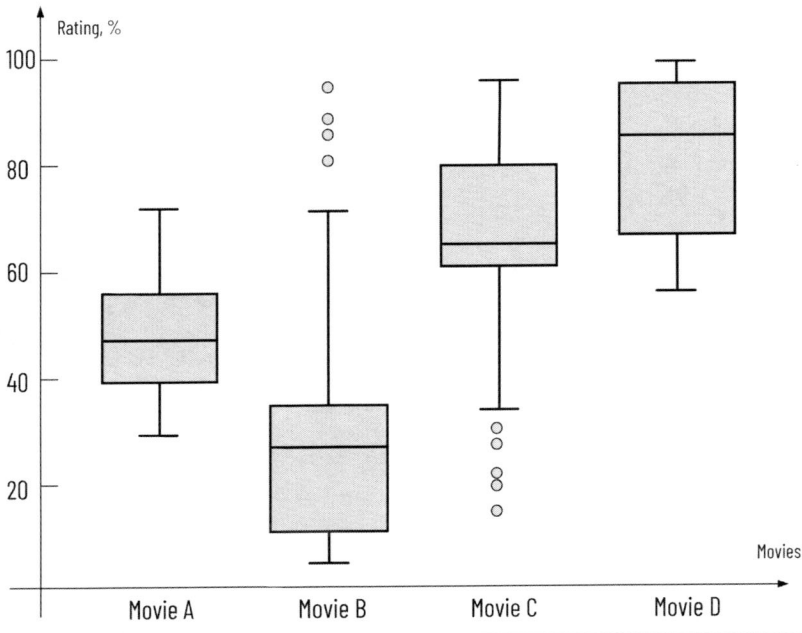

Figure 5.8 Multiple Box Plots—Example

To learn more about various statistical measures, refer to the resources mentioned in the Recommended Readings.

📖 **TIPS ON TERMS**

What Is an Average?

Average could very well be the most frequently and loosely used term when referring to data. A reference to an average implies one of the measures of central tendency—mean, median, or mode. While we often assume it is the mean (the total of all values divided by the number of observations), calculating the mean is only applicable to numerical values.

When analyzing a population of law school applicants, a reference to the *average age of applicants* can be clarified as a mean. However, a reference to *average education* is unclear and ambiguous. Are we measuring the number of years of education? In that case, a mean would be applicable. If we are interested in the education levels such as high school, bachelor's degree, master's degree, or PhD, then we are dealing with a categorical ordinal variable and should be looking for a median.

When you hear the word *average*, clarify and define explicitly which measure is to be used.

Summation versus Summarization

Summation refers to adding up the amounts to determine the total. *Summarization* is a more generic term referring to the expression of important information about something in brief. A summary can be textual, such as an executive summary or a report, or require performing of mathematical operations, such as calculating a weighted average.

⚙️ EXAMPLE

Selecting an Appropriate Descriptive Metric

Depending on what needs to be measured or summarized, some metrics are more suitable, and some can be downright misleading. For example, a manufacturer needs to analyze a problem of defective parts and wants to examine the trend. Measuring the number of defective parts produced monthly supplied the following information:

Defective Parts – Monthly Trend

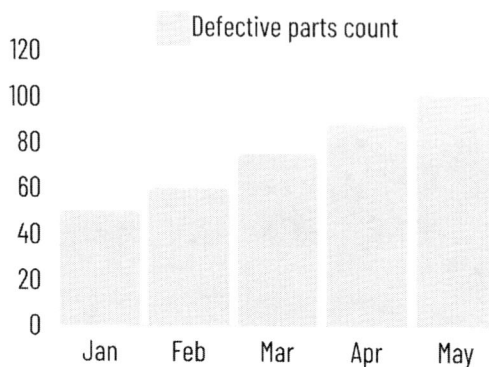

Figure 5.9 Trend Visualization: Number of Defective Parts

This may look like a worrying trend, but is it? It depends on the total number of parts manufactured every month. In a scenario where the production numbers rise (perhaps because the plant is ramping up new production), the situation may look different if we consider another metric—the ratio of defective parts per million manufactured.

Defective Parts - Monthly Trend

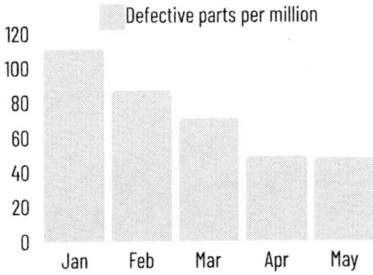

Defective parts per million

Month	Manufactured (million)	Defective parts	Defective parts per mln
Jan	0.45	50	111
Feb	0.69	60	87
Mar	1.05	75	71
Apr	1.80	88	49
May	2.10	101	48

Figure 5.10 Trend Visualization: Rate of Defective Parts

Breakdown and Aggregation

Another approach to summarizing data is to break observations down based on certain criteria and aggregate the data in each group. For example, the data for all retail purchases in a store can be aggregated into daily sales totals, or the number of new customers in each location can be aggregated to summarize customer growth by region.

Grouping must be based on meaningful dimensions such as time, geography, product categories, or expense types. It can be univariate, bivariate, or multivariate, depending on the number of variables used for breakdown or aggregation.

The simplest example is a **frequency table**—a table that shows the number of times different groups of values appear in a dataset.

The observations are grouped, counting the number of observations in each group. The grouping must be based on meaningful criteria, such as nominal groupings or ranges of numeric values. For example, Table 5.4 shows the distribution of YardExperts' landscaping survey respondents by property type.

Table 5.4 Distribution of Homeowners—Frequency Table

Property type	% of responses
Urban	32
Suburban	55
Rural	13
Total	**100**

This data can also be presented graphically, for example, with a pie chart:

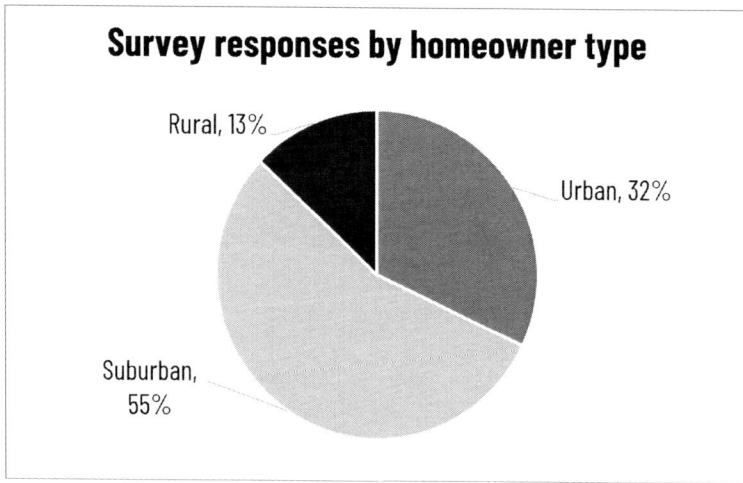

Survey responses by homeowner type

Figure 5.11 Distribution of Homeowners—Pie Chart

Frequency tables are also called *distribution tables* or *summary tables* and can be used for nominal data, as in Table 5.4, as well as for numeric data. When dealing with numeric data, the analyst must determine appropriate groupings, which may be referred to as *ranges* or *bins*. For example, analyzing all retail purchases by transaction amount, the following frequency table summarizes the total number of purchases with transaction amount within each of the pre-defined ranges. Each row represents a range (bin) of transactions.

Table 5.5 Distribution of Retail Purchases by Transaction Amount

Transaction amount	Number of purchases
Under $50	320
From $50 to under $100	140
From $100 to under $250	64
From $250 to under $500	16
$500 or more	20
Total	**560**

Frequency tables may refer to the absolute numbers (total number of occurrences) and/or percentages (contribution of each group to the total).

A frequency summary can be presented visually: as a column chart for nominal data, or as a histogram for numeric data. A *histogram* is a column chart that shows the frequency of the distribution of a numeric variable in a dataset, where the height of each column corresponds to the number of occurrences in each numeric range.

A two-dimensional (or bivariate) frequency table can capture the breakdown across two dimensions.

Table 5.6 Distribution of Survey Responses—Bivariate Frequency Table

	Planning to spend on landscaping this year?		
Property type	**Yes**	**No**	**Total**
Urban	15%	17%	**32%**
Suburban	48%	7%	**55%**
Rural	11%	2%	**13%**
Total	**74%**	**26%**	**100%**

Summary tables with more than two dimensions can be created using spreadsheet software, for example, utilizing the pivot table feature, and can also be referred to as *pivots*.

Multi-dimensional data is usually stored in specialized data marts (cubes). These cubes are designed to allow users to drill down and across dimensions to generate a variety of summary and detailed analyses (this will be explored more in Section 9.4).

CASE STUDY

The Pitfalls of Averages

YardExperts is facing the problem of lacking warehouse space in several locations. Sometimes, there is not enough space when new products arrive, and sometimes, the warehouse is underused while customers have to wait too long for their orders because products are not in stock.

To analyze this problem, the analytics team has produced some metrics for average product turnover in different warehouses, hoping to compare those locations that have frequent spacing issues to other locations that appear to be better utilized.

Unfortunately, the average product turnover, measured in days, proved to be an unhelpful metric. Why?

Average as a measure of central tendency is not useful when there are significant variations in a dataset. In the gardening and landscaping business, some products such as lawnmowers, prefabricated sheds, and garden furniture have a significantly longer turnover than tomato seedlings sold at the peak of planting season.

The inventory of YardExperts' business can be analyzed more effectively when it is segmented—that is, divided into groups with similar characteristics. Consider the turnover numbers of these product categories:

Table 5.7 Turnover by Product Category

Product category	Average turnover (days)
Lawn mowers	78
Lawn furniture	66
Garden tools	44
Seeds	102
Plant seedlings	15
Shrubs	31

Depending on the nature of the variable, averages within segments can provide better insight than population averages.

TIPS ON TERMS

Number, Count, Amount, and Total

The terms *number* and *count* apply to discrete (countable) variables (the number of new orders, defective parts count). The term *amount* applies to continuous (uncount-able) variables (the amount of time required to change a tire).

A *total* may apply to both discrete and continuous variables, such as the total number of retail locations (discrete) and the total annual grain production measured in millions of metric tons (continuous). The term *total* is used to distinguish the overall number or amount from summaries by subcategories or bins.

5.5 PRESENTATION AND VISUALIZATION

Descriptive analytics are developed for use by a variety of audiences and must be presented with care. The presentation format should adhere to best practices for clarity and ease of understanding.

The results of descriptive analytics can be presented as a single metric, table, or chart (see Figure 5.1).

Each of these can be embedded in different communication formats—reflected on slides of a presentation, included as a panel on a dashboard, illustrated in an annual report, or prominently displayed on a bulletin board.

What to summarize?	What is the population?	How to summarize?	How to present?
Metrics	**Selection criteria**	**Method**	**Presentation format**

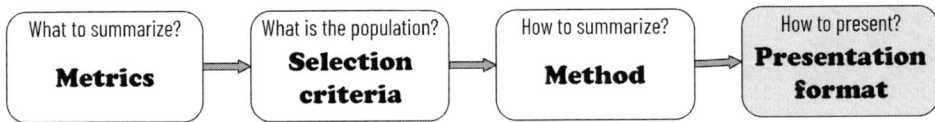

Figure 5.12 Descriptive Analytics Approach: How to Present?

With metrics and tables already discussed above, this section will provide an overview of visualization approaches. Refer to the Recommended Readings for a detailed study of visualization methods.

Visualization refers to the presentation of datasets and their characteristics in a pictorial or graphical format. It enables us to grasp visually the characteristics of the dataset, patterns, trends, and outliers.

Table 5.8 Types of Visualization

Type	Purpose	Examples
Comparative	Compare and rank data	Bar chart, column chart, radar chart
Contribution	Show the contributions of segments to a whole	Pie chart, donut chart, stacked area chart, stacked column chart, Marimekko chart, tree map
Relationship	Identify relationships between measures (correlations)	Bubble chart, scatterplot chart, correlogram, correlation matrix
Distribution	Show the distribution of value across the range	Box (box and whisker) plot, candlestick chart, histogram, density plot
Time-series	Examine data change over time	Line chart, area chart, column chart
Geographic	Overlay other visualization types on a map	Choropleth map, dot map, bubble map, flow map

Comparative visualization methods allow us to compare variables at a glance using the relative size of the chart elements such as bars or columns to aid the comparison. Bar charts are frequently used to visualize a ranking:

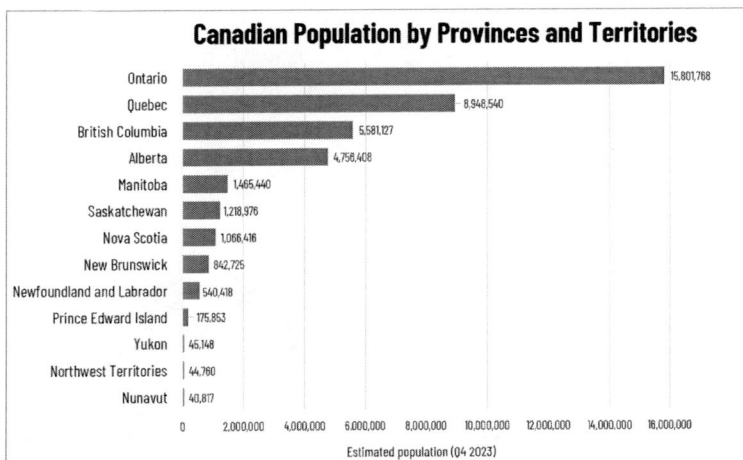

Canadian Population by Provinces and Territories

Province/Territory	Estimated population (Q4 2023)
Ontario	15,801,768
Quebec	8,948,540
British Columbia	5,581,127
Alberta	4,756,408
Manitoba	1,465,440
Saskatchewan	1,218,976
Nova Scotia	1,066,416
New Brunswick	842,725
Newfoundland and Labrador	540,418
Prince Edward Island	175,853
Yukon	45,148
Northwest Territories	44,760
Nunavut	40,817

Figure 5.13 Bar Chart Example
Data source: Statistics Canada[1]

Contribution visualizations can use different shapes to depict the whole. Apart from a circle that a pie chart and donut chart are based on, we can use columns when creating a stacked column chart or divide rectangles into smaller rectangles in proportion to their contribution to the whole as in Marimekko charts and tree maps.

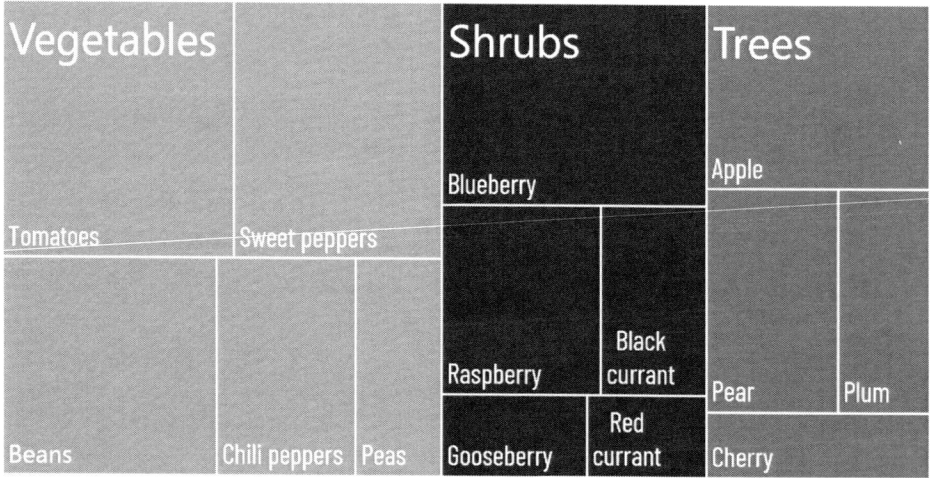

Figure 5.14 Tree Map Example

Some charts allow for the combination of multiple visualization types—for example, a stacked column chart illustrates both the comparison and contribution:

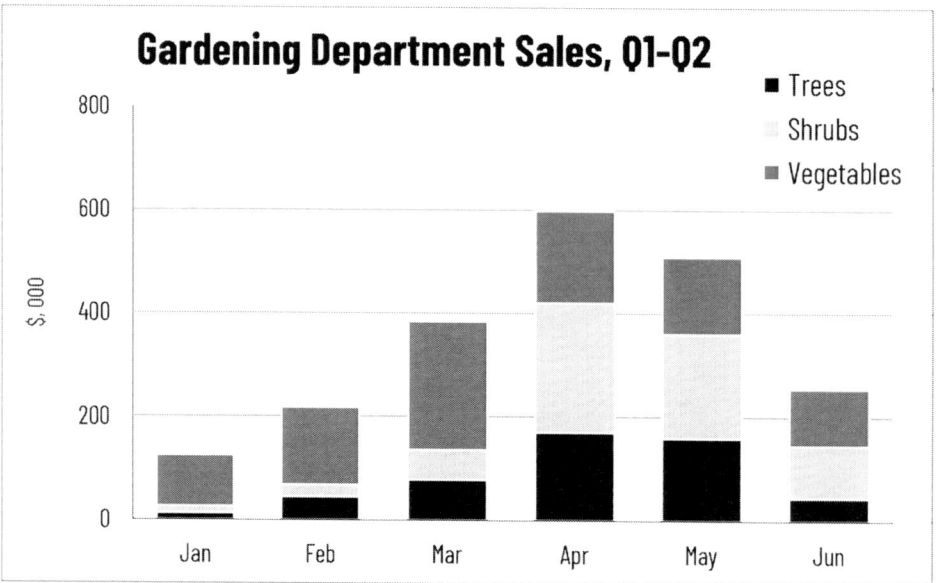

Figure 5.15 Stacked Column Chart Example

A comparative and contribution approach is frequently used on grouped data, such as grouping all sales in the Trees, Shrubs, and Vegetables categories in the stacked chart (Figure 5.15).

Relationship visualizations allow us to plot individual observations to identify potential patterns and correlations, such as during data profiling (discussed in Chapter 7).

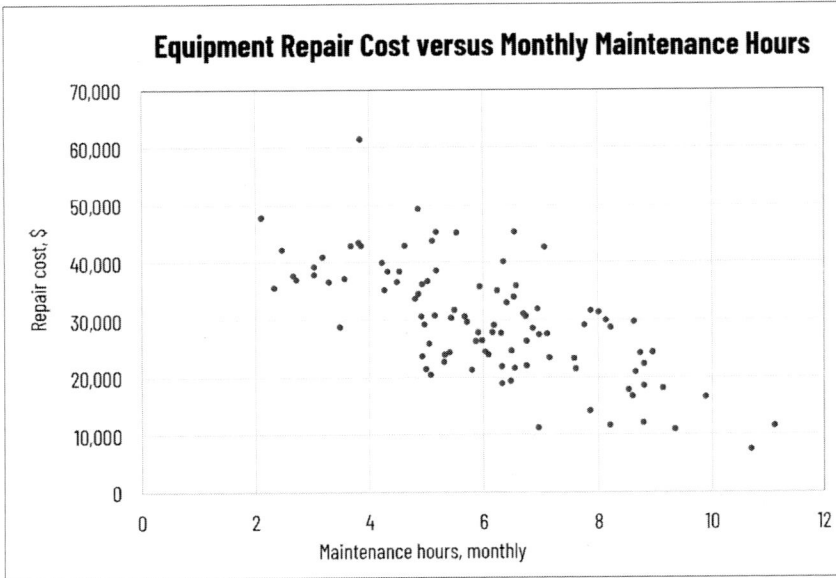

Figure 5.16 Scatterplot Example

Distribution visualizations focus on the distribution of a population. A histogram shows the distribution of data over a continuous interval divided into segments.

Figure 5.17 Histogram Example

Time-series visualizations are plotted over an x-axis that represents the time variable to show how other variables are trending over time.

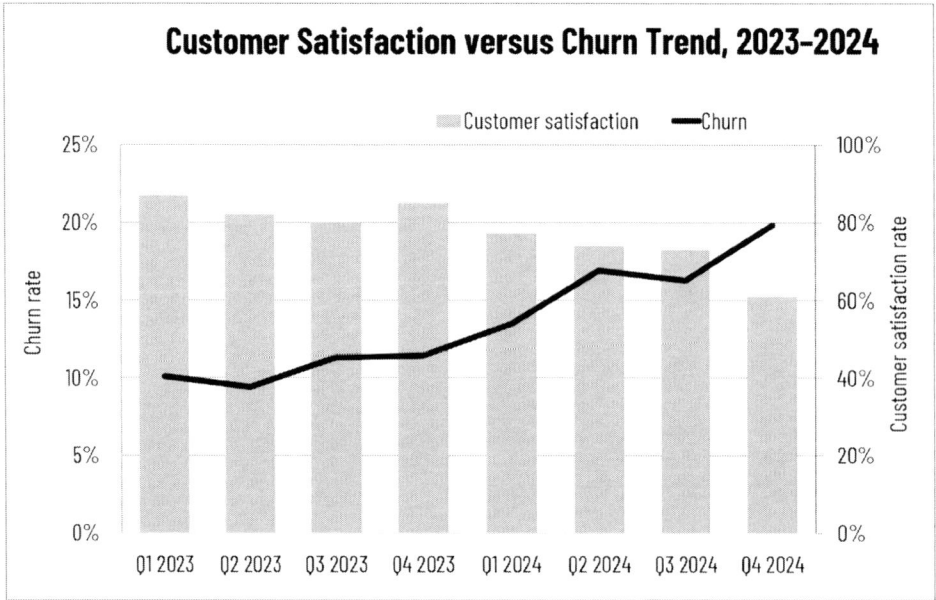

Figure 5.18 Time-Series Combination Chart Example

Apart from the chart type, visualizations can use additional visual elements to convey information, such as:

- Types of shapes
- Shape sizes
- Colours
- Axis scale
- Line width
- Shape fill styles

These elements can provide more depth to the visualization and allow more information to be condensed within. However, balance is critical. Including too much information can make charts confusing and hide important insights instead of highlighting them.

A good visualization is:

- Purposeful: answers relevant questions and addresses the needs of the intended audience
- Accurate: conveys the information without distortion or misleading the audience
- Clear: easy to understand, includes sufficient labels
- Uncluttered: does not contain unnecessary details
- Visually appealing: aesthetically pleasing, easy to look at

- Supported: the background information such as sources of data, assumptions, statistical analysis performed, and definitions of the chart elements are available to support the interpretation of the visual

A chart can become unhelpful or misleading if it is created without care—this can include making poor choices about the chart type or the range of values on the axes, including an excessive number of series or groupings, or mislabelling components. While modern analytics tools provide computing power and the ability to visualize large amounts of data, the person working on the visualization is responsible for ensuring that the visualization communicates the information accurately and clearly.

✓ **CHECKLIST**

Data Visualization Checklist

1. What is the purpose of the visualization?
2. Who will be the audience and what are they looking for?
3. How many variables do you need to visualize—one, two, or more?
4. What is the nature of the variables? Are they discrete or continuous?
5. What type of visualization would be appropriate for this data and the purpose of the visualization? Could this purpose be better served by a table than a chart?
6. Would the insights be clearer if you used more than one type of visualization or split the chart into multiple charts by segments of data?
7. If the dataset has a wide range, have you considered what subset requires analysis? Is there a need to visualize the full range? If visualizing a subset of data, have you included a clear annotation of the selection criteria?
8. When visualizing groups, what order makes sense? Is there a natural sequence? A hierarchy? Should the groups be sorted by a numeric variable or a statistic such as frequency?
9. If you are displaying more than one variable, how are they measured? Do they require separate y-axes?
10. Is the main message of the chart clear? Are there any misleading visual elements?
11. Did you follow accepted visualization conventions and best practices?
    - Bar charts and column charts start from zero.
    - The time variable is always on the horizontal (x) axis.
    - Every element that requires explanation is labelled, e.g., the chart title, axes labels, names of the data series.
    - Three-dimensional elements are avoided.
    - Numeric data have accurate relative proportions.

- All labels and text are concise, easy to read, and easy to relate to visual elements they describe.
- Important parts are highlighted using visual elements such as colours, labels, arrows, etc.
- Redundant information and unnecessary details are removed.
- Data is segmented into the smallest effective number of groups (e.g., no more than 7–10 sectors in a pie chart).
- There is sufficient white space; visual elements are not overcrowded.
- The source of data is referenced.
- Chart is tested for accessibility by colourblind viewers.

5.6 CHAPTER SUMMARY

Key Points to Remember

- The outcome of descriptive analytics is quantitative reporting of facts presented as tables, charts, or single metrics.
- Quantitative metrics state the facts but do not provide an interpretation or explanation. This requires diagnostic analysis.
- Some observations can be measured directly, while other, intangible concepts require indirect (proxy) measurements.
- The selection of descriptive metrics must be carefully based on what needs to be measured and who the audience is; metrics that can be ambiguous or misleading should be avoided.
- A good visualization must be purposeful, accurate, clear, and visually appealing.
- A visualization by itself may not be enough to make conclusions and important decisions. It must be supported by a commentary, including assumptions made, all definitions, sources of data, and their limitations.

Key Terms

Bivariate analysis: analysis involving two variables.

Calculated value: a value that is a result of performing arithmetic operations.

Change (delta): the difference between a variable's values at certain points in time.

Composite score: a metric derived from combining multiple variables.

Cumulative metric: a metric that accumulates value with time.

Derived value: a value obtained from other values by applying logical reasoning or rules.

Dimension: an attribute used for organizing, segmenting, and summarizing observations in a dataset.

Frequency table (summary table, distribution table): a table that shows the number of times different groups of values appear in a dataset.

Gauge: a metric that reflects a variable measured at a moment in time that may decrease or increase in value.

Indirect (proxy) measurement: a measurement believed to correlate with a variable that cannot be measured directly.

Key performance indicator (KPI): a metric created to track an organization's performance compared to established targets.

Mean: the average value of all the observations in a sample calculated as the total of all values divided by the number of observations.

Measure: a determined size or amount of a variable expressed in numeric units.

Measures of central tendency: summary statistics that characterize the whole dataset by identifying a single value as representative of the whole population.

Median: the middle value in the dataset when all the values are ordered.

Metric (operational metric): a measure of an operational activity or a business process.

Mode: the value that appears the most frequently in the dataset.

Multivariate analysis: analysis involving three or more variables.

Outlier: a value that differs significantly from other observations of a variable.

Rate: the occurrence of a variable over a specific interval expressed as a ratio.

Selection criteria: ranges, limits, or logical conditions that define what data is of interest for analysis.

Univariate analysis: analysis of a single variable.

Visualization: presentation of a dataset and its characteristics in a pictorial or graphical format.

Questions for Critical Thought

1. What is the difference between operational metrics and KPIs?
2. What are selection criteria, and how are they determined?
3. When will a ratio metric be more suitable than an absolute measure?
4. How are hierarchical dimensions used for analysis?
5. What are some of the pitfalls of relying on averages?
6. What are the most important considerations when choosing an appropriate visualization?

Test Your Knowledge

1. You need to summarize information about new landscaping contracts signed in the last quarter in the central region. What variables must be considered for the selection criteria?
   a. Contract type, contract status, and region
   b. Contract signed date, contract type, and region
   c. Region, contract type, and contract renewal date
   d. Start and end dates of the quarter, contract type, and region

2. You need to summarize information about equipment repair expenses across the whole company in the last 12 months to understand what classes of equipment and types of repairs are the costliest. What variables must be considered for the selection criteria?
    a. Equipment class, expense type, expense amount, expense date, and region
    b. Expense type, expense date, and expense amount must be greater than $1,000
    c. Equipment breakdown date, equipment repair date, equipment class, and expense amount
    d. Expense type and expense date

3. You are analyzing a dataset with customer survey responses. In the first question, the respondents are asked about their favourite type of vacation setting. The respondents can choose from one of the following values: Famous city, Beach, Forest, Cottage, Mountains, or Home. What measure of central tendency can be used to summarize the responses?
    a. Mean
    b. Median
    c. Mode
    d. All of the above

4. You are analyzing a dataset with customer survey responses. In the second question, the respondents are asked about the length of their most recent vacation. The respondents can choose one of the following values: 1–5 days, 5–9 days, 10–14 days, or more than 14 days. What metric can be used to summarize the responses?
    a. Mean
    b. Median
    c. Range
    d. Rate

5. A monthly order fulfillment report includes the number of open orders at the end of the month. What type of metric is this?
    a. Gauge
    b. Rate
    c. Composite score
    d. Change

Recommended Readings

Bergin, T. (2018). *An Introduction to Data Analysis. Quantitative, Qualitative and Mixed Methods.* SAGE Publications.

Cairo, A. (2019). *How Charts Lie: Getting Smarter about Visual Information.* W. W. Norton.

The Data Visualisation Catalogue: datavizcatalogue.com.

Gutman, A., & Goldmeier, J. (2021). *Becoming a Data Head: How to Think, Speak, and Understand Data Science, Statistics, and Machine Learning.* Wiley.

Knaflic, C. N. (2015). *Storytelling with Data: A Data Visualization Guide for Business Professionals.* Wiley.

Marr, B. (2014). *25 Need-to-Know Key Performance Indicators.* Pearson Education.

Wilke, C. (2019). *Fundamentals of Data Visualization: A Primer on Making Informative and Compelling Figures.* O'Reilly Media.

Note

1.   Statistics Canada. (2023, December 19). *Table 17-10-0009-01: Population Estimates, Quarterly.* Retrieved February 24, 2024, from www150.statcan.gc.ca/t1/tbl1/en/tv.action?pid=1710000901.

Chapter 6

Advanced Analytics

While descriptive analytics allow past and current performance to be summarized, this is not sufficient for future success. To adapt to ever-changing market conditions and achieve long-term goals, organizations use advanced analytics.

In this chapter, you will learn about:

- Methods and applications of advanced analytics
- Approaches to predictive modelling
- How advances in the development of AI can be used for business decision-making

6.1 DIAGNOSTIC ANALYTICS

Descriptive analytics provide a starting point for understanding what is happening, what is going well, and what is not. However, the numbers themselves—the descriptive metrics—state only the facts. They are the indicators pointing out what needs further attention. Descriptive analytics report on the information without interpreting it. To make changes, reverse a negative trend, or capitalize on a positive one, more is required. Decision-makers must understand the reasons behind the trends, or how observed outcomes are influenced by various factors.

Understanding the trends and the discovery of the contributing factors that affect business outcomes is the goal of root cause analysis, also known as diagnostic analytics.

CASE STUDY

Customer Churn: Investigating Contributing Factors

Last year's results show that YardExperts' total sales volume has decreased by 15% year-over-year.

If your goal is to reverse the trend and bring sales up again, how would you go about it? You start with diagnostic analytics—analyzing why sales have decreased.

Are we losing customers? What are they unhappy about?

Do our regular customers buy less? Why?

Can the decrease in sales be attributed to specific customer segments? If so, which ones and why?

Are there any correlations between the lower sales and external events?

Are there any seasonal patterns to the dips?

Does the sales slump affect particular geographic locales?

Does it have anything to do with the quality of our products? The prices? The competition? Bad press, good press? The latest TikTok trends?

A businessperson may have some ideas—hypotheses—about the root cause (or causes) of the sales decline. They may be right, and they may be wrong. Even if they have a good hunch, proving it will require data analysis.

The case study example highlights a key concept of diagnostics analysis: the hypothesis.

A **hypothesis** is a belief based on prior knowledge, experience, or intuition.

When we make a hypothesis about connections and relationships between variables, it must be validated using data.

Hypothesis testing is examining a hypothesis using available data in order to confirm, reject, or modify it.

Diagnostic analytics provides methods for testing hypotheses using data to see whether any statistical evidence exists to support the claim.

Diagnostics may require experimenting and testing out different venues of analysis, or different hypotheses. Sometimes, there is no obvious hypothesis, and diagnostic analysis may start with mining the data to identify patterns and trends to help form a hypothesis.

Several methods may need to be employed before pinpointing the most influential factors that impacted your sales in the prior year. This is what diagnostic analytics is about: exploring, mining, experimenting, coming up with hypotheses, testing them, and, through trial and error, zooming in on the significant factors that impact business performance.

Diagnostic Analytics Approaches

The first steps of diagnostics often involve manual data exploration and discovery by a data analyst:

- Exploring available datasets
- Eyeballing the quality and patterns within the data
- Performing simple summaries such as identifying minimum and maximum values, range, and central tendency for certain attributes
- Scanning data for outliers
- Filtering and sorting data by different dimensions

- Drilling down or across to explore potential associations and trends that contribute to particular outcomes
- Creating simple visualizations

These steps rely on descriptive analysis of the dataset, followed by more exploration to look for patterns that would be easy to detect by a human observer. This process is most effective when the analyst exploring the data understands the domain and therefore has enough background knowledge to "eyeball" the trends and outliers and interpret the data.

Thus, an initial hypothesis may be based on intuition, previous observations, obvious trends discovered through data exploration, or even a guess. It must be validated using rigorous statistical methods, some of which will be outlined further down.

If no viable hypotheses are discovered through the initial data exploration, data mining can be used to search for hidden patterns in the data—for instance, applying clustering or association algorithms. These patterns may not be detectable by a human observer due to data volume, variety, or veracity, or because the pattern is unexpected.

Figure 6.1 shows the typical steps in the diagnostic analytics process.

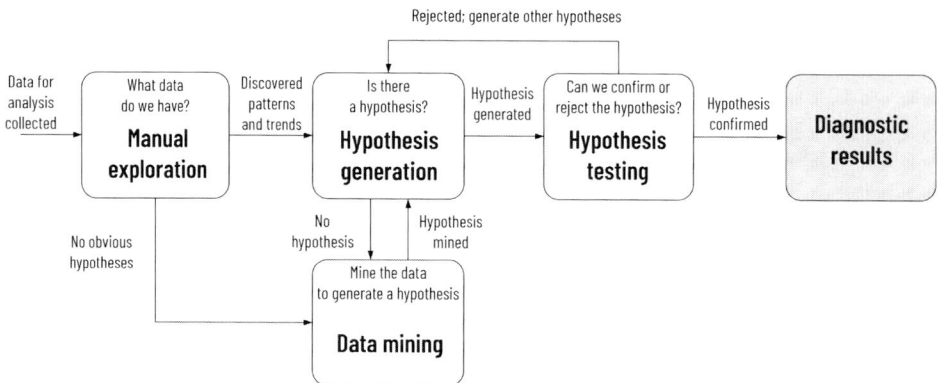

Figure 6.1 Simplified Diagnostic Analysis Process

Another difficulty may arise if the data is insufficient to prove or disprove a hypothesis—if there aren't enough observations, too much variability exists in the available sample, or important information is not in the dataset. Then the analysis may require additional data collection—either acquired from another source, such as a market research agency, or collected by running experiments.

While designing and conducting experiments is beyond the scope of this book, consider an example of A/B testing.

A/B testing is a type of research experiment to test the significance of one element by randomly changing its value between the control value (A) and the experimental value (B) and measuring the outcome. This experiment can be used to prove or reject a hypothesis that B is a significant factor that impacts the result.

A/B testing can be applied in many situations where it's possible to run a sufficient number of experiments, apply random sampling, and limit the change to only one element being tested. Some examples are:

- Testing whether one particular element of a webpage's design, such as a button label or position, a colour palette, or a specific word, impacts the click-through rate or how long a potential customer spends on a page
- Testing whether offering a sales incentive impacts the propensity to buy, or comparing the attractiveness of two incentives
- Confirming whether a courtesy call seven days before contract renewal increases the likelihood that the customer will renew the contract

CASE STUDY

A/B Experiment with Unexpected Results

At YardExperts, a high contract renewal rate is crucial. Attracting a new customer is expensive, while processing a renewal does not require a lot of effort. As part of battling the churn problem, one of the questions on the table was about the optimum time to place a courtesy call to remind customers about renewing their contract.

One camp believed that a two-week notice works better. Another camp suggested that a courtesy call closer to the expiry date may lead to better outcomes. There were arguments on both sides, and previous years' statistics were not helpful as previous practice was to make courtesy calls two weeks before expiration. No other data was available for comparison.

A new marketing manager suggested running an A/B test by randomly selecting about 50% of expiring contracts to call following the existing practice of two-week notice (the A group) and waiting until one week before the expiration for the other half (the B group). Both segments were picked to represent the overall population as closely as possible in terms of the size of the contract, the number of service calls, and complaints. The experiment was limited to one region to make data collection manageable.

The experiment was allowed to run for two months. The results surprised everybody. While Group A had about a 20% churn rate, in Group B, the churn rate was only 7%.

The improvement was significant enough to encourage YardExperts to run the experiment more broadly across all regions and for several months. The results were similar. When customers were contacted closer to the expiration date, they were more likely to renew their contract.

One may speculate that this can be explained by the unwillingness of customers to look for alternatives if there is less time left to renew a contract. Whether this is indeed the root cause might require more experiments. However, the results of the A/B testing convinced YardExperts' management to change the courtesy calls policy.

Diagnostic analysis also needs to deal with situations where a multitude of contributing factors exist and assessing their collective impact becomes challenging. The more factors there are, the more variations and interdependencies need to be considered. Making decisions about what to change to achieve a desired effect can become very difficult, especially when some factors are correlated. Building predictive models also becomes more complex and computationally taxing with a large number of variables.

In analytics, this is handled by identifying the most significant factors using factor analysis methods. The desired outcome of the diagnostic analysis is identifying a manageable number of the most significant factors (root causes) that influence a business outcome important to the organization.

Figure 6.2 shows how a more comprehensive diagnostic analysis process may require additional data collection, mining and testing of multiple hypotheses, and conducting factor analysis to identify key influencing factors.

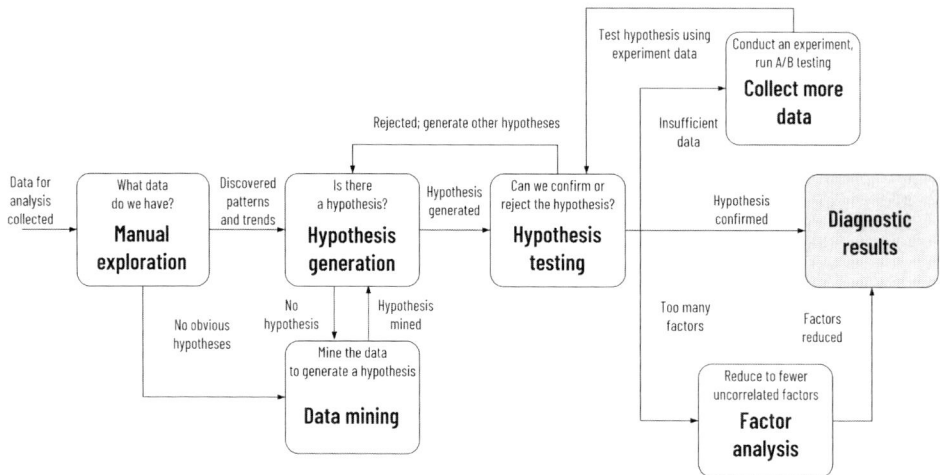

Figure 6.2 Comprehensive Diagnostic Analysis Process

Figures 6.1 and 6.2 each show a sample flow of diagnostics. Other variations are possible. The selection and sequencing of steps will depend on the nature and complexity of the problem, availability of data, and its volume and variety.

Statistical Methods

Statistical methods are widely used for diagnostics. Before introducing them, it's useful to recap some fundamental concepts of statistics.

Population refers to all members of a group of interest.

A **sample** is the part of the population with available data.

There are two main approaches to data analysis in statistics.

Descriptive statistics is concerned with summarizing and presenting sets of data.

Descriptive statistics describes the characteristics of a population numerically. These numerical results are called **parameters**. For example, the percentage of homeowners that reside in urban areas is a parameter of the homeowners population. Mean, median, mode, and standard deviation can also be population parameters.

While descriptive statistics analyze and describe the whole dataset, another approach becomes necessary when the analysis of data about the whole population is impractical or impossible.

Inference refers to making judgments about characteristics of a population based on a population sample.

A **representative sample** is a population sample selected to accurately represent the characteristics of a whole population.

⚙️ EXAMPLE

When a population census is undertaken, its goal is to collect data from all people who live in a country, hence the statistical term *population*. Censuses are slow and costly, and therefore can only be conducted once every few years.

When the government wishes to gather information or opinion from the population outside of a census, it is usually done through surveys using representative samples.

Similarly, during election campaigns, various election polls are performed on population samples. A typical size of an election poll sample is between one thousand and five thousand people.[1]

Using representative samples is essential for **inferential statistics**, which is concerned with studying smaller datasets to project these findings to a larger dataset (or infer the larger dataset characteristics from a sample).

Inferential statistics describe the characteristics of a population sample. When we calculate a numeric measure from a sample, we call it a **statistic** (singular). For example, the percentage of homeowners who were surveyed and responded that they allocated a landscaping budget for the upcoming summer is a statistic of the survey sample.

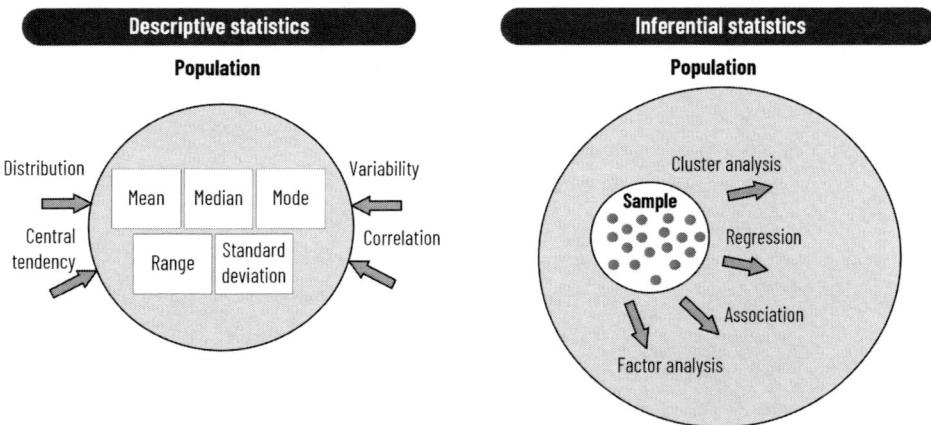

Figure 6.3 Examples of Descriptive and Inferential Statistics Methods

---

TIPS ON TERMS

Parameter versus Statistics versus Variable

A *parameter* is a measurable characteristic of a population, such as mean or median, which can take on a certain numeric value.

A *statistic* is a characteristic of a population sample (which may or may not apply to the whole population depending on the sample used). A statistic for a sample is what a parameter is for the whole population.

A *variable* is a characteristic of an object or a concept that will be analyzed and can take on different values.

For example, lot size would be a variable of interest when YardExperts tracks customer data. Their customers' minimum and maximum lot sizes would be a customer population metric. The median lot size of customers who said in a recent survey that they were planning a new gardening project would be a survey sample statistic.

Statistics versus Statistic

Statistics is a field of study that analyzes samples of data to make inferences about larger populations, whereas *a statistic* is a characteristic of a population sample. The plural of *a statistic* is *statistics*, but they should be distinguished from one another.

Representative versus Random Sample

A **representative sample** is a population sample selected to accurately represent the characteristics of the whole population.

In a *random sample*, every member of a population has the chance to be represented.

A random sample is not always representative.

Both descriptive and inferential statistics methods can be used for diagnostic analytics. Making inferences from a smaller dataset about the overall population can also be used for prediction.

Diagnostic analytics may employ a variety of statistical analysis methods to test a hypothesis. We will review a few of them.

Correlation analysis is the analysis of an association between two random variables.

Correlation can tell us whether two variables are linearly related—that is, whether or not they change together at a similar rate. Correlation between two observations can be positive (e.g., when the total number of product returns increases at the same rate as the volume of sales) or negative (e.g., when the number of complaints increases, the number of contract renewals decreases).

Correlation can only highlight the existence of an association between variables. It does not identify which variables are the causes and which are the effects in a causal relationship, nor that there is a cause-effect relationship in the first place.

> ⚙️ **EXAMPLE**
>
> A positive correlation was detected between boating accidents and ski purchases. As the number of boating accidents increases, so does the volume of ski equipment sales.
>
> Does this imply causation? Are those people who experienced a boating accident more likely to decide never to set their foot on a boat again and take up skiing instead?
>
> It's much more likely that both patterns are caused by a third factor: seasons. In many regions, boating is a summer pursuit, and therefore most accidents will happen in summer when boats are frequently used.
>
> Summer may also happen to be the season of the highest discounts on ski equipment when ski shops run sales on last season's products to free up the floor space for the new models.

This example illustrates a **spurious correlation** or a relationship where two variables appear to be correlated but do not have a causal relationship. This may happen if both variables have a causal relationship with a third variable. Some correlations are purely coincidental, as reflected in numerous examples published by Tyler Vigen.[2] This reflects a popular maxim: "Correlation does not imply causation."

It is also important to remember that when a sample is too small or variations in the population are too extreme, analysis of one sample can yield a coincidental correlation.

> 📖 **TIPS ON TERMS**
>
> **Correlation versus Causation**
>
> *Correlation* can tell us whether two variables are linearly related—whether they change together at a similar rate.
>
> *Causation* means that changes in one variable result in changes in the other variable.
>
> Correlated variables do not always have a causal relationship.

Cluster analysis refers to breaking data down into groups with similar characteristics. This approach supports diagnostics by enabling analysis and comparison of metrics and trends within and between clusters. Clustering can play a crucial role in behavioural analysis such as spending patterns or reading preferences. Dividing customers into clusters for behavioural analysis is also called *customer segmentation*.

Cohort analysis is a specific approach to clustering based on common characteristics that cohort members will retain for a certain period. These could be demographic characteristics such as age, nationality, or belonging to stable social groups, such as universities, neighbourhoods, or religious communities. A well-known example is the determination of population cohorts by year of birth: Baby Boomers, Generation X, Millennials (Generation Y), and Generation Z.[3]

Another example of clustering is **stratification**, which is when population members are divided into strata (layers) based on an ordinal characteristic. For example, the population of a country can be divided into strata by wealth or education level.

The variables that define which group a particular population member will be sorted into are called **discriminants**. For example, year of birth is the discriminant for segmenting the population into generations X, Y, and Z. If there is a significant difference in the outcome when the population is divided into clusters, then the discriminants used for sorting the population into groups may indicate the root causes and can be used as candidate predictive factors for predictive modelling.

When there is a difference in the outcome between different groups in a population, the population is called **heterogeneous**. When no significant difference is detected, the population is considered **homogeneous**.

Regression analysis refers to the examination of a relationship among quantitative variables.

A statistically significant relationship will indicate the influence of certain factors on a variable of interest. **Statistically significant relationships** are those that are unlikely to be due to chance.

For example, regression analysis can be used to determine the relationship between total equipment maintenance hours and the cost of equipment repairs.

Regression can be used for diagnostics, when identifying factors contributing to an observed outcome, and for predictive modelling, when the same relationship is projected into the future.

Association analysis refers to searching for interesting associations within a dataset, such as the co-occurrence of certain values. For example, in market basket analysis, the researcher may be interested in grocery items frequently bought together.

This method can be used to search for associations between two sets of data—for example, between customer attributes such as family status or profession and the types of products (e.g., books, movies, cereal bands) that customers prefer.

Association analysis can be used to form a new hypothesis—for example, a hypothesis that customers who purchase a certain type of product will be interested in another product.

Factor analysis is used to select variables (factors) that have the highest influence on specific outcomes among multiple candidate variables. For example, many factors may contribute to a customer's decision not to renew a landscaping contract. Factor analysis can be used to identify a smaller number of factors that have the strongest influence, such as multiple missed service appointments, customer chargebacks, or logged complaints about rude behaviour.

Factor analysis supports the reduction of a large number of potentially interdependent variables to a smaller number of minimally correlated factors. These methods play a role in feature selection (discussed in more detail in Section 7.3) when the goal is to select the smallest possible number of predictive factors that will provide sufficiently accurate predictions.

Note that this section highlights only a few of the many statistical methods; refer to specialized statistics textbooks for in-depth study of the subject.

Diagnostic Analytics Questions and Use Cases

How can you ask clear, specific, and relevant diagnostic analytics questions?

✔ **CHECKLIST**

Asking Diagnostic Questions

1. Clarify the goals of diagnostics.

   Have a clear understanding of the business results that require diagnostics, such as lower customer churn, reduced rate of defective manufactured parts, or a higher proportion of positive customer reviews on a new product. Both favourable and unfavourable outcomes may be the subject of analysis.

2. Understand how to measure the outcome.

   Consider available descriptive analytics such as a KPI increase or decrease or recent trends that warrant further analysis. How is the target business outcome measured? What is considered a significant change?

   Diagnostic analysis is often initiated when business performance results are unexpected. If diagnostic questions are being asked before descriptive analysis is completed, descriptive statistics should be collected to confirm the problem. For example, a two-fold increase in customer churn in the last year may be a valid reason for further analysis. Having three more cancellations this month than the previous month may not be significant when compared to the total contract base or the expected seasonal fluctuations.

3. Determine the relevant segment(s) of the population.

   Another key aspect of diagnostics is the constraints on the analysis along one or more dimensions, such as time or location. For example, you might be asked to analyze the reasons behind a company's increase in customer churn in the Maritimes in the last three quarters. Note that the constraints are not always known. The analysis may include discovering whether the observed trend impacts the overall population or only specific segments of it.

4. Formulate the question.

   A diagnostic question may follow one of these patterns:
   - Why did … happen?
   - What caused …?

- What are the trends in …?
- Is there a relationship between … and …?
- What are the reasons for the increase/decrease of …?
- What are the similarities between group A and group B related to …?
- What groups have demonstrated a similar behaviour when …?
- What associations can we observe in …?
- Can … explain …?

5. Review the question. Is it sufficiently clear, relevant, and specific?

What business problems can be addressed with diagnostic analytics? Here are some sample applications:

- Root cause analysis: identifying significant factors influencing the outcome. Examples: root cause analysis of manufacturing defects, customer churn, product returns
- Indicative pattern detection: detecting patterns in data that have strong correlations with the observed outcome. Examples: medical diagnosis, spam filtering, fraud or money laundering detection
- Population segmentation: grouping of population members with similar outcomes together to detect discriminating factors. Examples: customer segmentation, job candidate grouping, research results classification
- Trend analysis: searching for a relationship between variables that can explain the reasons for changes in the observable variable over time. Examples: sales trends analysis, stock price analysis, population growth trends
- Sensitivity analysis: detecting how changes in one variable affect another variable. Examples: price elasticity, stock price sensitivity to interest rate change, customer sensitivity to personalized offers
- Outlier detection: identifying data points located far from other points in a dataset that doesn't seem to follow the main pattern in the dataset; analysis of outliers may pinpoint interesting dependencies

IMPORTANT

One of the challenges of diagnostic analytics is to assess whether we can make an inference from a statistic determined on a sample to the larger population. What you observe in a sample may not be reflective of the larger population if:

- The size of the sample is too small to be statistically significant. As is well described by Darrell Huff in the book *How to Lie with Statistics*,[4] if you try a few times, you can always find a small sample that displays the desired trend.

That particular trend can be completely accidental, and we must be careful not to assume statistical significance without testing it.

- The variability in the population is high. In this case, a larger sample may be required to identify trends.
- Lack of representation of some groups may create a biased sample, such as a gender imbalance, or a poorly designed survey that results in one of the groups disproportionately refusing participation, resulting in a non-representative sample.

Diagnostic analytics are valuable as a means of not only explaining past trends and occurrences but also providing a foundation for predicting the future.

6.2 PREDICTIVE ANALYTICS

The value of prediction for a business is in the opportunity to capitalize on correctly forecasted future outcomes. It gives organizations an opportunity to take advantage of trends before their competitors, prepare for what might happen, and minimize the impact of undesirable events. Smart businesses understand the value of prediction in building winning strategies, gaining competitive advantage, and capitalizing on market trends. This is why more and more organizations invest in predictive analytics capabilities.

These capabilities can be applied to predict:

- Customer behaviour and purchasing preferences
- Customer satisfaction and the likelihood they will recommend the company's products to others
- Likelihood that a transaction is fraudulent
- Demand for a particular product in specific seasons and markets
- Expected arrival time of an order
- Time when a piece of equipment is likely to break down

These predictions can provide a foundation for making better decisions and for the automation of various aspects of operations.

We will explore the use cases of predictive analytics later, but first, let's consider how predictions happen.

Predictive Modelling

What is prediction? Simply put, prediction is about using information you have to generate information you don't have.[5]

In analytics, **prediction** is the application of mathematical methods to determine the probability of certain outcomes under specific conditions.

Predictions are generated through predictive modelling.

An **analytical model** is a simplified mathematical representation of an object or a process. Modelling means creating a set of mathematical equations representing the relationships we want to predict. For example, we can model customer response to a reduction in price, or a dependency between the quality of materials, the number of quality checks, and the defect rate of the products.

Predictive modelling is the process of using mathematics to analyze and find patterns in data that allow us to calculate the probability of future outcomes.

Predicting is based on identifying the relationship between predictor variables (what we know) and response variables (what we want to predict). Predictive modelling discovers predictive factors and examines how they influence the likelihood of a target outcome.

A **predictor variable** is the known variable used to predict the outcome. It may also be referred to as an *independent variable, feature, attribute, X variable, explanatory variable, input variable, control variable*, or *leading indicator*.

A **response variable** is the variable being predicted. It may be referred to as a *dependent variable, outcome, target, Y variable, output variable*, or *lagging indicator*.

⚙ EXAMPLE

Imagine how a streaming platform might make movie recommendations to its users by predicting what they might be enticed to watch. Table 6.1 captures a hypothetical dataset with instances of movie recommendations to different users at different times of the day, taking into account their age group and some movie attributes. The table also captures the outcome of each recommendation: whether the movie was selected by the user or not.

Table 6.1 Sample Dataset for Training a Predictive Model: Movie Recommendations

Age group	Time of day	Genre	Won awards	Average rating	Year released	Similar to previously watched	Selected?
18–29	Evening	Comedy	No	6.7	2023	90%	Y
18–29	Afternoon	Non-fiction	No	7.8	2021	45%	N
18–29	Evening	Comedy	Yes	8.0	2005	78%	N
30–49	Evening	Drama	Yes	8.4	2022	60%	Y
30–49	Afternoon	Drama	Yes	7.4	2020	75%	N
50–64	Morning	Thriller	No	4.4	2019	66%	N
30–49	Evening	Thriller	No	4.4	2019	74%	Y
18–29	Morning	Thriller	No	4.4	2019	88%	Y
65+	Afternoon	History	Yes	5.6	2015	76%	Y

We'll assume that each of these factors has been clearly defined, such as the criteria for determining how two movies are similar. The target outcome must also be measurable—for example, the movie was selected for watching within 48 hours of seeing the recommendation.

Of course, real movie recommendation algorithms rely on more parameters than this, but for simplicity, we will not consider them in this example.

If this dataset were to be used to train a predictive model, all the attributes except whether the user selected the movie (the last column) would be treated as potential predictive factors. Whether the movie was selected is the target outcome, or the response variable.

Where do predictor variables come from? How are they discovered? The process works best when based on the domain knowledge—understanding the prediction problem, its context, and what is likely to influence the target outcome.

Predictive analytics can utilize diagnostic insights and meaningful factors discovered through diagnostics. When searching for root causes and relationships between variables, we identify significant factors: variables with a strong influence over the outcomes we wish to predict. When grouping a population based on an outcome such as preference for certain types of movies, we discover discriminants that make members of the group similar and different from other groups. These variables then become candidate predictor factors.

As will be further explored in Chapter 7, the predictive modelling process includes testing various candidate predictive factors to select those most suitable. This process is referred to as feature selection.

That said, sometimes a prediction of complex phenomena may utilize machine learning methods to discover unexpected predictive factors that human experts would never think of—ones that lead viewers to select movies very different from anything they've watched before.

CASE STUDY

Diagnostic Results as Potential Predictive Factors

A previous case study example noted how the root cause analysis of customer churn may provide significant factors for predicting future churn.

Diagnostic analysis was concerned with the factors that influenced customers' decision to stay or leave in the past.

The analysis highlighted several interesting relationships:

- Reduction in renewals of snow removal contracts if the previous winter was mild
- A clear pattern of churn increase among customers with more than one complaint

- More mid-term landscaping contract cancellations than the historical average in several neighbourhoods, which are still a bit of a mystery (a special customer survey is in the works to collect more data)

In addition, A/B testing revealed that the likelihood of contract renewal increases if the renewal courtesy call is made closer to the date, 7 days instead of 14 days before the contract renewal date.

A spike in new contracts was also observed in response to the new holiday promotion of snow removal contracts as gifts for parents or neighbours.

All these insights suggest potential predictive factors for customer churn modelling.

How can domain knowledge be used for identifying potential predictors? A few potential sources of knowledge can supply candidate predictive factors for analysis.

Table 6.2 Using Domain Knowledge as a Source of Predictor Variables[6]

Domain knowledge	Sources of predictor variables
Subject matter experts working in operational areas	• Accumulated experience and intuition of the workers that support business processes day after day
Current decision-making process	• Data currently used to make business decisions, e.g., existing procedures and business rules • Parameters and attributes included in business reports and operational analytics that management uses to make decisions
Existing metadata	• Existing documentation that describes business data, relationships, and constraints
External data sources	• External sources such as credit rating agencies or business associations with rich knowledge of relevant data and its importance for prediction
Research/peer experience	• Data used by industry, competitors, and peers for solving similar business problems • Research papers may indicate interesting relationships tested using rigorous academic research guidelines

Predictions involve uncertainty, and it is important to consider various sources of uncertainty when working with predictive analytics.

One of the unavoidable sources of uncertainty is human behaviour. Any business outcome that involves human actions will have an element of uncertainty, dependent on people's emotions, inclinations, and decisions. Models that involve human behaviour aspects may use a variety of information about a person, their interests and emotions, as outlined in Table 6.3.

Table 6.3 Using Personal Data as Sources of Predictor Variables[7]

Type of predictor data	Description
Geodemographic data	Information about a person's state of being, such as age, income, occupation, appearance, education level, and location
Associate data	Information about a person's associates such as partners, family, and close social circle, including their geodemographic data and behaviours
Personal network data	Information about a person's network of connections and their characteristics such as social media followers or professional network
Sentiment data	Information about a person's attitudes, feelings, and opinions, such as social media likes/dislikes, approvals/disapprovals, comments, blog posts, or survey answers
Behavioural data	Information about a person's past behaviour (observed actions) that may be indicative of the future behaviour, including: • **Primary behaviours:** past behaviours of the same type as the behaviour being predicted • **Secondary behaviours:** past behaviours that are similar (but different) to the one being predicted • **Tertiary behaviours:** past behaviours without an obvious connection to the behaviour being predicted

In behavioural data analysis, the choices made by humans are considered *hard data*, while sentiments are referred to as *soft data*. It distinguishes what people say they might do (e.g., when leaving comments on social media when responding to a survey) from what they actually do (observed and measured actions).

TIPS ON TERMS

Associate versus Personal Network Data

Associate data relates to people who are closely associated with an individual, such as family, friends, and colleagues. If we want to target someone for travel advertising, having information about a person's family demographics (associate data) can help determine what type of family travel they prefer.

Personal network data relates to the reach of an individual through their social connections, including people with whom they have very superficial or no relationships. If we care how many people a particular individual can influence when posting a negative review of our product, we care about their personal network data—social media connection and followers that may see and share their review or post.

CASE STUDY

YardExperts' Experience with Soft and Hard Data

Customer surveys are popular tools for collecting market research, but relying on them can be misleading. YardExperts learned this the hard way.

As part of the company's environmental, social, and corporate governance (ESG) strategy, they decided to introduce more environmentally friendly products. A survey was designed to ask customers whether or not they would be willing to pay a little more for an environmentally friendly product. The survey was run under the slogan "Let's help the environment," and the response indicated that the majority of customers were quite comfortable with paying more.

Encouraged by these results, YardExperts increased its assortment of environmentally friendly merchandise. On average, a comparable product labelled "environmentally friendly" was about 30% more expensive than its regular counterpart.

The results were disappointing. In most cases, customers purchased a cheaper product when available and were more likely to buy nothing if only the more expensive version with an "environmentally friendly" label was on the shelf.

What happened? We can make several hypotheses. One is that when responding to a survey, many people were already primed to think of themselves as noble and willing to contribute to a good cause. However, when faced with two similar products at two very different prices, most customers focused only on the numbers. Primary behaviour data (what was purchased) can be a better predictor than soft data like survey responses.

We could also hypothesize that the price difference plays a role. When someone says they are willing to "pay more," the range of prices they consider acceptable for a better environmental choice may be different from the actual price difference: 5–10% may be acceptable, but 30% is not. To test this theory, the company might have to run some experiments with different product pricing to study the elasticity of customers' readiness to pay more for products labelled as less harmful to the environment.

While Tables 6.2 and 6.3 suggest a variety of sources of predictive variables, in reality, the most interesting and relevant data may not be available.

Sometimes, organizations have to plan for additional data collection through their operational systems or surveys. For example, if YardExperts does not know the reasons why customers cancel their service contracts because they have never asked them, then an exit survey could be implemented to start collecting this information.

The process of predictive modelling includes testing predictive factors using various methods, with the goal of reaching the desired prediction accuracy. Methods used for predictive modelling are selected based on the complexity of the problem, how well understood the predictive factors are, and the relationships between predictive and response variables. Predictive modelling methods can utilize regression, data mining, and machine learning, as some examples.

Some models can make accurate predictions based on small data. Other models may utilize a machine learning algorithm to train on very large datasets. The next section explores machine learning in more detail.

Machine Learning

Machine learning (ML) is the development of algorithms that can learn patterns from data, apply these patterns to new data, and adapt ("learn") from the new data received by the algorithm. ML algorithms are widely used for predictive modelling.

The process of the algorithm extracting ("learning") patterns from data is called **training**. The datasets used to train ML algorithms are called **training data**.

Training data may be **labelled**. This is possible when the outcome of each scenario in the training dataset is known. Labels represent the value of the response variable for each scenario.

The example of the training dataset for movie recommendations in Table 6.1 represents labelled data since it indicates whether or not the user chose to watch the recommended movie in each instance.

When training data does not have the answers (the response variables), this data is called **unlabelled**.

Machine learning algorithms can be broadly divided into supervised and unsupervised learning.

Supervised learning happens when the ML algorithm is trained on labelled data. In this case, the label captures the connection between the predictor variables and the response variable, and this relationship is learned by the algorithm. Understanding the relationship between input data (predictor variables) and the labels (response variables) enables the algorithm to predict the outcomes of new scenarios.

Unsupervised learning happens when the algorithm is trained on unlabelled data—that is, when the correct answers for each observation are unknown. This approach can be used to model underlying structures, distributions, or relationships in the dataset. As the algorithm learns from the training dataset, it will group observations into categories based on similarities.

Sometimes, unsupervised algorithms can be used to label data by grouping similar observations for labelling. This process would involve a machine learning expert reviewing the results of the unsupervised grouping and assigning labels. Human review, especially for borderline cases where label fidelity is insufficient, allows us to adjust and improve the labelling algorithm.

Supervised machine learning is computationally simpler and can provide more accurate predictions than unsupervised methods do.

Figure 6.4 summarizes popular supervised and unsupervised algorithms.

Machine learning

Supervised: using labelled data

Classification	Regression
Predict a category for a given input.	Predict a quantity / amount.
Response variable is discrete.	Response variable is continuous.

Unsupervised: using unlabelled data

Clustering	Association
Find a pattern in a collection of uncategorized data.	Discover relationships between variables.
Group observations by similar properties.	Identify co-occurrence and correlations in large datasets.

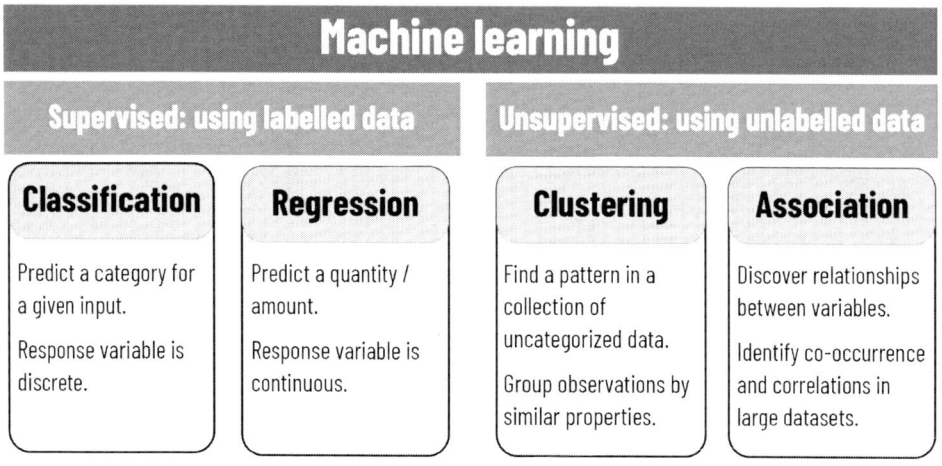

Figure 6.4 Supervised and Unsupervised ML Models

Classification ML models are intended to solve classification problems—that is, determine the probability that an observation belongs to one of the limited categories (classes). The response variable may be Boolean (e.g., accepted/rejected, pass/fail) or may have a limited number of possible values (e.g., vehicle class, blood type).

Regression ML models are concerned with finding a function that fits the data with the least error. They are used to estimate numeric outputs from given inputs (e.g., share price, sales volumes). There exist several regression techniques that can be chosen based on the number of predictor variables, types of data, and relationships between variables.

Clustering ML models look for patterns in data to organize it into groups with similar characteristics (clusters). Clustering may be applied on unlabelled data to create labels with the goal of using a supervised ML model thereafter. For example, a large number of pictures of different flowers may be grouped using a clustering algorithm so that an expert can assign labels to each group. This labelled dataset can then be used for training a classification algorithm to identify new images of flowers.

Association ML models look for interesting relationships between variables. They may help identify unexpected correlations without a pre-existing hypothesis, such as discovering that air passengers who pre-order vegetarian meals are more likely to board their flight[8] or that people who live next to recent lottery winners are more likely to go bankrupt.[9]

Along with supervised and unsupervised machine learning, there are other methods, such as:

- **Semi-supervised learning:** machine learning on datasets that contain a mix of un-labelled and labelled data. The model must organize and structure the data to create the missing labels which would then allow to use supervised learning for predictions.
- **Reinforcement learning:** algorithms that learn through trial and error. These models receive responses from the outside environment providing answers that the model uses for learning.

Table 6.4 Machine Learning Model Examples

ML model	Examples
Classification: Predict the probability of the event from a discrete list of possibilities	• The probability that an email is spam/not spam • The probability that a customer will place a new order within the next month • The probability that a student will pass the course • The probability that a credit card transaction is fraudulent
Regression: Predict a quantity from given inputs	• Estimated customer lifetime value (CLV) • Estimated amount of rainfall in a given location and period • Predicted value of a real estate property
Clustering: Group similar observations together	• Identify groups of customers with similar interests or behaviours • Identify groups of images containing a similar object • Identify audio segments played by the same musical instrument
Association: Find relationships between variables in a dataset or between different datasets	• Identify products frequently bought together (basket analysis) • Detect a relationship between movies people watch and the types of restaurants they prefer • Search for a relationship between customers' age groups and the types of garden plants they purchase

Table 6.5 Comparison of Machine Learning Models

Supervised models	Unsupervised models	Semi-supervised models	Reinforcement models
Trained on labelled data	Trained on unlabelled data	Trained on a smaller volume of labelled data and a large volume of unlabelled data	Trained on responses from the environment through trial and error
Lower complexity	Higher complexity	Medium complexity	Varied complexity
Higher accuracy of predictions	Less accurate predictions	Higher accuracy of predictions than unsupervised	Accuracy of predictions improves with time
Used for predictive modelling	Used for diagnostic analysis to identify hidden relationships and patterns	Used for picture recognition, natural language processing	Used in gaming and robotics

Deep learning (DL) is a set of machine learning methods that use artificial neural networks to imitate the process of human learning to model and solve complex problems. DL methods may belong to any of the above-mentioned categories—for example, they can be supervised, unsupervised, semi-supervised, or based on reinforcement learning.

The development of machine learning algorithms frequently relies on data mining as a foundation. Data mining enables exploring the existing data to discover meaningful patterns and relationships. This process is often referred to as *knowledge discovery* or *information harvesting.* Data mining insights—in particular, the discovery of significant factors, relationships, and trends—can in turn be used for predictive modelling.

Sometimes, data mining is conflated with machine learning. Many interdependencies exist between them. Machine learning techniques can be used for mining data. Machine learning algorithms often rely on data mining techniques for the identification of patterns.

The main distinction between data mining and machine learning is that data mining is applied to known sets of data. It is most frequently used for diagnostic analytics, as its scope is the analysis of data that's already collected and available.

Machine learning allows us to learn patterns from an existing set of data to apply them to new, previously unknown data and continue to refine and adapt the algorithm without (or with very little) intervention from the engineers. This is where the term *machine learning* comes from, referring to the algorithms being designed to run continuously and "learn" from new data. Machine learning methods are not explicitly programmed to produce certain results. Rather, the algorithms are designed to search for patterns that a human engineer may not even suspect exist.

EXAMPLE

Data Mining for Equipment Breakdown Patterns

In most cases, preventative maintenance is more cost-effective than fixing things after they break.

When equipment is difficult or expensive to service, it is beneficial to be able to predict what is likely to break down and when. This allows the scheduling of preventative maintenance to be optimized.

This is a good use case for data mining, provided that sufficient data is available. A data mining algorithm may use measurements related to the state and functioning of equipment (e.g., temperature, pressure, vibration, or noise level, along with breakdown events and their characteristics) to search for patterns that may indicate a likely breakdown and even predict the expected severity of the breakdown.

This example is a reminder that data mining and machine learning models can only be successful if the training dataset contains the most significant predictive factors. If a water pipe breaks down because of a specific chemical in the water, no algorithm could predict it unless the chemical composition of the water has already been measured and made available to the algorithm.

Predictive Analytics Questions and Use Cases

How can organizations use predictions to solve business problems? The answer is not always apparent. If your company has been losing money, simply asking "How can we increase our revenue?" will not lead to a meaningful prediction.

To be actionable, analytics insights must help the organization determine what steps to take to achieve the objectives. For that, a business problem must first be reframed as a prediction problem.

If the company is losing revenue, consider what is most likely to bring about the revenue increase: changes in pricing, product features, marketing techniques, or post-sales services.

🏷 CASE STUDY

Tackling the Customer Churn Issue with Predictive Analytics

The problem of customer churn is a top priority for the YardExperts analytics team. The company already recognized an undesirable trend: the increase in the cancellation rate. How can this trend be reversed?

To tackle this issue, they must first reframe it as a prediction problem. Consider what changes YardExperts can make to increase the likelihood of contract renewal. Potential factors in the company's control include whether:

- Service fees stay the same or change upon renewal
- The range of services covered by contracts decreases, increases, or stays the same
- Loyal customers are offered a discount on renewal
- A particular customer had a good experience last year or filed multiple complaints
- The biggest competitor is running a marketing campaign offering large discounts

Identifying these discriminating factors can lead to more meaningful and specific analytics questions, such as:

- How likely is a customer to renew their annual service contract if the contract conditions do not change?
- How likely is a customer to renew their annual service contract if service fees decrease by X%?
- How likely is a customer to renew their annual service contract if they filed a service complaint in the last 12 months that was resolved (or not resolved) within X days?
- How likely is a customer to renew their annual service contract if they filed a service complaint that took more than a week to resolve if we offer them an X% discount?

If the YardExperts analytics team has already conducted a thorough diagnostic analysis indicating the dependency between unresolved service complaints, fee increases, service discounts, and customer loyalty as measured by the renewal rate, the answers to these questions might recommend potential business decisions. This is how predictions become a foundation for prescriptive analysis, as further explored in the next section.

It is important to note that the most useful predictions are specific—they predict the behaviour of a particular group of customers under a constrained set of circumstances.

Consider customers who are moving. Diagnostic analysis may indicate whether a customer is more likely to cancel the contract when they move, even if YardExperts has good service coverage at their new location. Possible reasons include:

- Having a similar service available as part of a new rental agreement
- The presence of a local service provider that goes the extra mile to win new business
- The move being a convenient opportunity to get out of a contract that the customer felt was not a good value but unmotivated to do something about before

Based on any such discovery, the company may consider making special offers to customers who are moving in order to mitigate the risk of losing them.

This brings us to the important concept of *personalization*: the ability to offer personalized services or products to customers, which analytics makes possible. This is one of the use cases of predictive analytics, discussed further down.

As shown in the case study example, in predictive modelling, we need to take a business problem and reframe it as a prediction problem. Predictive modelling allows us to estimate the likelihood of an outcome under a specific set of circumstances (predictive factors). To benefit from predictive analytics, consider what predictions will help your organization make the right decisions.

✓ **CHECKLIST**

Asking Predictive Analytics Questions

1. What is the target variable, and how can you measure success?

   For example, the target may be to improve the first call resolution rate—the percentage of customers who get their issue resolved on the first call.

2. What are known significant factors, such as those discovered through diagnostic analysis?

   For example, review whether previous call resolution analysis points to influencing factors such as different types of requests, customer problems, the time of the day, who was assigned to the ticket, or the duration of the call.

3. What activities and outcomes can be improved by prediction?

Not all influencing factors are in our control; improvements must focus on feasible goals. In the case of service calls, assigning the call to the appropriate technician right away may decrease the overall call duration. Can we predict the nature of the call from customer history, the products they purchased, and typical issues that other customers reported with the same products, to assign the call to the most appropriate person?

4. What segment of the population is the prediction about?

Clustering, such as in customer segmentation, can tell us what groups may be influenced by different factors. Predictions can be more precise and actionable when they are specific to an individual segment.

If the first call resolution rate is significantly lower for less technically savvy customers, ask an analytics question specific to this segment.

5. Formulate your questions as specifically as possible, referencing the target variable, population segment, and potential predictors (if known).

Here are some patterns to reframe problems as prediction problems when asking predictive questions:

- What is the probability that <observation> belongs to <category>?
- What is the likelihood of <event> if <scenario>?
- When is <event> likely to happen if <scenario>?
- What is <someone> likely to do if <scenario>?
- What is the likelihood that <someone> will choose <something> if <scenario>?
- What is the expected <metric> at <time> if the existing trends continue?
- What is the expected <metric> at <time> if <specific change> happens?

To use these patterns, replace the <parameters> in angled brackets with specific conditions, factors, and segments relevant to the problem. See further down for examples.

6. Review the question. Is it sufficiently clear, relevant, and specific?

Following are sample analytics questions that can be posed for various predictive analytics use cases.

Use Case: Detection of Undesirable Events

- Spam detection: learn from commonalities among many labelled spam messages to classify emails as spam.
- Fraud detection: examine many examples of fraudulent and non-fraudulent transactions to detect patterns that may be associated with fraudulent activity.
- Flagging data errors: identify likely data errors based on previous data quality patterns.

- Early disease detection: identify early signs of disease onset based on patterns found in previous patients' data.

Analytics question: What is the likelihood that this <email, transaction, data point, patient> is <spam, fraudulent, invalid, belongs to a risk category for a certain disease>?

Use Case: Survival Analysis

- Estimate the probability of a patient's survival over a certain period.
- Estimate the expected time of customer attrition.
- Estimate the time when the customer is likely to make the next purchase.

Analytics question: What is the probability that <patient, customer> will <survive, attrite, make a purchase> within <time period>?

Use Case: Prevention of Undesirable Events

- Credit risk assessment: determine the likelihood of a credit line default based on customer profile and loan details.
- Preventative maintenance: predict potential equipment breakdown by analyzing root causes and early detection signals.

Analytics question: What is the likelihood that this <loan, device> will <be paid on time/default, function properly/break down> during <time period>?

This use case may use a classification approach, for example, asking whether an undesirable event may happen (loan paid or not), or a survival analysis, asking when it is likely to happen. This may lead to a decision to recall the loan early or do unscheduled preventative maintenance.

Use Case: Behaviour Prediction

- Predict customer needs: predict what products and product features customers are likely to be interested in.
- Predict buying behaviour: examine factors that influence a customer's behaviour when they search for information and make purchases in order to influence their purchasing decisions.

Analytics question: What is a <customer segment> likely to <want, buy, rent, view, select> when <given choices>?

Use Case: Scoring Alternatives

- Lead scoring for marketing purposes based on the lead's propensity to buy.
- Score incoming calls for prioritization of responses based on the likelihood that a prompt response can significantly influence customer retention or CLV.
- Score job candidates for interview selection and hire based on the estimation of which candidate is likely to be the most advantageous hire.

Analytics question: Which <alternative> has the highest expected <propensity to buy, CLV, skills match>?

Use Case: Forecasting

- Weather prediction
- Expected electricity consumption
- Required staffing levels
- Expected demand for product
- Cash flow forecast

Analytics question: How much <precipitation, product demand, liquid cash> is expected in <time frame> provided that <conditions>?

Natural Language Processing (NLP)

- Sentiment analysis: predict the most likely emotion or sentiment in a segment of text.
- Speech recognition: identify the most likely interpretation of a sound pattern and predict the intention of a speech segment.
- Chatbots: predict the intention of a natural language question and match it to the most likely answer.
- Typing autocomplete: predict the most likely words that the customer is typing based on the context and first letters.

Analytics question: What is the most likely <meaning, intention, sentiment> of a <natural language segment>?

📌 **IMPORTANT**

Limits of Predictive Modelling

In predictive modelling, as we identify relationships between the most important factors, other factors will be discarded.

For example, consider modelling the dependency between the quality of materials, the number of quality checks, and the defect rate of the products. In real life, there will be other factors that may affect the defect rate on a given day—the weather, the absence of the most experienced worker, the general mood after a holiday party, or an unexpected faulty parts batch from a supplier that is usually very reliable.

Developing a model that accounts for hundreds instead of dozens of predictive factors will be more complex, time-consuming, and costly. In real business situations, any predictive model is a result of balancing the cost of developing and supporting the model versus the expected rewards from using it.

Since no predictive model can include every possible factor, decision-making may require a combination of prediction, expert judgment, and reinforcement learning. This will be further discussed below.

6.3 PRESCRIPTIVE ANALYTICS

Prescriptive analytics closes the gap between prediction and decision. It involves assessing possible courses of action and choosing or recommending the path most likely to affect the desired outcome.

From Prediction to Decision

The value of prediction is in reducing the uncertainty of business decisions. However, a prediction by itself does not equate to a decision. Business decisions can take predictions into account. However, additional judgment is usually involved in determining how to use the predictions to gain a business advantage.

The need to make a decision stems from having more than one alternative for the next step. If only one course of action is possible, no decision is necessary. But if indeed there are alternatives, then the decision-making process must assess the value of each. Which expected outcome is more valuable? What is the likelihood that this or that outcome can be achieved under the circumstances? What are the risks of each alternative, and do they outweigh the benefits?

⚙ EXAMPLE

Banks evaluate loan applications using customers' credit scores—external data purchased from a credit rating agency. A credit score is a numeric composite score designed to predict the likelihood that an individual will pay their bills.[10] For this example, we will convert numeric credit scores to percentages for simplicity.

Table 6.6 Loan Approval Example

Customer	Credit score	Approve loan?
A	95%	?
B	80%	?
C	80%	?
D	60%	?
E	60%	?
F	85%	?

While a credit score represents the predicted likelihood of timely repayments, is this prediction alone sufficient to make a decision? Will customers with the same credit score (B and C, D and E) be treated the same way?

Banks typically consider multiple factors before approving loans, such as the loan amount and whether collateral is available to mitigate that risk.

The decision is not always binary (approve the loan or not). Depending on the factors mentioned, a bank might vary the maximum amount they are willing to lend and raise or lower the interest rate depending on the loan risk. This is why banks sometimes make different decisions for customers with the same credit scores, as shown in Table 6.7.

Table 6.7 Loan Approval and Conditions Example

Customer	Credit score	Loan amount	Collateral	Approve loan?	Loan conditions
A	95%	$1,000,000	Yes	Yes	8% interest
B	80%	$50,000	Yes	Yes	10% interest
C	80%	$5,000	No	Yes	20% interest
D	60%	$300,000	Yes	Yes, reduced amount	Max. $100,000 12.5% interest
E	60%	$800	No	Yes	20% interest
F	85%	$250,000	No	No	N/A

The example emphasizes that most business decisions require the evaluation of multiple factors, including multiple predictions. How big is the risk of approving the loan? How well do we know this customer? How important is this customer? What loan conditions would be acceptable to the bank?

More than that, the same loan request may be approved or denied at different times depending on the state of the bank's loan portfolio. From the bank's perspective, no loan decision is a standalone task, as each contributes to the overall task of the bank's loan portfolio optimization.

Optimization is identifying the combination of variables that will enable the maximization of the desired result.

Depending on the complexity of the optimization task, automation of decision-making may pose a challenge.

For the example above, how will the bank decide to approve a loan and determine acceptable loan conditions? Depending on how sophisticated the bank's loan approval process is, the decision could be automated, especially in straightforward cases where the overall risk is low enough to approve or high enough to decline automatically. Some cases in the middle may require human intervention, review of additional information, or even a meeting with the customer.

This example illustrates different levels of decision automation that can be achieved using advanced analytics:

Table 6.8 Degrees of Decision Automation with Analytics

Degree of automation	Description
Decision support: not automated	The algorithm assists human decision-making by providing analytics and prediction scores; requires human judgment to make the decision (human-in-the-loop)
Decision augmentation: partially automated	The algorithm recommends decisions; flow may be automated for flowthrough (standard) behaviours while allowing (or requiring) human operators to make decisions for complex (exceptional) cases
Decision automation: fully automated	The algorithm makes the decisions based on scores from the models and manages the automated execution of the process steps (autonomous execution)

With different types of analytics, different levels of human involvement are required for making decisions, as shown in Figure 6.5.

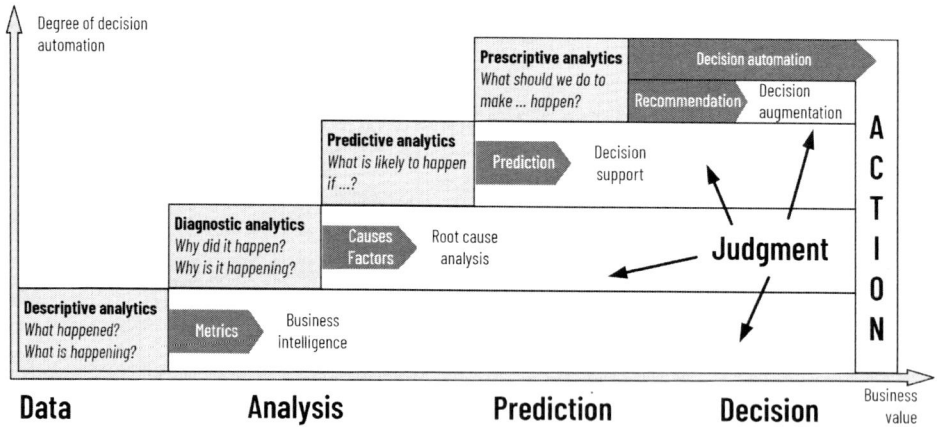

Figure 6.5 Degrees of Decision Automation with Analytics

With descriptive analytics, decision-makers will have to use their judgment, relying on the metrics that measure past performance. Diagnostic analytics will further inform decision-makers about trends, root causes, and important relationships between variables.

Predictive analytics will supply the likelihood of various outcomes—for example, when assessing alternative courses of action. Human judgment will be required to evaluate these predictive insights, such as:

- The probability of various outcomes with their prediction accuracy
- Risks associated with each alternative ("What's the worst that could happen?")
- The expected payoff from taking one alternative over another

The more advanced the analytics, the more decision support it provides. Decision augmentation and automation require the most advanced, prescriptive analytics.

Keep in mind that decision automation is not always feasible or desirable.

For complex decisions, the number of relevant variables may be so large that building predictive models that take them all into account would either be impossible or prohibitively expensive. Simplified predictive models could be substituted to provide decision support, while human expertise would be used to handle the most complex cases or those in which predictions are not precise enough. This is an example of a decision augmentation model.

Another scenario in which decision support would be preferred is when developing predictive models in a company that is lacking in analytics maturity. When workers have little prior experience with predictive and prescriptive analytics, they might be wary of algorithms making business decisions.

One way to gradually build trust in algorithms, as well as to validate their performance, is to get human experts to review algorithm recommendations. This human-in-the-loop model can be gradually transitioned to decision augmentation, and eventually, with a sufficient level of comfort and established monitoring, to decision automation. At the same time, some decisions may never be fully automated if the accountability for the decision must be taken by a human for legal or ethical reasons.

Decision augmentation mode can also be used for reinforcement learning, allowing the algorithm to learn from human experts making decisions in complex scenarios and using this new data to improve the algorithm. In this case, the algorithm is further trained by human operators taking over complex cases or providing feedback on the decisions. Not every organization has achieved sufficient analytics maturity to rely on prescriptive analytics for making important business decisions. We can evaluate a company's analytics maturity level based on how much of the decision process is automated and how much human intervention in the decision-making process is required. See Section 11.1 for additional perspective on analytics maturity.

Prescriptive Analytics Methods and AI

Prescriptive analytics can utilize deterministic or stochastic (probabilistic) methods.

Deterministic methods of prescriptive analytics do not require predictions and instead are rule-based. They use a pre-programmed set of rules to derive decisions from a set of required inputs. The deterministic nature of the decision reflects that the decision is determined by the inputs—that is to say, the same inputs will always result in the same decision.

For example, a deterministic rule may state that any loan below $10,000 with a collateral value exceeding 120% of the loan amount will be approved if the customer's credit score is above 60%.

Deterministic systems that rely on explicit rules are also referred to as *expert systems*. Such systems require that an expert provide all the rules to handle possible variations of the inputs and the required decision for each combination. Early attempts to create AI in the 1970s and 1980s used expert systems that relied on extensive knowledge based on pre-programmed rules and inference engines capable of applying these rules to different scenarios.[11] Expert systems have found limited application due to the explicit programming efforts required and the need for human engineers to continuously update the knowledge base and rules.

Probabilistic methods rely on predictive insights to estimate the best possible decision when deterministic rules cannot be used due to the complexity of the optimization task or the stochastic nature of the input variables.

Probabilistic methods of prescriptive analytics use machine learning algorithms. In this case, the same input parameters may result in different decisions based on the algorithm learning from new data. For example, if a significant percentage of loans given to customers with a credit score between 60% and 70% have not been repaid in time in the last year, the algorithm may learn to increase the threshold for loan approval to credit scores above 70%.

The main difference between deterministic (rule-based) and probabilistic (machine learning) methods is that in the first case, the logic must be modified by the programmer, and in the case of machine learning algorithms, the algorithm itself may learn from the data and adjust the thresholds for loan approval decisions, possibly without any human intervention.

Prescriptive analytics methods can be quite complex, and their detailed study is beyond the scope of this book. Some examples are:

- Stochastic optimization
- Graph analysis
- Simulation
- Complex event processing
- Neural networks
- Network analysis
- Evolutionary computation
- Reinforcement learning

CASE STUDY

YardExperts Implements a Chatbot

In many areas of business, customer questions will likely follow the 80-20 rule: 80% of customer inquiries will be about the same 20% of frequently asked questions. This is the premise for introducing chatbots trained to respond to typical customer questions consistently.

There are two approaches to designing a chatbot: deterministic and machine learning.

A deterministic, or rule-based, chatbot, will be pre-programmed with a set of questions to ask in a particular sequence until getting to an answer. For example:

Are you a current YardExperts customer?
Do you have a question about gardening, snow removal, or other services?

If the customer selects *gardening* as a response, then the chatbot will ask a further series of questions related to gardening.

Rule-based chatbots are reliable but limited. They don't learn—new questions and branches of inquiry must be programmed in by an engineer. After using a rule-based chatbot for a while, YardExperts discovered that about 70% of all chatbot conversations ended up with customers selecting the "I would like to speak to someone" option, often after the first two or three questions. The company is now implementing a new machine learning chatbot.

A machine learning chatbot uses a reinforcement learning approach to continuously learn from every customer dialogue. After the first three months of training, the chatbot learned how to answer 80% of questions about YardExperts services without any intervention, such as "Does your company do tree removal?" The remaining 20% of questions were directed to the call centre. This is a typical decision augmentation scenario, where only complex or exceptional cases require human involvement.

The chatbot also learned when to schedule service calls without human intervention—for example, when a customer wanted to reschedule to another date and qualified technicians were available. As the chatbot is monitored by the engineers and its model adjusted when required, YardExperts expects to implement a higher degree of automation. Customer service representatives will spend less time responding to routine inquiries and will be able to provide more customized and personalized service for non-routine questions.

Making decisions under uncertain circumstances is a human intelligence task. We are constantly making decisions, big and small. We choose products to buy, music to listen to, career paths, and life partners. Getting a machine to make decisions with human-like intelligence is one of the aspects studied by the broad field we call artificial intelligence (AI).

When we develop prescriptive analytics algorithms for automating tasks and making decisions without human intervention, are we in fact creating AI? The answer depends on the depth of meaning behind the term, and on making distinctions between narrow and general AI.

Prescriptive analytics algorithms designed to automate certain tasks are examples of **narrow AI**—algorithms designed to perform a single task or a narrow set of tasks. Every example in this chapter represents narrow AI, which should be distinguished from the concept of **general AI**—machines intended to perform a broad set of tasks that usually require human intelligence. All general AI examples we have come from science fiction books and movies.

While narrow AI relies on prescriptive analytics and building quantitative predictive models using large amounts of data, general AI would require what is commonly referred to as *cognitive analytics*, or the capability of making human-like decisions, drawing conclusions, and self-learning.

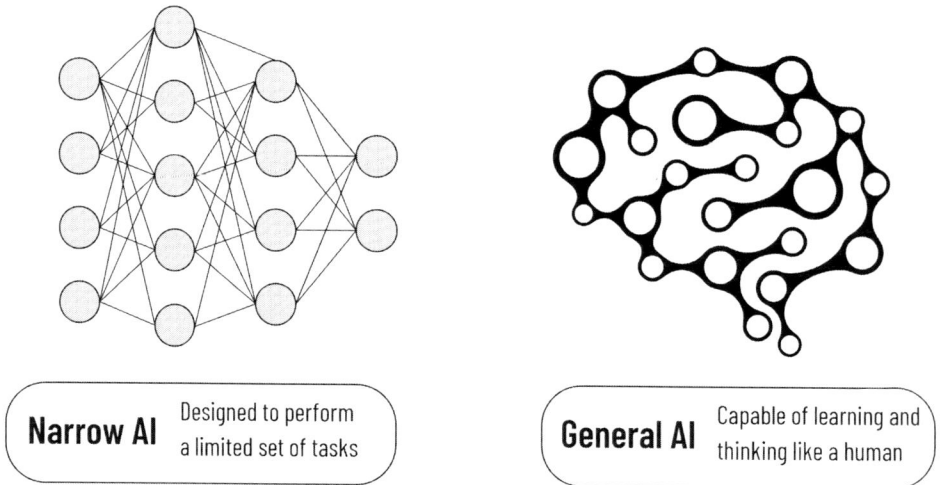

| **Narrow AI** | Designed to perform a limited set of tasks |

| **General AI** | Capable of learning and thinking like a human |

Figure 6.6 Narrow versus General AI

At present, general AI development is in its early stages; no general AI, in its broad sense, has been demonstrated. The multitude of AI applications used in research, science, and business today represent narrow AI of various degrees of complexity. These include:

- Robots: machines able to perceive and interact with their physical environment without human supervision
- Autonomous vehicles: vehicles able to operate without human intervention
- Generative AI: models capable of generating content such as text, music, video, or images (such as image-generating DALL-E and Midjourney)
- Large language models (LLMs): deep learning generative AI models capable of performing various natural language processing tasks; examples include generative pre-trained (GPT) models developed by OpenAI (such as ChatGPT chatbot), as well as Bard and PaLM by Google and Llama by Meta, among others
- Virtual assistants: advanced chatbots that are capable of accessing various digital resources to execute tasks such as scheduling, creating records, and making purchases
- Smart devices such as fitness trackers or internet-connected home appliances
- Autonomous agents such as stock trading bots and travel agents
- Game-playing algorithms such as AlphaGo and DeepMind

- Translation engines
- Computer vision systems

Table 6.9 Narrow AI versus General AI

Narrow AI	General AI
Designed to perform a limited set of tasks	Capable of performing a potentially unlimited set of tasks associated with human intelligence
Knowledge limited to the domain used to train the model	Can leverage knowledge to apply to new, unfamiliar domains
Learns from data, makes quantitative predictions, and solves problems that are framed as prediction problems	Replicates or imitates human cognitive process; capable of self-learning and reasoning
Does not have self-awareness	Expected to have self-awareness, emotions, and creative expression
Weak/shallow/applied AI	Broad/strong/full AI
All AI that exists today is narrow	Hasn't been demonstrated; all examples are in science fiction books and movies

Today's AI applications all fall into the category of narrow AI, and yet they deliver remarkable results. How can these algorithms beat human chess and Go champions, compose poetry, recognize images, and translate texts between multiple languages without being explicitly programmed?

To understand their success, we must first establish that these impressive successes of narrow AI are not based on deterministic logic. In other words, there is no comprehensive knowledge base programmed into them by human engineers that determines their behaviour. These algorithms use machine learning to extract and learn patterns from vast stores of data. The number of interrelationships they are capable of extracting is far beyond what can be explicitly programmed by the largest team of engineers. The success of translation engines, LLM chatbots, virtual assistants, and many other examples is a function of the enormous training datasets used for training the models.

As highlighted by three Google scientists in their famous article "The Unreasonable Effectiveness of Data,"[12] "the biggest successes in natural-language-related machine learning have been statistical speech recognition and statistical machine translation."[13] Training a translation engine on a huge training set of existing texts that have already been translated and verified by qualified human translators had better results than attempting to explicitly program dictionaries and grammar rules into a translation engine.

These algorithms use probabilistic approaches, predicting the most likely word combinations based on the training data—and the more data, the better the predictions. The conclusion of the above-mentioned article was that "simple models and a lot of data trump more elaborate models based on less data."[14] Thus, the **unreasonable effectiveness of data** refers to the idea that the size of the training dataset may matter more to the success of the prediction than the choice of the prediction model.

Prescriptive Analytics Questions and Use Cases

The goal of prescriptive analytics is to recommend or prescribe the action, and this is reflected in the ways we ask prescriptive analytics questions. The emphasis is on the action to be performed and the target outcome.

Here are some sample applications of prescriptive analytics and questions it answers.

Recommendation Engine

This algorithm decides what content, offers, or products to recommend (or include in the user's feed) based on their profile, preferences, past history, and behaviour of similar users.

The target outcome is to maximize sales, usage, or time on the platform.

Analytics questions: Which products should we offer to the customer to maximize the expected purchase? What content should be presented to the user to maximize their engagement?

Targeted Advertising

This algorithm determines which users to target with specific advertising messages based on their propensity to buy, interests, past behaviour, and sentiments.

The target outcome is to optimize the advertisement return on investment (ROI).

Analytics question: Which customers should be targeted with a <particular promotional message> to maximize the advertising ROI?

Personalization

This algorithm determines the parameters and features for tailoring an individual customer's experience to their needs.

The target outcome is to maximize customer satisfaction and customer lifetime value.

Analytics question: What should we offer this particular customer <from the available choices> that they will <like, buy, enjoy, use often>?

Process Automation

This algorithm makes automated decisions and selects the next best action, taking into consideration various factors that impact the desired process outcome.

The target outcome will depend on the process being optimized and may be related to decreasing cost, reducing the time to process, reducing the likelihood of defects, or increasing resource utilization.

Analytics question: What should be done next in this case in order to <minimize, maximize, or optimize the desired outcome>?

Dynamic Pricing

This algorithm sets optimal prices for various products based on the demand forecast, price elasticity, and scarcity of the resource.

The target outcome is to optimize overall profitability.

Analytics question: What price should we present to this customer for this product at this time to maximize our revenue?

Inventory Management

This algorithm determines when, what, and how much of each product, material, or ingredient to order for optimized inventory management.

The target outcomes combine having sufficient stock to fulfill the demand while minimizing the cost of storage and restocking.

Analytics questions: When should we order a particular product or material to ensure optimal stock levels? What products and in what quantity should be ordered <at a specific time> to ensure optimal stock levels?

Resource Allocation

This algorithm determines the optimal matching of available resources to the tasks to be done to maximize the utilization of resources and task completion.

The target outcomes may include completion of tasks on time, minimizing the cost, and optimized matching of resources to the tasks. The most frequent resources are people but could also be equipment, premises, and so on. The outcome of resource allocation may be a schedule.

Analytics question: How should we assign tasks to resources to optimize resource utilization and task completion?

Logistics Optimization

This algorithm determines the optimal allocation of goods to be delivered to available transportation options and determines the delivery routes.

The target outcomes could include timely delivery, minimized delivery cost, avoidance of risk, and maximizing of space utilization in the containers or trucks.

Analytics question: How should we allocate delivery tasks to available resources to minimize the time and resources required?

Route Optimization

This algorithm determines the best route under specific constraints.

The target outcome could be to minimize the time required to reach the destination.

Analytics question: What is the optimal route from A to B <at a specific time> to achieve the earliest arrival time?

📌 **IMPORTANT**

Prescriptive analytics is based on optimization—finding the best alternative that delivers desired results. Therefore, prescriptive analytics requirements must clearly state the desired outcome—the goal to which the algorithm should optimize.

For example, route optimization results may be different if the algorithm prioritizes the expected time of arrival over fuel consumption or the cost of using toll roads.

6.4 CHAPTER SUMMARY

Key Points to Remember

- Diagnostic methods can identify causal relationships that can then be used to generate predictions.
- Correlation does not imply causation.
- When a sample is too small or variations in the population are extreme, analysis of one sample can yield a coincidental correlation.
- Predictions are made for specific scenarios, conditions, or sets of circumstances.
- A machine learning algorithm looks for patterns in data without requiring an explanation behind the patterns.
- Predictions are meaningful when they are created for a specific set of constraints.
- Training datasets must be representative of the population. For instance, a training dataset for a classification model must include a representative number of labelled observations from each class.
- The need for a decision stems from having more than one option for the next step. If there is only one course of action possible, no decision is necessary.
- A predictive model is always a simplified representation and therefore cannot include all possible predictive factors.

Key Terms

A/B testing: a research experiment to test the significance of one element by randomly changing its value between the control value (A) and the experimental value (B) and measuring the outcome.

Analytical model: a simplified mathematical representation of an object or a process.

Associate data: information about a person's associates such as partners, family, and close social circle, including their geodemographic data and behaviours.

Association analysis: searching for interesting associations within a dataset, such as the co-occurrence of certain values.

Behavioural data: information about a person's past behaviour (observed actions) that may be indicative of the future behaviour.

Classification model: a machine learning model created to solve a classification problem—that is, to determine the probability that an observation belongs to one of the limited categories (classes).

Cluster analysis: breaking data down into groups with similar characteristics.

Cohort analysis: an approach to clustering based on common characteristics that the cohort members will retain for a certain period.

Correlation analysis: analysis of an association between two random variables.

Deep learning (DL): machine learning methods that use artificial neural networks to imitate the process of human learning in order to model and solve complex problems.

Descriptive statistics: a group of methods and approaches concerned with summarizing and presenting sets of data.

Deterministic method (expert system): a method that derives decisions from inputs based on a set of pre-determined rules.

Discriminant: a variable that defines which group a particular population member will be sorted into.

Factor analysis: selecting variables (factors) with the highest influence on specific outcomes among multiple candidate variables.

General AI: the ability of a machine to perform a broad set of tasks that usually require human intelligence.

Geodemographic data: information about a person's state of being, such as age, income, occupation, appearance, education level, and location.

Heterogeneous: a population with a large degree of variation in characteristics that impact the outcome of interest.

Homogeneous: a population with minimal variation in characteristics that impact the outcome of interest.

Hypothesis: a belief based on prior knowledge, experience, or intuition.

Hypothesis testing: examining a hypothesis using available data to confirm, reject, or modify it.

Inference: making a judgment about characteristics of the population based on studying a population sample.

Inferential statistics: a group of methods and approaches concerned with studying smaller datasets in an attempt to project these findings to a larger dataset.

Labelled data: a training dataset where the outcome of interest for each record is known (records are labelled, i.e., include response variables).

Narrow AI: an algorithm designed to perform a single task or a narrow set of tasks.

Optimization: identifying the combination of variables that will enable the maximization of the desired result.

Parameter: a descriptive statistic that describes a characteristic of a population numerically.

Personal network data: information about a person's network of connections and their characteristics such as social media followers or professional network.

Population: all members of a group of interest.

Prediction: an application of mathematical methods to determine the probability of a certain outcome under specific conditions.

Predictive modelling: the process of using mathematics to analyze and find patterns in data allowing to calculate the probability of future outcomes.

Predictor variable (independent variable, feature, attribute, X variable, explanatory variable, input variable, control variable, leading indicator): a known variable used to predict a future outcome.

Primary behaviour: in predictive modelling, a past behaviour of the same type as the behaviour being predicted.

Probabilistic method: a method relying on prediction to estimate the best possible decision.

Regression analysis: an examination of a relationship among quantitative variables.

Reinforcement learning model: an algorithm that learns through trial and error by using the responses from the outside environment as training data.

Representative sample: a population sample selected to accurately represent the characteristics of the whole population.

Response variable (dependent variable, outcome, target, Y variable, output variable, lagging indicator): the variable being predicted.

Sample: the part of the population with available data.

Secondary behaviour: in predictive modelling, a past behaviour similar (but different) to the one being predicted.

Semi-supervised learning: machine learning on datasets that contain a mix of unlabelled and labelled data.

Sentiment data: information about a person's attitudes, feelings, and opinions.

Spurious correlation: a relationship where two variables appear to be correlated but do not have a causal relationship.

Statistic: a numeric measure that describes a characteristic of a population sample.

Statistically significant relationship: a relationship between variables that is unlikely to be due to chance.

Stratification: dividing population members into strata (layers) based on an ordinal characteristic.

Supervised learning: machine learning on datasets containing labelled data.

Tertiary behaviour: in predictive modelling, a past behaviour without an obvious connection to the behaviour being predicted.

Training: a process of a machine learning in which an algorithm extracts ("learns") patterns from data.

Training data: a dataset used to train a machine learning algorithm.

Unlabelled data: a training dataset that does not contain known outcomes of interest (records are not labelled, i.e., do not include response variables).

Unreasonable effectiveness of data: the idea that the size of the training dataset may matter more to the success of the prediction than the choice of the prediction model.

Unsupervised learning: machine learning on datasets containing unlabelled data.

Questions for Critical Thought

1. How can we test a hypothesis using data?
2. What circumstances require the use of inferential statistics methods versus descriptive methods?
3. What is the purpose of A/B testing?
4. What considerations should be taken into account when selecting the most important predictive factors?
5. How can a prediction help solve a business problem?
6. Where would you look for predictor variables?
7. Can we generate predictions with small data?

8. What is the benefit of audience segmentation in advanced analytics?
9. How can a predictive model help a company with decision-making?

Test Your Knowledge

1. A data scientist is working on a model to predict the number of patients expected to be re-admitted within a month after surgery using the data about re-admittance rates in the past five years.
   Which machine learning algorithm will be more suitable for this task?
   a. Association
   b. Clustering
   c. Regression
   d. Classification

2. A data scientist is working on a model that will suggest the most likely diagnosis based on a large diagnostic database maintained by the hospital association that contains patient files, test results, and past diagnoses.
   Which machine learning algorithm will be more suitable for this task?
   a. Association
   b. Clustering
   c. Regression
   d. Classification

3. A data scientist is working on a model that will identify common characteristics of patients who tend to miss their appointments and medical tests.
   Which machine learning algorithm will be more suitable for this task?
   a. Association
   b. Clustering
   c. Regression
   d. Classification

4. A data scientist is working on a model to forecast doctors' workload in the cardiology clinic.
   What is a suitable response variable?
   a. Population growth in the area
   b. The expected length of the weekly clinic hours per cardiologist over the forecast period
   c. The number of cardiologists expected to retire in the near future
   d. The average age of the clinic's patients

5. A data scientist is working on a model to predict patient post-surgery rehabilitation success.

 What is a suitable response variable?

 a. Duration of the surgery

 b. Patient's heart rate one hour after surgery

 c. Number of days before the patient is able to return to normal activities post-surgery

 d. Patient's age

Recommended Readings

Broussard, M. (2018). *Artificial Unintelligence: How Computers Misunderstand the World*. MIT Press.

Haider, M. (2015). *Getting Started with Data Science: Making Sense of Data with Analytics*. Pearson Education.

Kaufmann, U. H., & Tan, A. B. C. (2021). *Data Analytics for Organisational Development: Unleashing the Potential of Your Data*. Wiley.

Levine, D., & Stephan, D. (2022). *Even You Can Learn Statistics and Analytics: An Easy to Understand Guide*. Addison-Wesley Professional.

Marr, B. (2020). *The Intelligence Revolution: Transforming Your Business with AI*. Kogan Page.

Pierson, L. (2021). *Data Science for Dummies*. Wiley.

Simply Artificial Intelligence. (2023). DK.

Taulli, T. (2019). *Artificial Intelligence Basics: A Non-Technical Introduction*. Apress Publishers.

Notes

1. Wikipedia. (n.d.). *Opinion Polling for the 45th Canadian Federal Election*. Retrieved June 14, 2024, from en.wikipedia.org/wiki/Opinion_polling_for_the_45th_Canadian_federal_election.

2. Vigen, T. (n.d.). *Spurious Correlations*. Retrieved January 15, 2024, from www.tylervigen.com/spurious-correlations.

3. Dimock, M. (2019, January 19). *Defining Generations: Where Millennials End and Generation Z Begins*. Pew Research Center. Retrieved February 14, 2024, from www.pewresearch.org/short-reads/2019/01/17/where-millennials-end-and-generation-z-begins/.

4. Huff, D. (1993). *How to Lie with Statistics*. W. W. Norton.

5. Agrawal, A., Gans, J., & Goldfarb, A. (2018). *Prediction Machines: The Simple Economics of Artificial Intelligence*. Harvard Business Review Press.

6. Finlay, S. (2014). *Predictive Analytics, Data Mining and Big Data: Myths, Misconceptions and Methods*. Palgrave Macmillan, p. 159.

7. Finlay (2014), p. 68.

8. Hardy, Q. (2012, March 28). *Bizarre Insights from Big Data*. Bits. Retrieved January 15, 2024, from archive.nytimes.com/bits.blogs.nytimes.com/2012/03/28/bizarre-insights-from-big-data/.

9. Evans, P. (2016, March 2). *Lottery Win Makes Neighbours More Likely to Go Bankrupt, Data Suggests*. CBC News. Retrieved January 15, 2024, from www.cbc.ca/news/business/bankruptcy-lottery-1.3472357.

10. Equifax. (n.d.). *How Are Credit Scores Calculated?* Retrieved January 15, 2024, from www
     .consumer.equifax.ca/personal/education/credit-score/how-are-credit-scores-calculated/.

11. Leondes, C. T. (2002). *Expert Systems: The Technology of Knowledge Management and Decision
     Making for the 21st Century.* Elsevier, pp. 6–21.

12. Halevy, A., Norvig, P., & Pereira, F. (2009). The Unreasonable Effectiveness of Data. *IEEE
     Intelligent Systems, 24*(2), 8–12. Retrieved January 15, 2024, from static.googleusercontent.com/
     media/research.google.com/en//pubs/archive/35179.pdf.

13. Halevy et al., (2009), p. 8.

14. Halevy et al., (2009), p. 9.

Chapter 7

Business Analytics Life Cycle

This chapter introduces the **business analytics life cycle**: the complete process from identifying the goals of analytics to implementing and using analytics solutions by business users. You will learn about:

- Each stage of the business analytics life cycle
- Data preparation and data wrangling techniques
- How analytics models are developed
- What is required for the deployment and operationalization of analytics solutions

7.1 ANALYTICS LIFE CYCLE AND PROBLEM DEFINITION

Each stage in the analytics life cycle contributes to the success of the analytics solutions: understanding the problem and formulating analytics questions, exploring and preparing the data, selecting predictive factors, testing the results, and designing the best way for sharing the insights and incorporating them into the business process. Figure 7.1 depicts these main stages as a cycle.

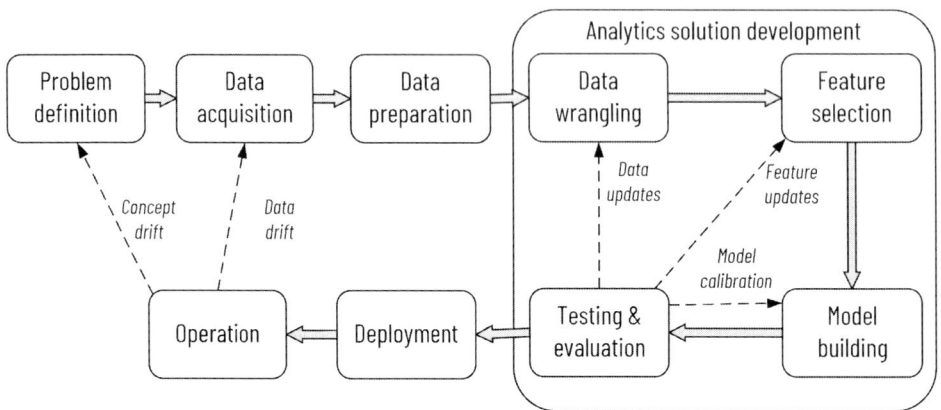

Figure 7.1 Business Analytics Life Cycle

The cycle starts and ends with business: from establishing the business need (*problem definition*) to the use of analytics solutions by business stakeholders and decision-makers (*operation*). Knowing how to understand business problems and ask good analytics questions lays the groundwork for being able to create effective solutions. This groundwork must manifest itself in quality business requirements. The process of identifying analytics requirements as part of analytics project activities will be reviewed in Chapter 10.

✓ **CHECKLIST**

Problem Definition Checklist

1. What does the organization want to achieve (e.g., increase revenue, reduce cost, gain competitive advantage, reduce risk)?
2. What problem is the organization facing?
3. Does the problem affect a specific part of the organization (e.g., sales, marketing, procurement, human resources)?
4. Does it have external impacts, such as on customers or service providers to the organization?
5. Do we know the root cause of the problem?
6. What insights would help the organization better understand its current state?
7. What would help decision-makers make better decisions?
8. What insights would help the organization make the necessary changes?
9. What would be considered a success?

The outcomes of this stage are:

- A clearly stated problem description, goal definition, or project scope statement
- Well-articulated analytics questions
- Business analytics requirements
- Success criteria

7.2 DATA ACQUISITION AND PREPARATION

Once we define the problem, the requirements, and the analytics questions, we can move onto the next stage in the analytics life cycle, which is about collecting data and preparing it for analytical use.

Data acquisition refers to the collection of data required for analytical purposes from appropriate sources.

The data you collect will not always be ready for analytical use. Depending on the nature and reliability of each source, it may require cleaning and further processing.

Data preparation refers to transforming data from the state in which it was acquired to a specified structure and quality standard. Its main objectives are to:

- Improve the quality of the data, which will ensure more accurate, trustworthy, and effective analytics solutions
- Transform data from multiple sources to a common structure and data model for storage and further analytical use

Cleaned, standardized, and fully integrated data can be stored in a centralized analytical system and made available for analytics purposes.

Further down the pipeline, using different analytics platforms and machine learning methods will require different data structures and data types, reduced datasets, or additional feature engineering. These subsequent manipulations are referred to as data wrangling or data munging.

Data wrangling is the process of transforming data into datasets suitable for analytical modelling and machine learning.

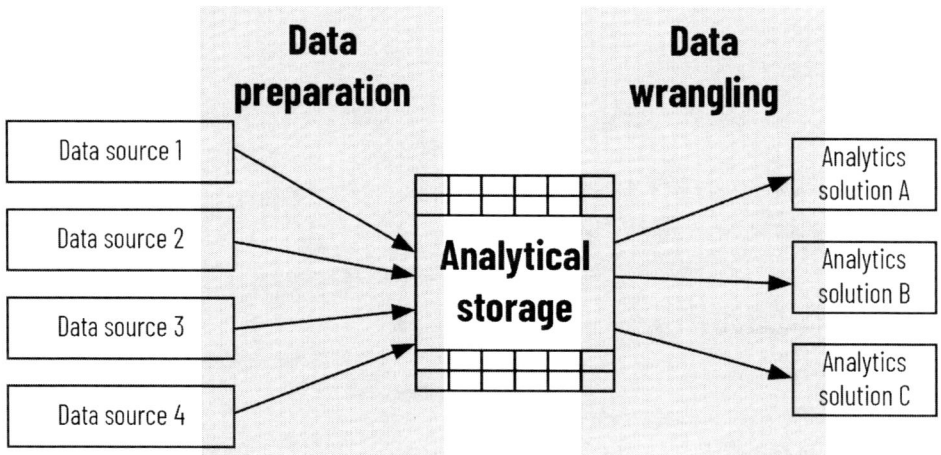

Figure 7.2 Data Preparation versus Data Wrangling

As the rest of the chapter will make apparent, while data preparation and data wrangling use similar methods, they have very different purposes:

- Data preparation is generic, as it prepares data for long-term storage and analytical use. Its destination is usually an enterprise data warehouse designed for storing historical data from all functional areas of the enterprise.
- Data wrangling is always performed with a specific purpose in mind. It involves manipulating the data to fit a particular analytics goal, such as preparing a dataset for training of a predictive model.

- Data wrangling may involve data that has not gone through any pre-processing, such as data introduced from an external source to enrich the training dataset. During feature engineering and model training, data scientists determine whether the new dataset provides value; if it doesn't, it will be discarded, never having touched the analytical storage system.

Figure 7.3 shows typical tasks involved in data acquisition and preparation. Some of these tasks may also be applied at the data wrangling stage, with different objectives.

Data acquisition & preparation

Acquire	Assess	Clean	Transform	Persist
Identify sources	Explore	Correct errors	Restructure	Validate
Collect	Visualize	Standardize	Reduce	Store
Stage	Validate	Handle missing data	Mask	Document
		De-duplicate	Consolidate	

Figure 7.3 Data Acquisition and Preparation Steps and Tasks

TIPS ON TERMS

Many Names for Data Acquisition and Preparation

The terms *data collection* and *data acquisition* can be used interchangeably.

The term *data ingestion* is sometimes used interchangeably with *data acquisition*. However, other sources give narrower meaning to the term *ingestion*, referring to the reception and storage of streaming data (e.g., real-time data collection).

Data cleaning is sometimes used in place of the broader term *data preparation*, along with *cleansing*, *scrubbing*, and *data remediation*.

The terms *data remediation*, *pre-processing*, and *scrubbing* may also refer broadly to all data preparation activities, including restructuring and handling missing data.

Depending on the data sources and analytics architecture, acquisition and preparation activities can be meshed closely together or be distinctly separated in space and time. Not all the steps depicted in Figure 7.3 must always be performed, and not necessarily in such a linear manner. The variety and veracity of data will affect the complexity of data preparation. Some exploration may be done before data collection begins, reformatting may be required before cleaning, and validation can be done in small increments after each activity.

The sequence of activities or the need to repeat some of the steps will be determined by the nature and quality of the data sources, as well as the analytics architecture used in the organization. For the purposes of understanding the analytics life cycle, we will review each step sequentially.

While discussing data preparation activities, keep in mind the typical data preparation challenges that affect timelines and data quality.

Table 7.1 Data Preparation Challenges

Challenge	Description
Volume, variety, and veracity of data	Data comes from multiple sources in different formats, managed by different rules, collected at different paces, and with different levels of confidence in its trustworthiness
Data quality at source	Bad data is introduced through defects, poorly designed operational systems, or human errors at data entry
Environmental factors	Measurements and data-capture devices are impacted by external factors such as weather, noise level, and pollution
Lack of master data management	Data from multiple sources lacks consistent common definitions and cannot be combined or compared directly, leading to integration and interpretation errors
Introduced data quality issues	Data is distorted, modified, or lost during processing and transformation, e.g., via defects in data preparation algorithms

Acquire

The purpose of data acquisition is to collect required data from various sources. To discover and better understand the data you need to collect, ask yourself a series of questions.

✓ **CHECKLIST**

Data Acquisition Checklist

1. What data is relevant to our understanding of the business problem?
2. What are the important data entities and their relationships?
3. Is the data available?
4. What are the sources of data?
5. Is there any documentation or metadata available for the data sources?
6. How can data be collected from the sources?
7. Is the data sensitive? What protection does it require?

Answering these questions will provide direction for data collection and its further processing. In the process, data may be stored in a temporary location to facilitate preparation and cleaning, which is referred to as **data staging**. Conversely, it may be collected and stored in data lakes indefinitely, without any pre-processing. The choice of approach will depend on an organization's information strategy and analytics architecture, which will be discussed further in Chapter 8.

Table 7.2 Data Acquisition Tasks

Task	Examples
Identify sources: systems, databases, repositories, and external sources from which to collect the data for further analysis	• Determine operational systems where the transactions requiring analysis are tracked • Identify master sources of data about customers, suppliers, products, or materials relevant to the business activities being analyzed • Consider external sources of data that may provide additional relevant information not available internally
Collect: extract and gather data from the sources	• Copy data from operational systems or databases • Receive data files from third parties • Collect data through surveys or A/B testing
Stage: Store collected data in a temporary location for data preparation	• Store collected datasets in a staging area until data preparation is completed

When we discuss data acquisition in the context of the analytics life cycle, the usual assumption is that data already exists and needs to be found, assessed, and acquired. Thus, a significant portion of data used in analytics is secondary data. However, existing data may not be sufficient, recent, or trustworthy. Depending on the goals of analytics, there may be a need to collect new primary data through surveys, A/B testing, observation, interviews, or focus groups. While primary data collection is more expensive and time-consuming, it may be a necessary step in the data acquisition stage.

Collection of primary data may involve:

• Designing A/B experiments, forms, or survey questions
• Identifying a population sample
• Devising a data collection procedure (through observation, email communication, personal interactions, or recording of clickstream data)
• Capturing and storing the raw data for cleaning and processing

Assess

Data preparation involves cleaning, transforming, and persisting the data, and begins with an assessment of what needs to be cleaned and transformed.

Table 7.3 Data Assessment Tasks

Task	Examples
Explore: view and study the collected data	• Analyze the documentation and metadata such as a data dictionary, schema, or data specification • Interview business domain experts about data • Query and sample data to assess its content and quality • (See the Data Exploration Checklist)

(continued)

Table 7.3 Data Assessment Tasks (*continued*)

Task	Examples
Visualize: create charts and diagrams from the data	• Visualize data to view patterns, trends, and distribution • Visualize data using statistical methods to detect unexpected results, erroneous values, and outliers • Use visualization to identify data issues
Validate: query data to detect quality issues and missing or duplicate values	• Check whether data falls within the valid range • Find values in incorrect format or containing invalid characters • Search for unexpected values • Check whether data conforms to pre-defined specifications, e.g., to a data dictionary • (See the Data Validation Checklist)

The following checklists can be used to guide data exploration.

✓ **CHECKLIST**

Data Exploration Checklist

1. Is the data human or machine generated?
2. Does it come from an internal or external system?
3. Is it structured, semi-structured, or unstructured?
4. What do we know about the data structure and format in the source system?
5. How trustworthy is the data source?
6. If the data is generated by a business process, where in that process are the data collection points?
7. Does the data undergo any transformations before acquisition?
8. Is the data complete? What may be missing and why?
9. Do you expect or observe data quality issues?
10. Does the data match the specification?

To answer these questions, you will use exploratory or statistical analysis. Exploratory analysis is performed without trying to identify statistical significance and may not use representative samples. Statistical analysis relies on representative samples and focuses on statistically significant findings.

After exploring the data, focus on identifying data quality issues that must be addressed. At this point, data visualization can be used to highlight the areas requiring further investigation and validation (refer to the Visualization Checklist in Section 5.5).

Based on the initial exploration and findings, a more pointed data validation approach should be used to find data issues that require validation or correction, as outlined in the next checklist.

The results of the assessment determine the scope of data cleaning and transformation.

✔️ **CHECKLIST**

Data Validation Checklist

1. Is the data accurate—i.e., are the observations captured correctly?

    Examples of inaccurate data:
    - Erroneous instrument readings
    - Errors in human input
    - Information on the form entered in the wrong field

2. Are the data values and format valid?

    Examples of invalid values or format:
    - Data is outside the acceptable range
    - Incorrect data type (negative value in a count field, fractional value where a whole number is expected, text instead of a numeric value)
    - Syntax or formatting errors, invalid characters

3. Is the data consistent—i.e., values are compatible and do not contradict each other?

    Examples of inconsistent data:
    - Year of birth is not consistent with a person's age
    - Street address is incompatible with postal code

4. Is the data complete—i.e., expected data points are not missing?

    Examples of incomplete data:
    - Skipped survey questions
    - Missing mandatory attributes
    - Failed instrument readings

5. Is the data relevant—i.e., useful for the purpose?

    Examples of irrelevant data:
    - Corrupted data that cannot be recovered
    - Attributes that have no analytical value, e.g., inventory ID of equipment that was used for measurement
    - Fraudulent data such as customer reviews from fake accounts

6. Does the data contain duplicates—i.e., is the same information duplicated in multiple places?

    Examples of duplicate data:
    - The same event recorded by two sources
    - The same request erroneously processed twice
    - The same transaction captured by multiple systems

Clean

Cleaning data implies modifying the data to correct errors, fix irregularities, and improve its quality.

Table 7.4 Data Cleaning Tasks

Task	Examples
Correct errors: update, repair, or remove incorrect or invalid data	• Correct erroneous values by getting more accurate data from another source or deriving it from other data • Correct formatting errors • Remove extraneous or invalid characters such as spaces or special characters • Remove data points outside of the valid range (e.g., incorrect instrument readings)
Standardize: modify data to conform to common rules and definitions	• Replace different values, codes, or spellings with a standard value—e.g., convert all currency codes to standard ISO currency codes[1] • Bring values to the scale or measurement unit—e.g., convert all distances to metres, all temperature readings to Celsius • Standardize the phone number field to a common format
Handle missing data: detect and handle missing values according to established rules	• Fill in missing customer attributes from the master source of customer data • Replace blank survey responses with a default value of "NA" • Populate missing observation values from records captured just before or just after
De-duplicate: detect and handle duplicate records according to established rules	• Remove identical duplicate information • Detect and correct discrepancies created by duplicate information

The purpose of data cleaning is not only to improve the quality of data, but also to remove data points that have no analytical value and may interfere with accurate analysis. However, data cleaning must be well planned and executed to avoid introducing additional issues.

Whether the issue is with invalid, incorrect, or missing data, correcting it must be based on an understanding of the reasons for inaccuracy and the location of the master source of data. If the issue relates to data inconsistency across enterprise systems, such as using different codes and values to capture the same value, cleaning will involve replacing inconsistent values with standard entries using enterprise reference data.

When data quality issues are caused by systemic issues, such as a lack of validation procedures during data collection, or enterprise systems not using proper reference data, the organization should make an effort to fix the root cause of the data issue. This is an example of applying data governance to improve data quality.

The optimal approach to handling missing values will depend on several considerations.

✓ **CHECKLIST**

Handling Missing Data

1. Identify what and how much is missing.
2. If records consist of multiple attributes, which of them are missing?

   Is there a pattern—e.g., the same attribute missing in many records? Are there sparse records where a large number of attributes is missing?
3. Is there an explanation for the pattern of missing data?

   Possible reasons:
   - Information unknown when data was collected
   - Attribute not mandatory on collection
   - Data difficult or costly to collect
   - Faulty data collection method

   Take these reasons into account when deciding on the appropriate way to handle the missing data. A pattern may also indicate the need to address the root cause of the issue. For example:
   - If the missing attribute is not mandatory on input and is not available from other sources, there may be nothing to be done at the data cleaning stage. If you believe this attribute is required for analysis, make a recommendation to enforce collection at the source or find another source.
   - If the same survey question is frequently skipped by respondents, ask whether the question is confusing or intrusive, or if the response options are insufficient.
   - If there is a pattern of missing data from a particular demographic, such as a lack of responses from female respondents or from a certain age group, investigate why. Lack of representation of a particular segment may lead to biased survey data and biased analysis.
4. Draw a distinction between missing and non-existent data.

   E.g., if a person is not married, the "name of spouse" attribute will be empty. This should not be considered missing data, as in this case, an empty value has a meaning (no spouse exists).

   Whether an empty value is valid for a particular attribute should be defined through data governance and captured in the organization's data dictionary or data catalogue.

   Note that an empty (non-existent) value may also be referred to as blank, or when referring to data storage, as the NULL value. NULL is different from a zero in a numeric field or a space-filled string as it signifies no value. When NULL values are not acceptable, they might need to be replaced by a default value such as "NA."

5. What is the importance of missing data for analysis?

   Consider the value of missing data points versus other attributes in the records. For instance, if a customer's gender is missing but other useful data is available, is it acceptable to use the imperfect record for analysis?

   How valuable is each record for analysis? If the volume of available data is large, discarding random records with missing data points may not have much impact. In this case, records may be removed from the dataset and omitted from analysis, provided that this does not create a sample bias as noted above.

   If there is a risk of losing too much data or statistically significant records in a dataset, then discarding imperfect records may not be an option. Instead, consider imputing values or flagging records as having missing data.

6. Is there a feasible way to impute missing data?

   Imputing refers to calculating or deriving missing data points from other observations. Consider whether imputing is possible: what information can be used to infer missing values?

   - Can missing data points be derived from other attributes (e.g., obtaining a postal code from a street address)?
   - Can missing data points be derived from other data sources (e.g., retrieving a missing customer address from the customer relationship management system)?
   - Can a measurement be imputed using statistical methods (e.g., substituting with a mean, median, or average from nearby observations)?
   - Can a value be copied from similar records (*hot deck method*) (e.g., copying a missing soil type survey response from the answers of customers who live in proximity)?
   - For time-series data, can a value be interpolated (e.g., using the last-observation-carried-forward or the next-observation-carried-backward methods)?

   Note that using a default value for imputing may not be advisable. If many observations are missing and all are replaced by the same default value, the algorithm might mistakenly learn a non-existent pattern or assign higher importance to the default.

   In some instances, there is no reasonable default. For example, if gender is missing, using a default can lead to creating a dataset with a skewed distribution or a gender bias.

7. Agree on a consistent procedure for handling missing data.

   Whether the decision is to discard, impute, or flag missing data, this must be applied consistently and documented.

   When flagging records with missing data, this must be clearly documented to inform decisions on how flagged records should be handled during analysis.

The problem of duplication deserves additional attention, as this is not a challenge with individual records but one that compromises the quality of the dataset. Even identical duplicate records may cause confusion—for example, counting the same event or transaction twice inflates the numbers. This could result in misleading or contradictory metrics.

✓ **CHECKLIST**

Handling Duplicate Values

1. Determine what duplication scenario you are dealing with.

   Referring to "duplicate records" can be ambiguous; be clear about what type of duplication you are dealing with.

   a. Identical: identical duplicate records of the same transaction or data entity

   b. Complimentary: records of the same transaction where different data sources supply different attributes

   c. Conflicting: records of the same transaction or data entity with some attributes having conflicting values

2. Determine suitable handling of duplicates based on the scenario.

   a. Identical duplicates

   This is the redundancy scenario. At the data acquisition stage, there is no reason to ingest multiple copies of the same transaction into an analytical system as it does not provide any value and can cause an incorrect count. All identical copies should be discarded.

   The criteria used to identify identical records are important, as two records may look identical (if only a few attributes are considered) but in actuality represent two different valid transactions. Consider what attributes or metadata are required for detecting duplicates. For instance:

   - When two customers buy the same product in the same store on the same date, a customer identifier, the four last digits of the payment card used, or a timestamp will indicate whether these were similar but separate transactions.
   - When a customer buys something at a store and immediately decides to buy another item at the same price, a timestamp or unique item identifier such as a barcode will indicate that these were similar but separate transactions.
   - When a customer places multiple calls to the customer service centre in quick succession and does not get a response, the precise timestamp of the call will allow each call to be recognized as a different event.

   b. Complimentary duplicates

   This is an example of distributed data storage encountered when multiple transactional systems are used to manage end-to-end processes. For example, one system captures the customer inquiry date, time, and reason for the call, and another obtains information about the resolution of the case.

In this scenario, the records can be either merged or linked to allow retrieval of all attributes related to the same transaction. Sometimes, data will continue to be stored in separate data entities if this is required for normalization and avoidance of data redundancy. It is the data architect's or data modeller's job to optimize the analytical system data models and guide how the data should be structured. The key outcome is for related attributes or records to be reliably linked.

c. Conflicting duplicates

This scenario points to data quality issues in the organization, inconsistency of data definitions, or lack of integration.

For example, the customer address in the order management system is different from the address captured in the order delivery tracker. Was there a problem with a delivery? Has the customer had a recent address change? Or did the delivery driver record the new customer address when calling them to confirm the delivery time, creating a conflicting record?

This is a data governance concern and must be handled in a systematic way. However, since changes to operational systems may take a long time, a decision must be made on how to handle such conflicting records during data acquisition. This may include, for example:

- Determining what system is the master source of data and giving preference to values from the master source
- Selecting the value with the latest timestamp, with the assumption that it is the most up to date
- Flagging records with conflicting values for investigation, manual correction, or exception processing
- Discarding both conflicting values

3. Document the decision and logic for handling duplicate values for each scenario. Document both the steps taken and the rationale behind the decisions.

4. Address systemic issues that are causing duplicates.

Report the finding as a data quality issue, providing examples to support the analysis and resolution. The resolution process may include:

- Investigating for potential design defects
- Enhancing the source systems to eliminate the root cause of the issue, e.g., adding a data entry validation
- Improving master data management processes to ensure master data changes are shared with all affected systems

Many data issues become recurring because individuals tasked with cleaning the data perform the narrow task only, without bringing up the need to make improvements in the source systems.

Transform

Data collected from multiple sources may differ in structure and format. A variety of unstructured, semi-structured, and structured data from different sources may need to be consolidated and blended into a more uniform format as required by the analytical system in use. Modern data acquisition and preparation platforms offer a broad range of tools and libraries to handle various data transformation scenarios, such as the examples noted in Table 7.5.

Table 7.5 Data Transformation Tasks

Task	Examples
Restructure: change the structure of datasets, columns, or rows	• Convert semi-structured or unstructured datasets to structured datasets • Convert structured data from multiple systems into a common schema (data model) • Merge (concatenate) columns • Split (parse) data in columns into multiple fields • Separate heterogeneous datasets into separate tables of homogenous data
Reduce: remove unnecessary or irrelevant data	• Discard records not needed for analytical purposes, e.g., temporary data • Discard irrelevant attributes, e.g., control sums generated for audit purposes
Mask: transform sensitive data to protect it from unauthorized use	• Mask credit card numbers by replacing all but the last four digits with asterisks
Consolidate: combine data from multiple sources into a common structure	• Once data from disparate sources is reformatted to the same schema, consolidate it into the records in the same database • Combine and add rows and/or columns into the new structures

Persist

The final step of data preparation is **persisting data**—storing the prepared data in a permanent storage system.

Table 7.6 Tasks Involved in Persisting Prepared Data

Task	Examples
Validate: check the results of data manipulations for quality and integrity	• Check the number of records after transformations • Validate the final format and structure of transformed data
Store: save prepared data in an analytical system	• Move the transformed data from the staging area to the permanent storage
Document: capture the data preparation logic	• Capture the design of each transformation step and the sequence of steps

It is important not to skip the documentation step. Capturing the logic behind various data preparation activities is necessary to support:

- Audit requirements
- Future changes, e.g., when data sources change or the analytical needs of the company evolve
- Testing and issue investigation if defects are discovered in the processed data or if invalid analytics results are received
- Understanding of the data to support intelligent development of analytics solutions

The documentation step may be supported by the creation of or updates to a data catalogue, data dictionary, data models, or other types of data documentation mentioned throughout this book.

7.3 DATA WRANGLING AND FEATURE SELECTION

In this section, we explore various wrangling activities. As with data preparation, not all transformations will apply to all individual scenarios. It will depend on the analytics requirements, the availability, volume, variety and veracity of data, and the capabilities of different analytical tools.

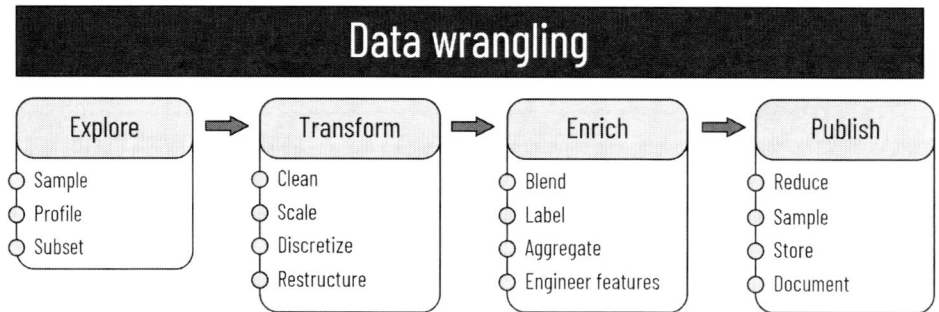

Figure 7.4 Data Wrangling Steps and Tasks

Explore

Pre-processed data is usually stored in enterprise data warehouses and other analytical storage solutions. Organizations maintain these solutions as repositories of historical data and analytical storage (see Chapter 8).

Prepared and cleaned historical records must be maintained and protected from unauthorized changes and misuse. When specific analytics goals are set, data wrangling will be performed on a copy, a subset extracted from the main analytical storage. The first step is to explore the data and assess its suitability for a specific analytical purpose. This will require **data profiling**—examining and evaluating the data and its statistical properties to better understand it and guide data transformations

Table 7.7 Data Exploration Tasks

Task	Examples
Sample: select a subset of data for profiling	• Select records in one product category or from a subset of locations for further assessment
Profile: examine and evaluate the data and its statistical properties	• (See Data Profiling Checklist)
Subset: select a part of a dataset for analytical or machine learning purposes	• Based on profiling results, identify a dataset to perform further wrangling on • Filter on specific criteria and discard irrelevant records and/or attributes • Select a representative sample as a training set

The steps involved in data wrangling, like those of the overall analytics process, will be iterative. At any time, the analytics team may identify a lack of crucial data, requiring more discovery and acquisition. Profiling activities may indicate deficiencies in data or interesting relationships that will suggest adjustments to data selection and training dataset composition.

Before introducing the Data Profiling Checklist, it is important to note that wrangling may involve data that has not gone through any pre-processing. Data could be coming from new sources, including external sources, having never been stored in a centralized analytical storage system in a structured format. The iterative nature of developing advanced analytics presumes that at any time, the researcher may introduce a new dataset as part of experimentation and feature engineering.

Therefore, some data profiling questions in the checklist assume profiling is performed on a new dataset in its raw format.

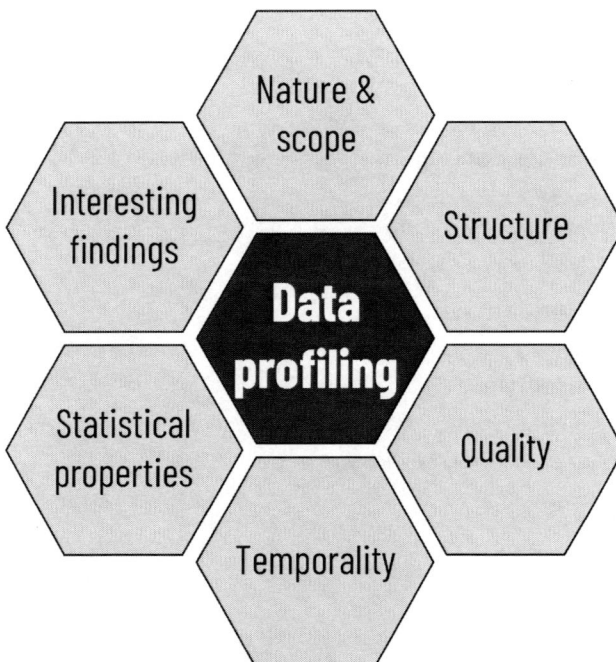

Figure 7.5 Aspects of Data Profiling

Data Profiling Checklist

1. Nature and scope of the data

   What data entities are captured in the data?

   What is the relationship between these entities?

   Does the dataset contain records about different data entities (making it a heterogeneous dataset) or the same entity (making it a homogeneous dataset)?

   What attributes of data entities are included?

   What is the granularity of records? Does the dataset include detailed or aggregate information?

   Is the dataset complete? Does it contain all the records expected?

   Are there any missing records?

   Is the data unique or are there duplications?

2. Data structure

   Is the dataset structured, semi-structured, or unstructured?

   What is known about the data structure? Is there a data model? What about documentation?

   Is the dataset homogeneous or heterogeneous?

   Do all records in the dataset contain the same fields?

   How can you access specific fields—by position or by name?

   How is the data encoded—using human-readable text, binary numbers, hexadecimal values, hash keys, or codes?

   Is the data compressed or encrypted?

3. Data quality

   Are there records in the dataset that do not match specifications?

   Are there invalid fields in the records?

   Are there known data quality issues?

   (Refer to the Data Validation Checklist)

4. Temporality of data

   When was the data collected?

   Were all the records and fields collected at the same time? What time range is reflected in the data?

   Does the dataset contain the date and time of data collection? Is this information captured at the record or field level?

   Was the data modified? When? Is this information available at the record or field level?

   Is it possible to determine which data is current and which is stale?

5. Statistical properties

How is the data distributed? Does the distribution look right (as would be expected based on domain knowledge)?

What are the ranges of values, minimums, maximums, means, and medians of particular fields? Do they match reasonable expectations, given the dataset parameters?

Are there detectable patterns?

Are there outliers?

6. Interesting findings and relationships

Are there detectable correlations between attributes for further analysis?

Are there any redundant attributes that can be discarded to reduce the size of the dataset?

Does the dataset have any potential keys that can be used to uniquely identify each record (key analysis)?

Profiling methods may be individual or set-based.

Individual profiling validates individual records, fields, or values, such as syntax or semantic checks:

- **Syntax checks** are concerned with whether values are within the permissible range and satisfies the formatting rules of the field—e.g., is the date field in the correct format? Is the country code valid?
- **Semantic checks** are concerned with whether values make sense based on the expected meaning of the data—e.g., if all the company's stores are closed on New Year's Day, no purchases should have a date of January 1.

Set-based profiling allows us to assess a dataset and its parameters. This involves applying statistical analysis or visualization to the dataset by:

- Building a histogram
- Creating a frequency table for categorical values
- Plotting geospatial data on a map
- Plotting time-stamped data on a timeline
- Building a scatter plot
- Checking a dataset for duplicate records
- Comparing values of two attributes for consistency

Data profiling provides valuable information about properties of data that will determine what you need to do with the data next.

CASE STUDY

Interesting Data Profiling Findings

The YardExperts analytics team has been poring over the latest national landscaping survey data. Some of the interesting results include a significantly higher proportion of rock gardens in the western region compared to the rest of the country.

As the team plotted the data on a map, a certain geographical area began to stand out. It had three to four times more houses with rock-garden-style landscaping than anywhere else in the country, while the distribution of landscaping styles in rest of the western region looked similar to the national averages.

This was an intriguing finding that eventually led to more discoveries.

The team created a data mining algorithm to do some association analysis. They discovered that in those neighbourhoods, having a rock garden was highly correlated with requests to transform them into regular flower beds. It turned out that a local contractor ran a successful promotional campaign on discounted rock garden installations some time back, only to plant unsuitable perennials. Now the contractor was gone, and house owners were unhappy with the unruly appearance of their rock gardens and wanted to replace them with something more conventional.

Since this pattern was only evident in one location, it paid to investigate this idiosyncrasy before making wide-reaching assumptions that rock gardens were going out of fashion. It also paid off to be able to discover this pattern in the first place, as it led to useful diagnostic analysis and may help YardExperts to come up with a special promotion for many potential customers with a similar problem.

Transform

Data wrangling often requires further data transformation to make datasets more suitable for analysis and machine learning.

Note that some of these transformations will result in changing the type of data. As machine learning models work with numeric data, qualitative data must be converted to quantitative data. When using numeric variables with very different scales (such as the 1–10 range for one variable vs. the 1–1,000,000 range for another), variables may need to be rescaled to the same scale to avoid the algorithm assigning more weight to values with a larger range.

Enrich

Data enrichment refers to adding new values to the dataset to enhance the data with additional details, context, or metrics.

Data can be added from:

- Other sources
- Calculations and derivations from existing values

Table 7.8 Data Transformation Tasks—Wrangling Stage

Task	Examples
Clean: handle data issues to make a dataset suitable for analytics and machine learning	• Impute missing values or remove records with missing fields • Standardize values to conform to common rules and encoding • Clean data from new sources that did not undergo any data preparation (refer to Section 7.2 for descriptions of data cleaning tasks)
Scale: transform values to fit into a specific range (scale)	• Rescale data to 0–1 range according to the minimum and maximum value of the variable
Discretize: convert a continuous variable to discrete values	• Assign continuous values to discrete ranges (bins), e.g., age ranges or income ranges
Restructure: change the structure of datasets, columns, or rows	• Convert semi-structured and unstructured data to structured • Convert structured data from multiple systems into a common schema (data model) • Split or merge columns or rows • De-normalize data, e.g., for a data mart with a dimensional data model

Table 7.9 Data Enrichment Tasks

Task	Examples
Blend: merge data from multiple datasets	• Combine attributes from two datasets by linking them to the same records, e.g., add customer demographic attributes to the customer review details • Add records from multiple datasets to increase the scope of the set, e.g., add customer reviews from two social media platforms into the same set for sentiment analysis
Label: add labels to records to create a dataset for supervised learning	• Label images intended for training an image recognition model • Add a "fraudulent" label to all credit card transactions reported as fraud • Add "Silver," "Gold," and "Platinum" labels to a set of customer records
Aggregate: create groupings, aggregations, and pivots to improve performance and reduce the need for redundant calculations	• Create new records with daily sales totals to supply to a frequently used sales dashboard • Group and link records of all household members to enable frequent analysis with a household grouping
Engineer features: create new attributes (features) from the available data	• Derive a sentiment score from a chatbot transcript • Calculate elapsed time from the start and end timestamps • Assign a location identifier to a geolocation such as a neighbourhood identifier • Create multiple Boolean values to replace a categorical value (one-hot encoding)

Feature engineering becomes important when available data is not in the right format or not sufficient to generate a model with the required accuracy or performance. The need for feature engineering and to test models using different features underscores the experimental and iterative nature of model development.

CASE STUDY

Feature Engineering with One-Hot Encoding

Among the data collected through the YardExperts landscaping survey is the prevalent type of property landscaping. The team wants to use it to develop a machine learning model to predict customer needs during the next gardening season. However, this data is qualitative and cannot be used as is. Each value in the "Landscaping needs" attribute contains a list with a variable number of selections, separated by commas.

Table 7.10.a Feature Engineering Example—Survey Response Data

Customer ID	Landscaping needs
504895	lawn, hedge, planters
456012	rock garden
465221	flower border, planters
404899	lawn, window boxes
404578	lawn, hedge, planters, rock garden

One-hot encoding can be applied to assign a value of 0 or 1 to each of the possible values for each customer, thus converting one qualitative attribute into multiple Boolean features.

Table 7.10.b Feature Engineering Example—One-Hot Encoding Results

Customer ID	Lawn	Hedge	Flower border	Window boxes	Planters	Rock garden
504895	1	1	0	0	1	0
456012	0	0	0	0	0	1
465221	0	0	1	0	1	0
404899	1	0	0	1	0	0
404578	1	1	0	0	1	1

Publish

Publishing data refers to making data available for processing by the next component in the data pipeline. This step is required when wrangled data must be stored elsewhere, such as a data mart or an analytical sandbox. Depending on the tools being used, model building can be done on the same platform as data wrangling, which would make some of these steps unnecessary.

Table 7.11 Data Publication Tasks—Wrangling Stage

Task	Examples
Reduce: reduce the size of the dataset while retaining the most important information	• Remove less important or redundant features from a dataset • Remove attributes for anonymization purposes • Combine multiple features into one
Sample: select a smaller dataset for modelling that preserves the required characteristics	• Select a subset of survey responses with a representative distribution of households by region and income range • Select a training dataset of job candidates with an unbiased gender distribution
Store: move or copy wrangled data to the target location for storage and model building	• Store the transformed version of the dataset in the analytical tool
Document: capture data wrangling steps to enable testing, issue investigation, and future changes	• Capture the sequence and logic of each transformation step • Store the scripts that generate the refined datasets • Store the scripts that generate profiling statistics and insights

Feature Selection

When doing advanced analytical modelling, we should be ready to experiment with different features and algorithms as part of iterative model building.

When selecting features to be used, it is always preferable to keep the number of features (predictive factors) small, as it makes it easier to set up hyperparameters, as well as to train, tune, and fit the model. The number of features will also affect the model's performance: the fewer features, the less computing power will be required.

Remember to ask yourself:

- Are there any dependent features in the dataset? If so, omit them from selection.
- Which variables are important in a practical sense (e.g., can be controlled by the company)? Using these as features for prediction will make it more actionable.
- Which variables are more reliable, i.e., which are missing less frequently, and which have higher accuracy at the source? Variables that require significant cleaning or imputing are less reliable, as the imputing process might skew the results.

TIPS ON TERMS

Data Wrangling

There are many terms used to refer to data wrangling, including *data munging* and *advanced data preparation*.

The term *exploratory data analysis* can be a synonym for *data exploration* or *data profiling*.

Consolidation of prepared data can be called *blending* or *merging*.

Coding may refer to *labelling* or *discretizing*.

7.4 MODEL BUILDING AND TESTING

Models are built and trained using algorithms. An **algorithm** is a set of instructions and rules designed to accomplish a task, usually by a computer. A **machine learning algorithm** is a set of instructions and rules provided to the computer to generalize relationships and patterns from the data provided to the algorithm.

Algorithms—such as Linear, Polynomial, or Logistic Regression; Decision Tree; Classification and Regression Tree (CART); Random Forest; Naïve Bayes; Support Vector Machines (SVM); k-Nearest Neighbour (kNN); k-Means; and Artificial Neural Networks (ANN), to name a few—are selected based on the characteristics of the data being used and the purpose of the model.

For each algorithm, engineers will select *hyperparameters*, which are model configurations required by each algorithm, such as the number of layers in an ANN or the k value in kNN.

Without delving into specific machine learning algorithms, this section summarizes the key steps in model building as part of the overall analytics life cycle. Model building can also be called *engineering* and *training*.

Table 7.12 Model Building and Testing

Task	Examples
Prepare training and test sets	• Split the set into two parts—training and testing sets (e.g., 70% for training and 30% for testing)—aiming for a comparable distribution of data in each set • Randomize the sequence of records in the training set (sorted records may mistakenly lead the algorithm to assume a trend pattern)
Select an algorithm and hyperparameters	• Select a candidate model based on the characteristics of the data and the objective • Set a starting set of hyperparameters for the model (to be tuned and modified as part of model training)
Train the model	• Develop the model using the training dataset • Check and correct inaccurate predictions as part of training • Experiment with the algorithm, features, and their weights • Tune the model, adjust its hyperparameters
Evaluate the model	• Test the model using the test dataset • Assess model fit and the accuracy of predictions
Select model for deployment	• Repeat steps until reaching the desired accuracy • Select the best-performing model and its parameters to be deployed to production

How are the models evaluated? The goal of machine learning and predictive modelling is to create a model that generalizes well—that is, a model that can make reasonably good predictions about new data by learning from past data. During the iterative and highly experimental machine learning (ML) process, data scientists and engineers must be aware of and actively mitigate the following challenges.

If a sample chosen to train the machine learning model was biased toward a certain range of variables (biased training set), the model may overestimate their significance. For example, if more male than female job candidates are present in the training set, the model may assume that gender is important.

Overfitting in machine learning happens when the model becomes too complex by learning too much from the training set, including parameters that are not important. *Noise* is what we call irrelevant or random data that cannot help in making more accurate predictions, such as street numbers in the customer address. Streets can be short or long, include single dwellings and multi-residential buildings, have different numbering systems, and reach into neighbourhoods of different characters. As a result, the model performs very well on the training set but does not generalize well when given new data because it learned incorrect patterns from the "noise" in the training set.

Underfitting happens when the model is oversimplified and does not learn enough from the training set—that is, it is not able to predict well either on the training set or on new data. While overfitting may happen if a model uses too many features, underfitting may result from using too few features.

The best outcomes are achieved when machine learning models are balanced between overfitting and underfitting and generalize well the relationships in a dataset while disregarding the noise.

TIPS ON TERMS

Model Parameters versus Hyperparameters

Model parameters are "learned" by the model, or determined through machine learning—for example, when the model selects weights of features or coefficients in a regression model.

Hyperparameters cannot be learned from the data and are set by a human operator, data scientist, or ML engineer. An example is the selection of the ML algorithm or specific tuning metrics.

7.5 IMPLEMENTATION

After some experimentation with features, algorithms, and hyperparameters, a solution will have been developed and tested to satisfactory results. It must now be deployed for use by the business. **Implementation** refers to the deployment of the scalable solution into production, supported by the activities required for the successful adoption by intended users.

The *scalability* of a solution refers to its ability to handle an increasing processing load. For example, while the ML model was developed in a sandbox environment, it was fed a small number of records from a test set for validation. If this model were to be deployed to support embedded analytics in a transactional system required to manage thousands of simultaneous transactions, the analytical components of the solution must be able to manage a much larger workload. It is the job of machine learning engineers to ensure that ML models are scalable.

When new solutions, systems, or tools are deployed, the success of the implementation will depend on whether or not the intended users are ready and know how to utilize the analytics solution.

Thus, the implementation stage may include the tasks in Table 7.13.

Table 7.13 Model Implementation Tasks

Task	Examples

Interpret the results	• Meet with stakeholders to discuss the insights and explain:
	  • How to interpret the insight, the parameters, and the accuracy of the prediction
	  • What the limitations of the models are, and when and how to incorporate user judgment
	  • What the result means for the business process
	  • How to use the insight to make decisions, and what the decision-making approach will be
	• If the model was unsuccessful, explain the reasons, conduct a review of lessons learned, and discuss next steps

Train users	• Record training videos, create user documentation • Train users on the analytics solution and its features • Conduct demonstrations
Share the results	• Communicate results to key stakeholders in the form of a presentation, storytelling, or an executive summary • Publish the results, e.g., reports or visualizations • Create a video demonstrating the features of a dashboard
Document the solution	• (See Model Documentation Checklist)
Deploy the solution	• Launch the dashboard in the production environment and provide access to business users • Schedule a regular job to generate and deliver new reports • Deploy the machine learning model embedded in a workflow
Operationalize the solution	• Incorporate analytics into the business process • Set up a feedback mechanism to assess the accuracy of predictions by collecting data and outcomes of the business process • Launch a support model, e.g., a process for users to report issues and get help

✔ **CHECKLIST**

Model Documentation Checklist

1. When was the model designed, and by whom?
2. What was the original purpose of the model and the analytics questions?
3. What are the model dimensions (time horizon, regions, and groups of data included)?
4. What algorithms and hyperparameters were tested, and which were deployed to production?
5. What are the potential issues to monitor?

At this stage, no matter the outcome, it is especially important to communicate the insights and the results of the model to the business stakeholders. Knowing how to effectively communicate analytics insights using narratives, sometimes referred to as **data storytelling**, is an important skill for all analytics professionals.

✔ **CHECKLIST**

Communicating Analytics Insights: Data Storytelling

1. Know your audience.
   Who are you presenting to?
   What are their interests?
   Are they only interested in the main insight, or would they also be interested in the details of how this insight was generated?
   What is the stakeholders' level of expertise? Would they prefer a simple message using business terms, or would they be interested in more technical details?
2. Identify the main message.
   Focus on the objective and the original analytics questions you asked yourselves.
   What is the main insight? Why is it important?
3. Explain what is being measured.
   State clearly what is measured, what the main variables are, and how metrics and KPIs were defined. Never assume that everyone already knows and has the same interpretation.
4. Tell the story in business language.
   Present to businesspeople in business terms. Keep statistics and technicalities to a minimum or risk losing your audience. Consider using narratives to

complement data and visualizations and to help them interpret the insights—for example:

- "Our model shows that a price reduction of 10% can generate 20% growth in the value of new contracts."
- "When we fail to clean the snow within a six-hour window, there is an 85% chance that the customer will not renew the contract."

5. Explain the data.

Provide an overview of what data was used and how it was prepared, what issues were found, and the main data preparation challenges. Keep it high level but ensure that the importance of data preparation comes through. You want to ensure that your next project gets adequate support and resources for data preparation, especially if this was a problematic step.

6. Prepare clear, purposeful, and unbiased visualizations.

Where possible, deliver one message per visualization. Do not cram many ideas into one visual.

Check your visualizations for bias. It is very difficult for human beings to un-see what they have seen, and it may be hard to undo the damage of a poorly executed or misleading diagram.

7. Consider different formats for presenting.

Will you create slides? Animations? Animated visualizations? Video visualizations? A live demo of the new dashboard?

There are many options, so consider which format would be most suitable for each audience.

8. Be prepared to answer questions.

Prepare references such as appendices, links to the documentation, sample data extracts or data exploration, and profiling results.

Have on hand a list of the assumptions, data sources, features engineered, features used, hypotheses tested (with results), and other information relevant to the analytics tasks completed. These can not only be used to answer questions but provided to interested parties.

Remember the documentation tasks in the analytics life cycle? This is another reason to document diligently.

9. Be open about model limitations.

Models cannot include all possible factors from real life. Business users must understand the limitations of the models, and when and how to incorporate judgment. Outline recommendations on how the model can be used for decision-making and explain how the model will be monitored and maintained.

10. Prepare to speak on legal and ethical issues.

You may have to explain how the private data was protected and how the team ensured the model was not biased (refer to Chapter 11).

11. Include the "What Next?" part.

    What have we learned? What can we predict? How could it help make deci-
    sions? Can these insights be embedded into the process, and what should be
    the next steps for using the results? Focus the audience's attention on these
    questions.

It is important to consider what to do in case of failure, such as if the predictive model
never achieved the desired accuracy, the source data could not be sufficiently enhanced, or
the training dataset was found to have serious bias issues. Not all analytics and data science
initiatives succeed. It is a good practice to hold "Lessons Learned" sessions to discuss what
went wrong, what could be done differently next time, and what improvements should be
made to the data life cycle or source systems.

7.6 OPERATION

The business analytics life cycle is made complete by the *operation* stage, in which we
use analytics solutions to make business decisions. The operation of any solution requires that we monitor its efficiency, measure results, and identify required changes and
improvements.

The most important aspects of monitoring analytics models are:

- Measuring the effectiveness of the model: tracking prediction accuracy and calculating success metrics
- Assessing how the model adapts to changing business conditions and data
- Monitoring for **model decay (model drift)**—degradation of the model's prediction accuracy over time, leading to inferior decisions

A model may experience decay, or a deterioration of its performance, for several
reasons.

Data drift (feature drift) is caused by changes in features (independent variables)
such as:

- Changes in the statistical properties of independent variables
- Data quality or scarcity issues—when data needed by the model deteriorates in
  quality or becomes unavailable
- New/better data becoming available

Concept drift is caused by changes in the relationship between dependent and independent variables—for example:

- The definition (or business interpretation) of the dependent (target) variable
  changes
- The effectiveness of the predictor variables used in the model starts degrading

- The organization's objectives change, so the model no longer fits the purpose
- Trends, customer behaviours, and prevailing market preferences change

As business conditions change and models drift, you will have to:

- Communicate with business stakeholders to explain changes in model effectiveness
- Prune models with little business value
- Tune, improve, and optimize the models
- Retrain models periodically when significant drift occurs (may involve relabelling old data or retraining on new data)
- Update documentation as the model is enhanced or modified

7.7 CHAPTER SUMMARY

Key Points to Remember

- The objective of data preparation activities is to improve data quality before using it for a variety of analytical purposes.
- Project delays and cost overruns are frequently tied to underestimating time and resources required for data preparation.
- If data quality issues are being caused by a systemic problem, such as a lack of validation procedures when the data is collected, then that systemic problem must be addressed to avoid the recurrence of the data issues.
- The purpose of data wrangling is to give data a structure and format optimized for specific analytics purposes.
- Data wrangling processes and activities will be influenced by the selected analytics platforms and tools.
- The same dataset can be wrangled in different ways for different analytical purposes.
- It is important not to skip the documentation step of data preparation and wrangling. Capturing logic in documentation is necessary to support testing, issue investigation, and future changes.
- Training data and test data for predictive models should not intersect.
- The "acceptable" prediction accuracy will depend on the type of prediction, risk, sensitivity, and the price of errors.
- When selecting features for predictive models, consider which variables can be influenced by the organization.

Key Terms

Algorithm: a set of instructions and rules designed to accomplish a task, usually by a computer.

Business analytics life cycle: the complete process from identifying the goals of analytics to implementing and using analytics solutions by business users.

Consolidating data: combining data from multiple sources into a common structure.

Data acquisition: collection of data required for analytical purposes from appropriate sources.

Data cleaning: modifying the data to correct errors, fix irregularities, and improve its quality.

Data enrichment: adding new values to the dataset to enhance it with additional details, context, or metrics.

Data masking: transforming sensitive data to protect it from unauthorized use.

Data preparation: transforming data from the state in which it was acquired to a specified structure and quality standard.

Data profiling: examination and evaluation of data and its statistical properties.

Data publishing: making data available for processing by the next component in the data pipeline.

Data staging: storing data in a temporary location to facilitate data preparation and cleaning.

Data storytelling: communicating analytics insights using narratives (stories).

Data wrangling: transforming data into datasets suitable for analytical modelling and machine learning.

Discretization: converting a continuous variable to discrete values.

Feature engineering: creating new attributes (features) from the available data.

Implementation: deployment of the scalable solution into production.

Imputing: calculating or deriving missing data points from other observations.

Machine learning algorithm: a set of instructions and rules provided to the computer to generalize relationships and patterns from data.

Model decay (model drift): a degradation of the model's performance over time.

Overfitting: a situation in which a machine learning model becomes too complex by learning too much from the training set, including parameters that are not important.

Persisting data: storing the prepared data in a permanent storage system.

Reducing data: removing unnecessary or irrelevant data.

Restructuring data: changing the structure of datasets, columns, or rows.

Scaling data: transforming values to fit into a specific range (scale).

Semantic check: validating whether the values make sense based on the expected meaning of the data.

Syntax check: validating whether values are within the permissible range and satisfy the formatting rules.

Underfitting: a situation in which a machine learning model is oversimplified and does not learn enough from the training set, i.e., is not able to generate accurate predictions.

Questions for Critical Thought

1. What are the goals of data profiling?
2. How can we determine the best way of handling missing values?

3. What are some ways we can enrich the training dataset?
4. What might affect the accuracy of a predictive model?
5. What must we consider when communicating analytical insights?
6. What is the purpose of data storytelling?
7. Why might a model's performance deteriorate after it is launched?

Test Your Knowledge

1. While profiling a set of data collected from a weather station during summer in a sub-
    tropical climate, a data engineer identified and deleted records where the temperature
    reading was in the range –50 °C to –40 °C.
    What data preparation activity was performed?
    a. Standardization
    b. De-duplication
    c. Consolidation
    d. Cleaning

2. An e-commerce company has a very large dataset with data on all user browser ses-
    sions. For the purposes of analysis, records of all sessions for the same user during the
    same day will be collapsed into one record showing "Total browsing time per day."
    What data preparation activity was performed?
    a. De-duplication
    b. Aggregation
    c. Scaling
    d. Cleaning

3. A dataset with movie streaming session data has some records with a missing "Total
    session duration" attribute. The data wrangling algorithm populated missing values
    using the mean session duration during the given time of the day.
    Which method was applied?
    a. Imputing
    b. Enriching
    c. Scaling
    d. Blending

4. What factors can contribute to data drift?
    a. Lack of user documentation
    b. Business stakeholders don't want to use the analytics solution
    c. The distribution of the predictive factor is changing
    d. A data scientist wants to test whether a different algorithm will have a better
        accuracy

5. Which of the following challenges applies to the model building and testing phase of the analytics life cycle?
    a. Lack of user training
    b. Model overfitting
    c. Concept drift
    d. The solution cannot support a large number of end users

Recommended Readings

Finlay, S. (2014). *Predictive Analytics, Data Mining and Big Data: Myths, Misconceptions and Methods.* Palgrave Macmillan (p. 159).

Rattenbury, Y., Hellerstein, J., Heer, J., Kandel, S., & Carreras, C. (2017). *Principles of Data Wrangling: Practical Techniques for Data Preparation.* Trifacta/O'Reilly Media. Retrieved February 11, 2024, from www.fintechfutures.com/files/2017/10/Trifacta_Principles-of-Data -Wrangling.pdf.

Rose, D. (2020). *Artificial Intelligence for Business.* Addison-Wesley.

Tuulos, V. (2022). *Effective Data Science Infrastructure: How to Make Data Scientists Productive.* Manning Publications.

Note

1. International Organization for Standardization (ISO). (n.d.). *ISO 4217 Currency Codes.* Retrieved February 25, 2024, from www.iso.org/iso-4217-currency-codes.html.

Chapter 8

Analytics Architecture

The word *architecture*, just like the word *data*, can mean many things to many people. Architecture is the discipline of designing and building things—whether skyscrapers, bridges, or software solutions.

In this chapter, we will study the components of analytics architecture—systems, tools, and the connections between them—that enterprises use to manage data through its life cycle and to produce business analytics solutions.

You will learn about:

- Components of analytics architecture, their roles, and their characteristics
- Data pipelines
- Latency and its relevance for business analytics

8.1 COMPONENTS OF ANALYTICS ARCHITECTURE

Analytics architecture refers to the design and structure of systems and tools used by an organization to store and analyze data.

The purpose of these components is to get the data from its place of origin to the destination where the data insights are used for business purposes. This path is known as a **data pipeline**: a sequence of steps for collecting, transforming, and moving data from various sources to the intended destination.

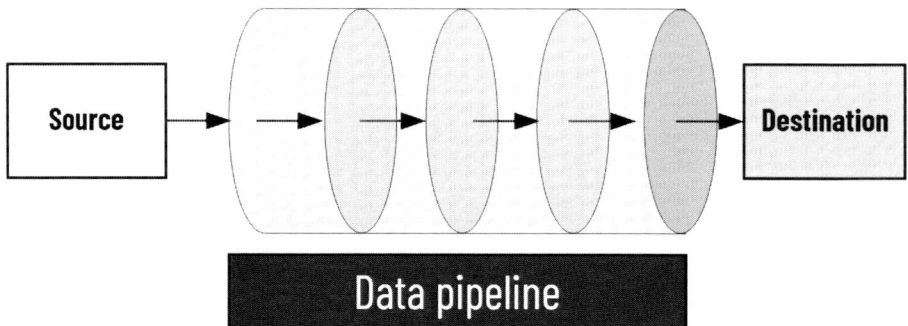

Figure 8.1 Data Pipeline

In business analytics, a data pipeline must be established for the collection and pre-processing of data for analytics purposes. Analytics architecture must support the flow and processing of data through every step of the analytics life cycle until it becomes available to an organization's decision-makers and embedded in the organization's business processes, as shown in Figure 8.2.

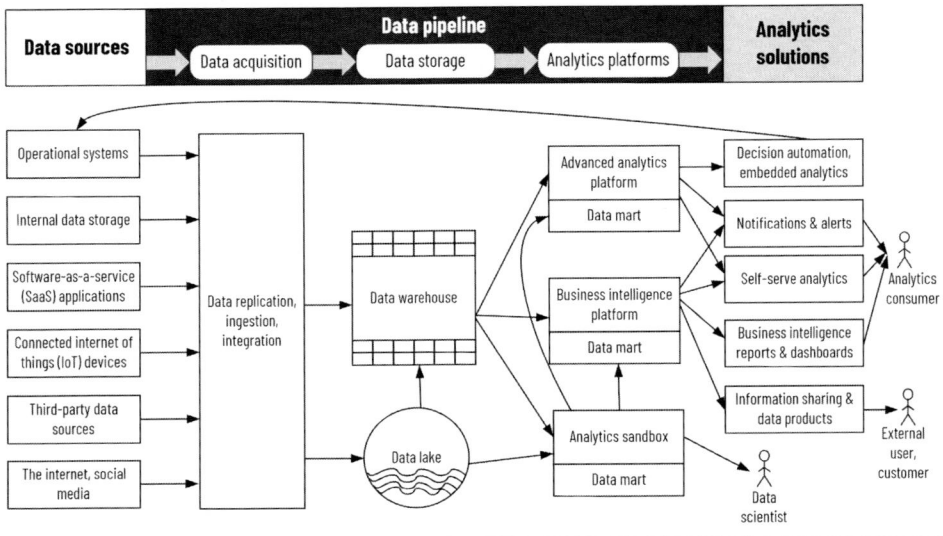

Figure 8.2 Analytics Architecture Components and Flows

Table 8.1 The Purpose of the Analytics Architecture Components

Component	Purpose
Data sources	Internal and external parties, systems, devices, and solutions that generate data to be used for analytical purposes
Data acquisition	Tools and solutions used for replication, ingestion, preparation, and integration of data
Data storage	Analytical systems intended for storing historical data for analytical purposes
Analytics platforms	Tools and applications for the design and development of analytics solutions
Analytics solutions	Developed and deployed solutions that deliver analytics insights to intended users

8.2 DATA ACQUISITION

A variety of methods may be utilized for data acquisition depending on the nature of data sources, as well as the volume, variety, and velocity of data.

Batch processing refers to the periodic extraction of data from the source and delivering it to the destination, with or without transformation. Variations include:

- **Replication:** copying data with minimal or no transformations

- **Extract-transform-load (ETL):** extracting data from the source, transforming it using pre-programmed methods, and loading it into the destination
- **Extract-load-transform (ELT):** extracting data from the source, loading it into the destination, and transforming it using pre-programmed methods at the destination

Batch processing is used more frequently for large, complex datasets, such as those extracted from hundreds of tables of an operational system. They are generally processed at pre-set intervals or schedules, such as every 15 minutes, every hour, once a day, or even, in extreme cases, once a month.

Most often we encounter batch processing as a method of data acquisition for traditional business intelligence purposes such as daily, weekly, and monthly operational or financial reporting.

Data streaming refers to the real-time ingestion of data from the source as soon as it is created.

In many cases, data streaming ingests and replicates data at the destination with minimal or no transformation as the ingestion occurs in real time and often deals with high-velocity data, such as data generated by connected devices, mobile phones, or social media.

However, in some use cases, highly advanced real-time analytics occurs as the data is streamed, for example, to enable security monitoring or support real-time fraud detection for payment card transactions.

Change data capture (CDC) refers to the selective replication of source data that applies only to changes, including newly created, updated, or deleted records.

This method allows the volume of data being transported or processed to be minimized and can occur in either batch or streaming mode. This method is the opposite of full replication, which may be acceptable for small volumes of data but becomes prohibitive with high volumes.

One way to implement these data acquisition methods is through an **application programming interface (API)**—a coded routine (program) that allows computer systems to exchange data. APIs are developed to standardize data exchange between systems, in particular, when servicing a large volume or a variety of data requests. They are used frequently when acquiring data from external systems and third parties.

⚙ EXAMPLE

Many commercial-off-the-shelf (COTS) software products develop proprietary APIs to allow companies that purchase their products to build integrations between these products and their other systems. For example, a company may purchase a new marketing automation product and use its APIs to integrate it with their existing customer relationship management (CRM) solution. These APIs may be used to share contact information between the systems, create a new contact in the CRM when a new lead responds to a marketing email sent by the marketing automation system, or delete a contact.

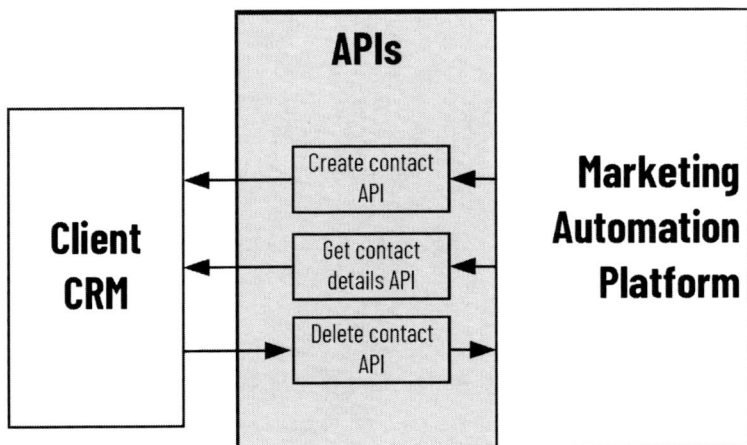

Figure 8.3 Exchanging Data via API

Many platforms also offer free (public) APIs so that any company or a developer may use it to connect and use the data from the platform. For example, Google offers a large selection of public APIs such as Google Maps API,[1] which allows acquiring of geospatial data and displaying of embedded maps in other systems and apps.

CASE STUDY

Data Acquisition for Customer Churn Analysis

YardExperts' analytics team is adding new sources of data to support the analysis.

Sales data is already loaded into the enterprise data warehouse daily via *ETL*. The team will conduct gap analysis to review whether all transaction attributes required for churn analysis are already available. If not, they will need to modify the existing ETL jobs to expand data extraction and transformation.

Customer surveys collected by canvassing neighbourhoods were processed by the administrative team and entered into a specially prepared spreadsheet. This data will be loaded into the data warehouse as a one-time *batch upload*.

Current service contract data will be loaded into the data warehouse from the contract registry daily via *replication*. The volume of data is small, and tracing the most recent changes is difficult due to the number of steps involved in contract negotiations. The team has determined that the replication approach would be the simplest to use, and so far, it has not created any issues.

Service history is tracked in a new software as a service (SaaS) tool that the company started using last year. To extract data from this system, the team must use *partner API* provided by the SaaS platform. The APIs utilized for this purpose use the *CDC* method to receive the data about new tickets and every service ticket update. This will be a real-time integration as the YardExperts team would like to start utilizing this information for another purpose: to prioritize customer service calls.

As for customer reviews and social media comments, this is high-velocity data that must be consumed in data streaming mode from each social media platform utilizing their *APIs*.

8.3 DATA STORAGE

Enterprise data collected from the sources discussed in Section 2.4 must be stored somewhere to make it accessible for analytical use. This section will introduce different types of analytical data storage and their features, advantages, and challenges.

Different approaches to analytical data storage are offered by a variety of modern technologies and analytic architecture configurations.

A **data warehouse (DW)** is a centralized data repository for storing consolidated data from multiple sources. This data storage solution, typically a relational database for storing structured data, has been around since the 1980s[2] and is still central to the analytics architecture of many large enterprises. The main concept of a data warehouse as it was originally conceived was for it to be a "single source of truth," or a consolidated database containing the historical records for all key data of the enterprise. Data warehouses have come to be known as centralized data warehouses (CDWs) or **enterprise data warehouses (EDWs)**.

Table 8.2 Data Warehouse Characteristics

Characteristic	Description
Integrated	Stores data gathered and made consistent from one or more source systems
Separated	Separated from operational (transactional) systems
Subject-oriented	Organized by data subject rather than by application
Enterprise scope	Sources data across the whole enterprise
Time-variant	Stores data captured at a moment in time; preserves timestamps to capture how attributes change over time
Non-volatile	Data is non-modifiable; once it is stored, it becomes read-only to serve as a historical record

A **federated data warehouse** is a variation of an EDW where multiple data warehouses conforming to the same data model are separated physically:

- For technical or performance reasons, e.g., a geographically distributed set of data warehouses
- For compliances reasons, e.g., due to legislative data protection requirements

A perfect DW would have all the data needed to support any type of business intelligence and cross-functional reporting of the organization clean, well organized, and integrated. The EDW of any large organization requires a complex data model that covers various lines of business, daily transactions, and activities of all departments.

To build an integrated data warehouse, data from a multitude of data sources, possibly built or purchased at different times for different purposes, needs to be consolidated. With this ambitious goal and an ever-increasing number of business applications used by organizations, the complexity of building data warehouses presents a major challenge and often results in unmet expectations.

Table 8.3 Data Warehouse Challenges

Challenge	Description
Development cost and complexity	Building a data warehouse that integrates data from many (possibly hundreds) applications requires complex data modelling, numerous data processing programs, and significant resources and budgets to complete
Partial completion	Due to high costs and long timelines, many data warehouses never achieve the desired scope, instead containing only a fraction of data from selected applications; this incompleteness makes them less useful and encourages the creation of independent data marts
Obsoleteness	Due to the complexity of data models and the difficulty of making changes to large systems, data warehouses may not reflect the latest changes in operational systems, thus making the data less useful or obsolete; this may be exacerbated when the original developers leave the organization and take their expertise with them, making subsequent changes more challenging
Cost of storage vs. utilization	The cost of storage and maintenance of large volumes of data may not be justified due to the low utilization of data
Not suited for unstructured data	Traditional data warehousing technologies are designed for storing structured data in relational databases and cannot support semi-structured and unstructured data without significant pre-processing effort to structure it; in addition, most companies do not wish to invest too much into pre-processing big data without clear use cases and with uncertain payback
Lacking real-time analytics capabilities	Pre-processing, integrating, and loading data into a data warehouse requires time, and these steps are frequently done through batch processing, thus creating barriers for real-time analytics

One of the proposed answers to a data warehouse challenge is a data mart—a scaled-down version of a data warehouse.

A **data mart** is an analytical data repository built specifically to serve a particular business unit or line of business. Data marts typically have a smaller scope and more manageable data model than most enterprise DWs and can be built through small or medium-sized projects.

While both data warehouses and data marts can be built using similar technologies such as relational databases storing structured data, they will have several key differences, which are outlined in Table 8.4.

Table 8.4 Data Warehouse versus Data Mart

Parameter	Data Warehouse	Data Mart
Scope	Data about the whole enterprise	Data about a specific area (by business process or department)
Objective	Provides an integrated environment with a full picture of the enterprise; may be used for many different purposes	Provides information for a specific purpose or a project
Sources	Multiple source systems	One or a small number of sources
Size	Very large; from 100 GB to many TB	Smaller than DW, usually below 100 GB
Data model and design	Complex; may include thousands of tables	Relatively simple; can be less than 100 tables
Implementation	Long and risky; can take several years	Faster and less risky; can be built in a few months
Historical data	Time-variant, historical repository	May not include full history, only what's required for the purpose it was built for
Granularity	Details stored to create historical records	May be consolidated for specific purposes, discarding some detail
Cost	Very expensive	More affordable

Data warehouses and data marts are not mutually exclusive analytical storage solutions. They may co-exist in various configurations as parts of an organization's analytics architecture.

A **dependent data mart** receives data from an EDW, thus serving as a subset of an integrated data warehouse for use by a specific business group. Figure 8.1 shows an example of dependent data marts feeding from a central hub—that is, a data warehouse. This pattern is also called **hub-and-spoke**, where a central hub for data storage such as EDW distributes data for further analytical purposes.

An **independent data mart** pulls data directly from source systems, rather than being dependent on a centralized hub. As shown in Figure 8.4, independent data marts can be introduced as analytical data storage on a smaller scale, receiving data from one or a small number of operational systems directly. As these data marts are not reliant on a hub of integrated data, they sometimes get developed using different and, in extreme cases, incompatible data models and rules.

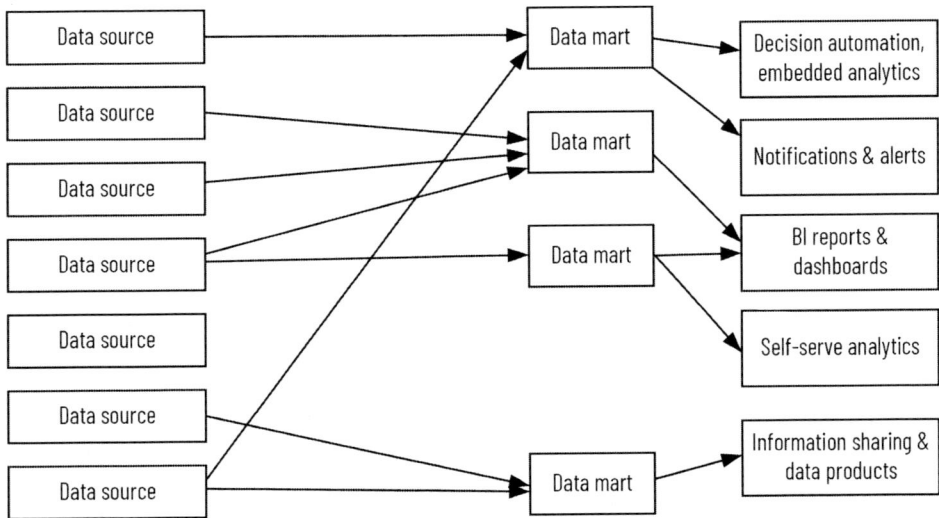

Figure 8.4 Independent Data Mart Pattern

While independent data marts provide an alternative to the more resource-intensive and lengthy undertaking of building an EDW, this solution comes with drawbacks.

Table 8.5 Independent Data Mart Challenges

Challenge	Description
Redundant data	Copies of the same enterprise data are stored in multiple data marts
Inconsistent data	Consistency of data and metrics across different solutions is not enforced, resulting in conflicting information and having multiple "versions of the truth"
Redundant processing	Different data preparation processes get developed for the same groups of data for each data mart, resulting in wasted resources and a lack of reusability
Lack of scalability	Changes in data sources require changes in multiple data marts and data pre-processing, creating a larger impact from each source system change, greater divergence of data, and a higher likelihood of overlooking required changes

In most cases, data warehouses and data marts receive data through batch processing and, as a result, don't support real-time analytics. Other solutions emerged in response to the timeliness challenge of a data warehouse.

An **operational data store (ODS)** pulls data directly from source systems in real time, or as close as possible to real time, to support business processes and enable operational reporting. This solution is built specifically to address operational reporting needs close to real time by capturing snapshots of current operational data for simple and fast analysis.

An ODS contains only current data for a limited period, such as from several minutes to a few days, to feed operational reports. The data is regularly replaced with new,

Table 8.6 ODS Characteristics

Characteristic	Description
One location	All the data is loaded into one location for ease of access
Separated	Separated from operational (source) systems
Minimum integration	Data loaded without extensive data integration or transformation—"as is"
Simplicity	Designed to support simple queries from one application or a small number of applications
Close to real time	Data is replicated as soon as it's created to enable close to real-time analytics and reports
Current data	Contains current data for a defined short period; not intended as historic data storage

refreshed snapshots. An ODS may also serve as a staging area for the data warehouse, with data continuing to flow through the pipeline to a data warehouse for further processing, integration, and long-term storage.

As a result of a variety of data warehousing, operational reporting, and analytics initiatives, a company's analytics architecture may look very different from the diagram presented in Figure 8.2. It may resemble a variation on the layout depicted in Figure 8.5. Such configurations are sometimes referred to as **accidental architectures**—collections of solutions developed and connected without following a well-thought-through plan for the overall enterprise architecture and streamlined data integration.

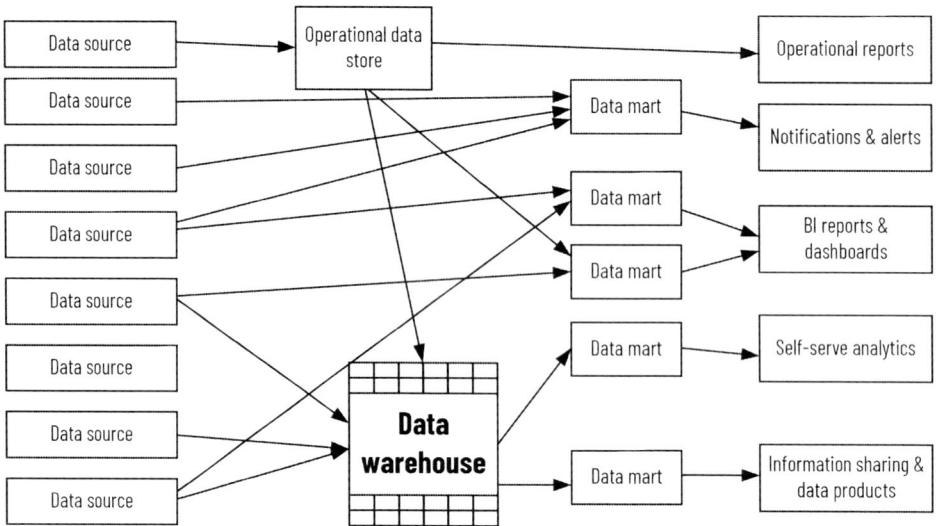

Figure 8.5 An Example of Accidental Data Architecture

Data warehouses, data marts, and ODSs are all solutions for storing structured data. Different solutions are required for storing unstructured and semi-structured data.

NoSQL databases are used for managing non-relational data. The term *NoSQL* means "not only SQL" and encompasses semi-structured and unstructured data—for example, data that does not conform to the tabular rows-and-columns format. Some examples of NoSQL databases are document-based databases, key-value stores, wide column-oriented databases, and graph databases.

A **data lake** is a repository for holding vast amounts of raw data in its native format without pre-processing.

Data lakes are highly flexible in allowing storage of any type of data: structured, semi-structured, and unstructured. Data received from a variety of sources can be stored as is, without integration or standardization, until it's needed. At that point, data required for a defined purpose is extracted and processed according to the type of data and intended usage.

For example, if data is intended to be used for machine learning, it should be structured and reduced as part of feature engineering. If it will be used for business intelligence purposes, it should be structured and standardized for storage in the data warehouse or data marts feeding the respective analytics platform.

If an organization is unsure of how to use its data, data lakes make for suitable solutions, as they allow data storage for future analysis with minimal upfront costs. The data can be stored in a data lake until the organization has resources, expertise, and a clear business case for further analysis.

Figures 8.6 and 8.7 show a simplified data warehouse and data lake pattern, respectively, to highlight the main differences between the two.

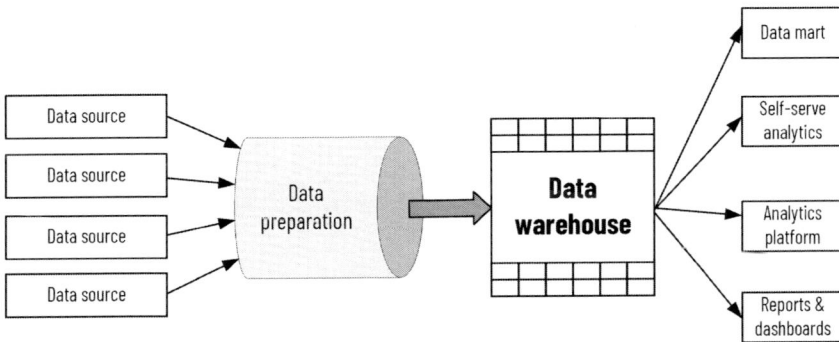

Figure 8.6 Data Warehouse Pattern

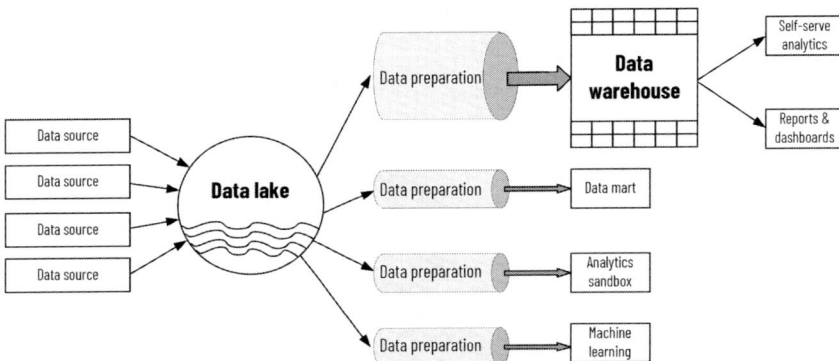

Figure 8.7 Data Lake Pattern

Naturally, whenever there are alternative solutions with pros and cons, hybrid solutions arise with the intention of combining the best of both worlds. Thus, the **data lakehouse** pattern was born, a data management platform that combines the advantages of a data lake with data warehouse features. Data lakehouse architecture typically consists of a unified platform with three layers:

- The storage layer, where structured, semi-structured, and unstructured data is stored in a data lake
- The metadata and governance layer, which has warehouse-like capabilities that facilitate consistency and adherence to schemas, data governance, and optimization
- The data access layer, which supports a variety of application programming interfaces (APIs) for accessing subsets of data

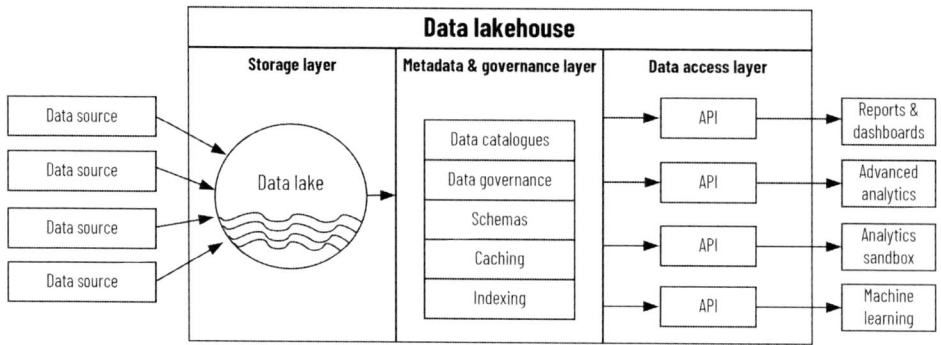

Figure 8.8 Data Lakehouse Pattern

The main characteristics of these data storage architecture patterns are summarized in Table 8.7.

Table 8.7 Data Warehouse versus Data Lake versus Data Lakehouse

Characteristic	Data warehouse	Data lake	Data lakehouse
Types of data	Structured	Structured, semi-structured, and unstructured	Structured, semi-structured, and unstructured
Data structure	Processed, standardized, follows a common schema	Raw, any variety of native formats	Raw, any variety of native formats, with metadata captured
Interconnectedness of data	Connected and cross-referenced through keys and relationships	Datasets are not connected with each other, and data is not cross-referenced across datasets	Some interconnectedness facilitated by the metadata layer; less rigid and restrictive than in a data warehouse

Table 8.7 Data Warehouse versus Data Lake versus Data Lakehouse
(*continued*)

Characteristic	Data warehouse	Data lake	Data lakehouse
Data preparation	Data must be processed and prepared before storing in a data warehouse; large upfront effort	Stored unprocessed; preparation and structuring done as part of analysis for specific purpose and subset of data	Minimal upfront processing; data preparation and extraction for analytics facilitated and standardized with the metadata layer
Purpose of data	Currently in use	Not yet determined	Combines storing actively used data with storage for future use
Data accessibility	Complex; relies on pre-processing and a common schema	Easy to access in raw format; more processing required based on need	High accessibility supported by data access layer APIs
Adding new data sources	Difficult, costly, time-consuming	Easier and cheaper	Easier and cheaper than DW, with some metadata management
Complexity, technical expertise	Technologies are well established; expertise easier to obtain; some organizations have in-house expertise	Technologies are more recent, somewhat established; more expertise required when the need for extraction and analysis arises	Relatively new and still emerging technology; lack of experts; complex; requires good data governance

Apart from a variety of data storage patterns to choose from, organizations can also choose to deploy and maintain their analytical storage either:

- **On premise**, where the solutions are deployed on the infrastructure owned by the company and hosted at the company's locations, or
- **On cloud**, where the organization's data is stored on servers managed by a third party and accessed via the internet

Both hosting approaches have advantages and disadvantages based on offered levels of control, security, cost, scalability, performance, and disaster recovery.

Keep in mind that different analytical architectures are not always the outcome of purposeful planning. They often emerge as the result of many projects led by different groups, or as a consequence of mergers and acquisitions of companies, each of which have their own analytical storage solutions.

Revamping a large organization's application architecture is almost always a risky, expensive endeavour. Business value is not always apparent; it may require significant upfront investments. As a result, companies tend to maintain accidental architectures, only making small, incremental changes when their resources permit it. Any professional working in an analytics field must be ready to deal with a variety of architectures and data pipelines, and to design data acquisition and preparation solutions under imperfect conditions.

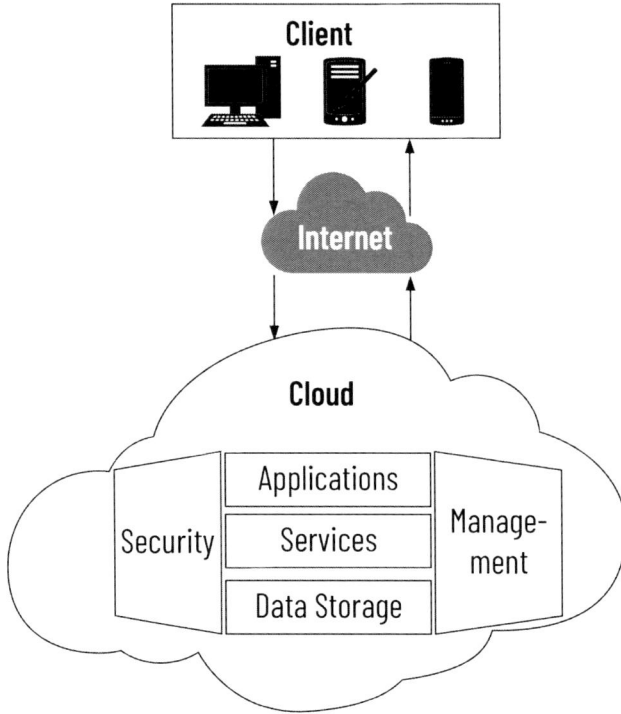

Figure 8.9 A Simplified Cloud Computing Architecture

8.4 ANALYTICS PLATFORMS AND SOLUTIONS

An analytics platform is an ecosystem of solutions for supporting the analytics life cycle. These platforms allow enterprises to design, develop, test, and deploy business analytics solutions, which will be discussed in greater detail in the next chapter.

There are many powerful analytics platforms on the market (see Appendix B), and some enterprises will choose to deploy more than one. These decisions will depend on the size of the company, the scope of its analytics needs, and its overall architecture. Some analytics platforms may be chosen for the performance of selected analytical tasks—for example, Google Analytics for web analytics, SAS or SSPS for statistical analysis, or Tableau for business intelligence (BI) dashboards and visualization. Other platforms provide a broad range of analytical capabilities suitable for users with different levels of expertise. Best-in-class analytics platforms usually include a large range of features, such as:

- Data exploration, profiling, and statistical analysis tools
- Working environments for exploring and experimenting with data and algorithms (called **sandboxes**)
- Tools for data preparation, cleaning, and transformation
- Data modelling capabilities
- Data marts

- Tools for designing business intelligence solutions such as reports, dashboards, and visualizations
- Collaboration and configuration management for versioning and sharing programs
- Predictive modelling and machine learning capabilities
- Security features
- Support for data governance and documentation

Besides using governed data and integrating analytics platforms into the enterprise data pipeline, some companies develop **data shadow systems**: spreadsheets and databases that are created and used by individual business groups and are not integrated into the enterprise analytics architecture. They may become an individual department's tool for collecting and exploring data and creating business intelligence solutions for departmental needs, whether instead of or in addition to enterprise solutions. Data shadow systems can also be called *spreadmarts*, as they are often created in spreadsheet applications such as Microsoft Excel.

Analytics platforms are used to develop analytics solutions—the final deliverables created for business users looking for analytics insights. These deliverables can come in many forms, from daily reports emailed to the company's managers, to executive dashboards, real-time analytics, or predictive models embedded in the business process. We will explore this topic in detail in the next chapter.

8.5 LATENCY

Up until now we have only asked ourselves what questions analytics should answer, where to get the necessary data, and how to process it. It's time to ask *when*. When do we need answers to analytics questions? Generally speaking, for insightful answers to be useful, we need them *before* making any decisions based on the information under consideration. If getting these answers takes too long, insight becomes hindsight.

This brings us to the concept of latency. In computing, **latency** means a delay—the time it takes for a message or a packet of information to move from one point to another—but in business analytics, it is the delay between when data is captured and when action is taken based on analysis of said data.

How long does it take to produce an analytics insight and act upon it? This will depend on several types of latency contributing to the overall reaction time from the event to the action. The total reaction time is sometimes called *reaction latency* or *business latency*.

The overall business latency depends on:

- Analytics architecture and the data pipeline design
- Data quality and required data preparation
- Type of analytics used (descriptive, diagnostic, predictive, or prescriptive)
- Analytics maturity of the organization

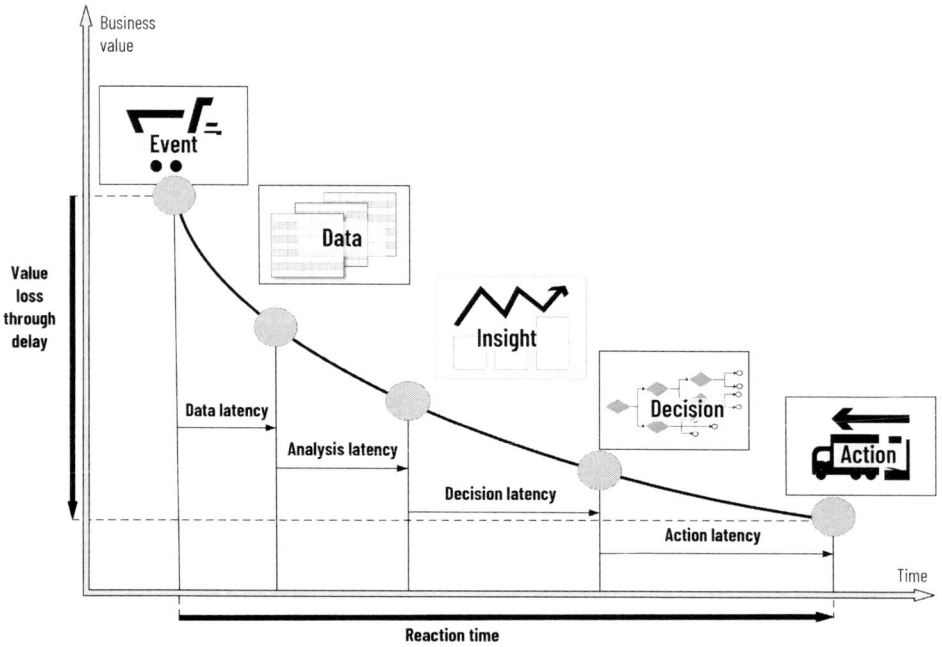

Figure 8.10 The Impact of Latency on Value

Table 8.8 Types of Latency in Analytics

Type of latency	Description
Data latency (capture latency)	The time it takes to collect and store the data
Analysis latency	The time it takes to analyze the data and generate an insight
Decision latency	The time it takes to make a decision using the insight
Action latency	The time it takes to implement a decision into action

If an organization mostly relies on descriptive and diagnostic analytics, overall latency will depend on how the decision-makers use analytical insights, how they make decisions, and how quickly these are implemented.

Predictive analytics can help an organization prepare for different predicted possibilities, allowing decision-makers to respond to different courses of events with a minimum delay.

Prescriptive analytics allows the organization to further reduce the decision latency by providing decision recommendations and eliminate the latency by implementing process automation.

> **CASE STUDY**
>
> ### Reducing Latency
>
> YardExperts uses weather prediction to plan snow removal operations. This allows the field teams to deploy the snow removal fleet—fuelled, checked, and ready to go—before a major snowfall hits the area.
>
> To avoid running out of stock and losing sales, the new prescriptive model automatically creates replenishment orders based on when each product is likely to run out and the expected delivery timelines.

When working on analytics solutions, we must understand what levels of latency are acceptable. Real-time analytics may not be feasible and, even when it is feasible, will likely be more expensive. Depending on use cases, different levels of latency will be deemed acceptable.

Table 8.9 Acceptable Latency Levels for Different Use Cases

Latency level	Decision-making approach	Examples
Real time: information is captured and analyzed and insights presented or actioned upon immediately	Decision automation, mission critical	• Banking and payments (fraud monitoring) • Telecommunication • Autonomous vehicles
Near real time: information is captured and analyzed at set intervals rather than instantaneously, aiming to be as close to real time as needed ("good enough" for business needs)	Decision automation (not mission critical), decision augmentation	• Operational reporting • Social media monitoring for hate speech • Email and SMS delivery and spam filtering
Batch: information is captured and analyzed in batches at pre-defined times, e.g., daily or every few hours; usually requires significant time to process and reach the destination	Decision support, descriptive and diagnostic analytics	• Month-end management reporting • Competitive trends analysis • Payroll and billing

> **EXAMPLE**
>
> ### Acceptable Latency
>
> When a large publicly traded company is preparing its quarterly results for external reporting, latency will be measured in days, as this reporting requires information from many sources, extensive reconciliation, and approvals. There is too much risk in getting

it wrong, as it may affect the company's share price and reputation. Most companies publish their quarterly results within a few weeks after quarter-end.

On the other hand, high-frequency trading relies on ultra-low latency access to market data to take advantage of mispricing and price discrepancies. To achieve ultra-low latency, high-frequency traders rely on stock exchange co-location, such as at the Nasdaq's data centre in Carteret, New Jersey.[3]

8.6 CHAPTER SUMMARY

Key Points to Remember

- A robust analytics architecture is fundamental to the success of analytics in any enterprise.
- Different data sources will require different methods and approaches to data extraction and pre-processing.
- To support embedded analytics, analytics solutions may need to be integrated into operational systems of the enterprise.
- Different types of analytical storage may co-exist, serving different purposes or supporting different analytical functions.
- Analytics professionals must be ready to deal with a variety of architectures and data pipelines, as well as to design solutions under imperfect conditions.
- Advanced analytics—in particular, big data analytics—requires suitable technologies beyond traditional data warehousing. Unstructured data cannot be treated as structured.
- When working on analytics solutions, we must understand what levels of latency are acceptable. Real time is expensive.

Key Terms

Accidental architecture: a collection of solutions developed and connected without following a well-thought-through plan for the overall enterprise architecture and streamlined data integration.

Action latency: the time it takes to implement a decision into action.

Analysis latency: the time it takes to analyze the data and generate an insight.

Analytics architecture: design and structure of systems and tools used by an organization to store and analyze data.

Application programming interface (API): a coded routine (program) that allows computer systems to exchange data.

Batch processing: periodic extraction of data from the source and delivering it to the destination, with or without transformation.

Change data capture (CDC): a selective replication of source data that applies only to changes, including newly created, updated, or deleted records.

Data lake: a repository for holding vast amounts of raw data in its native format without pre-processing.

Data lakehouse: a data management platform that combines data lake and data warehouse capabilities.

Data latency (capture latency): the time it takes to collect and store the data.

Data mart: an analytical data repository built specifically to serve a particular business unit or line of business.

Data pipeline: a sequence of steps for collecting, transforming, and moving data from various sources to the intended destination.

Data shadow system (spreadmart): spreadsheets and databases created and used by individual business groups that are not integrated into the enterprise analytics architecture.

Data streaming: real-time ingestion of data from the source as soon as it is created.

Data warehouse (DW) (enterprise data warehouse [EDW]): a centralized data repository for storing consolidated data from multiple sources.

Decision latency: The time it takes to make a decision using an insight.

Dependent data mart: a data mart that receives data from a central hub or EDW.

Extract-load-transform (ELT): the process of extracting data from the source, loading it into the destination, and transforming it using pre-programmed methods at the destination.

Extract-transform-load (ETL): the process of extracting data from the source, transforming it using pre-programmed methods, and loading it into the destination.

Federated data warehouse: a variation of an EDW where multiple data warehouses conforming to the same data model are separated physically.

Hub-and-spoke: an architecture pattern where a central hub for data storage, such as an EDW, distributes data for further analytical purposes.

Independent data mart: a data mart that pulls data directly from source systems rather than being dependent on a central hub.

Latency: in business analytics, a delay between when data is captured and when action is taken based on the analysis of this data.

NoSQL ("not only SQL") database: a database used for managing non-relational data.

On cloud: a method of hosting an organization's data and software on servers managed by a third party and accessed via the internet.

On premise: a method of hosting an organization's data and software on the infrastructure owned by the company and hosted at the company's locations.

Operational data store (ODS): a data repository that pulls data directly from source systems as close to real time as possible to enable operational reporting.

Replication: copying data with minimal or no transformations.

Sandbox: a working environment for exploring and experimenting with data and algorithms.

Questions for Critical Thought

1. Why would it take a long time to build a data warehouse?
2. What types of data can be stored in a data warehouse?
3. What is a trade-off of using independent data marts instead of hub-and-spoke architecture?
4. How might a data pipeline be impacted if a new source system must be added?
5. What are the differences between a data warehouse and an ODS?
6. What factors may impact the latency of analytics-based decisions?
7. When is real-time analytics necessary?

Test Your Knowledge

1. What statement best represents the function of a data warehouse?
   a. It stores all incoming data until the company decides how to use it.
   b. It stores the data from a specific application for operational reporting close to real time.
   c. It stores integrated data from accounting applications for financial reporting.
   d. It stores integrated data from the main enterprise applications to support multiple analytics solutions.

2. What description best describes a data mart?
   a. It is smaller and easier to build than a data warehouse.
   b. It is more expensive and complex than a data warehouse.
   c. It combines features of a data warehouse and a data lake.
   d. It is designed for storing unstructured data.

3. What statement is the most applicable to a data lake?
   a. It stores structured data in a rigid pre-defined format.
   b. It is designed to store unstructured data and is not suitable for structured data.
   c. It can store any type of structured, semi-structured, and unstructured data.
   d. It requires a metadata layer to provide data warehouse–like functionality.

4. When the weather station captures current wind speed, it takes about two seconds to record each measurement for transmission.
   What type of latency is described?
   a. Data latency
   b. Analysis latency
   c. Decision latency
   d. Action latency

5. When a sales manager requests a new ad hoc analysis of reasons for customer churn on the last month's data, it takes the data analyst four days to complete the diagnostics and pinpoint three contributing reasons for the churn increase.

    What type of latency is described?

    a. Data latency
    b. Analysis latency
    c. Decision latency
    d. Action latency

Recommended Reading

Sherman, R. (2015). *Business Intelligence Guidebook: From Data Integration to Analytics.* Morgan Kaufmann (Elsevier).

Notes

1. Google. (n.d.). *Google Maps Platform.* Retrieved June 21, 2024, from https://mapsplatform .google.com/maps-products/.
2. Hayes, F. (2002, April 15). *The Story So Far.* Computer World. Retrieved January 3, 2024, from web.archive.org/web/20080708182105/http://www.computerworld.com/databasetopics/data/ story/0%2C10801%2C70102%2C00.html.
3. Nasdaq. (n.d.). *Why More Trading Firms Are Considering Co-Location with Nasdaq.* Retrieved June 21, 2024, from https://www.nasdaq.com/articles/why-more-trading-firms-are -considering-co-location-with-nasdaq.

Chapter 9

Business Analytics Solutions

By this point, you have an understanding of different types of analytics used to answer analytics questions and solve business problems.

How does this happen in practice? How will analytics questions get answered? This requires developing, implementing, and using analytics solutions.

A **business analytics solution** is a solution intended to provide answers to analytics questions required to make business decisions.

In this chapter, you will learn about:

- Styles of analytics solutions
- Types of users (personas) these solutions are intended for
- Features and examples of analytics solutions

9.1 BUSINESS ANALYTICS PERSONAS

When we design any solution or product, we must keep in mind the intended user—who will be using it and for what purpose. The same applies to analytics solutions. We will refer to the users of analytics solutions as *business analytics personas*.

A **business analytics persona** is a user of analytics solutions with a specific level of expertise and requirements for business analytics.

We will categorize these personas along two dimensions: type of use and skill level.

By type of use, analytics personas can be divided into two groups:

- Operational: workers who require analytics to do their job, whether as operational staff or at the managerial and executive level. To these workers, analytics are the *tools* to help them do their jobs, manage the day-to-day responsibilities of their department, or make business decisions.
- Analytical: workers who are responsible for creating analytics as part of their job, i.e., in service of operational and executive staff. For these workers, analytics solutions are a *product* they create for others.

These personas will have different skill levels.

Basic users do not have time and/or desire to access advanced analytics features. They prefer:

- Simple-to-use solutions with easy-to-understand features and interfaces
- Predictable solutions—pre-defined design and parameters
- Minimum choices to get what they need quickly
- Solutions that reduce the likelihood of mistakes through built-in constraints and limits

Intermediate users have the knowledge and skills to explore available data in different ways to look for new insights. They require:

- More choices for accessing, grouping, aggregating, and disaggregating data
- Flexible solutions that allow ad hoc analysis or customization of existing solutions
- The ability to analyze the data across dimensions, as well as to add and change dimensions and measures
- Access to multiple data sources and the ability to bring in new data sources on demand for the enrichment of datasets and exploring various hypotheses

Advanced data and analytics professionals have the skills to apply advanced data wrangling and statistical and predictive modelling methods. They require:

- Access to raw data for advanced exploration, discovery and visualization
- The ability to manipulate and transform data in different formats
- Access to advanced data mining, statistical analysis, and machine learning tools

Using these two dimensions—type of use and skill level—we define the following analytics personas.

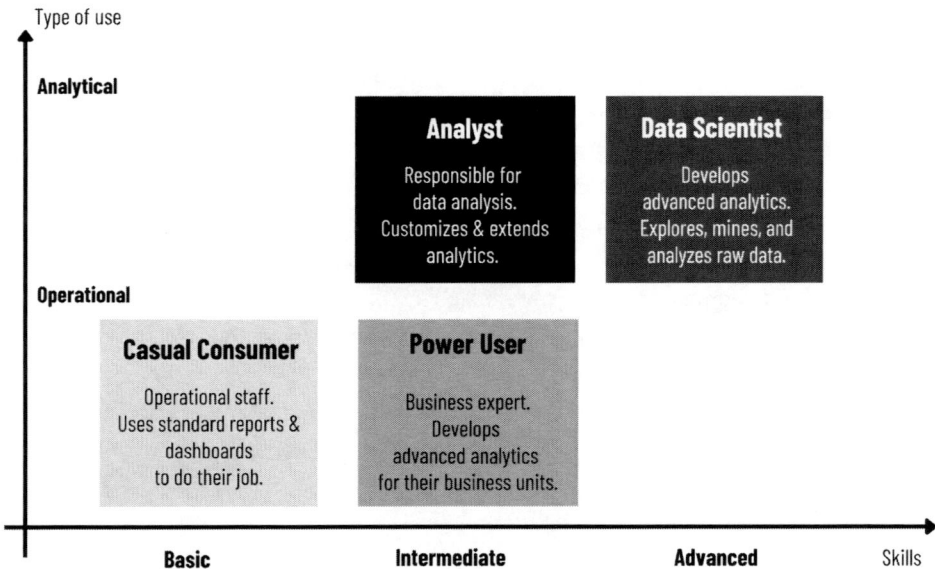

Figure 9.1 Business Analytics Personas

- **Casual consumers:** Operational and managerial staff who use standard reports and dashboards to get the information needed to perform their jobs. Casual consumers may range from individual contributors to the executive management level.
- **Analysts:** Staff specializing in exploring and analyzing data. They use analytical systems for ad hoc data analysis and to enhance, modify, and customize existing analytics solutions.
- **Power users:** Departmental experts in business intelligence; sophisticated users who utilize their business and data analysis knowledge to provide custom analytics to their departments. Power users are often also the developers of data shadow systems.
- **Data scientists:** Professionals with specialized knowledge to handle, explore, and mine raw data of varied nature and complexity, and to gain insights from big data. They design and train machine learning models and interpret findings for business stakeholders.

In this matrix, there is neither a persona that possesses only basic skills in an analytical job, nor one with operational focus and advanced analytics skills comparable to a data scientist. This would be quite a mismatch between the job and the worker's capability.

CASE STUDY

Analytics Personas at YardExperts

Gurpreet manages a customer service department. It is a part of her job to monitor and ensure that all customer calls are answered on time, plan required staffing levels, and create shift schedules.

Gurpreet needs a real-time dashboard that shows her important indicators such as the average wait time, average call time, number of service representatives available to take the next call, and their total call time per shift.

Gurpreet is a *casual consumer*: she is busy with her work and needs to monitor the same indicators daily and hourly without effort. If she needs to investigate certain anomalies in call centre activities, she will ask a data analyst to do some digging.

Nick is a customer service analyst working for the customer service support team. His job is to help all customer service department heads across the region with their analysis needs.

This time, he is asked to investigate a recent bottleneck in Gurpreet's department. Last Monday, they received a much higher than average number of calls and were unable to respond to all the calls on time. Some callers abandoned their place in the queue, and several complaints were made.

Nick will query multiple data sources for detailed information about the calls, the callers, their recent purchases, and the history of complaints, and will try to find some correlations. Nick will be doing a diagnostics analysis for his business customer, Gurpreet. Nick is an *analyst*.

Makena is the deputy head of the pricing department. Her job is to review and adjust pricing on products and service bundles. There are many factors to consider: how competitors change their prices, rising costs, customers' price sensitivity, and recent sales performance.

Makena designed some sophisticated calculations and scenario models in a spreadsheet application as she is quite proficient in it. She asked about developing a pricing dashboard, but her request never seems to get enough priority. Her requirements are quite complex and always changing, and besides, she would be the only user of this dashboard, so it's hard to justify the cost of development.

As a result, Makena has built her own "data shadow system" with several local databases where she stores competitive data purchased from another company and additional market data that she collects and enters herself. Everyone in pricing came to rely on Makena's models for pricing decisions. Makena is a *power user*.

Eva is spending a lot of time exploring the company's sentiment data, in particular, customer comments and reviews about the company's products. This data is collected from a wide range of social media and directed to the enterprise data lake. Eva is looking for ways to detect changes in customer sentiment that may be related to new product features, pricing changes, or logistics challenges.

Currently, she is exploring different types of visualizations to detect trends and direction of changes in sentiment for different types of products, correlating it with events that might have an impact on customer satisfaction. Eva is a *data scientist*.

As analytics solutions are discussed in this chapter, consider the needs of different personas as they will define the required features and flexibility of the solutions. Tables 9.1 and 9.2 highlight the distinctions between the personas that may get confused.

Table 9.1 Analyst versus Power User

Analyst	Power User
Gets requirements from business experts; may need expert support for understanding business specifics	Is an expert in a specific business function; has extensive domain knowledge
Creates on-demand analytics for use by business consumers	Creates analytics and business intelligence for their own use and for their business departments
Uses analytical tools to access, explore, and manipulate existing enterprise data	Sources and collects data for departmental use; may develop their own data shadow systems

Table 9.2 Analyst versus Data Scientist

Analyst	Data Scientist
Works with structured data	Works with all types of data including semi-structured and unstructured
Uses data that has already been organized and structured	Works with raw, unprocessed data; develops models for structuring data
Enhances and customizes existing analytics; builds new queries and reports relying on existing data models	Explores and mines data; builds new statistical and predictive models; develops machine learning algorithms; designs new analytics solutions

9.2 BUSINESS ANALYTICS STYLES AND FEATURES

There are many styles of analytics—ways of generating and presenting analytics to users. When we look at analytics solutions as a product, different features will be relevant depending on the type and goals of analytics.

A good product should have the features expected by the customers to make it useful, and it should not be overloaded with features they don't need, thus making it heavier, pricier, or more cumbersome to use and maintain. The description of styles and features of analytics in this section is platform-agnostic—that is, not tied to any particular analytics product on the market. Many market leaders in the field offer a comparable wide range of product features. See Appendix B for a summary.

The most common analytics styles can be grouped into four categories:

- Ready-to-consume
- Self-serve
- Advanced
- Embedded

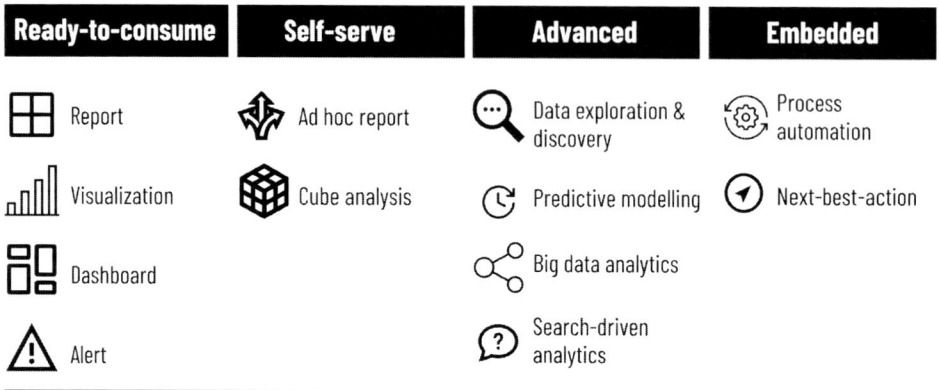

Ready-to-consume	Self-serve	Advanced	Embedded
Report	Ad hoc report	Data exploration & discovery	Process automation
Visualization	Cube analysis	Predictive modelling	Next-best-action
Dashboard		Big data analytics	
Alert		Search-driven analytics	

Figure 9.2 Business Analytics Styles

9.3 READY-TO-CONSUME ANALYTICS

Ready-to-consume analytics are reports, charts, tables, and visualizations generated from available data and arranged for viewing by business users based on requirements defined in advance. When business stakeholders use the term *business intelligence*, they usually mean and expect ready-to-consume analytics.

The main characteristics of these solutions are:

- They are consistent, predictable, and easy to understand.
- They are either available online on demand or generated and delivered on schedule (minimal effort required from the consumers' perspective to get the information).
- They require significant upfront work—data analysis, building of data pipelines, report design, and validation of prototypes with business stakeholders.

Reports are the most traditional way of presenting descriptive analytics. Reports have been used by humanity for millennia for purposes ranging from accounting and tax ledgers to population censuses and traders' inventories.

Reports are collections of information aggregated and presented in a pre-defined format, typically in tables, to make them easy to understand. They are intended and designed for recurring use, with groupings and summaries readily understood by the users. They summarize information using standard attributes and parameters.

A **reporting parameter** is a condition or dimension used to define the boundaries of the report or limit the data included in the report (report selection criteria). For example, a sales report may include parameters such as time period, region, and product category. The report consumer may then set parameters to limit the scope of the report to a certain combination of these dimensions, such as sales in the first quarter of the current year in the province of Ontario for all product categories.

While reports are a grid-like way of presenting information using text and numbers, there are many ways to present information visually. Visualizations such as charts, graphs, annotated maps, and infographics are widely used in ready-to-consume analytics. More sophisticated visualizations can utilize videos and animations. Refer to Section 5.5 for an overview of different types of visualizations.

Combining multiple visualizations can be beneficial for the user's understanding. It allows the consumer to compare and see the relationships and additional information visually without leafing through reports, clicking on links, and searching multiple pages on their digital device. Combining multiple analytics outputs on one page or screen is a distinct characteristic of dashboards and scorecards.

A **dashboard** is a combination of multiple analytics styles on a single panel or screen for the purpose of monitoring business performance.

Dashboards are usually designed to reflect current data (as close as possible to real time) and focus on specific areas of business. For example, they can be used for monitoring and managing operational activities in sales, order fulfillment, manufacturing, or customer service.

YardExperts' Quarterly Sales Report Example

This report has a standard format and two parameters: Region and Quarter. It requires daily or monthly sales revenue data as well as planned quarterly volumes for each category.

Quarterly Sales Report

Region   East   Generated: 01/15/2025

Quarter   Q3 2024 $, thousands

Category	July	August	September	Quarter	Actual/Plan
Retail					
Garden	42.1	54.2	35.8	132.1	87.0%
Home	87.1	76	56.7	219.8	102.0%
Retail total	129.2	130.2	92.5	351.9	95.8%
Snow removal					
First-year	0	0	0	0	NA
Recurring	0	0	0	0	NA
Snow removal total	0	0	0	0	NA
Landscaping					
First-year	123.4	98.1	165.9	387.4	104.0%
Recurring	432.9	306.2	769.5	1508.6	98.3%
Landscaping total	556.3	404.3	935.4	1896	99.4%
GRAND TOTAL	685.5	534.5	1027.9	2247.9	98.8%

Figure 9.3 Report—Case Study Example

All terms, labels, and metrics used in reports must be clearly defined, either in the data dictionary or in the report specification. There should be no room for ambiguity when creating standard reports—otherwise, they lose their value and may only create confusion.

Clearly defining business terms and metrics and sharing them across the organization is a best practice of data governance.

Dashboards typically include between four and a dozen panels in one view (page or screen), including charts, tables, and indicators. Just like other ready-to-consume analytics, they are designed around specific requirements and pre-defined parameters and formats.

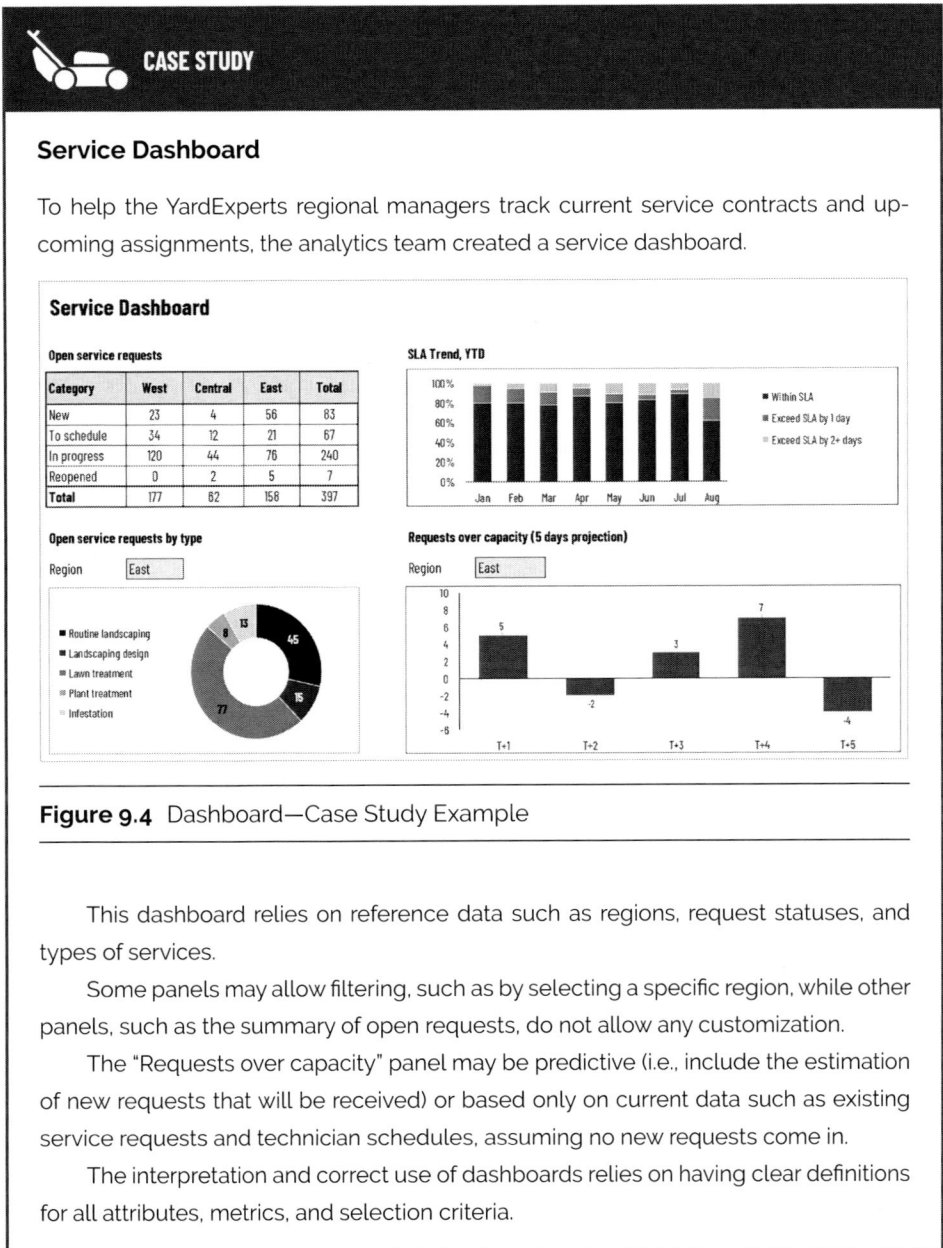

CASE STUDY

Service Dashboard

To help the YardExperts regional managers track current service contracts and up-coming assignments, the analytics team created a service dashboard.

Service Dashboard

Open service requests

Category	West	Central	East	Total
New	23	4	56	83
To schedule	34	12	21	67
In progress	120	44	76	240
Reopened	0	2	5	7
Total	177	62	158	397

Open service requests by type

Region: East

- Routine landscaping
- Landscaping design
- Lawn treatment
- Plant treatment
- Infestation

Requests over capacity (5 days projection)

Region: East

Figure 9.4 Dashboard—Case Study Example

This dashboard relies on reference data such as regions, request statuses, and types of services.

Some panels may allow filtering, such as by selecting a specific region, while other panels, such as the summary of open requests, do not allow any customization.

The "Requests over capacity" panel may be predictive (i.e., include the estimation of new requests that will be received) or based only on current data such as existing service requests and technician schedules, assuming no new requests come in.

The interpretation and correct use of dashboards relies on having clear definitions for all attributes, metrics, and selection criteria.

Modern business intelligence (BI) and analytics tools provide a variety of features to support interactive dashboards, such as:

- The ability to change parameters and filters (affecting the dashboard selection criteria)

- Drill-down (drill-in) features that enable viewing of more detailed information for a subset of data within the same dashboard
- Drill-through (drill-across) features that allow for viewing of different sets of information or indicators for a subset of data by taking the user to a different report or panel
- Drag-and-drop features that allow the users to select, drag, and drop certain data subsets, dimensions, and attributes to create new dashboards using a visual interface or move around the individual panels of a dashboard to create a custom view

A *scorecard* is a special type of dashboard. Scorecards are also designed to combine multiple analytics insights in one view. However, the purpose of a scorecard is different.

A **scorecard** is a visual snapshot of the organization's KPIs. Rather than monitoring operations and making day-to-day business decisions, scorecards are used to highlight company performance by tracking KPIs and comparing them to targets. You may encounter monthly, quarterly, or annual scorecards. The information in scorecards is usually static—it is accurate as of a certain date. How organizations use scorecards depends on their preferred performance measurement systems (refer to the Section 11.3 for an overview).

CASE STUDY

When an Alert Saves the Day

In the past two days, YardExperts' western region call centre received an unusually high number of urgent customer requests for mosquito treatment. Looking at the service dashboard would reveal that the number of available service teams for a particular week is lower than the number of requests. This means that the company will not be able to fulfill all customer commitments next week.

This is a situation that the business needs to avoid. But what if all operational managers are so busy that nobody has the time to check the dashboards? The vital insight about the projected lack of service teams may go unnoticed until it's too late to do anything about it.

This is a scenario when an alert would be a more effective analytics tool.

An **alert** is a notification sent to interested parties when specific criteria are met.

Analytics alerts are designed to be communicated automatically upon meeting certain criteria determined from data analysis. In the case study example, it could be generated when the planned workload for the upcoming week exceeds a certain threshold. This would allow the manager to either negotiate different service dates with some customers or search for part-time resources for help during that particularly busy week.

The criteria and thresholds for the alerts may be set up by the consumers (alert subscribers). For example, you may set up a minimum bank balance threshold in your banking app to receive a notification when your bank balance falls below a certain amount.

In other situations, alert criteria are standardized. For example, the government of Canada establishes specific threshold criteria for issuing weather alerts such as extreme cold warnings. These criteria depend on the location; in south-central and southwestern Ontario, the alert is issued when the temperature or wind chill is expected to reach –30 °C for at least two hours.[1]

> **📌 IMPORTANT**
>
> Requirements and thresholds for alerts must be sensible and validated by experts. Alert feature should be reserved for situations when an alert is warranted. Nothing decreases the effectiveness of alerts as quickly as too many false positives.
>
> A **false positive** is a test result that incorrectly indicates that a particular condition was satisfied.
>
> A **false negative** is a test result that incorrectly indicates that a particular condition was not satisfied.

9.4 SELF-SERVE ANALYTICS

Self-serve analytics refers to solutions that allow users to access, query, and analyze prepared data for creating new business intelligence and diagnostic insights. Self-serve options should support ad hoc analysis and allow for investigation into exceptions and unexpected occurrences or responses to new analytics questions.

Diagnostics is not as straightforward as following a set of instructions. It requires experimenting, testing different hypotheses, using statistical analysis, and comparing the influence of different factors. It is a trial-and-error process, as described in Section 6.1. This is where the flexibility offered by self-serve analytics is crucial. These solutions must enable users to:

- Choose datasets and attributes from available options
- Filter, subset, group, or segment data for further analysis
- Disaggregate data by multiple dimensions ("slicing and dicing")
- Apply aggregations and statistical analysis
- Create **pivots**—summary tables that group and aggregate values from a larger table across one or more dimensions
- Create custom visualizations

These are the features of **ad hoc analysis**: analysis performed to respond to new analytics questions. Ad hoc queries are utilized to select and extract data based on criteria specific to a new situation when the need arises. This is in contrast to pre-defined and recurring data queries, which are used to create standard reports.

Ad hoc reports are reports that are not produced regularly and get generated for a specific purpose or to answer a new analytical question.

When standard reports are insufficient, creating an ad hoc report is often the next step. An analyst may experiment with a variety of ad hoc queries to get the right dataset, including pulling data from additional sources. Then, they could design a new report or customize and modify an existing report template to generate a new version. The main purpose of such a report is to answer a one-off question related to new observations, events, or outliers.

Power users frequently use ad hoc reports to respond to new analytical needs of their department when no suitable enterprise analytics solutions exist.

Successful ad hoc reports and visualizations that respond to emerging analytical needs may become prototypes for new standardized (ready-to-consume) analytics solutions.

Approaches to self-serve analytics range from running SQL queries to extract datasets from enterprise systems and uploading results into a spreadsheet for further analysis to using data cubes such as online analytical processing (OLAP) cubes and data exploration features of advanced analytics platforms.

A **data cube** is a data structure organized along multiple dimensions that describe business transactions captured in the cube. Data cubes are essentially data marts designed to support fast, multi-dimensional analysis of specific transactions.

Data in a cube is organized in a dimensional structure where the facts—transactions, orders, sales, or service requests—are the key business events to be analyzed. The dimensions in a cube are the main attributes of the business events; most cubes support a multi-level dimension hierarchy.

Table 9.3 Data Cube Dimension Hierarchy

Dimension	Hierarchy
Time	Year → quarter → month → week → day → hour
Location	Region → country → province/state → municipality → area code
Product	Product type → category → product line → Universal Product Code (UPC) → stock keeping unit (SKU)
Customer	Customer type → segment → household account → household member

Data cubes are not limited to three dimensions; the structure used to store data in cubes can support a large number of hierarchical dimensions. A data cube with more than three dimensions can also be referred to as a **hypercube**.

Business users can be given access to analyze data in a cube through a specialized analytical platform or by utilizing a method called *spreadsheet integration*, where a spreadsheet application like Excel is integrated with the data cube to provide a familiar user interface for summarizing and visualizing data from a cube.

OLTP versus OLAP versus OLAP Cube

Online transaction processing (OLTP) is an approach to designing systems for handling large volumes of real-time transactions, such as ATM transactions, hotel reservations, bank payments, and e-commerce purchases. OLTP design is optimized for handling a large number of database read-and-write transactions in real time, at high speed, and with minimal downtime. OLTP relies on relational databases and supports operational systems.

   Online analytical processing (OLAP) is an approach to using databases to query and retrieve large volumes of data by organizing the data into a multi-dimensional cube (*OLAP cube*). OLAP can support storing large volumes of data (which could be transactional data from OLTP) for analytical purposes and enables fast responses to complex multi-dimensional queries. OLAP supports analytical systems.

Self-serve analytics is a double-edged sword. On one hand, it allows analysts and power users the freedom to conduct ad hoc analysis, especially when delays in analysis can have negative consequences for business. On the other hand, self-serve analytics may result in the proliferation of similar reports created by different users, buried on individual computers without documentation, which will not be reused but never get pruned. Some small to medium companies end up with thousands of obscure reports over the years that, instead of supporting better decision-making, become a distraction and digital clutter.

An additional risk is that the datasets generated by these reports may end up residing in unprotected storage at risk of exposure, especially if the reports contain any confidential or private information. Data security in organizations must take into account these off-the-books reports and ad hoc query results and create policies and procedures around managing analytics generated by ad hoc analytics solutions.

🚜 **CASE STUDY**

Data Cube Analysis

The YardExperts analytics team is using a sales data cube for analysis. The dimensions shown in Figure 9.5 are standard in many data cubes and represent time, location, and product categorization. Depending on how granular the data stored in the cube is, it can be sliced and diced along one or more dimensions to answer questions like:

- What was the total retail sales volume in January?

- What was the sales volume in the western region in February?
- What was the retail sales volume in the western region on February 1?

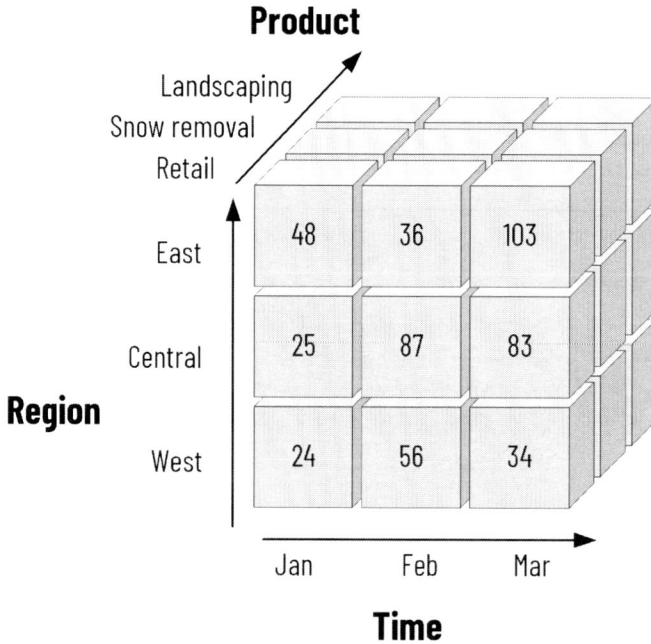

Figure 9.5 Data Cube—Case Study Example

9.5 ADVANCED ANALYTICS

Advanced analytics as a style of analytics refers to various solutions for exploring, mining, and analyzing large volumes of raw data for patterns with the goal of predicting the future and prescribing the best course of action to achieve specific goals. These solutions are most frequently used by personas with advanced skills such as data scientists, and to some extent by power users.

Data exploration and discovery refers to the viewing and profiling of datasets to learn more about their nature, structure, and patterns.

This type of analysis is performed to:

- Assess the quality, completeness, and depth of data sources
- Uncover statistical characteristics of datasets
- Detect trends, patterns, and outliers in data
- Identify subsets of data for further analysis for a specific analytical purpose

Data discovery usually involves data profiling, statistical analysis, and visualizations. The most sophisticated tools are capable of auto-suggesting visualizations that highlight specific patterns or anomalies.

```
CASE STUDY
```

Customer Sentiment Analysis

Textual analytics can be complex and imprecise and require the investment of time and resources. Before including customer reviews sentiment analysis in churn modelling, the data scientist at YardExperts, Eva, wants to determine whether this will enrich the analysis.

Eva starts with developing an algorithm that identifies prevailing sentiments in customer reviews, as well as comments and posts on social media. This initial analysis will be captured in visualizations similar to those shown in Figure 9.6.

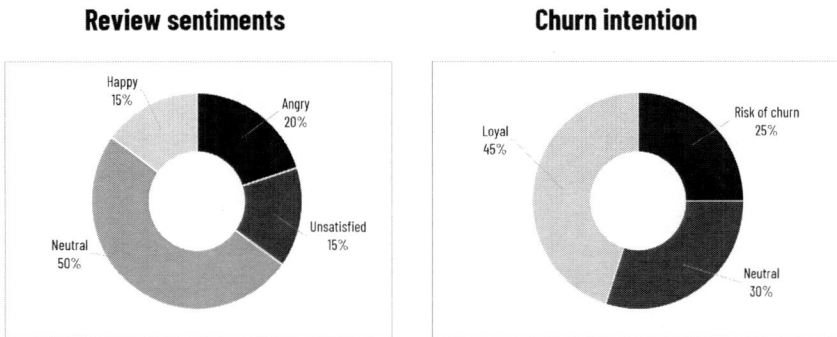

Figure 9.6 Sentiment Analysis—Case Study Example

Further, Eva wants to create a data mining algorithm to search for any meaningful correlation between contract cancellation rates in different locations and customer sentiments in those locations. Eva is also curious whether correlations exist between these sentiments and other factors such as region, season, or type of service.

Eva's findings will determine whether to bring in customer sentiments as a feature for predictive churn modelling. This sentiment analysis can also be used to cluster similar reviews together for further analysis and identify the most negative (extreme) cases that may require further investigation.

Sentiment analysis is an example of big data analytics as the source data represents large volumes of unstructured data—review comments, posts, reactions, and likes on social media.

Big data analytics is an aggregate term for discovering patterns and trends in large amounts of raw data, including unstructured data. Big data analytics can be applied to searching for patterns in satellite images, analyzing GPS traffic or internet of things streaming data, social network analysis, and more.

Data discovery, data mining, and machine learning allow us to find meaningful patterns in big data and discover predictive factors. These insights become a foundation for building predictive models to support decision support and automation.

Predictive modelling is the development of computational models for calculating probabilities of future outcomes and trends based on past and current data.

As outlined in Chapter 7, predictive modelling involves model selection and development, testing, parameter tuning, and performance analysis until the desired accuracy is achieved. Predictive modelling, along with other advanced analytics methods, may not by itself produce an insight ready for consumption by decision-makers. Advanced insights require interpretation and embedding into a business process.

If a data scientist makes a valuable discovery from big data analytics, they might first share this discovery with business stakeholders (using storytelling techniques). Then, it must be determined how the insights can be used, from enhancing existing models to developing new prescriptive analytics or further investigation of outliers and conducting of A/B experiments to test new hypotheses. We've discussed many such examples throughout this book.

To conclude this section, let's talk about the holy grail of advanced analytics. It goes by several terms: search-driven analytics, search-based analytics, natural language analytics, or BI search.

Search-driven analytics refers to solutions that allow users to get analytical insights in response to analytical questions asked using natural language.

It's best to explain this with a story.

EXAMPLE

Andrea is the new CEO of a major children's clothing company. She needs to grasp the current state of affairs quickly. She is very busy and does not have the patience to explore the multitude of dashboards and scorecards that her management team provided her. Instead, what she really wishes is to be able to type a question into a search box and receive an answer to her question, including the relevant numbers and metrics.

For example, imagine that Andrea types her question into a search box:

Which customer segment experienced the highest growth in the last quarter of 2024 by total sales revenue?

In response, she receives the following insight:

The highest revenue growth in Q4 2023 was recorded in the "Urban Parent" customer segment.

Below this response, she also receives a relevant visualization showing the sales revenue growth in Q4 2024 by customer segments, with the "Urban Parent" segment showing the highest value.

This type of analytics solution would be quite advanced. First, it requires powerful natural language processing capabilities to interpret complex analytical queries.

Then, the solution must retrieve or calculate the relevant response using a well-designed and fine-tuned analytical platform and generate a clear and user-friendly presentation of the results.

This example illustrates the ultimate user-friendly analytics: the ability to simply ask a question, as you would ask a human analytics expert, and in response, receive the best insight that can be achieved with available data.

This analytics style is still in its early stages and no doubt will be the focus of the field as analytics solutions become more advanced. Ways of asking questions can start as computer assisted and eventually become free form. Responses may be generated incrementally, validating the interpretation of the question with the customer with each iteration. Finally, the style of analytics responses can range from natural language to descriptive reports, visualizations, and predictions. The possibilities are endless.

9.6 EMBEDDED ANALYTICS

Embedded analytics refers to analytics solutions integrated directly into the business process. It differs from other analytics styles in the method of delivery. Analytics personas do not need to make an effort to find and retrieve analytics insights by navigating dashboards, clicking links, or running analytics models. Instead, the insights are supplied to the users in the context of the business process—that is, as they are doing their jobs.

Embedded analytics can be incorporated into enterprise applications to manage workflows, select the next task, or execute a decision, with or without human intervention. The key advantage of embedding analytics into the business process is that it becomes contextual, with relevant insights delivered where the user needs them. Embedded analytics provide contextual insights at the right place and the right time.

These insights may be descriptive, such as providing the user with relevant information to perform the next activity. For example, as a customer calls the contact centre, the system detects the caller's phone number and automatically provides a summary of recent orders, dates, and previous interactions to the customer support representative.

Embedded analytics are rarely of a diagnostic nature, as diagnostic results may require a trained eye and expertise for further interpretation and comparison. Diagnostics will not always be helpful to a casual analytics consumer who needs to make a quick decision—it may be a case of "too much information."

The value of predictive embedded analytics is in providing contextual insights to help the user make a decision, as in decision support scenarios. For example, when a loan officer is reviewing loan application information, supplying a "loan repayment score" that predicts the likelihood of the requested loan repayment would be helpful for decision-making.

Prescriptive embedded analytics are sometimes referred to as **next-best-action**: real-time prescriptive analytics aimed at optimizing the next activity in a business workflow. The algorithm predicts the likelihood of a desired outcome for each alternative, selects the best alternative, and either recommends the next action (providing decision support) or executes it (realizing decision automation).

To summarize, embedded analytics are intended for operational users. Personas such as data analysts and data scientists may assist in designing these solutions and test them as part of the development process, but they are not the intended users.

CASE STUDY

Embedded Analytics Potential in Customer Service

Recall Gurpreet, who manages a customer service department. One of her responsibilities is to ensure that customer calls are answered on time and in accordance with company standards.

Gurpreet receives daily call performance reports for her department. Every morning, she can review the key performance indicators for the day before, as well as month-over-month trends.

One morning, she observed that one of her senior staff, Amber, had a very unproductive day; her calls were completed much slower than usual, and she had a lot of downtime, where she was not on the phone with customers while there were calls waiting in a queue. This was quite unusual. As it was a very busy day yesterday, Gurpreet couldn't see the problem immediately as she had to step in and take some of the calls to relieve the queue.

Of course, Gurpreet, being a good manager, would find a moment to chat with Amber the next day and find out what happened.

What if instead, the call management software was smart enough to detect an unusual pattern in Amber's call queue? If the duration of her calls was well outside the expected range, the software could provide this information to Gurpreet, as it may require the manager's attention. Was the system directing only difficult customers to Amber as the only senior representative that day? Was there something wrong with her computer? Or was she not feeling well and struggling to focus?

Whatever the reason, the productivity of the department, and potentially the well-being of an employee, could benefit from an analytics insight delivered close to real time and within the operational system. Remember that Gurpreet had to take some customer calls—she did not have idle time to browse self-service dashboards and reports in search of potential problems. She is much more likely to take action if analytical insights are provided to her in the right place and at the right time.

9.7 HOW TO SELECT THE APPROPRIATE ANALYTICS STYLE

With so many styles of generating and presenting analytics insights, how can the right approach be selected? The most suitable style will depend on many factors, including the intended user (persona) and how the analytics will be used.

A business analytics professional does not just develop analytics solutions. They often act as an advisor, helping their customers choose the style of analytics most suitable for the task.

Businesspeople may have specific ideas about desired solutions in mind, often shaped by their prior experiences. Someone who is used to receiving daily reports may favour this approach; a management scorecard or a dashboard will be a preferred style of receiving business intelligence for an operations executive using similar tools for day-to-day management.

However, as the capabilities of analytics platforms expand and the uses of analytics become more advanced, many more solutions become available to choose from. Experienced professionals can improve the analytics outcomes by suggesting the most suitable styles and features of business analytics solutions to satisfy business needs.

On the other hand, for business users—customers using analytics solutions—understanding the capabilities, limitations, and important factors helps provide better requirements, create reasonable expectations, and extract the most value from enterprise data.

What factors should be considered when choosing the most appropriate analytics style?

Table 9.4 Factors for Selecting the Appropriate Analytics Style

Factor	What to consider
Expertise and level of interest of analytics personas	• Which personas are asking analytics questions? • Who will use analytics solutions, and what for? • What decisions will they make using the insights?
Data domain	• What is the subject, e.g., what is the data about?
Impacted business process	• What process is the data concerned with? • How will insights be used to manage the business process?
Volume and structure of data sources	• Is the data structured, semi-structured, or unstructured? Is it big or small data? • Is the data homogenous or heterogeneous? • Are there many data sources in different formats?
Data velocity	• Is the data received in real time, i.e., streaming data?
Depth of analysis required	• What is the level of detail expected by intended users? • Do they need information summarized, grouped, and aggregated by categories? Or disaggregated, with access to granular data?
Acceptable latency	• Is there a need for real-time or near-real-time analytics? • What level of decision automation is required?

Now, let's be practical. Sometimes, there isn't one right answer. If options have been narrowed down to two or three styles, use a "test and learn" approach—a frequent feature of analytics projects. Create prototypes of each style and demonstrate them to your customers, using a sample of real data or test data statistically similar to production data.

Many people respond better when explanations and descriptions are complemented by visual representations. Seeing the prototype of a solution and being able to play with it and try out its features will give your customers an opportunity to reflect and crystallize what they really need. Another benefit is that this approach lets customers discover new features that they may not have known about, so wouldn't know to ask for.

In this respect, an analytics developer would use the same best practices as any software developer: creating prototypes is one of the ways to elicit in-depth requirements, especially related to presentation and usability.

Through prototyping and user demonstrations, you might determine:

- Required drill-down and drill-across features
- The level of detail required when drilling down (grain of data)
- The visualization sequence—based on a logical sequence of exploring data
- Additional dimensions required for enrichment
- More accurate terms for labels and titles
- Design features that are too complex and require simplification
- Missing information important for decision-making

In the next chapter, you will explore how these solutions are delivered through analytics projects and learn about the fundamentals of managing an analytics project.

9.8 CHAPTER SUMMARY

Key Points to Remember

- When designing analytics solutions, the requirements and skill level of the intended users play a key role in selecting the appropriate analytics style.
- Analytics solutions to support operational needs must be standardized and simple to use.
- Giving users too many choices and options is not always a good thing: a good solution must satisfy the user's requirements without overloading them with unnecessary features.
- The interpretation and correct use of reports and dashboards rely on having clear definitions for all attributes, metrics, and selection criteria.
- Successful ad hoc reports and visualizations that respond to emerging analytical needs may become prototypes for new standardized analytics solutions.
- The purpose of embedded analytics is to inject analytics insights directly into the workflow.

Key Terms

Ad hoc analysis: analysis performed to respond to new analytics questions.

Ad hoc report: a report that is not produced regularly and is generated for a specific purpose or to answer a new analytical question.

Advanced analytics: solutions for exploring, mining, and analyzing large volumes of raw data for patterns with the goal of predicting the future and prescribing the best course of action.

Alert: a notification sent to the interested parties when specific criteria are met.

Analyst (as an analytics persona): staff specializing in exploring and analyzing data.

Big data analytics: discovering patterns and trends in large amounts of raw data, including unstructured data.

Business analytics persona: a user of analytics solutions with a specific level of expertise and requirements for business analytics.

Business analytics solution: a solution intended to provide answers to analytics questions required to make business decisions.

Casual consumer (as an analytics persona): operational and managerial staff who use standard reports and dashboards to get the information needed to perform their jobs.

Dashboard: a combination of multiple analytics visualizations on a single panel or screen for the purpose of monitoring business performance.

Data cube: a data structure organized along multiple dimensions that describe business transactions captured in the cube.

Data exploration and discovery: viewing and profiling of datasets to learn more about their nature, structure, and patterns.

Data scientist (as an analytics persona): a professional with specialized knowledge to handle, explore, and mine raw data of varied nature and complexity, and to gain insights from big data.

Embedded analytics: analytics solutions integrated directly into the business process.

False negative: a test result that incorrectly indicates that a particular condition was not satisfied.

False positive: a test result that incorrectly indicates that a particular condition was satisfied.

Hypercube: a data cube with more than three dimensions.

Next-best-action: real-time prescriptive analytics aimed at optimizing the next activity in a business workflow.

Online analytical processing (OLAP): an approach to using databases to query and retrieve large volumes of data by organizing the data into a multi-dimensional cube.

Online transaction processing (OLTP): an approach to designing systems for handling large volumes of real-time transactions.

Pivot: a summary table that groups and aggregates values from a larger table across one or more dimensions.

Power user (as an analytics persona): sophisticated business users who utilize their business and data analysis knowledge to provide custom analytics to their departments.

Ready-to-consume analytics: reports, charts, tables, and visualizations generated from available data and arranged for viewing by business users based on requirements defined in advance.

Report: a collection of information aggregated and presented in a pre-defined format.

Reporting parameter: a condition or dimension used to define the boundaries of the report or limit the data included in the report.

Scorecard: a visual snapshot of an organization's key performance indicators.

Search-driven analytics: solutions capable of providing analytical insights in response to questions asked using natural language.

Self-serve analytics: solutions that allow prepared data to be accessed, queried, and analyzed for the purpose of creating new business intelligence and diagnostic insights.

Questions for Critical Thought

1. How will persona requirements influence the choice of the analytics style?
2. Should every user have access to self-serve analytics?
3. What are the advantages of search-driven analytics?
4. How would operational users access embedded analytics insights?
5. How would you determine the right style of analytics for a new project?

Test Your Knowledge

1. Prefers reports that are predictable and easy to understand, to help them fulfill their daily duties.
   Which analytics persona is described?
   a. Casual consumer
   b. Analyst
   c. Power user
   d. Data scientist

2. Accesses and analyzes data in many formats to find patterns, build machine learning models, and recommend methods for using unstructured data for analytics.
   Which analytics persona is described?
   a. Casual consumer
   b. Analyst
   c. Power user
   d. Data scientist

3. Specializes in working on structured data, creating reports and dashboards, augmenting existing reports, and creating new reports based on ad hoc needs of the business.

   Which analytics persona is described?

   a. Casual consumer

   b. Analyst

   c. Power user

   d. Data scientist

4. When sales numbers in a region hit an unexpected low, the sales manager requests some diagnostic analysis to investigate what factors may have impacted the sales.

   Which analytics style is described?

   a. Ad hoc report

   b. Dashboard

   c. Predictive analytics

   d. Alert

5. A city infrastructure engineer takes measurements on a routine water pipe inspection, and the data is fed into the central data hub in real time. Immediately after scanning the next section of the pipe, the engineer's device displays a pipe breakdown prediction that shows the likelihood of a leak within the next seven days.

   Which analytics style is described?

   a. Ad hoc report

   b. Dashboard

   c. Embedded analytics

   d. Cube analysis

Recommended Readings

Schwabish, J. (2021). *Better Data Visualizations: A Guide for Scholars, Researchers, and Wonks.* Columbia University Press.

Sherman, R. (2015). *Business Intelligence Guidebook: From Data Integration to Analytics.* Morgan Kaufmann (Elsevier).

Wexler, S., Shaffer, J., & Cotgreave, A. (2017). *The Big Book of Dashboards: Visualizing Your Data Using Real-World Business Scenarios.* Wiley.

Winston, W. (2020). *Analytics Stories: Using Data to Make Good Things Happen.* Wiley.

Note

1. Government of Canada. (n.d.). *Criteria for Public Weather Alerts.* Retrieved February 23, 2024, from www.canada.ca/en/environment-climate-change/services/types-weather-forecasts-use/public/criteria-alerts.html.

Chapter 10

How to Deliver Analytics Solutions

To implement a new solution—whether it's a custom enterprise application, off-the-shelf accounting software, website, mobile app, or recommendation engine—companies organize their efforts and resources into projects.

A **project** is a temporary endeavour undertaken to create a unique product, service, or result.[1]

In this chapter you will learn:

- How to approach analytics projects
- Key project roles and their responsibilities
- What is involved in the planning and execution of analytics projects
- What makes these projects successful

10.1 ANALYTICS PROJECTS

Two categories of projects deliver analytics solutions:

- Projects undertaken to solve business problems, change business processes, or implement new tools where business intelligence, reporting, or embedded analytics are required to support the change
- Projects where the main objective is the design and implementation of analytics solutions—analytics projects

The goals of analytics projects (or analytics components of larger enterprise projects) can be as varied as the different types of analytics solutions discussed in this book:

- Building a new operational dashboard from the data already collected by operational systems
- Designing a data pipeline for collecting the data from operational systems into a central data warehouse, and designing new management reports using this data
- Creating a tool for regional managers to explore and analyze information about sales performance and customer segmentation in their region

- Exploring big data collected by the enterprise to discover what information can be used to predict customer loyalty and churn and build a predictive model for that
- Setting up a regular process for monitoring social media comments about the company's products and services to measure sentiment change and drive reputation management decisions
- Developing a chatbot for the company's website that will answer frequently asked questions and triage more complex questions to the service representatives while continuously improving using previous chat interactions
- Developing a pricing optimization engine to modify prices dynamically with the goal of maximizing revenue and customer retention
- Exploring big data sources to discover new monetization opportunities

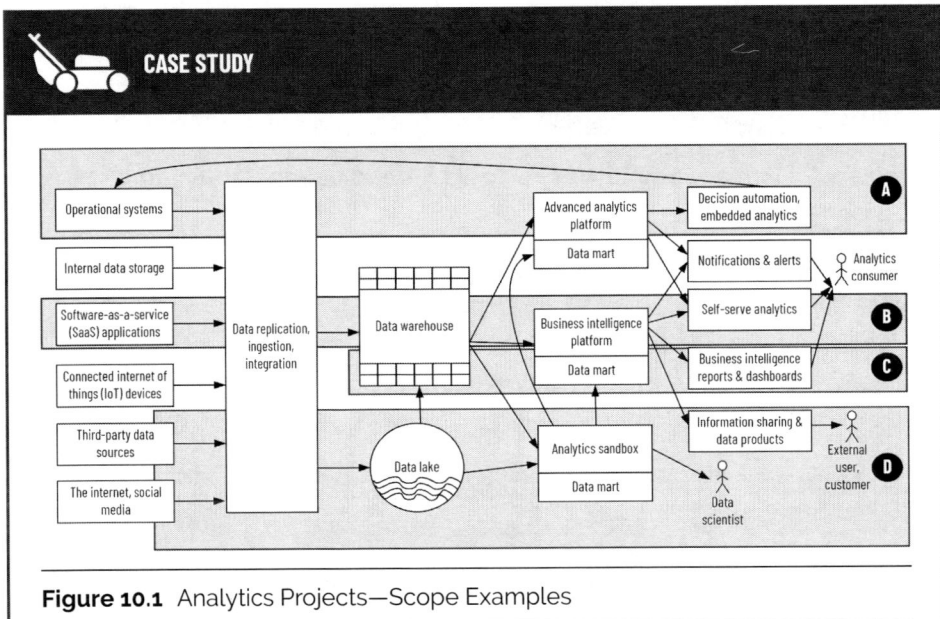

Figure 10.1 Analytics Projects—Scope Examples

Figure 10.1 outlines the scope of four hypothetical projects.

Project A: Increase Customer Service Process Automation

The current customer portal allows customers with premium landscaping contracts to create service requests, which are then reviewed by a triage team and assigned to different service technicians for resolution.

The goal is to develop a new prescriptive analytics solution that will:

- Identify simple service requests that can be resolved automatically, such as changing the date or time of the next visit

- Automatically assign the remaining requests to service technicians based on the complexity of the case, each technician's experience, and their predicted availability—this would apply to more complex cases such as an infestation, a plant disease, or a front yard redesign

The prescriptive model must be embedded into the business process so that customers receive almost instantaneous responses to simple service requests or notifications about the assignment of their request to a service technician with the expected response time. The new business process may involve notifying technicians if their input is required to assign and schedule a request, updating their work schedules, or reassigning other services to accommodate emergency requests.

The scope of this project will involve developing a new prescriptive analytics model on the company's advanced analytics platform as well as embedding the recommendations from the model into the steps for assigning and responding to requests. This will be embedded into one of the operational systems, the YardExperts Order Management System (YOMS).

Project B: Enhance Employees' Access to Weather and Gardening Season Predictions

The rationale of this project is that access to this information can help optimize service schedules for watering, pruning, fertilizing, and pest treatments, ultimately leading to improved customer satisfaction.

YardExperts purchased a third-party tool that provides detailed local forecasts and recommendations for managing different types of plants. The goals are to:

- Make this data available to employees through the organization's self-serve analytics platform
- Allow landscaping technicians to get the insights they need to improve landscaping service plans for their customers

This project involves:

- Acquiring data from the third-party application
- Preparing this external data for storage in the data warehouse (DW), which may require an update to the DW data model
- Further integrating the required data into the business intelligence platform data mart
- Modifying existing self-serve solutions, or creating new ones, based on business requirements

In this example, third-party data is too valuable to store it directly in the business intelligence (BI) platform data mart, bypassing the DW. It is possible that the same data, once it is acquired, can be used for other scenarios and other analytics use cases—for example, for predictive modelling for the next season. Once the data is in the DW, it can be used by multiple consumers.

Project C: Improve Tracking of Customer Churn Indicators

The goal of this project is to improve the tracking of customer churn indicators.

An existing customer satisfaction dashboard tracks service levels and customer review sentiments; however, summarized churn statistics are currently not available. Information about contract cancellations and exit surveys is loaded into the DW, but it does not appear in any of the existing dashboards or analytics solutions.

The scope of this project includes:

- Uploading customer churn data from the DW into the BI platform that supports the existing customer satisfaction dashboard
- Designing new dashboard panels with churn analytics according to business requirements

Project D: Generate Ideas for Digital Products

This project starts as a research and development initiative. The main goal is to explore how to use existing data to create a new digital product for YardExperts' customers.

The company's data scientist studies data from a variety of internal and external sources stored in the company's data lake using an analytical sandbox. Several proto-types are reviewed with stakeholders, including the marketing and sales departments, to determine how to extract value from the available data.

Eventually, the team tests the idea of creating an app with personalized garden-ing tips. The app would require data about customers' location, soil characteristics, orientation of the lot, type of irrigation, and other attributes already collected by land-scaping technicians as part of customer onboarding. YardExperts also has access to various gardening databases and resources, as well as records about previous sea-sons' planting successes and failures in the area. The data science team is working on a machine learning model for recommending what to plant, when, and garden care recommendations.

This project involves:

- Building a prototype of the machine learning model and assessing its viability as a product
- Deciding whether or not to proceed with the development of a marketable app
- Identifying the appropriate platform for the development and deployment of the app (a typical analytics sandbox is not meant for this purpose)
- Developing and testing the solution
- Planning and executing the app launch

Running successful analytics projects requires applying a project management methodology to the business analytics life cycle. This will be the focus of the rest of the chapter.

10.2 METHODOLOGY

Most analytics projects involve engineering and software development efforts, such as building new programs or modifying existing programs for data acquisition, preparation, integration, report building, or machine learning algorithms.

Whether an analytics solution is developed through a standalone project or as a part of a larger enterprise initiative, it requires completion of the same fundamental steps as any software development project.

These steps, referred to as the **software development life cycle (SDLC)**, reflect the need for requirements analysis, design, development, and testing before making a solution ready for use by business users.

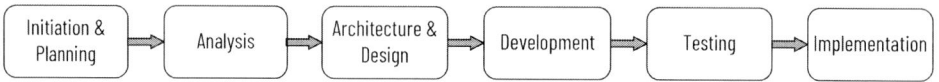

Figure 10.2 Software Development Life Cycle

There are several established methodologies for building new solutions that can be applied to business analytics development: most notably, the waterfall approach of upfront planning and the agile approach of building solutions iteratively.

With strict *waterfall* methodology, the SDLC steps are executed sequentially and align with project phases. The completion of each step is marked by an official *milestone* such as an approved project plan or requirements sign-off. Milestone completion is formalized, which means that a project will only proceed to the next phase once the milestone is achieved. The solution will be deployed and made available to users when the full scope of the project is complete.

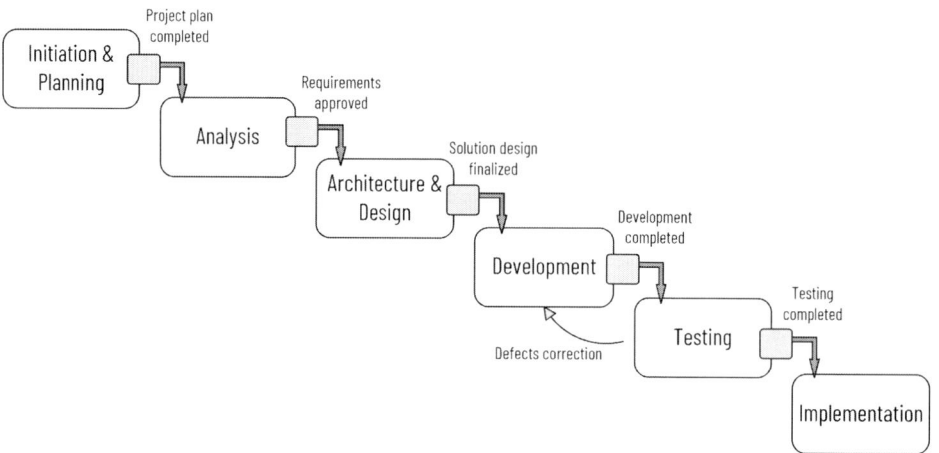

Figure 10.3 Waterfall Solution Development Approach

This is, of course, an ideal description of a waterfall project. In reality, many factors may affect the duration and scope of a project even after the project plan is approved, leading to changes. One of the major distinctions between a waterfall approach and an agile approach is how they manage change.

Waterfall projects rely on **change requests:** formal proposals to change the scope, time-line, or budget of the project due to new information or external influencing factors. There is usually a special process to follow when submitting and reviewing change requests, which may be time-consuming and cumbersome, but sometimes necessary in complex projects with a large number of stakeholders and parties involved, as well as contractual obligations.

With an agile approach, change is considered a normal and expected part of the SDLC. It is accepted that complete solution requirements may be impossible to define at the beginning of the project as some requirements emerge as a result of design discussions, prototyping, and testing of early designs with users. This approach is especially well suited to new product development, where it is crucial to understand user needs and preferences.

When using the agile approach:

- Requirements and development tasks are captured in a *backlog*, which is updated and groomed iteratively to reflect completed work, new findings, and user feedback.
- The work is done in *increments* (called *sprints* in the Scrum framework). Each increment iterates through the SDLC steps at a smaller scale.
- Detailed requirement analysis is done at the beginning of each development sprint, resulting in a groomed sprint backlog that captures all tasks to be completed in the sprint.
- Larger initiatives may have an upfront planning and design sprint.
- Building and testing are done in small increments, with emphasis placed on continuous testing.
- Each sprint delivers the next increment of the working solution. Some increments may be released to the users as early product releases.
- Larger deployment and implementation tasks are completed when the solution is ready for a major release to the user base.

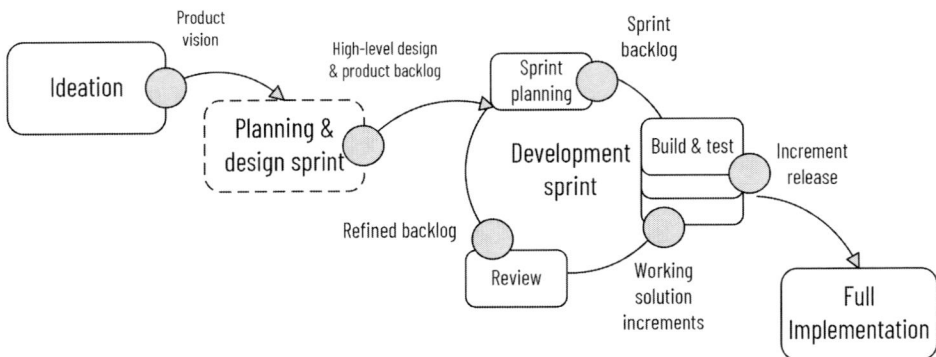

Figure 10.4 Agile Solution Development Approach

Table 10.1 Waterfall Methodology versus Agile Methodology

Waterfall	Agile
Sequential (linear) approach to software development	Requirements and deliverables evolve through cross-functional collaboration
The next phase starts as the previous phase is completed	Deliverables are defined and built in time-boxed iterations (sprints), typically 2-4 weeks each
Requirements are defined upfront and approved	Requirements are "groomed" in detail for the current and next sprints; less defined for future sprint (backlog)
Requires a formal process	Less formal but also well-defined "agile ceremonies"—regular meetings that provide structure to each increment of work (sprint)
A lot of documentation	Lightweight documentation
More often used for large projects with major integrations or by more formal and hierarchical organizations	More suitable for new product development utilizing the "test and learn" approach

What methodologies are suitable for analytics projects? There are a few important distinctions of analytics projects to consider in answering this question:

- Upfront architecture and design efforts are required to ensure proper data pipeline design.
- Business requirements may not be clear at the start of a project and must be refined iteratively.
- Analytics solutions rely heavily on visualization and presentation, which work best with active business stakeholder involvement and early solution prototyping.
- Data availability and quality are crucial and must be considered early in the project.
- Data preparation is an important phase, and it should be expected that it will require significant effort.
- Analytics projects rely heavily on access to domain knowledge, existing documentation, and previous analytics deliverables.
- Unanticipated changes to the existing architecture components such as the DW may be discovered during design or development.
- Solutions may rely on external data, requiring the involvement of third parties and vendors.
- Experimentation and research can become a significant part of the project, in particular, for advanced analytics solutions. Not every project starts with a viable hypothesis. A significant exploration and research effort may be required to mine for hypotheses before proceeding further to design and development.
- Data protection considerations must be integrated into the solution.
- Reinforcement learning solutions require a continuous feedback and improvement loop.

These characteristics of analytics projects emphasize the experimental and adaptive nature of analytics development, especially when it comes to predictive and prescriptive modelling. To accommodate these characteristics, many organizations use a **hybrid approach** that blends some of the waterfall elements and agile elements to reduce the inherent risks of large projects while ensuring the solution has a proper architecture foundation.

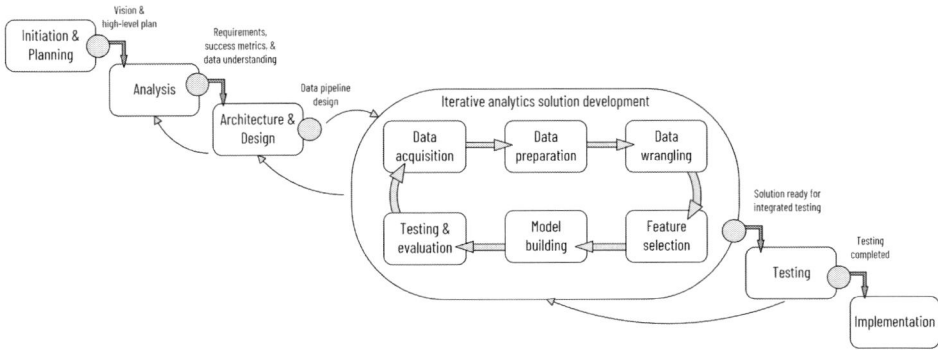

Figure 10.5 Hybrid Analytics Solution Development Approach

The next section will review project phases captured in Figure 10.5 as they apply to the development of analytics solutions.

10.3 ANALYTICS REQUIREMENTS

One of the persistent issues plaguing software projects is unclear, vague, or incomplete requirements, and the same applies to developing analytics solutions. Project requirements are necessary to direct the joint efforts of the project team toward the value expected by the stakeholders. **Stakeholders** are all people, departments, and entities interested in the solution, affected by it, benefitting from it, or having an influence over it.

A solution implemented without a clear understanding of the problem might produce some analytics, but not necessarily any insights that will make a difference. Therefore, every analytics effort must be based on clear objectives and business analysis.

Business analysis is the practice of analyzing organizations and their functions with the goal of identifying solutions to business problems and needs. Through the business analysis process, we identify **business requirements**—features and capabilities needed to solve a business problem or satisfy a business need.[2]

As discussed in the previous section, requirements for analytics solutions require an iterative approach. Even if the business problem is identified at the very beginning, its root cause and contributing factors might still be a mystery. It will be up to the analytics team to determine the root cause and then identify possible solutions.

This is why a hybrid or iterative approach is often necessary for analytics development: to enable discovery, research, and experimentation. The requirements and the solution are refined as the team continues to investigate, explore, and analyze. However, requirements remain necessary. As the investigation and analysis progress, the analytics team can refine their original hypotheses and inform detailed requirements.

CASE STUDY

The YardExperts Analytics Team Is Looking for Requirements

Everyone has been discussing the customer churn problem, and the analytics team has already helped to do some extensive diagnostic analysis to understand what makes customers leave.

After the team summarized and presented these results to the executive team, the YardExperts chief operating officer (COO) announced, "Now you have to build us an AI model to solve this."

The COO's request is just a *mandate*—a declaration of intention to find a solution. The real work will involve discussions with various stakeholders and the identification of business requirements. The analytics team lead starts planning a series of requirements workshops to understand them. They will discuss:

- Based on diagnostic findings, what are the most important factors, and which factors can the company control? This will help plan further analysis and design, as not all causes are equally important, nor is every cause in the organization's power to change.
- For selected causes of customer churn, what analysis is required to determine how to make improvements? This will direct analysis activities, such as business process mapping (if delays in a business process is what makes many customers unhappy).
- When is the optimal time to generate a customer churn prediction? In the middle of the contract, the last month, or the last week? Customer outreach planning must be done carefully since companies have limited resources and prefer to make customer calls at the best possible time.
- Based on past analysis and business expertise, what groups of customers are more likely to respond to different retention strategies such as customer care calls, discount offers, or complementary visits? This avenue of analysis may require additional data collection, making the creation of a survey or focus group one of the requirements.

Each of these questions might in turn require more analysis, reflecting the experimental nature of many advanced analytics projects. Throughout the whole project, the analytics team and the business stakeholders should work collaboratively on planning further analysis, reviewing the results, discussing next steps, and prototyping solution options.

This analysis process helps the YardExperts customer retention team define their requirements. They require a solution that will:

- Identify with reasonable accuracy customers with churn propensity in the range of 70–95% within two weeks before contract expiration.

- Based on customer characteristics and segmentation, recommend the best retention action to be applied to each customer. This must be adjusted based on current resource availability in the company, such as a temporary lack of staff in the contact centre.
- Automatically execute the retention action, such as an email, a promotional offer, or a customer care call.
- Continuously evaluate the accuracy of the churn prediction to improve the prediction model. This must include customers who were not contacted and churned.
- Continue to monitor for emerging causes of customer churn by analyzing customer reviews and social media.
- Evaluate the effectiveness of the retention actions for customers that were contacted to improve future retention recommendations.

Analytics requirements depend on the type of analytics desired and will evolve as the organization progresses to more advanced decision-making models. These requirements will revolve around the main themes in Figure 10.6.

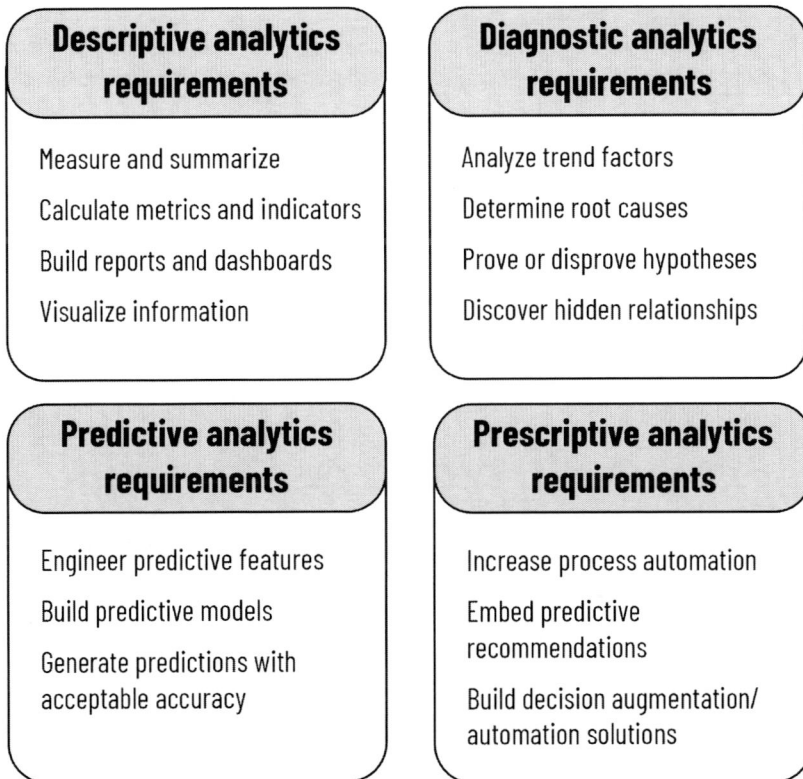

Descriptive analytics requirements

Measure and summarize

Calculate metrics and indicators

Build reports and dashboards

Visualize information

Diagnostic analytics requirements

Analyze trend factors

Determine root causes

Prove or disprove hypotheses

Discover hidden relationships

Predictive analytics requirements

Engineer predictive features

Build predictive models

Generate predictions with acceptable accuracy

Prescriptive analytics requirements

Increase process automation

Embed predictive recommendations

Build decision augmentation/ automation solutions

Figure 10.6 High-Level Requirement Themes by Types of Analytics

To translate these high-level requirements into detailed ones that will determine the design and features of the solution, several dimensions must be considered:

- Function: what should the analytics solution do?
- Data: what data must be analyzed?
- Stakeholders: who will use these solutions and for what?
- Latency: what is the acceptable analysis, decision, and action latency?

Figure 10.7 Analyzing Analytics Requirements as a Process

Analytics requirements will be identified and captured through various business analysis activities. Tools and techniques of business analysis, such as (but not limited to) the examples in Table 10.2, will be utilized.

Table 10.2 Business Analysis Techniques

Business analysis techniques	Expected results
Discussions with business stakeholders: interviews, workshops, brainstorming	• Clarification of business objectives and the problem to be solved • Understanding of the current business process and its pain points
Artifact analysis: existing business and technical documentation, reports, and problem evidence	• Business rules • Understanding of data and its sources • Descriptive analysis of the problem
Observation of the business process: job shadowing, immersion	• Understanding of hidden problems, manual and undocumented processes, exceptional scenarios • Discovery of pain points, data quality problems • Clarification of analytics goals
Process analysis and mapping	• Process maps indicating recurring sequences of steps executed to achieve specific results • Identification of inefficiencies, redundancies, or bottlenecks in the process • Discovered opportunities for using embedded analytics
Data modelling	• Conceptual and/or logical data models • Clarification of key data entities and their relationships • Identification of data gaps
Data collection and analysis: querying existing data sources, extracting data from systems for exploration	• Ad hoc analysis • Developed hypotheses for diagnostics • Scenario analysis • Data acquisition and preparation requirements
Validation and documentation	• Requirements captured in a document or a system • Report, dashboard, visualization specifications, and mock-ups • Acceptance criteria • Stakeholder agreement on requirements

Through the application of these techniques as part of the iterative solution development life cycle, the project team will ask more questions to add clarity and granularity to their understanding of the required solution—in other words, to determine analytics requirements.

✔ **CHECKLIST**

Analytics Requirements Checklist

Here are some examples of questions to guide iterative analytics requirements analysis.
For descriptive analytics:

- What should be measured and how?
- What information requires summarization? What variables are important?
- What is the scope of analysis? What segments are we interested in? What time frame should we analyze?
- How to summarize? What metrics and indicators are important?

For diagnostic analytics:

- What observations and trends need to be analyzed?
- Are there existing hypotheses to be tested or potential connections to be verified?
- What causal relationships or correlations have been discovered in the past?
- What has changed since then that may be relevant to the problem?
- What data can be used to source variables?
- What additional data should be collected, if any?

For predictive analytics:

- How can we reframe the problem as a prediction problem?
- What predictions are required to inform our business decisions?
- What data do we need for the prediction?
- What uncertainties will affect the prediction?
- What discriminating factors discovered through diagnostics should be considered?
- What is the acceptable prediction accuracy rate?

For prescriptive analytics:

- What decisions will help to solve the problem?
- How can a prediction be used to make better decisions?
- How should these decisions be embedded into the business process?
- What are the key considerations for optimizing these decisions?

- What type of decision-making model is required (decision support, augmentation, or automation)?
- Is reinforcement learning required?
- How should model drift be monitored?

For all analytics:

- What data is needed for these insights, and where can it be acquired from? What data preparation is required?
- Who needs these insights and what for? What types of analytics personas are they?
- How should the results be presented to the stakeholders?
- What additional information do they require to make decisions?
- What is the acceptable latency of the insights? How time-sensitive is the decision-making?
- What is the risk of making an incorrect decision?
- What mechanisms must be in place to mitigate errors?

10.4 PROJECT ROLES

When groups of people come together for a limited time to achieve a common goal, as in executing a project, a clear understanding of their roles, responsibilities, and interactions is necessary to project success.

Analytics projects must approach this from two perspectives:

1. Developing analytics solutions is a particular case of developing software solutions using specific platforms (analytics platforms) to deliver specific solutions (analytics solutions). As such, these projects will require roles similar to those of any other software development projects: ones related to the tasks of requirements analysis, design, and development, as well as testing of the solution and providing business domain expertise.
2. Developing analytics solutions involves a significant effort in collecting and processing data, establishing data pipelines, mining data, and designing sustainable analytics solutions. As such, these projects will require resources to design, build, and maintain data pipelines, as well as conceive and develop advanced analytics.

Project roles will vary from company to company, subject to the preferred methodology and whether the project is executed in house or in collaboration with a vendor or a consulting partner. However, key roles are required for every project (Figure 10.8, Table 10.3).

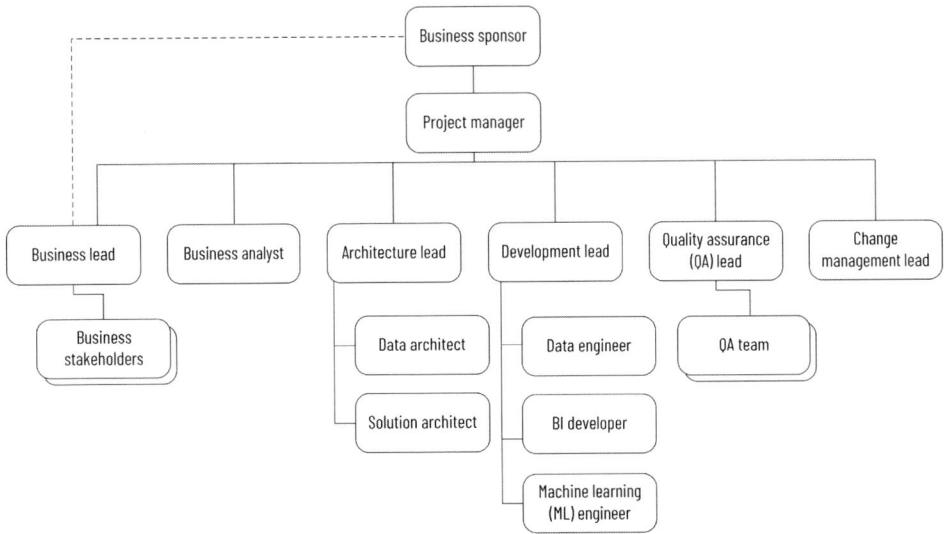

Figure 10.8 Analytics Project Structure

Table 10.3 Analytics Projects Roles and Responsibilities

Project role	Variations	Responsibilities
Business sponsor	• Executive sponsor • Steering committee	• Set objectives • Secure funding and resources • Oversee execution • Ultimate accountability for success
Project manager	• Analytics or data science lead for specialized projects	• Plan activities • Request and manage resources • Request and manage budget • Track execution and report progress • Remove impediments • Facilitate communication within the team
Business lead	• Product owner • Subject matter expert (SME)	• Supply domain expertise and business understanding of data • Clarify objectives of analytics • Key participant in requirements analysis
Business stakeholder	• Business domain expert • Process owner • Data owner	• Provide expertise in business processes and data • Contribute to analytics requirements

(*continued*)

Table 10.3 Analytics Projects Roles and Responsibilities (*continued*)

Project role	Variations	Responsibilities
Business analyst	• Business systems analyst • Product owner • Data analyst for special-ized projects	• Elicit, analyze, and capture analytics requirements • Validate requirements with all stakeholders • Explore data • Provide ad hoc analysis and visualizations • Clarify and manage requirements throughout the project • Support business acceptance testing and change management • Facilitate communication with business stakeholders
Architecture lead	• Design lead • Data scientist for ad-vanced analytics or re-search and development (R&D) projects	• Design data pipelines and solutions • Direct design activities • Ensure solution architecture meets requirements and constraints
Data architect	• Information architect • BI architect • Big data architect	• Design data models • Design data integrations and analytical storage solutions • Create blueprints, diagrams, and design documentation
Solution architect	• Technical architect • Technical lead • May play the role of the architecture lead	• Design integrations of the analytics solutions with other systems (e.g., for embedded analytics) • Ensure the solution integrates with the existing architecture • Architect infrastructure and platforms required to support the solutions
Development lead	• Lead developer • Lead programmer	• Coordinate solution development • Ensure developers follow best practices and resolve issues • Oversee the integration of solution components
Data engineer	• Database developer • ETL developer • API developer • Data services developer	• Design and optimize databases • Create programs for data integration and transformation • Develop and manage data storage solutions
BI developer	• Reports developer • BI analyst • Data analyst	• Provide exploratory data analysis • Create ad hoc reports • Build reports, online analytical processing (OLAP) cubes, and other analytics solutions • Design visualizations and dashboards
ML engineer	• Big data engineer • Data scientist	• Develop data wrangling programs and engineer features • Develop data mining and ML algorithms • Build predictive and prescriptive models and inte-grate them into enterprise systems • Track model performance and recommend improvements

Table 10.3 Analytics Projects Roles and Responsibilities (*continued*)

Project role	Variations	Responsibilities
QA lead	• QA manager • Lead tester	• Create test strategy, test plan, and test cases • Oversee test plan execution and coordinate between the QA team
QA team	• Tester • QA engineer	• Execute test cases • Investigate and report issues
Change management lead	• Change manager • Implementation lead	• Plan and coordinate change management activities (training, user documentation, communication) • Ensure end users are prepared to use the solution • Organize training • May coordinate business acceptance testing

In addition to the core project members, other specialists will support the project as needed, engaged by the project manager or leads:

- Infrastructure experts such as systems or network administrators or database administrators (DBAs) to support the infrastructure needs of the project and test, deploy, and maintain database solutions
- Security specialists to provide security and data protection requirements
- Data governance leads to provide support and ensure that data governance processes are followed
- Legal counsel to advise on potential legal or ethical implications, in particular, for big data analytics and AI algorithms

10.5 PLANNING AND EXECUTION

The main approach to planning projects is to create a **work breakdown structure (WBS)** by breaking down the work into smaller tasks that are easier to understand, estimate, and execute. The result of this exercise is a visual representation of the work required to achieve the goal, split into smaller pieces that may be separately estimated, assigned, and scheduled, forming the foundation of a project plan.

In this section, we will review typical tasks and sample deliverables in an analytics project WBS. Work breakdown of a particular project in a particular organization will depend on the nature of the project, methodology and standards used in the organization, analytics architecture and technology, and the organization's maturity level.

To learn more about individual project deliverables and how to create them, refer to specialized project management books and resources.

Table 10.4 Analytics Project Sample Work Breakdown Structure

Work breakdown: Project tasks	Sample deliverables
Project phase: Initiation and planning	
Identify project scope: a brief description of the project objectives and expected deliverables	Scope statement Project overview
Identify project stakeholders: individuals or entities with an interest in the project	Stakeholder list, stakeholder matrix
Request and justify project financing	Approved budget or financing guidelines
Secure resources: individuals or partners who will execute project tasks, technology, or assets required	Resourcing requirements Roles and responsibilities matrix
Plan the project: detail and precision of the planning will depend on the methodology and project specifics	Project plan, work breakdown structure, detailed project schedule
Project phase: Analysis	
Conduct due diligence: research and collect existing artifacts such as glossary, data dictionary, existing analytics and reports, data source documentation, market research, customer survey results, etc.	Collected artifacts available for analysis
Analyze business requirements: clarify stakeholder needs and expectations and capture them as project requirements	Business requirements document (BRD), diagrams, mock-ups, backlogs
Prioritize requirements, plan iterations	Prioritized requirements and iterations
Define measurement approach for reporting and performance measurement	Definition of metrics and KPIs
Capture expected business results: based on business requirements, clarify stakeholder expectations and what success looks like	Success metrics
Identify data requirements: based on business requirements, identify required groups of data to use for analytics	Conceptual data model High-level data requirements Business glossary
Explore data: consider and explore available sources of data and their applicability to the business problem	Data sources evaluation and profiling Data flow diagram Source systems data models or dictionaries
Determine data availability and gaps: compare required and available data, identify gaps and the need for new data acquisition	Data gaps identification; required sources of data
Project phase: Architecture and design	
Architect data pipeline: what components or integrations must be added, removed, or modified to support project scope	Architecture diagrams and documents for the data pipeline design

Table 10.4 Analytics Project Sample Work Breakdown Structure
(*continued*)

Work breakdown: Project tasks	Sample deliverables
Analyze current and future state data models: identify required changes	• Logical data model (entity relationship diagram) for the current and future state
Data exploration and mining: explore data sources, in particular, for projects acquiring data from new sources	• Data profiling results, visualizations, discovered patterns, data issues
Design for data acquisition and preparation: identify required components, integrations, and transformations	• Design specifications • Data mapping
Architect the solution: determine the future components and integrations for the deployment of the analytics solutions and how to embed them into the business process	• Architecture diagrams and documents for the overall solution • Future state process flows capturing embedded analytics requirements • System requirements document or functional design document
Prototype: create early prototypes to test design ideas and receive early feedback from stakeholders	• Sketches and storyboards • Early prototypes with feedback
User interface design: create wireframes and design specifications for user-facing features	• Wireframes • Dashboard, report design specifications • Stylesheets, colour schemes
Project phase: Development	
Analytics storage development: create new storage solutions such as data warehouses, data marts, etc., if required for the project and defined through the architecture and design phase	• New or modified analytical storage
Data acquisition and preparation: develop programs and scripts for acquiring and preparing the data	• Transformation logic specifications • Programs, scripts, or API • Changes applied to analytical storage solutions (DW, data mart, data lake)
Data wrangling: extract and wrangle data for feature selection and analytics solution development	• Wrangling logic specifications • Programs, scripts, or API • Creation of new data marts to accommodate new wrangled data
Feature engineering: development of new features if required	• Documented logic • Updated or new training datasets
Report and dashboard development: build programs for generating reports, visualizations, summarizations, and dashboard features	• Developed reports and dashboards
Model building: develop algorithms and programs for data mining, machine learning, predictive and prescriptive models	• Developed algorithms and programs

(*continued*)

Table 10.4 Analytics Project Sample Work Breakdown Structure (*continued*)

Work breakdown: Project tasks	Sample deliverables
Embedded analytics: build the mechanisms to integrate analytical insights into business process	• Developed integrations between operational systems and analytics solutions
Project phase: Testing	
Test planning: create test strategy, test plan, and test cases	• Test strategy, test plan, and test cases
Environment preparation: determine the requirements for the test environment(s) and set up the environments for all QA activities	• Test environment specification • Prepared test environments
Acquire sample data or synthesize test data	• Test data populated to enable functional testing
Conduct component testing: test each component separately	• Test results, issues corrected
Conduct integration testing: test the integration between components	• Test results, issues corrected
Conduct business acceptance testing (BAT): validate that business users get expected results from the solution	• Test results, issues corrected
Project phase: Implementation	
Prepare, translate, and distribute user documentation	• Documentation distributed
Conduct user training	• Training completion
Load initial data into production (e.g., historical data load into the new data mart)	• Historical data available for analysis
Communicate the launch of the solution to stakeholders	• Communication announcements, presentations, videos
Prepare the production environment for deployment of the solution	• Environment readiness
Deploy the solution into production (including all components and integrations)	• Solution ready to be used in the production environment
Conduct final tests	• Test results, go/no-go decision
Present results to stakeholders	• Visualization, presentations, storytelling
Set up a feedback loop for monitoring model effectiveness	• Monitoring analytics, maintenance procedures
Measure the benefits: measure the improvements achieved through using new analytics solutions such as the reduced product return rate, savings on repairs or marketing expenses, the value of cross-sales or retaining customers	• Estimated benefit from using analytics solutions

While Table 10.4 outlines typical project tasks, other activities may be included in the WBS depending on the scope and players in the project, such as:

- Purchasing of new software products, e.g., an analytics platform or a data extraction tool
- New software installation, licence acquisition, set-up, and technical training
- Purchasing and installation of hardware for on-premises solutions
- Negotiation and signing contracts with vendors and service providers
- Acquiring API documentation and testing with a third party when acquiring external data for analysis
- Migrating data from one solution to another, e.g., from legacy data storage to a new enterprise data warehouse
- Communicating with customers when developing customer-facing solutions, e.g., preparing an email campaign and educational videos to promote new expense analytics features of a bank app

The work breakdown presented in Table 10.4 provides the suggested structure and can serve as a checklist. The actual project may require these tasks to be broken down further. When the solution involves a number of components, tasks are broken down by components to enable the assignment of project tasks to individual project members.

The WBS becomes the foundation of a project plan created and monitored by the project manager. Project plans will track other attributes for each task:

- Person responsible for execution
- Projected start and end date, duration of the task in hours or days
- Dependencies—what tasks must be completed in advance
- Percentage of completion once the task is started
- Completion status

As the project gets underway, a project manager will coordinate and track project activities and ensure that every team member knows what to do and has the necessary resources. While in-depth study of project management practices is out of scope for this book, in the next section, we focus on why analytics projects fail or succeed, and how to improve chances of success.

TIPS ON TERMS

There are many interchangeable, similar, official, and colloquial terms related to software development projects.

The *development* phase can be called *build* or *construction*.

Architecture is the discipline; an *architect* is a role or a job title.

The *analysis* phase can be called *requirements analysis* or *requirements definition*.

Business requirements may be captured in *user story* format.

A *design document* may be called a *blueprint* or a *system specification*.

User interface (*UI*) development such as building screens, dashboards, and online reports can be collectively called *front-end* development, whereas developing databases, integrations, scripts, and API are examples of *back-end* development.

An engineer may specialize in front-end or back-end development or may be an expert in both areas, therefore becoming a *full stack* developer.

User interface design may also be called *UX* (*user experience*) design.

Software *defects* are called *bugs*.

White box and *black box testing* are different approaches where the tester either has access to the logic and structure of the programs they are testing (white box) or conducts testing while treating the program as a black box with inputs and outputs.

QA (*quality assurance*) refers to *testing* in a broad sense, including developing a test strategy and considering the quality of the final product during the design.

Business acceptance testing (*BAT*) may be called *user acceptance testing* (*UAT*).

10.6 ANALYTICS PROJECTS SUCCESS FACTORS

Projects centred around data science and analytics deliverables have a lot in common with operations-centric software development projects, but at the same time, they differ from them in several aspects.

Table 10.5 Characteristics of Operations-centric versus Analytics-centric Projects

Operations-centric projects	Analytics-centric projects
• Support of business operations and daily activities	• Management, planning, and innovation objectives
• Create and manage master and transaction data • Deal with highly volatile current data • Unlikely to involve predictions	• Aggregate, transform, and query data • Analyze current and historical data • Experiment with predictive modelling and using predictions to improve operations
• Well-defined in terms of data and functionality • Requirements defined at the beginning of the project with more confidence	• Change, experimentation, research, and development are expected • Requirements evolve and may depend on analytical findings
• Rely on established technologies such as enterprise resource planning systems and traditional databases • Reducing risk to operations is paramount	• Often explore experimental and cutting-edge technology • Results harder to predict, higher uncertainty
• Budget estimates rely on prior experience, higher confidence in timelines	• More difficult to assess resource and funding needs for new, complex, or unproven technologies • Shifting timelines more likely
• More in-house expertise	• Lack of qualified workers more likely
• Benefits are easier understood by users and stakeholders	• Benefits not always obvious • Require complex metrics or a longer time horizon to bring value

Many of the inherent characteristics of analytics and data science projects are explained by the experimental nature of advanced analytics. Sometimes, you don't know what you'll find in the data until you find it. Planning what to do with the diagnostic findings remains hypothetical only until the diagnostic analysis is complete—one of the amazing values of machine learning can be finding patterns and dependencies that human experts never expected.

Therefore, it is important to recognize how to support and accommodate analytics initiatives to make them more successful.

✔ **CHECKLIST**

Analytics Projects Success Factors Checklist

1. Set clear objectives.
   - Clarify the purpose of the project and the problem it should solve.
   - Ensure project vision is communicated and clear to all project team members.
   - Establish success criteria at the start and calibrate all project activities to them.
   - Define clear and specific analytics questions.
2. Involve business stakeholders early and keep them engaged through the whole project.
   - The success of analytics solutions depends on understanding the business, its operations, and business rules.
   - Ensure the project has access to business expertise and engage SMEs in requirements analysis, interpretation of data analysis, design, prototyping, review of test results, and change management.
3. Allow time for due diligence and requirements analysis.
   - Collect information and artifacts relevant to the problem.
   - Identify impacted stakeholders and involve them as early as possible.
   - Engage a business analyst to facilitate requirements analysis.
   - Recognize that while requirements will be refined throughout the project, clear requirements for each upcoming project iteration are necessary.
   - Ensure there is a shared understanding of requirements among all stakeholders.
4. Provision early access to data.
   - Never assume that data is available.
   - Provide access to data as early as possible. Legal and security approvals always take longer than even the most pessimistic estimate.
   - If external partners are involved in the project, initiate preparation of non-disclosure agreements (NDAs) as soon as possible.
5. Engage legal and security stakeholders early.
   - Discuss project scope, implications, and risks at the initiation stage.
   - Capture legal, privacy protection, security, and auditability requirements.
   - Clarify what legislation is applicable, including other countries' laws.

- Be clear what European Union legislation is applicable, as it is likely to have the strictest laws and requirements when it comes to the use of data, privacy protection, consumer rights, and AI regulations.

6. Plan for ample time for data exploration, acquisition, and preparation.
   - Never assume that the data will be clean, consistent, conformed, current, and comprehensive.
   - Allocate time and resources for data preparation and cleaning.
   - Consider privacy protection; if anonymization of datasets is required, it will add to the overall effort.

7. Have a strategy for acquiring test data.
   - Analytics solutions require test data with similar properties and characteristics as the production data.
   - If production data will be used, it must be properly sanitized.
   - If synthetic data is required, its acquisition must be planned.
   - Ensure the test data strategy is approved by security stakeholders.

8. Involve the architecture team early.
   - Analytics development requires significant upfront planning and design to ensure proper data architecture.
   - Data pipeline design must be considered early in the project as part of the overall planning and architecture activities.

9. Get data governance on the team.
   - Analytics models rely on quality data. Engage data governance stakeholders to help achieve the best possible data quality.
   - Communicate any data issues to the data governance team to get issues fixed at the source.

10. Recognize the R&D phase of the project.
    - If a significant R&D component is expected, recognize the timelines as estimates.
    - Allow room for generating, testing, and rejecting multiple hypotheses.
    - Expect multiple iterations of advanced modelling to retrain models, change hyperparameters, and experiment until achieving satisfactory results and prediction accuracy.

11. Use early prototyping to validate ideas.
    - Most analytics projects have visualization requirements to enable business-people to access and use the insights.
    - Early prototyping allows solutions to be designed in collaboration with intended users, taking into account their needs, opinions, and sentiments in order to increase solution adoption.
    - Adopt the "test and learn" mindset and continuously test ideas with future customers.

12. Don't rely on software to be the solution.
    - Purchasing a best-in-class analytics platform does not equal success.
    - Without quality data, clear requirements, and sensible design, there will be no successful solution.
13. Build up organizational data and analytics literacy.
    - Invest in training and learning for both business and technical stakeholders.
    - Build a culture of data ownership.
14. Treat each type of data appropriately.
    - Do not treat big data as traditional structured data. Secure adequate expertise and architecture for handling big data.
    - Ensure the availability of appropriate methods, tools, and expertise for managing semi-structured and unstructured data.
15. Apply project management discipline.
    - Manage analytics efforts as projects while accommodating their special needs:
        - Keep project scope realistic; don't overpromise.
        - Communicate diligently and manage stakeholder expectations.
        - Ensure executive support and project resources.
        - Deal with politics and conflicts before they become a problem.
16. Integrate analytics insights into business process
    - Don't stop at collecting and analyzing data—analytics must be used to improve business processes and support decision-making.
    - Consider how to embed analytics in operational processes and how to measure its effectiveness (create a feedback loop).
17. Prepare to deal with unexpected results.
    - What if a data mining insight contradicts management belief? Will executives be open-minded about accepting the unexpected? Will business stakeholders trust a solution that makes counterintuitive decisions? Would this undermine the project?
    - Depending on the organization's maturity, a prolonged adoption process may be necessary, starting with decision support and decision augmentation models to allow stakeholders to assess the benefits of the predictive models before they are comfortable with higher levels of automation.
    - Even with sufficient stakeholder adoption of the solution, monitoring, tuning, and maintenance of the models are still vital.
18. Monitor and improve.
    - As part of the project, develop mechanisms for monitoring the performance of analytics models.
    - Plan for periodic review of the metrics or a reinforcement learning model to ensure concept, data, and model drift are addressed.

The reality of a complex project in an organization—which may face monetary or resourcing challenges, disruption, market fluctuations, or changes in leadership—is such that not everything will go according to plan. The maturity of an organization doesn't determine just how successful an analytics project is likely to be but also how the company and its employees learn from each new experience. Learning from past mistakes is a foundation of future success, along with building organizational knowledge and expertise.

Here is what organizations can do to learn from analytics initiatives:

- Analyze project gaps and failures—what went wrong and why, and what can be done differently next time.
- Create reusable artifacts such as glossaries, data dictionaries, data preparation and wrangling specifications, data models, and business process diagrams.
- With every data-heavy project, strengthen the data governance function.
- Reuse wireframes and prototypes to create libraries and templates for reuse.
- Refine visual presentation styles for reuse and stakeholder familiarity.
- Capture and retain security, privacy protection, and auditability requirements as they are likely to be similar on the next project.
- Capture and share the outcomes of data exploration, data mining, and data science experimentation. A certain result that was beyond the scope of one project might be a good starting point for the next one.
- Plan for reuse of code and components, scalable integrations, and extendable APIs. Get architecture and software design expertise to create the foundation for scalable solutions.

10.7 CHAPTER SUMMARY

Key Points to Remember

- An analytics solution may be the main goal of an analytics project, or one of many deliverables of an enterprise software development project.
- Analytics projects may involve changes to the company's analytical storage solution, acquisition of new data sources, or a data pipeline development.
- Whether a project uses waterfall, agile, or hybrid development methodology, its success depends on using the methodology best practices consistently.
- Understanding of analytics goals and business requirements play a key role in designing successful analytics solutions.
- Many project roles on analytics projects are similar to software project roles, with additional needs for data and analytics expertise.
- Many analytics projects, in particular, those involving big data analytics, will require time for experimentation and research.
- Analytics solution development must take into account legal, ethical, and security aspects.

Key Terms

Business requirement: a feature or capability needed to solve a business problem or satisfy a business need.

Change request: a formal proposal to change the scope, timeline, or budget of a project.

Hybrid approach: an approach to solution development that blends the waterfall and agile methodology elements.

Project: a temporary endeavour undertaken to create a unique product.

Software development life cycle (SDLC): fundamental steps required to deliver a software development project.

Stakeholders: people, departments, and entities interested in the solution, affected by it, benefitting from it, or having an influence over it.

Work breakdown structure (WBS): deconstruction of the scope of required work into smaller tasks that are easier to understand, estimate, and execute.

Questions for Critical Thought

1. What phases are essential to any software development project?
2. What project roles are essential for an analytics project?
3. What is a work breakdown structure, and what is its purpose for managing projects?
4. Who determines business requirements for an analytics project?
5. When is the right time to involve business stakeholders in the analytics project?
6. Discuss analytics project success factors that can pose the biggest challenge for advanced analytics development.

Test Your Knowledge

1. What project role is best suited for the task of creating a data model for the new data warehouse?
   a. BI developer
   b. Data architect
   c. Project manager
   d. Business analyst

2. What project role is best suited for the task of validating requirements with business stakeholders?
   a. BI developer
   b. Data architect
   c. Project manager
   d. Business analyst

3. What project role is best suited for the task of creating a project WBS?
    a. BI developer
    b. Data architect
    c. Project manager
    d. Business analyst

4. What is the reason for involving business stakeholders in the project early?
    a. To get their requirements captured as quickly as possible and allow them to go back to their regular work
    b. To ensure that the project objectives are clear and that each phase of the project aligns with business needs
    c. To provide the background and the information needed to understand business requirements and design the solution
    d. a, b, and c
    e. b and c

5. What project phase is most likely to contain activities related to the validation that summaries and KPIs on a new dashboard developed by the project are calculated correctly?
    a. Initiation and planning
    b. Architecture and design
    c. Testing
    d. Implementation

Recommended Readings

Archer, S., & Kaufman, C. (2013). *Accelerating Outcomes with a Hybrid Approach within a Waterfall Environment.* Paper presented at PMI® Global Congress 2013—North America, New Orleans, LA. Project Management Institute (PMI).

Barrett, D. (2024). *Understanding Project Management: A Practical Guide* (3rd ed.). CS Business Press/Canadian Scholars.

Scrum.org. (n.d.). *What Is Scrum?* Retrieved February 21, 2024, from www.scrum.org/resources/what-scrum-module.

Notes

1. Project Management Institute. (2008). *A Guide to the Project Management Body of Knowledge (PMBOK® Guide)* (4th ed.). Project Management Institute, p. 434.
2. Kosarenko, Y. (2019). *Business Analyst: A Profession and a Mindset*, p. 30.

Chapter 11

Analytics in an Enterprise Context

Business analytics solutions are created by organizations with specific goals in mind. The success of these solutions should be measured by the extent they help the organizations achieve these goals. In this chapter, we look at what is required to build analytics-driven organizations:

- What affects analytics maturity
- Performance measurement approaches
- The risks, legal concerns, and ethical concerns of using data and analytics

11.1 ANALYTICS MATURITY

The degree to which a company can be successful in using data to make better decisions is a factor of its **analytics maturity**—the competency in managing its data and transforming it into meaningful and actionable insights.

Analytics maturity depends on a company's ability to:

- Organize, manage, and govern enterprise data
- Enforce standards, consistent definitions, and understanding of data
- Create a sense of ownership and accountability for data quality
- Hire, retain, and train knowledgeable people
- Support robust technology and architecture capabilities
- Promote the value of analytical insights from the executive leadership level
- Use analytics to innovate and gain competitive advantage

Every data management and analytical activity discussed earlier in this book matters to the result—the quality of analytical insights and their effectiveness in supporting the company's decision-making. The ability of an individual organization to manage its data life cycle and utilize analytics for managing the enterprise can be reflected in the different levels of analytics maturity (Figure 11.1).

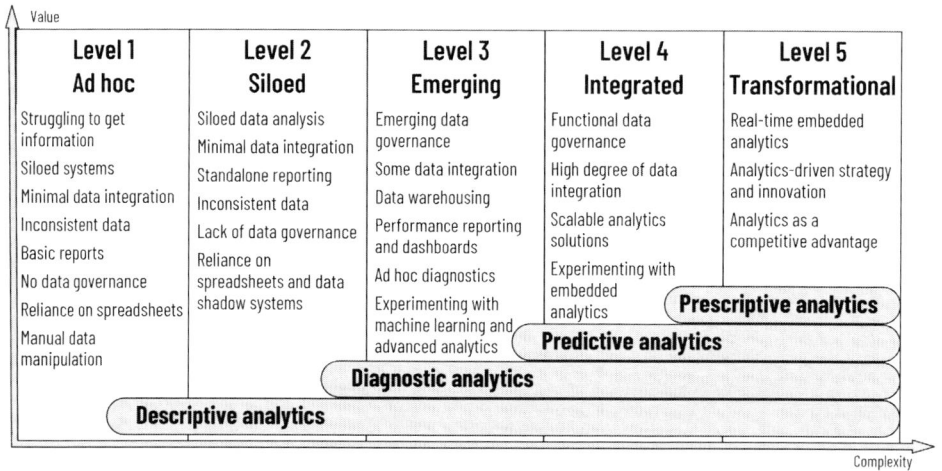

Figure 11.1 Analytics Maturity Levels

It takes time and conscious organizational effort to develop this maturity and transform data into a reliable resource to improve the decision-making process. The keyword here is *reliable resource*: the higher the risk of making a wrong decision, the more reliability will be expected by decision-makers to trust the analytics for decision support or augmentation. When it comes to decision automation, the level of trust in the solution must be very high.

This level of trust—that an analytics solution produces accurate results and makes reliable decisions—can only be achieved when all components required for managing the analytics life cycle are in place and effective.

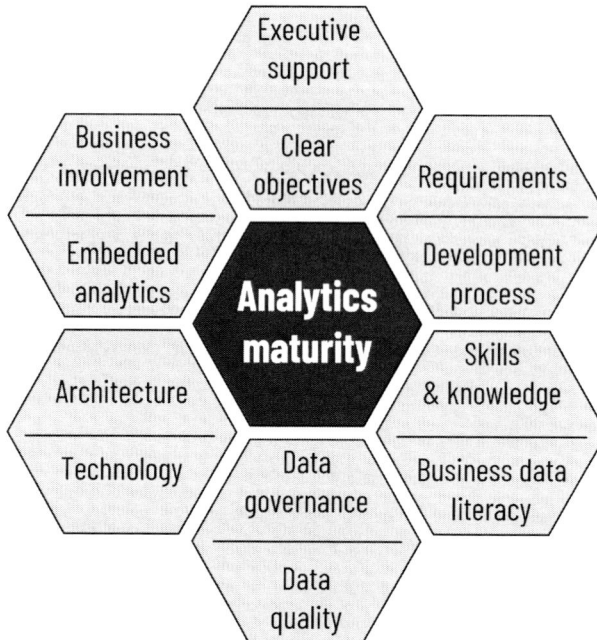

Figure 11.2 Analytics Maturity Factors

Table 11.1 Analytics Maturity Expectations

Factor	Best practices
Executive support	• The value of analytics and its potential as a competitive differentiator is understood and appreciated at the executive level • Funding and resources are provided for the development of analytics capability
Clear objectives	• Clear goals are established, empowering teams and providing targets and success metrics
Business involvement	• Business stakeholders are involved in all stages of analytics development, providing clear requirements and defining the decision-making process with analytics
Embedded analytics	• Analytics insights are actively utilized and embedded in the business process, and their effectiveness can be evaluated and improved using operational results • The organization has progressed beyond performance management to making analytics-driven decisions
Requirements	• Best practices of business analysis are applied to elicit business needs, analyze operational activities and processes to be supported by analytics, and determine analytics requirements
Development process	• Effective methodology and processes for the development of analytics solutions are in place • The organization uses best practices to deliver quality solutions, adapt to changes, and innovate
Skills and knowledge	• The organization consciously nurtures data and analytics expertise by hiring, training, and retaining qualified resources and developing an analytics centre of excellence • Knowledge development and sharing are embedded in the organization's culture • Solutions are well documented • Knowledge of employees leaving the organization can be captured and transferred without loss
Business data literacy	• A data-driven culture is supported and promoted, creating accountability for and a sense of ownership over the quality of data in business stakeholders • Business data ownership is established and functional
Data governance	• A functional enterprise data governance capability is established, developing and enforcing processes and controls for maintaining data quality and shared understanding of data entities, attributes, and metrics across the organization
Data quality	• Enterprise data quality is maintained and improved through effective data governance, master data management, integration, and effective data pipelines
Architecture	• Purposeful design of the analytics architecture and data pipelines • Architecture components and infrastructure are fit for purpose and scalable and satisfy reliability and security requirements
Technology	• Advanced analytical platforms and tools are available to enable enterprise analytics goals, minimizing decision latency and supporting scalability and future growth • Technology supports all types of data, including unstructured • Tools are available for experimentation, learning, and development of new analytics skills

11.2 ANALYTICS CAPABILITY IN ORGANIZATIONS

As analytics maturity depends on the data culture in the organization, placement of the analytics team or staff involved in producing analytics may also play a role. Organizations are hierarchical machines, driven not just by strategic goals, mission, and vision but also by forces such as reporting structure, performance measurements, and internal politics.

The success of business analytics depends on the involvement and contribution of business stakeholders as well as operationalization of analytics solutions into the business process. The effectiveness of the solution depends on well-formulated and understood requirements provided by stakeholders engaged in a project. The solution relies on the quality of data as there is only so much one can clean—and it is the business owners of the data who play a crucial role.

Successful operationalization of solutions requires trust. Is this solution reliable? Can we trust its predictions? It also requires a sense of ownership to be invested in measuring results and providing feedback for the model's maintenance, tuning, and future improvements. As a result, overall success depends on the relationship between an organization's analytics experts and business units. While historically, data and analytics functions were the purview of information technology (IT) organizations, many analytics-driven companies had success with other approaches that emphasized the role of analytics in the company as a trusted partner for business improvement and innovation.

Some of these approaches are depicted in Figures 11.3, 11.4, and 11.5. The models that refer to the business analytics unit as *analytics COE*, or centre of excellence, imply that:

- It may be comprised of more than one team, such as those dedicated to business intelligence (BI) and visualization, data science, machine learning operations, and data engineering.
- It supports the centralization of methodology, best practices, and knowledge-sharing for the use of data and analytics across the organization.

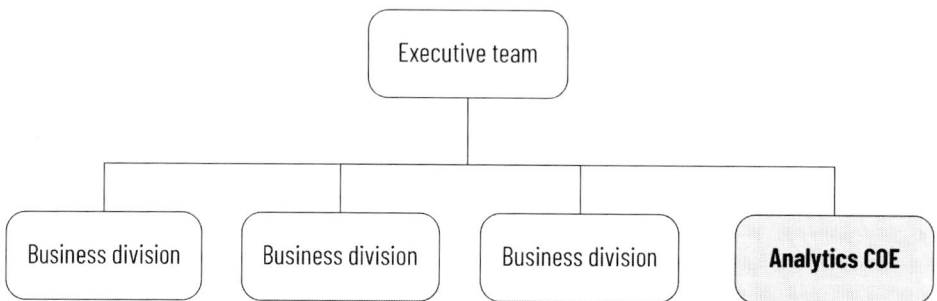

Figure 11.3 Analytics in an Organization—Centralized Model

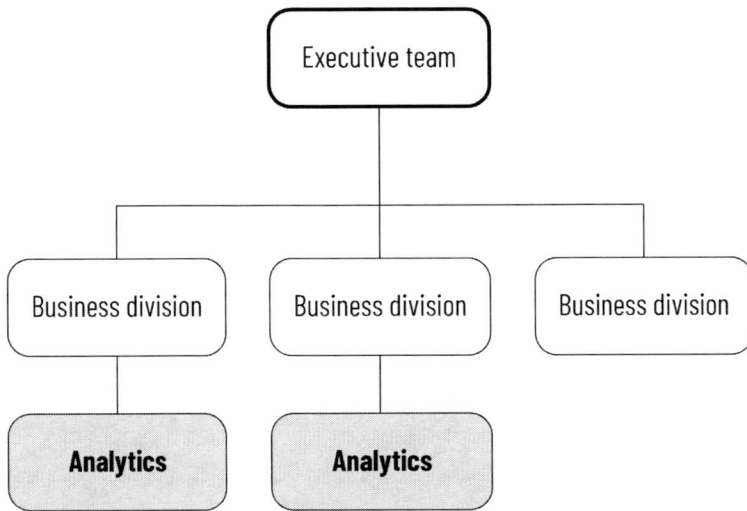

Figure 11.4 Analytics in an Organization—Decentralized Model

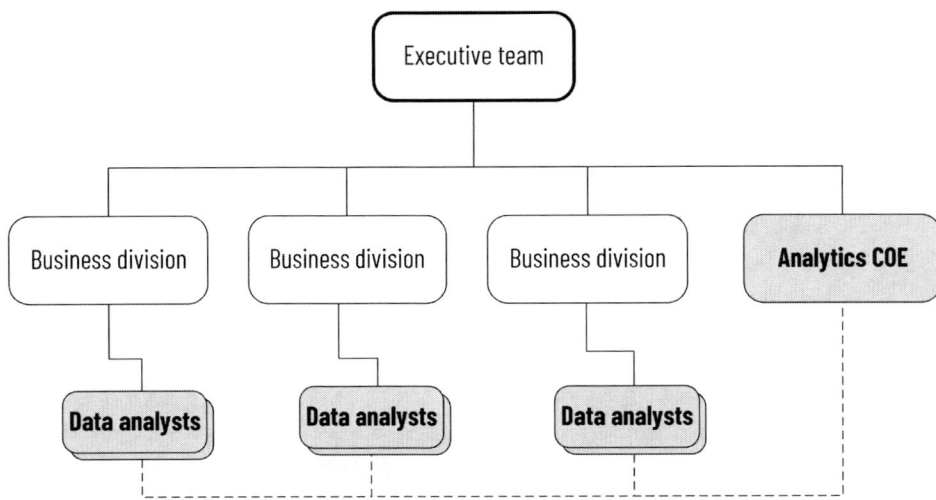

Figure 11.5 Analytics in an Organization—Hybrid Model

Table 11.2 Analytics in an Organization—Comparison of Models

Centralized model ("corporate" or "shared services")	Decentralized model	Hybrid model
Analytics resources are concentrated and assigned to work with business units	Some business units develop and fund analytics teams and capabilities	COE provides methodology, best practices, and expertise and collaborates with data analysts or teams dedicated to individual business units

Table 11.2 Analytics in an Organization—Comparison of Models (*continued*)

Centralized model ("corporate" or "shared services")	Decentralized model	Hybrid model
Rely on business units for functional and data expertise	In-depth functional and data expertise	In-depth functional expertise, unit analysts relied on for data expertise
Prioritization across the organization may lead to longer timelines for an individual unit	Faster turnaround on business unit-specific solutions	Faster delivery of BI, COE leads complex enterprise analytics solutions
Centralized budget, resources, and planning	Budget and resources funded by units, siloed planning	A mixed approach to budget and resources, planning requires the prioritization of shared resources
Shared best practices, standardization, cross-functional capabilities	Lack of standardization, duplication of effort, lack of integration, cross-functional solutions may be a challenge	Shared best practices, standardization, cross-functional capabilities

For a centralized analytics team, another factor is the executive chain of command—namely, whom the analytics function reports to:

- Chief Information Officer (CIO) or a Chief Technology Officer (CTO), when the analytics function is within an IT organization
- Chief Financial Officer (CFO), when the analytics function grows out of financial and accounting reporting
- Chief Data Officer (CDO), when data and analytics capabilities are considered strategic

The emergence of the CDO is a fairly recent phenomenon. The purpose of this executive role is to manage an organization's data strategy, from data governance to the strategic application of advanced analytics and AI. This role is usually found in organizations at the integrated and transformation levels of analytics maturity.

When will a company look at its analytics capabilities as strategic rather than supporting? It depends on how analytics can influence, define, and facilitate the execution of the enterprise strategy.

From a customer perspective, the approach will differ for B2B (business-to-business) and B2C (business-to-consumer) models. A B2C model will often lend itself more naturally to the use of consumer analytics to:

- Assess market trends and changing consumer preferences
- Use analytics for lead management, marketing automation, targeted advertising, and cross-selling to consumers
- Standardize and automate customer interactions and services such as via the use of virtual assistants, chatbots, and automated customer journeys

In a B2B business model, customer scale will define potential analytics use cases:

- When dealing with large volumes of small business customers, analytics-based automation and decision-making will be applied.
- Dealing with large strategic customers and partners may require a tailored approach and white-glove touch through account management, with analytics playing a supporting role.

From a product perspective, enterprises that market products with customer-facing analytics will consider analytics as part of their strategic research and development and product management capabilities. Consider some examples of digital products:

- Products that include analytics as a customer-facing function, e.g., a bank app with built-in expense or investment analytics
- Products based on collecting and processing customer data, e.g., wearables
- Products that deliver digital content, e.g., news, music, or video streaming
- Virtual services, e.g., online training or coaching
- Cloud platforms providing access to video editing, digital art, or generative AI capabilities on a subscription basis
- Data products, e.g., market research

Development of such products would be considered the intellectual property of the organization, the core of its competitive advantage. Product development groups will have a prominent position as they are not just developing analytics to support product marketing, sales, and services—they develop the product itself.

Can the analytics function be outsourced or provided by external agents?

While some companies use commercial-off-the-shelf (COTS) analytics platforms to provide the infrastructure, they frequently continue to maintain in-house teams to build solutions on these platforms. Other possible scenarios are:

- Using an external vendor to develop a reporting base, then in-house teams will maintain and update analytics solutions. This approach is often used when a company implements a new enterprise resource planning (ERP) system and requires a full replacement of the analytics and BI on the new platform. The implementation vendor with expertise in the new system builds the foundation, including the data pipelines, and then provides training and documentation to enable in-house maintenance and development.
- Purchasing a COTS product with sophisticated advanced analytics components that the company does not have resources to match. For example, if a COTS product includes access to market intelligence and competitive research, the organization may license and use the vendor product instead of developing its own solutions.
- Implementing a COTS solution with embedded analytics and AI capabilities that are part of the core product. In this case, the company may continue to develop other BI internally while relying on the product for advanced analytics and taking advantage of product releases and updates.

These scenarios will likely result in a hybrid analytics delivery model where COTS analytics is supplemented by internally developed BI. Full outsourcing of the analytics function is more likely for companies that are too small to sustain an analytics team while requiring access to sophisticated technologies and data storage solutions. While the analysis of the pros and cons of outsourcing can get quite complex, it is more likely to work for companies whose core business is not dependent on analytics.

11.3 ENTERPRISE PERFORMANCE MEASUREMENT SYSTEMS AND CHALLENGES

The goals of business analytics must be driven by the overall goals of the organization. As strategic and tactical goals are established, they define KPIs that the organization wants to achieve. This, in turn, determines what operational metrics to measure and monitor, and what target variables to select for predictive modelling.

CASE STUDY

Measuring Customer Satisfaction

YardExperts' goal of increasing customer satisfaction can translate into defining regularly tracked metrics such as:

- First call resolution rate
- First-year contract renewal rate
- Customer churn rate

These KPIs will be measured monthly and included in the company scorecard.

When the analytics team gets an assignment to create a model for customer retention recommendations, they start with establishing the target variable. After a consultation with the executive sponsor, they agree to use the first-year contract renewal rate as the initial target.

The first model will focus on new customers in their first year of a service contract and will aim to maximize the contract renewal rate by recommending various retention strategies, from courtesy calls to discounts to complimentary service visits.

Building on the success of this model, the team will next expand their target to the overall customer churn rate. This model will include both new and existing customers and will analyze the factors of customers' loyalty along with the first-year impressions. The target variable of the advanced analytics models will evolve. However, the success of analytics still needs to be measured using the performance indicators that matter to the enterprise.

Metrics and KPIs are descriptive analytics: they summarize information for easy consumption by businesspeople. They allow the establishment of the baseline against which to measure the performance of the organization, as well as the targets to strive for.

What descriptive analytics cannot do is tell the organization how to get to the targets. This is the job of advanced analytics, which assist the businesspeople in identifying discriminating factors and root causes, use these insights to build predictive models, and recommend what should be done to achieve the targets.

Nevertheless, it's important for organizations to have a consistent system for performance measurement. The goal of **performance measurement** is to provide a systematic approach to measuring and reporting the performance of the organization. There are several popular performance measurement frameworks.

Management by objectives (*MBO*) was originally proposed by Peter Drucker in 1954[1] and can be found in many organizations today, applied to measuring employee performance through a set of objectives and an annual cycle of performance reviews.

MBO involves setting organizational objectives that are then translated into departmental and individual goals. While the main ideas of MBO are still used in many organizations today to support annual performance assessment, the abbreviation itself is no longer widely referenced.

The *balanced scorecard* (*BSC*) considers a company's financial performance as the ultimate measure while balancing it with additional perspectives.[2] The four measurement perspectives of BSC are:

- Financial (profitability and use of financial resources)
- Customer (customer value, satisfaction, and retention)
- Internal business process (process efficiency and product quality)
- Learning and growth (capabilities that support the organization's growth such as human capital, IT, and culture)

Under the BSC framework, the organization will establish one or more KPIs for each of the four perspectives, establishing the goals and then tracking the performance toward those goals. The goals may be cascaded from the enterprise to parts of the organization, individual departments, or even individual employees.

BSC is used widely by businesses, governments, and nonprofit organizations around the world and is considered one of the most influential business ideas.[3]

The *objectives and key results* (*OKR*) framework focuses on defining measurable goals and tracking the results. It requires setting:

- A big, aspirational measurable goal (the *what*)
- Three to five measurable key results for tracking the achievement of the goal (the *how*)

OKR popularization is attributed to Andy Grove, who introduced it at Intel in the 1970s.[4] It was later popularized by John Doerr and adopted by Google and many other large tech companies.[5] It is considered more suitable for organizational goal setting and measuring performance at the strategic level rather than offering performance indicators applicable to individual departments or measuring employee performance.

One Metric That Matters (*OMTM*), or the "North Star Metric" approach, proposes that an organization chooses one important metric of growth that matters most at a given time. The OMTM approach was introduced in the book *Lean Analytics*[6] and was meant to help organizations focus on the most important indicators of growth without getting distracted by "vanity" metrics. A short-term goal may be selected as OMTM, replaced by another metric if the original OMTM goal is achieved.

While the original emphasis has been on helping startups maintain their focus to sustain growth and competitive advantage, a variation of OMTM called the North Star can be found used in many organizations. In contrast to OMTM, the North Star is usually established as a single long-term strategic metric.

Other than the frameworks mentioned above, many other variations and competing frameworks are described in books and articles, touted by competing management consulting companies, and introduced in organizations with the appointment of a new executive team. None are perfect, and implementation matters as much as the principles.

Eli (Eliyahu) Goldratt is credited with saying, "Tell me how you measure me, and I'll tell you how I will behave."[7] Any performance management system that rewards achievement of specific KPIs will encourage achievement of these indicators, potentially at the expense of other aspects such as product quality and longevity, infrastructure sustainability, or employee satisfaction.

Challenges may include:

- Measuring what is easy to measure instead of what is important
- Measuring against internal baselines without benchmarking, e.g., not comparing the company's churn rate against the industry average
- Measuring short-term achievement while not recognizing long-term performance trends, e.g., brand reputation
- Focusing on lagging indicators (past performance) versus leading indicators (metrics predicting future results)
- Measuring wrong metrics tied to rewards and punishment that leads to "gaming the metrics"

There are many well-documented examples of wrong metrics driving undesirable results.

In education, "teaching to the test" emphasizes the curriculum to help students pass standardized tests that educational institutions are being measured on instead of teaching them skills that are important for employability but more difficult to measure.

In medicine, surgeons may avoid taking on difficult cases if their remuneration and promotion are tied to the surgery survival rate.

When poorly chosen metrics are tied to rewards or punishment, it can lead to quite dramatic unintended consequences such as fraudulent behaviour—for example, the Wells Fargo scandal, in which company employees set up fraudulent accounts in response to impossibly high cross-selling targets.[8] Another famous example of a perverse incentive (an incentive that has an undesirable or opposite effect) is the Cobra effect.[9] When the British government offered a bounty for each killed cobra to reduce their numbers in Dehli, the initial reduction in cobra numbers was followed by entrepreneurial residents starting cobra farms as a source of income.

Choosing proxy measurements to measure intangible results is also a challenge. A proxy measurement should have a strong correlation with what we want to measure, and finding suitable metrics may pose a significant difficulty.

Another consideration, especially when measuring employee performance, is the impact of performance measurement and chosen performance rewards on employees' motivation. As discussed in Daniel Pink's book *Drive*,[10] the relationship between motivation, job satisfaction, drive to excel, and monetary rewards is not always straightforward.

CASE STUDY

Measuring Employee Satisfaction

The YardExperts management team has been debating how to measure employee satisfaction. What is a suitable proxy measure? The literature search yielded many suggestions; however, a consensus has not yet been achieved.

Some favoured the classic approach of an annual employee satisfaction survey with statements such as:

- I know about the potential career growth opportunities that my employer offers.
- I get recognition for a job well done.
- I have opportunities to learn new professional skills at my organization.
- My manager provides me with meaningful feedback.

Others argued that a landscaping and snow removal business is not the type of organization that offers many professional growth opportunities. Why do employees happily stay in the same job for many years or leave unsatisfied?

The analytics manager proposed a data-based approach to measuring:

- Average tenure by job type (with longer tenure indicative of overall satisfaction with the company)
- Employee participation in the pension and benefits plan (may be indicative of the employee's appreciation of the benefits package and intention to stay long enough to use the benefits)
- Participation in social committee activities (may be indicative of a positive climate and approval of company culture)
- The trend of employee referrals (assuming that employees are more likely to recommend the company to people they know if they are satisfied themselves)

> In the end, the management team decided to try both strategies and compare the results, segmenting them by the type of job and the regions, and to analyze potential relationships between metrics. It will be an interesting experiment, and it may suggest how to improve employee satisfaction measurement in the future and make it more meaningful.

11.4 LEGISLATIVE AND PRIVACY PROTECTION CONCERNS

Any technology can be used for good or bad, and this pertains to the advances in data science, machine learning, and the development of AI algorithms. Anyone who works closely with data or has privileged access to enterprise data sources can cause harm, intentionally or not.

This is why most jurisdictions establish legislative frameworks governing the use and protection of data, starting with privacy protection.

Privacy is a state of being apart from company or observation, or freedom from unauthorized intrusion.[11]

The purpose of **privacy legislation** is to establish the norms and boundaries for organizations' use of individuals' private data. Different jurisdictions—countries, states, and provinces—may have different laws in place. While the numbers fluctuate, according to data at the time of writing, 71% of all countries around the world had privacy legislation in force,[12] including (but not limited to):

- Personal Information Protection and Electronic Documents Act (PIPEDA) in Canada
- Privacy Act in the United States
- General Data Protection Regulation (GDPR) in the European Union (EU)

Privacy laws also exist at the state or provincial level (e.g., the California Consumer Privacy Act [CCPA] and the Personal Information Protection Act in Alberta, Canada) and the industry level (e.g., Health Insurance Portability and Accountability Act [HIPAA] in the United States); others are directed at specific population groups (e.g., Children's Online Privacy Protection Rule).

Privacy laws protect individuals' right to privacy by governing how organizations must handle the personal information of individuals in the course of their activities. The scope of these laws includes a wide range of personal information. For example, under PIPEDA, **personal information** includes any factual or subjective information, recorded or not, about an identifiable individual. This includes information related to:[13]

- Age, name, ID numbers, income, ethnic origin, blood type
- Opinions, evaluations, comments, social status, disciplinary actions

- Employee files, credit records, loan records, medical records, existence of a dispute between a consumer and a merchant, intentions (e.g., to acquire goods or services or change jobs)

When considering data about an individual that needs protection, privacy legislation goes beyond individual characteristics. While one or two pieces of information, such as first name and country of birth, may not be enough to pinpoint a particular person, when several attributes are collected together, they allow for identification of the person, and therefore constitute personal data, also referred to as **personally identifiable information (PII)**.[14]

PII examples include:

- First and last name, nicknames
- Email address(es)
- Phone number(s)
- Home address
- Date and place of birth
- Race, religion, gender
- Language preferences
- Physical description
- Biometric data
- Photos and videos picturing an individual
- Credit card numbers
- Medical file, genetic data
- Education
- Government-issued identification, e.g., driver's licence, social insurance, health card number
- Political affiliations
- Online identifications, e.g., username, password, cookie ID, Internet Protocol (IP) address of a device
- Spatiotemporal data, i.e., the location of an individual at a particular moment in time

At the same time, the information about an individual related to their official, public, or business role—for instance, an elected official's position or the titles and dates of a person's publications—is not considered personal.

HIPAA in the United States, which aims to protect patients from inappropriate disclosure of their health information, refers to **protected health information (PHI)**, defined as any information relating to a patient's condition, health care, or health care–related payments resulting from provisioning health care services for an individual.[15] Eighteen HIPAA identifiers require protection, which, along with the PII mentioned above, include medical record and health plan beneficiary numbers, vehicles, and device identification numbers.

The GDPR in the EU imposes the most stringent privacy and security laws in the world. Even companies outside the EU need to understand its requirements as it imposes obligations on organizations anywhere in the world as long as they collect data about EU residents. The GDPR establishes:[16]

- Data protection principles and accountability, including the required levels of security and encryption
- Instances when organizations are allowed to collect and process personal data
- Strict rules about what constitutes consent from a person to use their data
- Privacy rights of the individuals such as the right to be informed, the right to restrict process, and the right to erasure, also known as "the right to be forgotten"

Regardless of jurisdiction, the most fundamental principle of all privacy laws is that individuals have a right to privacy, and any organization that has access to private data is responsible for its fair use and protection.

For example, PIPEDA states that any collection, use, or disclosure of personal information must only be for purposes that a reasonable person would consider appropriate in the circumstances, which is reflected in PIPEDA's 10 fair information principles (Appendix C).

Privacy laws establish what is considered appropriate and inappropriate use of personal information. Under PIPEDA's guidance, inappropriate use may involve:

- Collecting, using, or disclosing personal information in ways that are otherwise unlawful
- Profiling or categorizing individuals in a way that leads to unfair, unethical, or discriminatory treatment contrary to human rights law
- Collecting, using, or disclosing personal information for purposes that may cause significant harm to someone
- Publishing personal information with the intent of charging people for its removal
- Requiring passwords to social media accounts for the purpose of employee screening
- Conducting surveillance on an individual using their own device's audio or video functions

---

TIPS ON TERMS

PI, PII, PHI, and PCI

The terms *PI (personal information)* and *PII (personally identifiable information)* are used by various privacy legislation to refer to the information that can lead to identification of an individual. In particular, PIPEDA and CCPA refer to PI, while GDPR refers to PII.

Protected Health Information (PHI) refers to information shared with or handled by health care providers in HIPAA jurisdiction (United States).

PCI (payment card industry) data refers to the data identified as sensitive by the payment card industry and includes information such as cardholder data (account number, cardholder name, expiration date) and sensitive authentication data (PIN, CVV code, magnetic stripe data).[17]

When determining what personal data will be collected by an enterprise for operational and analytical purposes, companies must ensure that their data collection is limited to what is considered the appropriate use of data and plan what data protection strategies to use. After data collection, further steps must be taken to protect data at different stages of the data life cycle. When discussing data protection, we also distinguish between data held in storage ("at rest") and while moving from one storage location to another ("in transit").

Table 11.3 Privacy Protection Strategies

Strategy	Description
Data minimization	Reducing data collected; personal data collected only if a specific and compelling purpose is defined
Pseudonymization	Identifiable data is substituted with a reversible, consistent value for operational purposes, while personal data is limited to the most protected storage and access (e.g., customer ID, account ID, token)
User access controls	Access to personal data is managed through access restriction and monitoring
Encryption	Data is altered (encoded) into unreadable form using an encryption algorithm that ensures the data can only be read by an agent that possesses the encryption key
Anonymization	Personally identifiable information is removed so that the data can no longer be linked to an individual
Synthetic data	Using datasets composed entirely of "fictional" individuals or altered identities that retain the statistical properties of the original dataset

From an analytics perspective, the last two strategies (anonymization and synthetic data use) are of special importance as they are primarily concerned with reducing the risk of exposure when using data for analytical purposes, while the other strategies apply to most of the data life cycle.

When data is anonymized sufficiently so that an individual cannot be linked to a particular record, such data is no longer under the purview of privacy legislation. Anonymized data can be shared and sold without permission from individuals. This is an approach used by market research companies that sell data products, such as for research on market trends and preferences.

There are several approaches to anonymizing data:

- De-identification: removing direct identifiers such as names and government-issued identifiers
- Removing indirect identifiers (quasi-identifiers) that may in combination allow to identify a person even without the direct identifiers—e.g., a combination of gender, date of birth, and street address
- Generalization (banding the data): replacing specific values with bands to reduce the exposure of personal details—e.g., income may be replaced with a category representing an income range, age of an individual can be replaced with an age group, and postal code can be trimmed to the first three characters

- Aggregating data: summarizing individual records if summary data will suffice
- Removing or masking outliers: discarding individual records with unique characteristics that make them easily identifiable or modifying their unique characteristics to allow the grouping of unique individuals with others to avoid identification
- Data perturbation: injecting random "noise" into datasets to provide a mathematical guarantee that the presence of any one individual will be masked

Anonymization of data is not perfect. With today's proliferation of open-source data sources and enormous amounts of personal data shared on social media, cross-referencing several data sources may result in a so-called **mosaic effect** or **de-anonymization**.

De-anonymization refers to identifying an individual from anonymized data by cross-referencing other data sources. It has been demonstrated many times that de-anonymization is possible:

- 87% of the population in the United States can be uniquely identified based only on five-digit ZIP code, gender, and date of birth.[18]
- More than 80% of Netflix movie rental service users could be uniquely identified by when and how they rated any three of the movies they rented.[19]

Organizations that release and share datasets must consider strategies for mitigating the risk of de-anonymization by applying multiple anonymization methods or utilizing synthetic data.

In addition, while the above strategies are mostly intended for structured data, unstructured data containing PII presents its own challenges outside the scope of this book. As most unstructured data is converted to structured data before being used for analysis, particularly for machine learning, the privacy protection strategies outlined above will apply to wrangled data.

TIPS ON TERMS

Pseudonymization is the replacement of personally identifiable data with another value that can be called a *pseudonym*, *alias*, *token*, or *identifier*.

Data perturbation can be called *noise injection*.

Anonymized data may be referred to as *sanitized* or *redacted*.

CHECKLIST

Data Protection during the Analytics Life Cycle

1. Identify user access controls and encryption requirements for the whole analytics life cycle.

Some companies place much more emphasis on the protection of data in operational systems while being more negligent with analytical systems. It is necessary to protect both.

2. Can you minimize exposure?

When exploring data sources during the acquisition stage, consider whether and what personal data is required for analysis. If particular sensitive attributes are not required (e.g., date of birth or social security number), exclude them during data acquisition.

Note that if personal data must be stored in a data warehouse or another analytical storage solution, then additional protection in the form of access controls and encryption must be applied during storage (when data is at rest). When subsets of data are extracted for further wrangling or machine learning purposes, all sensitive data that is not required must be stripped off before data is extracted and shared.

3. Can you use aliases?

If analytics requirements include the need for business users to drill into individual records, such as the details of a customer who filed a complaint, consider relying on pseudonyms such as customer ID or account ID and minimizing the exposure of personal data.

Remember that a numeric customer ID assigned by a computer system does not have a meaning outside of the organization, while a person's driver's licence number does and therefore requires a higher level of protection.

4. Protect data on the move.

Data must be protected both when stored (at rest) and when moving (in transit). While the need to protect the data stored in analytical storage solutions (data warehouses, data marts, and data lakes) is more obvious, ensure you secure data on the move (considering every component of the data pipeline, from ETL scripts to API security).

5. Use multiple anonymization strategies.

As outlined above, several choices are available when it comes to anonymization. Using multiple strategies, while not foolproof, helps reduce de-anonymization risks.

6. Continue to assess data protection and re-identification risks.

Implementation of data protection is not a one-and-done deal. The risks and the vulnerability of the data at rest and in transit must be re-evaluated regularly.

While privacy protection is the most significant legal concern for analytics, there are others.

Data Ownership

As creating and publishing data has become easy and accessible to any individual or organization with the ubiquitousness of the internet and social media, the question of unclear data ownership creates multiple concerns. When copying and distributing data created by others cannot be controlled by the originator, it creates a multitude of questions about accuracy, accountability, fair use, and using data for unintended purposes. Organizations must be aware of this complex environment and the development of new legislative frameworks and monitor their risks.

Intellectual Property

With the rise of generative AI, the debate about intellectual property versus fair use of information has been heating up. As new big data analytics and generative AI models are trained on data available online, legislative framework is lacking around the use of data shared by individuals, as well as the use of copyrighted materials such as books, movies, music, and visual art to train AI models.

Existing intellectual property legislation is not adequately equipped to deal with AI aspects, and no doubt updated legislation is expected and should be monitored and assessed by organizations to ensure their preparedness.

Another aspect of the intellectual property ownership challenge arises when companies use AI algorithms to create new inventions. If a pharmaceutical company used such a method to develop a new drug, the ownership of the patent and the ability to protect the invention may become a challenge due to lacking legal frameworks to regulate this scenario.

AI Risk Regulation

A major step to the regulation on AI is the first of its kind EU Artificial Intelligence Act (EU AI Act), approved by the Council of the EU on May 21, 2024. The act will regulate the obligations of AI providers based on the level of risk of the AI system. The act classifies AI according to its risk as follows:[20]

- Unacceptable: e.g., social scoring systems, manipulative AI, and certain uses of biometric identification; these AI systems are prohibited
- High-risk: e.g., systems profiling individuals, operating critical infrastructure, assessing eligibility for public services, administration of justice, and many others; these AI systems are regulated by the act
- Limited risk: e.g., chatbots and deepfakes; these are subject to lighter regulation, such as the requirements that users are made aware they are interacting with AI
- Minimal risk: e.g., spam filters and video games; these are not regulated

The act imposes strict requirements on the providers of high-risk AI systems related to transparency, security, human oversight, record-keeping, quality management, and more.

11.5 ETHICAL CONCERNS

The use of data for decision-making inevitably raises some ethical questions:

- Is it ethical for an enterprise to profit from the use of data about their customers?
- Can an employer look into their employee's social media posts to assess their suitability for promotion?
- Is it acceptable to give preference to job applicants of a certain gender based on the past performance of other workers?
- Is it ethical to suppress or promote social media posts based on criteria established by the platform, and under what circumstances is it acceptable?

These questions raise important ethical concerns related to the use of data and analytics by organizations and, in particular, by commercial, for-profit enterprises. What is the balance between striving to make a profit for its shareholders and ethical business conduct?

Ethical behaviour is not legislated—it is defined by accepted standards of conduct established by societies, professional organizations, or enterprises.

Table 11.4 Legal versus Ethical

Legal	Ethical
Acting in accordance with laws and regulations of a particular jurisdiction (country, province, international)	Complying with a code of ethics or professional conduct of a particular industry or organization
Compliance (must do)	Choice (should do)
Following the law	Doing what is right
Compliance is enforced; non-compliance is punishable by law	Adherence is voluntary; non-adherence is not usually punishable

Each organization must consider what constitutes ethical conduct and what guidelines it must follow. Unethical business conduct can have high-reaching implications for organizations, affecting the trust of the public and the company's reputation. The infamous Cambridge Analytica scandal in 2018 caused a significant loss of Facebook's market share and a mass exodus of users.[21] **Ethical** behaviour is behaviour conforming to accepted standards of conduct.[22] The standards may be set by an industry, by an international organization, or within a particular company. They set out ethical guidelines to follow from the perspective of public interest.

The concept of public interest is central to understanding ethical behaviour. **Public interest** is anything affecting the rights, health, or finances of the public at large.[23] It refers to the common good of the society and public welfare.

As commercial organizations are created with the goal of generating a profit for their shareholders, there is an inherent dilemma between maximizing the profit for a smaller population (owners or shareholders) and doing the right thing for the public at large. For example, is it ethical to raise the price of a product for a customer who desperately needs it? Is it ethical to modify a product to make it more addictive, even if the product is a video game or a social media app?

Every organization must consider how its activities may impact the trust and well-being of the public. The explosion of narrow AI solutions in the last several years has led to discussions of heightened intensity around the ethical aspects of using AI. As a result, the most powerful technology companies in the world now publish their ethical AI principles, covering aspects such as:

- Fairness: avoiding bias and discrimination, inclusiveness
- Safety: committing to safe design, product reliability, and a focus on putting safety first
- Privacy protection: prioritizing privacy when designing products
- Accountability and transparency: maintaining oversight and human direction over the development of AI, ensuring solutions are transparent and understandable
- Harm prevention: committing to not developing potentially harmful AI applications

It is not only organizations that must continuously assess their intentions and actions from an ethical perspective. This also applies to every individual, and particularly to professionals working with data and analytics. By the nature of their job, these professionals have privileged access to data and computer systems, which in turn gives them opportunities to cause harm to others by misusing data and solutions.

Professional behaviour must therefore be guided by codes of ethics that provide guidelines for ethical behaviour and the handling of difficult situations and ethical dilemmas. Large organizations develop their own codes of ethics for regulating decision-making, as well as codes of conduct for regulating behaviour, which employees must understand and comply with. Codes of ethics also exist at the industry level for a diverse range of professionals, from psychologists to finance professionals, with compliance required as a condition of maintaining professional qualifications and certifications.

IT professionals in general, and analytics and data science professionals in particular, must make themselves familiar with the applicable ethical codes of conduct—for example:

- The Data Science Association's *Data Science Code of Professional Conduct*[24]
- The *Code of Ethics for Certified Analytics Professionals*[25]
- The Institute of Electrical and Electronics Engineers Computer Society's *Code of Ethics and Professional Practice*[26]
- Canada's Association of Information Technology Professionals' *Code of Ethics*[27]

These codes address a range of aspects of professional behaviour, including:

- Accountability for professional competence and the quality of work
- Privacy and confidentiality

- Honesty and integrity
- Communication with clients
- Dealing with conflicts of interest
- Handling ethical dilemmas
- Respect for the work of others
- Falsification of results and bias prevention

Ethical issues are complex and multi-dimensional, and with the rise in applications of machine learning and AI, the need for ethical guidelines and frameworks will only increase. As of the writing of this book, the first regulation of its kind, the EU AI Act, proposing to legislate some acceptable and unacceptable uses of AI, is about to become law. The understanding of the ethical use of big data and AI will continue to evolve, so it is appropriate to leave this chapter open-ended. Every data professional and every organization that utilizes data science and big data analytics must consider the ethical aspects of their business conduct.

11.6 ANALYTICS RISKS

As analytics, data science, and AI methods and tools get more sophisticated and the volume of data that businesses wish to analyze increases exponentially, the risk of failure increases along with solution complexity. It is crucial for both analytics professionals and business leaders to understand the risks and mitigate them early. Some of these risks and scenarios to watch out for have been mentioned in previous chapters. Table 11.5 provides a summary and a foundation for further discussion when planning analytics and data science initiatives.

Table 11.5 Analytics Solution Risks

Risk	Description
Dependency on data quality and availability	- Untrustworthy sources, lack of data quality in operational systems, and lack of enterprise data governance result in untrustworthy or useless analytics and numbers that cannot be trusted and therefore will not provide business value
Data privacy and security concerns	- Handling and analyzing sensitive data require investment in data protection and security and lead to additional concerns and costs for managing big data
Model accuracy, overfitting and underfitting	- Lack of expertise, data challenges, unclear requirements, and other factors may lead to overfitted or underfitted models that do not yield acceptable accuracy of predictions and become cancelled projects
Bias	- When discovered, bias in models can lead to significant rework or project cancellation - If undiscovered until the launch, a biased model may result in causing harm, financial losses, reputational damage, and even lawsuits

(continued)

Table 11.5 Analytics Solution Risks (*continued*)

Risk	Description
AI errors and hallucinations	• While companies have policies and procedures for handling employee errors, the same may be lacking for AI errors, such as when a chatbot gives a customer incorrect information; public exposure of such errors can also lead to reputational damage and litigation • AI hallucinations—when AI models present incorrect information as facts, sometimes even supplying fake sources—can also result in serious repercussions
Explainability	• When an automated decision is made by AI-enabled decision models, it may not be possible to explain the scores resulting from complex machine learning algorithms, should the need arise
User trust	• Human perception, distrust, or apprehension about using AI tools or "trusting decisions to a machine" may undermine the value of even extremely well-performing models • The fear of losing a job and being replaced by AI can make AI initiatives unpopular from the start and result in a lack of support and acceptance
High price and low value	• Lack of expertise, technological capabilities, or overreliance on expensive external vendors may result in a high price tag for an analytics solution and its maintenance without sufficient return on investment
Premature analytics	• When companies rush to develop advanced analytics and AI solutions motivated by wrong reasons without proper methodology, data quality, and objectives, this results in a waste of money and resources; such solutions fall short of heightened expectations and will be unlikely to provide any value, instead creating a prejudice to analytics that may be hard to overcome later
Training data risk	• When AI models are trained on materials that are protected intellectual property such as books or visual art, the lack of legislative framework regulating intellectual property rights protection versus fair use can lead to legal challenges and future repercussions
Unlearning	• When AI models are trained on incorrect or private data, an alternative to re-training the model (which is not always feasible) is to make the model "unlearn" or "forget" certain knowledge; this research is still experimental, but with the development of AI regulations, it may become a necessity in the near future

Using sophisticated analytics solutions carries additional security risks. These risks extend beyond general cyber security concerns such as unauthorized access to data and data theft. The more an organization relies on analytics for its decision-making and process automation, the more critical these decisions are to the organization, and the higher the potential harm from a compromised analytics solution.

Mitigating these risks requires following cybersecurity best practices at every stage of the analytics life cycle, as well as comprehensive monitoring solutions. The ability to recognize and mitigate analytics risks is another characteristic of a company with well-developed analytics maturity.

Table 11.6 Analytics Security Risks

Risk	Description
Input data risks (data poisoning)	Vulnerability to fake data generation: hackers feeding the prediction machine or data lake with bad data
Untrusted mappers	Initial processing or reducing of collected data compromised by outside agents
Insider data mining	Employees gaining unauthorized access to sensitive data stored in analytical solutions that lack the same level of protection as operational systems
Trade secret leakage risks	Feeding confidential information into generative AI models (e.g., ChatGPT) may lead to the leakage of trade secrets into the public domain
Feedback data risks	Intentional feeding of the prediction machine with incorrect (manipulated) responses to "teach" the algorithm certain behaviour (reinforcement learning risk)
Prompt injection (instruction tuning)	Feeding generative AI models or virtual assistants with specially engineered malicious prompts to control the model output and elicit the desired—potential harmful—responses or actions
Surrogate model risks	Interrogating the model and using its output as training data, e.g., reverse engineering the algorithms to understand the predictive model (learning by imitation); once the attacker understands the prediction machine, it becomes more vulnerable or can be copied

11.7 CHAPTER SUMMARY

Key Points to Remember

- An organization's ability to develop and successfully use advanced analytics to support data-driven decision-making depends on its analytics maturity.
- Organizations establish consistent systems for performance measurement used to track and report business performance results. Their success depends on the choice of metrics and how these metrics are tied to evaluating and rewarding individual and organizational performance.
- The privacy of individuals is protected by laws in most countries, and all business enterprises must comply with these laws and protect private data from inappropriate use.
- Data anonymization significantly reduces the risk of identifying an individual. However, it is sometimes possible to reverse the effect and re-identify individuals by comparing data from multiple sources.
- AI regulations are still in their infancy. However, every analytics professional must familiarize themselves with the emerging AI regulations as they are likely to have a big influence on further developments in the industry and applications of AI in different areas of business.

- Using sophisticated analytics solutions carries additional security risks. Mitigation of these risks may require solutions as complex as the advanced analytics algorithms themselves.

Key Terms

Analytics maturity: the competency of an organization in managing its data and transforming it into meaningful and actionable insights.

Anonymization: removing personally identifiable information from data so that it can no longer be linked to an individual.

Data minimization: collecting data only if a specific and compelling purpose is defined.

De-anonymization (re-identification, reconstruction, "mosaic effect"): identifying an individual from anonymized data by cross-referencing other data sources.

Encryption: altering of data into unreadable form using an algorithm that ensures the data can only be read by an agent that possesses the encryption key.

Ethical: conforming to accepted standards of conduct.

Performance measurement: a systematic approach to measuring and reporting the performance of the organization.

Personal information (personally identifiable information, PII): any factual or subjective information, recorded or not, about an identifiable individual.

Privacy: a state of being apart from company or observation, or freedom from unauthorized intrusion.

Privacy legislation: legislation that establishes the norms and boundaries for organizations' use of individuals' private data.

Protected health information (PHI): any information relating a patient's condition, health care, or health care–related payments resulting from provisioning health care services for an individual.

Pseudonymization: substituting identifiable data with a reversible, consistent value for operational purposes, while personal data is limited to the most protected storage and access.

Public interest: anything affecting the rights, health, or finances of the public at large.

Synthetic data (artificial data): a dataset composed entirely of fictional individuals or altered identities that retain the statistical properties of the original dataset.

User access controls: a strategy for managing access to data through restriction and monitoring.

Questions for Critical Thought

1. What are the advantages and disadvantages of centralized versus decentralized analytics functions in an organization?
2. How can poorly chosen metrics influence the performance of an individual or a group?
3. How can the exposure of private data harm an individual?

4. What privacy protection strategies can be used to minimize the risk of exposing private data when developing analytics solutions?

5. Why does a data and analytics professional employed outside of the EU need to know about GDPR?

6. What is ethical behaviour, and how is it relevant to developing business analytics?

7. Which demonstration of analytics solutions risks have you encountered in the news recently?

Test Your Knowledge

1. What information about an individual is not considered personal?
   a. The date a person was elected to the municipal council
   b. Data of birth
   c. Dates of medical appointments
   d. Children's birth dates
   e. All of the above are personal information

2. What privacy protection strategy involves replacing real data with artificially created data with similar properties?
   a. Anonymization
   b. Minimization
   c. Synthetic data
   d. Encryption

3. How can an individual be re-identified in an anonymized dataset?
   a. By decrypting hidden primary keys
   b. By cross-referencing multiple sources of data
   c. By restoring removed data from backup sources
   d. De-anonymization is not possible once the dataset is anonymized

4. Which statement best describes the risk of prompt injection?
   a. Feeding the AI algorithm many similar prompts to confuse its answers
   b. Designing the prompts to uncover what sources the information is coming from
   c. Injecting confidential information into the prompts without realizing that this will cause sensitive data to leak into the outside world
   d. Feeding the AI algorithm specially engineered prompts to produce a desired malicious response or action

5. What is the main objective of privacy legislation?
   a. To establish the rules for protecting organizations' intellectual property from their competitors
   b. To establish the rules for protecting health-related information

c. To establish the rules for using the data about individuals by organizations

d. To establish the rules for encryption of sensitive data in transit

Recommended Readings

Doerr, J. (2018) *Measure What Matters*. Portfolio Penguin.

The EU Artificial Intelligence Act: artificialintelligenceact.eu.

H2O.ai. (2019, May 2). *Can Your Machine Learning Model Be Hacked?!* Retrieved February 18, 2024, from h2o.ai/blog/2019/can-your-machine-learning-model-be-hacked/.

Harvard Business Review. (2018). *HBR Guide to Data Analytics Basics for Managers*. Harvard Business Press.

Muller, J. (2018). *The Tyranny of Metrics*. Princeton University Press.

Ohm, P. (2010). Broken Promises of Privacy: Responding to the Surprising Failure of Anonymization. *UCLA Law Review, 57*, 1701–1777. Retrieved March 14, 2025, from https://papers.ssrn.com/sol3/papers.cfm?abstract_id=1450006.

O'Neil, C. (2016). *Weapons of Math Destruction: How Big Data Increases Inequality and Threatens Democracy*. Crown.

Schryvers, P. (2020). *Bad Data: Why We Measure the Wrong Things and Often Miss the Metrics That Matter*. Prometheus Books.

Notes

1. Drucker, P. (1954). *The Practice of Management*. Harper.

2. Kaplan, R., & Norton, D. (1992, January–February). *The Balanced Scorecard—Measures That Drive Performance*. Harvard Business Review. Retrieved September 4, 2024, from hbr.org/1992/01/the-balanced-scorecard-measures-that-drive-performance-2.

3. Balanced Scorecard Institute. (n.d.). *Balanced Scorecard Basics*. Retrieved February 16, 2024, from balancedscorecard.org/bsc-basics-overview/.

4. Bas, A. (n.d.). *A History of Objectives and Key Results (OKRs)*. Peoplelogic. Retrieved February 16, 2024, from peoplelogic.ai/blog/history-of-objectives-and-key-results.

5. Wikipedia. (n.d.). *Objectives and Key Results*. Retrieved February 16, 2024, from en.wikipedia.org/wiki/Objectives_and_key_results.

6. Croll, A., & Yoskovitz, B. (2013). *Lean Analytics: Use Data to Build a Better Startup Faster*. O'Reilly Media.

7. Goldratt, E. (1990). *What Is This Thing Called Theory of Constraints and How Should It Be Implemented?* North River Press. Retrieved February 16, 2024, from www.azquotes.com/quote/720399.

8. Wikipedia. (n.d.). *Wells Fargo Cross-Selling Scandal*. Retrieved February 16, 2024, from en.wikipedia.org/wiki/Wells_Fargo_cross-selling_scandal.

9. Dubner, S. (2012, October 11). *The Cobra Effect: A New Freakonomics Radio Podcast*. Freakonomics, LLC. Retrieved February 16, 2024, from freakonomics.com/podcast/the-cobra-effect-2/.

10. Pink, D. (2011). *Drive: The Surprising Truth about What Motivates Us*. Riverhead Books.

11. Merriam-Webster. (n.d.). *Privacy*. Retrieved February 8, 2024, from www.merriam-webster.com/dictionary/privacy.

12. United Nations Conference on Trade and Development (UNCTAD). (n.d.). *Data Protection and Privacy Legislation Worldwide*. Retrieved February 8, 2024, from unctad.org/page/data-protection-and-privacy-legislation-worldwide.

13. Office of the Privacy Commissioner of Canada. (2019, May 31). *PIPEDA Requirements in Brief*. Retrieved February 8, 2024, from www.priv.gc.ca/en/privacy-topics/privacy-laws-in-canada/the-personal-information-protection-and-electronic-documents-act-pipeda/pipeda_brief/.

14. General Data Protection Regulation (GDPR). (n.d.). *Personal Data*. Retrieved February 8, 2024, from www.gdpreu.org/the-regulation/key-concepts/personal-data/.

15. Health Insurance Portability and Accountability Act (HIPAA) Journal. (n.d.). *What Is Considered PHI under HIPAA?* Retrieved June 27, 2024, from www.hipaajournal.com/considered-phi-hipaa/.

16. GDPR.EU. (n.d.). *What Is GDPR, the EU's New Data Protection Law?* Retrieved June 27, 2024, from gdpr.eu/what-is-gdpr/.

17. Payment Cart Industry (PCI) Security Standards Council. (2018, July). *PCI DSS Quick Reference Guide: Understanding the Payment Card Industry Data Security Standard Version 3.2.1*. Retrieved June 27, 2024, from listings.pcisecuritystandards.org/documents/PCI_DSS-QRG-v3_2_1.pdf.

18. Sweeney, L. (2000). *Simple Demographics Often Identify People Uniquely*. Carnegie Mellon University, Data Privacy Working Paper 3. Retrieved February 8, 2024, from ggs685.pbworks.com/w/file/fetch/94376315/Latanya.pdf.

19. Narayanan, A., & Shmatikov, V. (2008). *Robust De-Anonymization of Large Sparse Datasets*. Presented at 2008 IEEE Symposium on Security and Privacy, Oakland, CA. *Institute of Electrical and Electronics Engineers*, pp. 111–25.

20. EU Artificial Intelligence Act. (2024, February 27; updated 2024, May 30). *High-Level Summary of the AI Act*. Retrieved June 27, 2024, from artificialintelligenceact.eu/high-level-summary/.

21. Wikipedia. (n.d.). *Facebook–Cambridge Analytica Data Scandal*. Retrieved February 11, 2024, from en.wikipedia.org/wiki/Facebook%E2%80%93Cambridge_Analytica_data_scandal.

22. Merriam-Webster. (n.d.). *Ethical*. Retrieved February 11, 2024, from www.merriam-webster.com/dictionary/ethical.

23. The Free Dictionary. (2008). Public Interest. *West's Encyclopedia of American Law* (2nd ed.). Retrieved February 11, 2024, from legal-dictionary.thefreedictionary.com/Public+Interest.

24. Data Science Association. (n.d.). *Data Science Code of Professional Conduct*. Retrieved February 18, 2024, from www.datascienceassn.org/code-of-conduct.html.

25. Institute for Operations Research and the Management Sciences (INFORMS). (n.d.). *Code of Ethics for Certified Analytics Professionals*. Retrieved February 18, 2024, from www.certifiedanalytics.org/code-of-ethics.

26. Institute of Electrical and Electronics Engineers Computer Society (IEEE-CS). (n.d.). *Code of Ethics and Professional Practice*. Retrieved February 18, 2024, from www.computer.org/education/code-of-ethics.

27. Canada's Association of Information Technology Professionals (CIPS). (n.d.). *CIPS Code of Ethics*. Retrieved February 18, 2024, from cips.ca/ethics/.

Chapter 12

Analytics Careers

For those studying business intelligence and analytics, understanding the boundaries and responsibilities of jobs in the field is key to professional development. For those involved in managing analytics teams and leading projects, recognizing the diversity of skills and accountabilities required for building successful analytics solutions is key to making projects successful.

This chapter covers:

- Types of analytics jobs and the knowledge and skills they require
- Career development paths in the analytics field
- An overview of future-proof knowledge and skills

12.1 JOBS IN ANALYTICS

As the influence of business intelligence (BI), analytics, and data science grows, so does the variety of jobs associated with them. And yet, with the increasing complexity of methods and tools and the emergence of new technologies, these jobs are becoming ever narrower and more specialized. As companies expand their analytics capabilities and explore technological advances, they create new titles and job descriptions to reflect their changing needs. This creates a proliferation of job titles and blurs the lines between them.

To make sense of this variety, we can outline the main themes and broadly divide jobs in this field into four types: architects, engineers, analysts, and data scientists. Their skills overlap with but are not always perfectly aligned with the domains of computer science, AI, and data science.

Engineers

Engineers build systems and solutions. They may be called programmers, coders, developers, or designers. In the world of data and analytics, they design, write, and test programs to:

- Build, modify, and optimize databases, data warehouses, and other data storage solutions

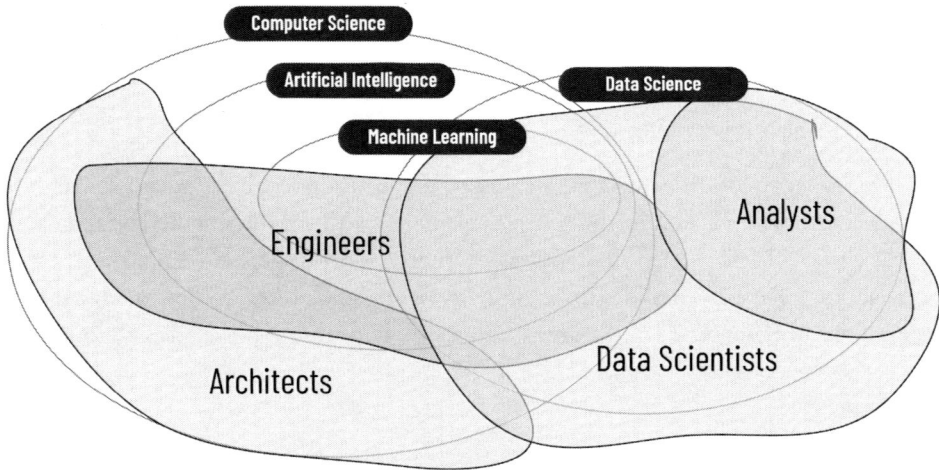

Figure 12.1 Analytics Job Types—Skills and Knowledge Overlaps

- Develop solutions for extracting, cleaning, transforming, and moving data from one system to another
- Deploy data mining, machine learning, and predictive algorithms
- Design and build reports and dashboards
- Monitor, maintain, and tune data integration and analytics solutions

Engineers must be skilled in programming and in multiple different computer languages, given that they will end up working in many different organizations with many different technologies. They must be proficient with databases, SQL, and the manipulation of structured data, as these are the most common requirements. Some engineers might be involved only with handling structured data, while others expand their expertise to handling big data and learning to work with tools like Hadoop and Spark. The programming of machine learning algorithms requires additional skills and may become another engineering specialization.

Engineers can specialize in multiple areas, leading to many job variations:

- Data engineers build and maintain data systems and pipelines and develop data transformation programs.
- Database administrators design, build, and manage databases. They are also often responsible for backup, monitoring, performance tuning, and sometimes for developing ETL and ELT programs.
- ETL developers specialize in the design and building of ETL programs, such as for enterprise data warehousing projects.
- BI developers design, build, and maintain analytics solutions such as reports and dashboards. They may be given a platform-specific title such as Tableau developer or Power BI developer.
- Machine learning (ML) engineers design, build, test, monitor, and maintain ML algorithms.

- Deep learning, computer vision, and natural language processing (NLP) engineers specialize in different areas of ML.
- ML operations engineers are responsible for the operation and maintenance of ML algorithms.

More generic job titles such as "developer" or "software engineer" may or may not involve analytics or machine learning requirements. As with any job search, job candidates should always review the job descriptions to understand what certain employers expect from employees in a given role. Current initiatives, prevailing technologies, and the placement of the analytics teams in the organization will shape the employer's expectations.

Analysts

Analysts specialize in extracting insights from data. They mostly work with structured data to:

- Prepare, clean, and transform it for analysis
- Apply statistical algorithms to analyze it
- Query, extract, and aggregate it for reporting
- Perform ad hoc diagnostic analysis
- Create reports, visualizations, and dashboards
- Present and explain analytics insights to business stakeholders

Data analysts work closely with business stakeholders to understand their requirements, translate business problems into hypotheses and analytics questions, and identify suitable metrics for aggregating and presenting insights. They can also help devise proxy metrics to support the measurement of complex phenomena by exploring and profiling data. Most of the time, they work with structured data manipulated using spreadsheets, SQL, or BI tools, producing descriptive and diagnostic analytics for their business stakeholders.

Data analysts are more likely than other analytics professionals both to be attached to business units and to specialize in business functions or types of analysis.

Data analyst job variations include:

- BI analyst
- Statistician
- Research analyst
- Data visualization specialist
- Financial analyst
- Risk analyst
- Fraud analyst
- Market research analyst
- Social media data analyst
- Sales support analyst
- Supply chain analyst

- Product analyst
- Operations support analyst

As mentioned above, the differences between individual titles may vary in different companies. A data analyst in one company, responsible for ad hoc analysis, data cleaning, and preparation of reports and dashboards, could have duties similar to those of a data visualization analyst or BI analyst in another company. A business analyst assigned to a data warehousing project might work on data modelling and data mapping as well as data cleaning and preparation. A BI analyst position in one organization might require programming skills and advanced SQL scripting, while in another, BI analysts are not involved in data preparation at all, and instead work with pre-processed data in the enterprise data warehouse.

The only way to discern the requirements of one particular job is to review the job description and ask questions during the interview.

Architects

Data architects plan and design data structures, systems, and integrations between them. They often work with other architects to optimize the overall system architecture of the organization and are responsible for:

- Designing databases, data warehouses, and data pipelines
- Selecting and designing appropriate data acquisition and integration methods
- Data modelling and recommending optimal data organization and structure for master, reference, and transaction data in the enterprise
- Ensuring that the physical design of data solutions meets business and architecture requirements

There are fewer job variations in the architecture space. However, we can distinguish such roles as:

- Data architect
- Data modeller
- Analytics architect
- Information architect
- Decision architect
- Big data engineer

In most organizations, the role of data architect is not limited to the analytics domain. Its mandate is quite broad, including data management and the alignment of data structures with enterprise, infrastructure, and security architecture. Some companies will designate their analytics architects or information architects as being focused on analytics and data science capabilities. Meanwhile, a decision architect's role is still quite rare and more likely to be found in very large, data-driven organizations.

Data Scientists

Data scientists—the newest member of the analytics job family—use advanced statistics and algorithms to solve business problems by gaining insights from big data. The role of a data scientist is to:

- Source, explore, study, and experiment with data
- Identify business challenges that can be solved with data
- Identify strategies for gaining insights from big data
- Design and optimize ML algorithms, including complex prescriptive optimization algorithms
- Recommend models for operationalizing and embedding analytics into the business process
- Detect anomalies in data
- Monitor model performance and decay
- Interpret and share analytical insights with stakeholders

Data scientists generally hold more advanced degrees in statistics, computer science, or data science; however, in addition to advanced mathematical and programming knowledge, they must also have strong business acumen and a strategic outlook. The problems they are tasked with solving are rarely either rigid or well-defined, so they must engage in experimentation and research to find innovative solutions or discover hidden value in large volumes of data.

As this job is relatively new, we should expect it to develop and change. Some of the job variations you may encounter include:

- Decision scientist
- Machine learning researcher
- AI research scientist
- Generative AI researcher
- Machine learning research scientist

Skills Overview

The job types mentioned in this chapter will inevitably overlap with one another, as they belong to the same job family, and will also share responsibilities with other jobs, such as that of the business analyst.

Data analysts and data scientists must have many skills in common, including the ability to present complex information in simpler terms to business stakeholders, to use visualizations and narratives, and to skillfully elicit analytics requirements. At the same time, they will likely work in different spaces. Data analysts work with small data, structured datasets, data marts, and spreadsheets, while data scientists work with any type of data (including unstructured data), explore large raw datasets stored in data lakes, and mine data using ML instead of SQL queries. Data scientists are more likely to conduct analysis on large, new problems while data analysts focus on smaller, more conventional tasks.

Data architects in larger companies rarely create and debug programs; rather, they are responsible for creating solution blueprints or design documents, which will then be used by engineers to write programs. Small companies might require hands-on architects to do some of the engineering or database administration tasks.

Table 12.1 summarizes the level of expertise in different areas of knowledge and skills required for different job types.

Table 12.1 Jobs in Analytics—Required Skills

Knowledge/skills	Analyst	Engineer	Architect	Data scientist
Solution architecture, data pipeline design	Not required	Advanced	Advanced	Intermediate
Software engineering	Not required	Advanced	Intermediate	Intermediate
Data modelling	Basic	Advanced	Advanced	Advanced
Database design	Basic	Advanced	Advanced	Intermediate
Scripting, SQL	Basic	Advanced	Advanced	Advanced
Spreadsheet tools, Excel	Advanced	Basic	Basic	Advanced
Reporting, dashboard management	Advanced	Basic	Not required	Intermediate
BI tools	Advanced	Basic	Basic	Intermediate
Visualization tools	Advanced	Basic	Basic	Advanced
Business acumen	Advanced	Basic	Basic	Advanced
Storytelling	Advanced	Not required	Not required	Advanced
Advanced math, statistics	Basic	Basic	Basic	Advanced
Data cleaning, manipulation	Not required	Advanced	Basic	Advanced
Statistical programming, R	Not required	Advanced	Basic	Advanced
Advanced programming: Java, Python, C, C++	Not required	Advanced	Basic	Advanced
Data mining	Not required	Intermediate	Not required	Advanced
Handling big data, Hadoop, Spark	Not required	Intermediate	Advanced	Advanced
Big data analytics	Not required	Intermediate	Not required	Advanced
ML modelling	Not required	Intermediate	Not required	Advanced

12.2 CAREER PATHWAYS AND JOBS OF THE FUTURE

Entering the job market, finding your first job, or making a major change in your career path might feel daunting. Gaining confidence in these things might take months or even years. At the same time, this is only the beginning of your career. What about the rest of it? What will you do in 5, 10, 20 years?

The fields of data science and AI are developing quickly, and careers in these fields will develop along with them. Nobody can truly predict where they will ultimately go. If you are new to this field, consider the career paths available to you now, which will help you decide what else to learn, what new skills to develop, and what to explore to continue developing as a professional. Understanding potential career advancement provides both motivation and easily visible milestones to aim for.

Your interests, inclinations, and strengths will define your career path. Opportunities available at your current company will define whether or not your career path can develop with the same employer. New opportunities and job variations will undoubtedly arise along with emerging technologies. We can only review a fraction of them in this chapter.

Figure 12.2 illustrates some potential career trajectories for those currently in analytics, including at the management and executive levels:

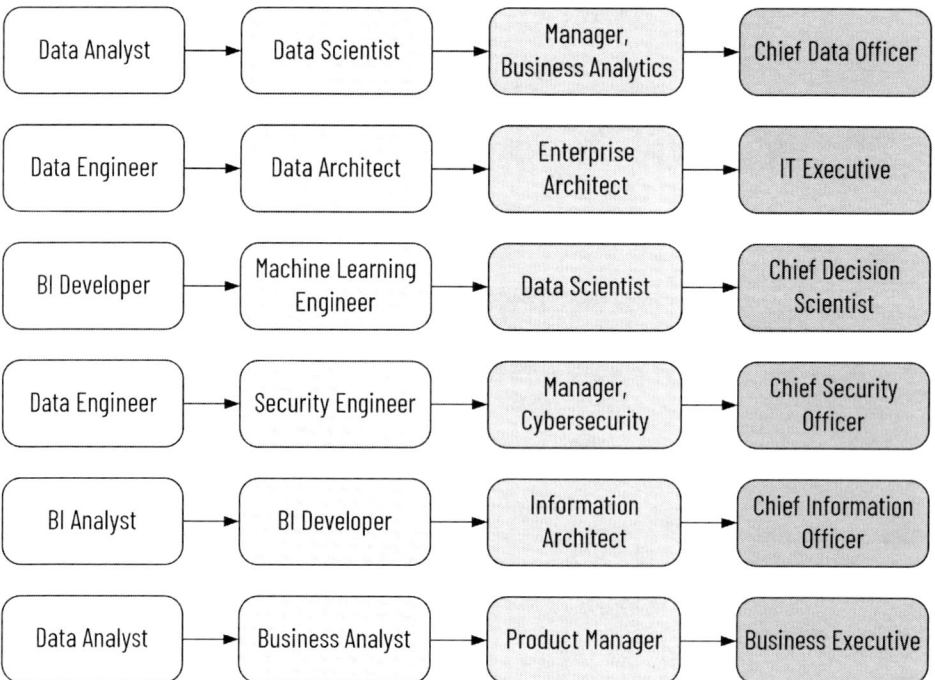

Data Analyst	Data Scientist	Manager, Business Analytics	Chief Data Officer
Data Engineer	Data Architect	Enterprise Architect	IT Executive
BI Developer	Machine Learning Engineer	Data Scientist	Chief Decision Scientist
Data Engineer	Security Engineer	Manager, Cybersecurity	Chief Security Officer
BI Analyst	BI Developer	Information Architect	Chief Information Officer
Data Analyst	Business Analyst	Product Manager	Business Executive

Figure 12.2 Analytics Career Pathways

As we follow ongoing developments in the fields of data science and AI, we can't help but wonder what the future will bring. What jobs will be in demand 5 or 10 years from now?

New types of jobs will undoubtedly arise, driven by factors such as:

- New technology developments
- Legislative frameworks around data protection and AI regulation
- The need to resolve current shortcomings and risks of AI applications
- The need to solve problems of increasing complexity
- Convergence of traditional and AI-augmented jobs

The rest of this chapter describes the jobs we can expect to appear or become more mainstream in the future, and how we understand them today. Both the jobs and our understanding of them will evolve along with the technical and human aspects of using data science and AI to change how we live and make things happen. While some of the expected directions of this evolution are mentioned in the next section, more innovation and novel ways of using the technology will emerge to serve humankind. You may be part of this evolution.

Data journalists are journalists using large datasets and open-source data to find news stories or to support existing stories with data-driven evidence. Data journalists need to have base knowledge in data science, statistics, data visualization, and coding.

Prompt engineers and problem formulation engineers specialize in creating text prompts that elicit the desired outputs from large language models (LLMs). As prompt engineering itself becomes more automated through more sophisticated AI algorithms, problem formulation emerges as an even more important skill for getting results from LLMs. A strong grasp of linguistics and semantics is required for this job.

AI trainers are engineers or domain experts training and tuning complex models, correcting algorithm errors, labelling data, and monitoring algorithm performance to improve it. In addition to coding and machine learning skills, this job often requires expert domain knowledge, such as a medical background for trainers of medical diagnostics models.

Along with AI trainers, *AI data engineers* and *data curators* work on creating and optimizing datasets for model training, focusing on data wrangling and feature engineering.

Knowledge engineers are involved in capturing and modelling knowledge for training AI, focusing particularly on complex layers of knowledge that represent a challenge for conventional ML approaches.

Roboticists and *robotics engineers* specialize in designing, constructing, and programming robots and robotic systems capable of functioning autonomously.

Swarm robotics engineers specialize in programming and coordinating the functioning of multiple robots working together (swarms), which involves research into decentralized control and collective algorithmic behaviour.

Robotics scientists are involved in advancing the robotics discipline and developing new technologies for the design of robots. All robotics specialties, in addition to computer science, programming, and machine learning skills, require a strong science, mechanical, and electrical engineering background.

Perception engineers specialize in robotic perception algorithms such as those required for robotic computer vision, self-driving vehicles, and artificial sensing. This area includes tasks such as gesture recognition and emotion recognition, which will also be central to human-robot interaction engineering.

Human-robot interaction engineers specialize in designing and testing solutions for interactions between humans and machines. There will be variations of this job specializing in NLP to study, design, and optimize conversations of AI models with humans, such as *AI linguists*, *NLP specialists*, or *conversation designers*. Like prompt engineers and problem formulation engineers, their jobs will also require a strong grasp of linguistics, semantics, and language studies, along with knowledge of psychology and user experience design.

AI augmentation designers will be engaged in devising ways to use AI to augment the work done by humans or work with humans. Examples include human-robot collaboration in agricultural, manufacturing, and health care settings. This job will have a strong emphasis on user experience design, ergonomics, NLP, and perception engineering.

An *AI therapist* or *machine psychiatrist* specialization involves machine learning and deep learning experts troubleshooting and tuning "misbehaving" AI models that exhibit signs of disbalance or unpredictable or unethical behaviour. This will be a demanding specialization where a strong knowledge of computer science and AI disciplines will be required, along with linguistic skills and knowledge in many other intersecting fields.

AI ethics officers or *AI ethicists* will be experts in AI regulations and ethical aspects of AI development. Their job would be to consult the development teams to ensure they follow the guidelines and recommendations for ethical AI. One interesting variation of this specialty would be a *quantitative AI ethicist*, whose job would involve using quantitative methods to measure and monitor bias in machine learning models, as well as to determine the potential impacts of bias on different population segments.

The job of a *data privacy expert* is not new; however, it will soon take on new responsibilities with the expanded use of AI technology. New threats to privacy will continue to arise from using big data and training LLMs on open-source data. These experts may evolve into *AI data compliance specialists* concerned with other data compliance aspects beyond privacy protection, such as intellectual property rights and the use of copyrighted materials in AI models.

The job of an *AI policy expert* requires in-depth knowledge of all AI regulations, as they will often be asked to advise companies on the development and use of AI to ensure compliance with policies and regulations.

Finally, we will also need *AI security analysts* and *AI defence engineers*—experts trained to detect threats and protect AI models from malicious attacks by external agents (such as in the examples outlined in Table 11.6).

These descriptions of future jobs outline but a few possible aspects where new expertise will be needed for designing, building, and supporting solutions in the emerging fields of advanced analytics and AI.

12.3 EMERGING TRENDS

Owing to the rapid development of the AI and data science fields, supported by the expanding capabilities of modern technology, we continue to witness how novel ideas become emerging technologies and new solutions.

This section provides an overview of new trends and innovative applications of analytics in various areas—from providing a better customer experience to increasing automation in manufacturing and improving public welfare outcomes. As you consider your future in analytics, these trends may provide you with inspiration for how to use your knowledge to make the world a better place.

Personalization

Collecting data on individuals and their online behaviour has become a lynchpin of marketing and customer analytics, as it allows us to more accurately gauge individual likes, dislikes, and desires. Access to this data, even within the guardrails established by privacy protection legislation, enables more refined customer segmentation and granularity as in the examples below.

What makes personalization possible? It is enabled by the extensive digital footprint that each individual leaves online—this is data that can be tracked, recorded, and mined. The ever-increasing volume of customer data such as browsing behaviour, search history, and social media comments provide a multi-layered view of their interests and sentiments and can help in the crafting of messages designed to speak to each person's needs.

Hyper-Personalization

As an extension of targeted marketing, personalization is about creating marketing messages tailored to a particular individual rather than to a customer segment. It considers the unique aspects of a person's online presence, such as preferences, previous purchases, sentiments expressed on social media, and browsing history.

The idea behind hyper-personalization is to tailor marketing messages to a person based not only on their history but also on the real-time context, such as a person's current location, the time of the day, and what is happening in the moment. Customized ads could be created and delivered to specific customers, at specific locations, and with discounts for specific products available at that location. For instance, as a customer walks along an unfamiliar street in hot weather, a customized notification to their phone might tell them that their favourite soft drink is on sale in the store they are approaching, already cold in the fridge.

Micro-Moments

The concept of micro-moments was first introduced by Google as "intent-driven moments of decision-making and preference-shaping that occur throughout the entire consumer journey."[1] The concept is based on changing consumer behaviour, where instant gratification has become an expectation, especially when consumers can have instant access to information and services through their mobile devices.

Google has introduced four crucial micro-moments: "I-want-to-know," "I-want-to-do," "I-want-to-go," and "I-want-to-buy." Capturing a micro-moment when a consumer has an immediate need allows a brand to deliver its marketing message at the right time when the consumer is ready to act.

Immersive Technologies

Immersive technologies create new user experiences by interacting directly with users' senses.

Augmented reality (*AR*) creates an interactive experience that layers computer-generated information over the physical world, creating enhanced inputs for a user's vision, hearing, or sense of touch. It can be used in many areas—from retail to immersive training methods to helping customers visualize how a new product will fit into their environment.

Virtual reality (*VR*) allows users to experience a digitally rendered environment where their senses of vision, hearing, touch, and even smell are fed computer-generated information. VR is used for gaming, training simulations, health care, retail, and entertainment, to name a few examples.

These technologies use AI algorithms, such as deep neural networks and generative AI, for rendering digital content, NLP for receiving auditory input and communicating with the consumer, and machine learning to respond to the situations and adapt to the user's behaviour.

AR and VR are delivered to the individual consumer through *augmented consumer interfaces*, which enhance how consumers may interact with products. For example, a virtual fitting room can show a consumer how a particular piece of clothing will fit them.

Furthermore, *human augmentation* refers to using technology to enhance human abilities, such as sensory (e.g., through implants) or physical (e.g., via robotic limbs) abilities. The future and the viability of human augmentation are yet to be proven, not only from technology but from ethical, medical, and legal perspectives.

Continuous Intelligence

While statistical process control is nothing new, and measuring process inputs and outputs is ubiquitous, technology now allows for data to be collected at much higher velocity and volume. The ability to automate data collection, support frequent measurements, capture a gigantic number of observations, and process them in real time has led innovators to the idea of continuous intelligence.

Continuous intelligence is a design pattern in which real-time analytics are integrated into business operations. Current and historical data are processed to prescribe actions in response to business moments and other events.[2] Continuous intelligence requires the embedding of analytics into the business process and the building of reinforcement learning algorithms that continuously adapt to changing environments.

Many terms refer to the various levels of process automation and continuous intelligence. *Robotic process automation (RPA)* refers to deterministic algorithms that are programmed to automate repetitive tasks such as data entry, form processing, or routine ticket management. *Process mining* refers to extracting large volumes of data from multiple systems to model and analyze business process performance, used in particular when a process is supported by multiple operational applications. Process mining enables *process intelligence*—by using insights from process mining and advanced analytics, organizations can improve and optimize their processes to improve efficiency and reduce costs. Process intelligence is an example of continuous intelligence.

Process automation can be further enabled by the use of robots and cobots.

Robots and Cobots

While robots are designed to execute tasks autonomously, without human intervention, cobots (collaborative or companion bots) are designed to work alongside humans. Robots are used more and more extensively in environments that may be hazardous to humans, or to execute tasks with a high demand for constant speed, precision, and power, from painting, drilling, and welding to cutting, loading, and parcel sorting.

Cobots are designed to share space with humans. They have enhanced safety features to function in these spaces and are used for tasks that cannot be fully automated.

Robots require complex and extensive programming including advanced algorithms for computer vision and task optimization through machine learning. An advantage of cobots is the reduction in algorithm complexity if a human operator is available to manage or guide the cobot in exceptional circumstances. Humans can also "teach" cobots by guiding them in task execution, thus using reinforcement learning. The robotics industry will continue to develop, relying on technological advancements, particularly in machine sensing and reinforcement algorithms development.

Internet of Things

The idea of the IoT as a network of objects connected to the internet is no longer new to us. Wearable fitness trackers, smart homes, and connected appliances are all examples of objects capable of collecting and receiving data. These devices use sensors to collect data and execute commands such as displaying information, generating voice communication, or sending signals to other devices, such as turning your thermostat down by one degree.

The complexity of IoT technology is increasing, enabling the design of, for example, smart multi-residential buildings, where all building systems, from heating to lighting to door locks, can be controlled through the network from a central command centre. In a smart building, sensors will collect data from different pieces of equipment and infrastructure such as plumbing, smoke detectors, window frames, and solar panels to enable efficient operation, energy conservation, and preventative maintenance.

The future of the IoT is even more digitized and interconnected. From smart vehicles, the next step is smart highways. From smart robots, the next step is smart plants and smart warehouses. From smart buildings, the next step is smart cities. According to some estimates, the number of IoT devices is expected to reach 30 billion by 2030.[3] A higher level of IoT penetration will allow us to use data and machine learning to monitor, control, and optimize the use of increasingly complex systems, such as manufacturing facilities or municipalities.

While we call IoT devices "smart," this might be something of a misnomer, as most devices do not actually make autonomous decisions. They don't store and process data—instead, they send information to data centres in the cloud. These become the command centres in which big data is stored and processed, decisions are made, and instructions are generated. This centralization of operations brings its own challenges, particularly regarding safety. When a self-driving car's battery runs out, or an apartment with a digital lock cannot be unlocked due to software issues, the human user may face serious risks. Safety requirements and guardrails will play a significant role in the future of IoT technology. Some of these challenges will be solved by giving more autonomy to the devices on the periphery of the network, which brings us to the discussion of a different approach: edge computing.

Edge Computing

One of the innate characteristics of IoT is the need for internet connection and latency resulting from sending data back and forth between the device and the data centre. This can become a weakness, and in situations when latency tolerance is very low, edge computing comes into play.

Edge computing is a model whereby data processing and analytics are executed as close as possible to the data source, with latency reduction and avoiding connectivity issues being the primary advantages. Computations must be performed locally—at the "edge" of the network. Edge computing can be used in designing autonomous vehicles, farming techniques, manufacturing, inventory monitoring, and network optimization.

Edge computing requires using machine learning algorithms that can be run on a single computer with much less processing power than data centres in the cloud. This gives rise to the need for edge ML, also called TinyML—machine learning algorithms that can run on low-capacity computers at the periphery of the network.

Biotechnology

AI is increasingly being used for the discovery of new drugs, protein engineering, and genome sequencing. Next-generation sequencing, for instance, utilizes massively parallel sequencing of DNA and RNA, supported by extensive use of machine learning, and deep learning algorithms in particular.[4] A significant increase in speed and efficiency of genome sequencing enables broad applications in genomics, as well as in the study of genetic diversity, evolutionary biology, and human genetic disorders.

Personalized Medicine (Precision Medicine)

The goal of personalized medicine, also known as precision medicine, is to prevent, diagnose, and treat diseases using people's individual genome, lifestyle, and environment data.

It may involve using AI algorithms for diagnostics, which has already shown remarkable results, in particular in the area of genome mapping and diagnostic imaging, allowing for earlier disease detection.

Patient data can also be used for treatment personalization by tailoring of medical interventions to the patient's medical history, genetic makeup, response to medications, observed reactions, and treatment complications.[5]

Geospatial Technologies

Geospatial technologies are those that have a geographic or locational component—that is, they allow data to be connected to certain locations or geographical coordinates.

Geographic information systems (GISs) are computer systems that capture, store, verify, and display data related to positions on earth's surface.[6] Geospatial data (data that contains information about a location on earth's surface) can be used in many applications, from remote sensing and navigation to forest management and insurance. While GISs have been used for decades to store and manage geospatial data, machine learning and AI have advanced them to unprecedented levels of precision.

Geospatial big data analytics enables more precise geographic segmentation and identification of geospatial factors—for example, to determine the influence of the location on target variables. It can be used in complex tasks such as urban planning by allowing the researcher to study geospatial aspects of foot and vehicle traffic, cell phone and credit card use, as well as pollution and noise levels.

With the use of drones, geospatial data can be collected from previously inaccessible places, enabling detailed topographic surveying and data collection. This can be used for land management, construction, wildlife protection, landslide and avalanche monitoring, and disaster response. Other industries with a growing reliance on geospatial technology include autonomous vehicles, environmental monitoring, forestry management, and agriculture.

New applications become possible when multiple technologies are combined. One notable combination being that of geospatial technologies and AR, referred to as *geospatial AR*. This may involve layering digitally rendered content over the real-world environment, such as aligning three-dimensional (3D) imagery with specific locations while using a smartphone or AR glasses. Geospatial AR can be used for navigation and tourism applications, simulation, gaming, and emergency response.

Another example of combined technologies is the use of GIS systems to develop digital twins of natural and human-built environments.

Digital Twins

A *digital twin* is a virtual model designed to represent a real-world object, process, or system as accurately as possible. Digital twin models can be used to study real objects or processes, run simulations, and predict the future behaviour of the system's elements.

A digital twin can be used to test different design options, identify potential flaws and bottlenecks, predict breakdowns, and optimize the operation of complex processes.[7]

Digital twins can utilize IoT technology to receive real-time sensor data from the real object, thus enabling its accurate real-time representation. This would allow a digital twin to monitor the real object for potential issues, run complex analytics using the computing power of the digital model, and, if necessary, control the behaviour of the object or system.[8]

The use of digital twins is growing in many industries, especially those that involve large and complex equipment: power generation, construction, aerospace, offshore drilling, agriculture, and urban planning.

Data for Social Good

While using analytics for business, analyzing customer data, or creating new products has enormous potential, data can and should be used for social good—to benefit the public in general. The discourse around using big data to solve social problems generally tends to focus on:

- Analyzing the impact of social policies for evidence-based policy-making
- Using big data to address issues in underserved communities
- Identifying vulnerable groups for accessibility to social programs and supports
- Detecting and eliminating race, ethnicity, and gender biases in public programs and law enforcement
- Tracking media misinformation
- Using data to analyze the impacts of climate change and the effects of sustainability initiatives
- Nonprofit planning and allocating of resources
- Improving accessibility, e.g., by using AR/VR technologies
- Providing open data for public use

Shift toward Non-Financial Metrics

The shift to focus on social good and well-being is also reflected in many organizations that are giving more attention to non-financial metrics, such as those measuring company reputation, customer satisfaction, employee well-being, and innovation.

Measuring these intangible things can be a complex and ambiguous process, requiring the mining and analysis of a variety of proxy measures. This task becomes more realistic with further advances in big data analytics and NLP, such as by applying sentiment analysis to customer feedback, employee comments, or social media chatter.

One important category of non-financial metrics is referred to as environmental, social, and governance (ESG) metrics. ESG metrics are growing more relevant to investors and stakeholders when assessing the risks and growth of investments. According to the Chartered Financial Analyst Institute, while "ESG metrics are not commonly part of mandatory financial reporting, … companies are increasingly making disclosures in their annual report or in a standalone sustainability report."[9]

ESG metrics pertaining to the environment may include:

- Carbon emissions
- Air and water pollution
- Biodiversity
- Deforestation
- Energy efficiency
- Waste management
- Water scarcity

Some of the above environmental metrics are made possible by IoT technologies such as water meters, and others by the advances in geospatial analytics or drone-based data collection and analysis.

Many social and governance metrics, however—such as those related to data protection and privacy, human rights, labour standards, and lobbying—are indirect; there may be no established consensus on how they should be measured. Metrics for measuring carbon emissions come with complexity and ambiguity that may result in lack of agreement and low confidence in the resulting scores. While several ESG index providers have emerged, they each tend to use different approaches to calculating ESG scores, and even the question of how to combine environmental, social, and governance scores into one composite score is controversial.

In the future, we will see more attention paid to non-financial metrics, and much remains to be done to make them comparable and meaningful.

Data and Analytics as a Service

Cloud computing can provide organizations with access to potentially unlimited storage, but it doesn't stop there. Through the cloud, a business can rent not only space to store their data but also services, from software as a service (SaaS) and platform as a service (PaaS) to predictive maintenance as a service, leading to the collective term *anything as a service* (XaaS). This can include:

- Data as a service—leveraging the cloud for storing, integrating, and managing data
- Analytics as a service—cloud-based BI, data mining, and predictive analytics software

The growths of XaaS, essentially a subscription-based model to access services hosted and managed by service providers on the cloud, allows even smaller companies, potentially unable to afford complex and demanding analytics infrastructure on premises, to have access to the modern analytical technology and tools.

Decision Intelligence

Business decision-making has always been an integral part of the management discipline. However, the level of analysis that the decisions are based on, and the reliance on data, is evolving with the advancements in ML and AI. Where previously, decision-makers relied more on descriptive analytics for a summary of what happened, applying their judgment to make decisions, advanced analytics methods provide opportunities to make this process more analytics-driven.

Where measurements were previously often discrete (e.g., scores from annual customer satisfaction surveys), they can now be measured continuously. Where rule-based expert systems once supported deterministic decisions based on programmed rules, we can now rely on stochastic approaches and ML algorithms to learn patterns from data from a multitude of sources as quickly as it is generated.

The progression along the analytics value chain from descriptive to diagnostic, predictive, and finally prescriptive analytics supports higher levels of automation in decision-making. Gartner defines *decision intelligence* as a discipline for advancing decision-making, by explicitly understanding and engineering how decisions are made and how outcomes are evaluated, managed, and improved via feedback.[10] It is considered an engineering discipline that draws on theory from multiple fields—from decision theory, economics, and managerial science to computer science and its AI applications.

In the future, organizations will seek to advance their decision intelligence capabilities to gain competitive advantage.

Data Democratization

Business decisions are made not only by a handful of executives. Every day, businesspeople at all levels, from floor supervisors to vice-presidents of sales, make big and small decisions that affect the rest of their organization. A shift toward analytics-based decisions requires decision-makers at all levels to have access to data and analytics.

Data democratization is the process of empowering all employees to use data to support their daily activities and decision-making. It requires employees to have easy access to data along with a good understanding of what the data means, and the ability to extract useful and timely analytics insights independently, without asking IT professionals, submitting requests, or going through approval bureaucracy and wait times.

To achieve this lofty goal, companies must have robust data architecture, functional data governance, effective access management, and privacy protection, and they must provide education, training, and tools. To empower employees in such a way, we need to promote analytics styles that enable flexibility and experimentation, such as self-service analytics and search-driven analytics.

While these examples give us a glimpse of the amazing capabilities of technology, data science, and AI, we must remember that powerful technologies come with greater responsibilities. Ethical considerations regarding the applications of AI and privacy protection must remain paramount in our minds.

12.4 FUTURE-PROOFING YOUR KNOWLEDGE AND SKILLS

Which skills are likely to become obsolete and replaced by technology and AI solutions, and which will remain in demand? This final section considers the importance of professional skills and considerations for future-proofing your career.

Domain Knowledge

Understanding the business aspects of and having expert knowledge in a specific field or industry will be required for accurate problem formulation, model training, and optimization of the decision-making process. Many analytics professionals of the future will also be experts in specific business domains.

Computer Science and Software Engineering

The development of advanced algorithms may enable the automation of routine coding, yet more advanced software engineering knowledge will be required for designing complex hardware and software.

Data Structures

Understanding how to model and organize data will remain foundational knowledge for data science. This includes knowledge of different types of data, databases, SQL and NoSQL storage solutions, and their development and optimization.

Math and Statistics

A strong grasp of these fields will continue to be the foundation of algorithmic design and data science.

Information Security

With the development of more and more sophisticated technologies and algorithms, and with continued research in quantum computing, the role of cybersecurity will only grow more vital. Beyond protection of data itself, the new task of protecting AI algorithms from being compromised by malicious attacks will demand that this field keeps pace with the latest technology developments.

Legal and Ethical Frameworks

All professionals working in data science and AI fields will be required to be conversational in the legal and regulatory aspects of using data and AI.

Decision Theory

If the ultimate goal of using analytics in an enterprise is to make better decisions, the study of decision theory provides a foundation for approaching and optimizing decision-making.

Business Analysis

The ability to analyze enterprise processes and operations, capture and clarify objectives and business requirements, and model the interactions between users and solutions will continue to be an integral part of the process of solution development.

Accessibility and User Experience Research

AI augmentation and human-machine collaboration, which centre on enabling effective interactions and "understanding" between humans and machines, both require a great deal of expertise. Humans have a wide spectrum of capabilities, so these interactions must always take into consideration an equally wide range of accessibility requirements.

Psychology and Neuroscience

The future of AI will centre around optimizing human-machine interactions and designing the approaches to the augmentation of human activities with AI while keeping the well-being of humans front and centre. These disciplines provide tools for the research and development of solutions to improve the quality of life of humans everywhere.

Collaboration Skills

Technology might be developing fast, but one area in which AI falls short is people skills. The ability to collaborate, lead, engage, and empathize is a human quality that will always remain in high demand.

Communication, Visualization, Presenting, and Storytelling

The importance of effective communication will never fade. Communication and visualization experts will be especially important when it comes to teaching machines better communication and visualization skills, as well as using creative approaches to tell stories. True creativity, after all, is a uniquely human trait.

12.5 CHAPTER SUMMARY

Key Points to Remember

- Jobs related to working with data and analytics represent a job family with different job titles, accountabilities, and skill requirements.
- As the variety of job titles increases, the best way to understand a particular job's requirements is to read the job description and ask questions during the interview.
- There are many types of jobs with *analyst* in the title, some of them related to the field or data analysis and business analytics, and some that can be quite removed. Read the job description.
- Skills required for different jobs in the same job family inevitably overlap. Investing in learning new skills, even when not mandatory for your job, is one of the best strategies for career advancement.
- The development of machine learning and AI technologies will not only change existing jobs but bring about new types of jobs with new expectations and responsibilities.

Key Terms

Analyst (data analyst): a professional specializing in extracting insights from data.

Architect (data architect): a professional specializing in planning and designing data structures, systems, and integrations between them.

Data scientist: a professional specializing in using advanced statistics and algorithms to solve business problems by gaining insights from big data.

Engineer (computer engineer, programmer, developer): a professional specializing in building, testing, implementing, and maintaining hardware and software systems.

Questions for Critical Thought

1. What type of job in analytics are you most interested in? Why?
2. Have you ever had work responsibilities similar to the responsibilities of an analyst? What did you analyze? What methods have you used for analysis?
3. If you had a data analyst job now, what new methods learned from this book would you apply?
4. What skills will you prioritize when considering the next steps in your career?
5. Are you interested in any jobs listed in the "Career Pathways and Jobs of the Future" section (12.2)? What can you do today to develop your career in that direction?

Test Your Knowledge

1. A professional spends a lot of time discussing business challenges with operations managers and extracting and aggregating data from different systems to help them get more data for investigating operational issues.
   What is this professional's most likely job type?
   a. Analyst
   b. Architect
   c. Engineer
   d. Data scientist

2. A professional spends a lot of time tuning and maintaining machine learning algorithms embedded into the service workflow. When the model shows an increasing drift, this professional will change the model's parameters or work on retraining the model.
   What is this professional's most likely job type?
   a. Analyst
   b. Architect
   c. Engineer
   d. Data scientist

3. A professional uses a big data query language and advanced visualization tools to explore data stored in the data lake, searching for interesting patterns that can help solve an emerging business challenge. Finding a new pattern may lead to developing a new customer segmentation model.

   What is this professional's most likely job type?

   a. Analyst

   b. Architect

   c. Engineer

   d. Data scientist

4. A professional recommends the best approach to storing and managing streaming IoT data from a recently introduced new product line. They will oversee the changes to the data pipeline design and ensure that the data is stored in accordance with the established standards and data model.

   What is this professional's most likely job type?

   a. Analyst

   b. Architect

   c. Engineer

   d. Data scientist

5. What skills are essential for a data analyst working as part of a marketing team and responsible for collecting and manipulating marketing statistics and customer survey data?

   a. Database design and maintenance

   b. Machine learning algorithm design

   c. Data cleaning and report generation

   d. Visualization and storytelling

   e. a and b

   f. c and d

Recommended Readings

British Computer Society (BCS). (2024, January 23). *AI and the Future of Work*. Retrieved March 2, 2024, from www.bcs.org/articles-opinion-and-research/ai-and-the-future-of-work/.

Coulton, C. J., Goerge, R., Putnam-Hornstein, E., & de Haan, B. (2015). *Harnessing Big Data for Social Good: A Grand Challenge for Social Work* (Grand Challenges for Social Work Initiative Working Paper No. 11). American Academy of Social Work and Social Welfare. Retrieved June 25, 2024, from grandchallengesforsocialwork.org/wp-content/uploads/2015/12/WP11-with -cover.pdf.

Robinson, E., & Nolis, J. (2020). *Build a Career in Data Science*. Manning.

Rotman, D. (2024, January 27). *People Are Worried That AI Will Take Everyone's Jobs. We've Been Here Before.* MIT Technology Review. Retrieved March 2, 2024, from www.technologyreview .com/2024/01/27/1087041/technological-unemployment-elon-musk-jobs-ai/.

United Nations. (n.d.). *Big Data for Sustainable Development.* Retrieved June 24, 2024, from www.un .org/en/global-issues/big-data-for-sustainable-development.

United Nations Principles for Responsible Investment (UN PRI). (n.d.). *What Are the Principles for Responsible Investment?* Retrieved June 24, 2024, from www.unpri.org/about-us/ what-are-the-principles-for-responsible-investment.

Notes

1. Ramaswamy, S. (2015, April). *How Micro-Moments Are Changing the Rules.* Think with Google. Retrieved June 23, 2024, from www.thinkwithgoogle.com/marketing-strategies/app-and-mobile/ how-micromoments-are-changing-rules/.

2. Gartner. (n.d.). *Continuous Intelligence.* Retrieved June 24, 2024, from www.gartner.com/en/ information-technology/glossary/continuous-intelligence.

3. Vailshery, L. S. (2024, June 4). *Internet of Things (IoT)—Statistics & Facts.* Statista. Retrieved June 24, 2022, from www.statista.com/statistics/1183457/iot-connected-devices-worldwide/.

4. Alharbi, W. S., & Rashid, M. (2022). A Review of Deep Learning Applications in Human Genomics Using Next-Generation Sequencing Data. *Human Genomics, 16,* Article 26. doi .org/10.1186/s40246-022-00396-x.

5. Ramalingam, G. K. (2024, April 4). *AI-Enabled Precision Medicine.* Retrieved June 24, 2024, from ssrn.com/abstract=4783598.

6. National Geographic. (n.d.). *GIS (Geographic Information System).* Retrieved June 25, 2024, from education.nationalgeographic.org/resource/geographic-information-system-gis/.

7. O'brien, S. (2023, August 1). *5 Digital Twin Use Cases.* IEEE Computer Society. Retrieved June 25, 2024, from www.computer.org/publications/tech-news/trends/digital-twin-use-cases.

8. IBM. (n.d.). *What Is a Digital Twin?* Retrieved June 25, 2024, from www.ibm.com/topics/ what-is-a-digital-twin.

9. Chartered Financial Analyst (CFA) Institute. (n.d.). *What Is ESG Investing?* Retrieved June 25, 2024, from www.cfainstitute.org/en/rpc-overview/esg-investing.

10. Gartner. (n.d.). *Decision Intelligence.* Retrieved June 24, 2024, from www.gartner.com/en/ information-technology/glossary/decision-intelligence.

Appendices

Appendix A: Data Storage Units

Table 13.1 Data Storage Units

Unit	Short form	Size	Description and examples
Bit	b	2^0 (1) bit	The smallest data storage unit, represents either 0 or 1 Can store a single Boolean value
Byte	B	2^3 (8) bits	Base unit of data storage measurement Can store a single character E.g., ASCII code for *B* is 01000010
Kilobyte	KB	2^{10} bytes (1,024 bytes)	Used to measure the size of text files or small images E.g., 2 KB: one typewritten page
Megabyte	MB	2^{20} bytes (1,024 kilobytes)	Used to measure the size of digital images or music files E.g., 5 MB: the complete works of Shakespeare or a high-resolution photo[1]
Gigabyte	GB	2^{30} bytes (1,024 megabytes)	Used to measure the size of video files of photo collections E.g., 1 GB: a symphony in high-fidelity sound,[1] 3 hours of high-definition video, or 250 digital photos[2]
Terabyte	TB	2^{40} bytes (1,024 gigabytes)	Used to measure the size of large databases E.g., 1 TB: 50,000 trees made into paper and printed[1] or 500 hours of high-definition video[2]
Petabyte	PB	2^{50} bytes (1,024 terabytes)	Used to measure the size of large data centres E.g., 1 PT: 500 billion pages of standard printed text[1] or 13 years of high-definition video[2] E.g., 200 PT: all printed materials ever[1]
Exabyte	EB	2^{60} bytes (1,024 petabytes)	Used to measure the size of massive data storage E.g., 1 EB: 3 billion high-resolution photos[2] E.g., 5 EB: all words ever spoken by human beings[1]
Zettabyte	ZB	2^{70} bytes (1,024 exabytes)	Used to measure global internet traffic E.g., 1 ZB: estimated volume of data generated by the internet in one year[2] E.g., 175 ZB: the expected volume of data created globally by 2025[3]

Table 13.1 Data Storage Units (*continued*)

Unit	Short form	Size	Description and examples
Yottabyte	YB	2^{80} bytes (1,024 zettabytes)	Exceeds the entire internet's data by several orders of magnitude[2] The volume of data that would fit on DVDs stacked all the way from Earth to Mars It is suggested that by the 2030s, the world may generate about one yottabyte of data per year[4]
Ronnabyte	RB	2^{90} bytes (1,024 yottabytes)	The second largest data storage unit, introduced in November 2022[5]
Quettabyte	QB	2^{100} bytes (1,024 ronnabytes)	The largest data storage unit, introduced in November 2022[5]

Notes

1. Puiu, T. (2023, July 28). *How Big Is a Petabyte, Exabyte or Yottabyte? Let's Look at the Largest Units of Data Storage*. ZME Science. Retrieved February 15, 2024, from www.zmescience.com/feature-post/technology-articles/computer-science/how-big-data-can-get/.

2. Farrell, B. (2024, March 16). *Data Storage Units of Measurement Table*. Data Driven Daily. Retrieved June 8, 2024, from datadrivendaily.com/data-storage-units-of-measurement-table/.

3. Reinsel, D., Gantz, J., & Rydning, J. (2018, November). *The Digitization of the World from Edge to Core*. International Data Corporation (IDC). Retrieved February 17, 2024, from www.seagate.com/files/www-content/our-story/trends/files/idc-seagate-dataage-whitepaper.pdf.

4. Gibney, E., & Nature Magazine. (2022, November 23). *How Many Yottabytes in a Quettabyte? Extreme Numbers Get New Names*. Scientific American. Retrieved June 8, 2024, from www.scientificamerican.com/article/how-many-yottabytes-in-a-quettabyte-extreme-numbers-get-new-names/.

5. The General Conference on Weights and Measures (CGPM). (2022, November 18). *On the Extension of the Range of SI Prefixes*. Resolution 3 of the 27th CGPM. Retrieved June 8, 2024, from www.bipm.org/en/cgpm-2022/resolution-3.

Appendix B: Technology and Tools Overview

Technology, tools, and software solutions evolve faster than book editions. This appendix provides a snapshot of some widely used technologies and products available on the market at the time of writing this book.

Some are open-source while others are licensed by the big technology companies. Some are specialized, intended to support specific tasks of the analytics life cycle such as visualization. Others are end-to-end platforms able to support the full cycle from data acquisition and data pipeline design to data warehousing and advanced analytics tools.

While Table 13.2 organizes them by categories, there are inevitable overlaps as many products are marketed as comprehensive solutions and continue to add features in a fierce battle for market domination. The largest market players buy out startups and rebrand their products. Anyone tasked with researching the functionality and advantages of various tools and technologies must do their research using the latest updates and product descriptions provided by the companies that developed the products.

The examples of software, products, and tools are sorted alphabetically, and no ranking or recommendation is implied.

Table 13.2 Analytics Products and Tools

Function	Products and tools
Small data manipulation and analysis	Airtable, Google Sheets, Microsoft Excel
Structured data manipulation and querying	SQL
Database management and data warehousing	IBM Db2, Microsoft SQL server, MySQL, Oracle
Cloud-based data warehousing	Amazon Redshift, Google BigQuery, Microsoft Azure, Snowflake, Teradata
Programming languages and environments	Julia, Jupyter Notebooks, Matlab, Python, R
Analytics platforms supporting data preparation, business intelligence (BI), statistical analysis, and advanced analytics	Azure Synapse Analytics, ClicData, Cognos, GoodData, MicroStrategy, Power BI, Qlik, SAS, Sisense, SPSS, Thoughtspot, TIBCO Spotfire
Visualization	Chartblocks, D3.js, Datawrapper, Fusioncharts, Google Charts, Grafana, Infogram, Klipfolio, Looker, Plotly, Qlik Sense, Tableau, Zoho Analytics
Data mining, machine learning	Anaconda, Apache Spark, Azure Databricks, Big ML, Cloudera, Dataiku, Datarobot, H20.ai, IBM Watson, Keras, KNIME, PyTorch, RapidMiner, TensorFlow, Weka

Table 13.2 Analytics Products and Tools (*continued*)

Function	Products and tools
Big data storage, management, and processing	Amazon S3, Apache Cassandra, Apache Hadoop & MapReduce, Cloudera, Google Cloud Storage, Microsoft Azure data lake, MongoDB
Big data query languages	Cloudera Impala, CQL (Cassandra Query Language), GoogleSQL, HiveQL (Hive Query Language), Presto, SparkSQL
Data integration, transformation, and data pipelines	Alteryx, Apache Kafka, Domo, Fivetran, Google Cloud Dataflow, Informatica, Microsoft Azure Data Factory, Mulesoft, Talend, TIBCO
Specialized data analytics	Google Analytics (web analytics), Hubspot (marketing analytics), Kinaxis RapidResponse (supply chain analytics), Sprout Social (social media sentiment)
Enterprise performance management and analytics	Oracle Analytics Cloud, Salesforce Einstein Analytics, SAP Analytics Cloud

Appendix C: PIPEDA Fair Information Principles[1]

The 10 fair information principles of the Personal Information Protection and Electronic Documents Act (PIPEDA) form the ground rules for the collection, use, and disclosure of personal information, as well as for providing access to personal information. They give individuals control over how their personal information is handled in the private sector.

Principle 1: Accountability

An organization is responsible for personal information under its control. It must appoint someone to be accountable for its compliance with these fair information principles.

Principle 2: Identifying Purposes

The purposes for which the personal information is being collected must be identified by the organization before or at the time of collection.

Principle 3: Consent

The knowledge and consent of the individual are required for the collection, use, or disclosure of personal information, except where inappropriate.

Principle 4: Limiting Collection

The collection of personal information must be limited to that which is needed for the purposes identified by the organization. Information must be collected by fair and lawful means.

Principle 5: Limiting Use, Disclosure, and Retention

Unless the individual consents otherwise or it is required by law, personal information can only be used or disclosed for the purposes for which it was collected. Personal information must only be kept as long as required to serve those purposes.

Principle 6: Accuracy

Personal information must be as accurate, complete, and up to date as possible in order to properly satisfy the purposes for which it is to be used.

Principle 7: Safeguards

Personal information must be protected by appropriate security relative to the sensitivity of the information.

Principle 8: Openness

An organization must make detailed information about its policies and practices relating to the management of personal information publicly and readily available.

Principle 9: Individual Access

Upon request, an individual must be informed of the existence, use, and disclosure of their personal information and be given access to that information. An individual shall be able to challenge the accuracy and completeness of the information and have it amended as appropriate.

Principle 10: Challenging Compliance

An individual shall be able to challenge an organization's compliance with the above principles. Their challenge should be addressed to the person accountable for the organization's compliance with PIPEDA, usually their Chief Privacy Officer.

Note

1. Office of the Privacy Commissioner of Canada. (2019, May). *PIPEDA Fair Information Principles.* Retrieved February 16, 2024, from www.priv.gc.ca/en/privacy-topics/privacy-laws-in-canada/ the-personal-information-protection-and-electronic-documents-act-pipeda/p_principle/.

Appendix D: Test Questions Answer Key

Chapter 1: 1-c, 2-d, 3-a, 4-d, 5-b
Chapter 2: 1-a, 2-b, 3-c, 4-a, 5-d
Chapter 3: 1-c, 2-d, 3-b, 4-b, 5-c
Chapter 4: 1-a, 2-d, 3-c, 4-b, 5-a
Chapter 5: 1-b, 2-d, 3-c, 4-b, 5-a
Chapter 6: 1-c, 2-d, 3-a, 4-b, 5-c
Chapter 7: 1-d, 2-b, 3-a, 4-c, 5-b
Chapter 8: 1-d, 2-a, 3-c, 2-a, 5-b
Chapter 9: 1-a, 2-d, 3-b, 4-a, 5-c
Chapter 10: 1-b, 2-d, 3-c, 4-e, 5-c
Chapter 11: 1-a, 2-c, 3-b, 4-d, 5-c
Chapter 12: 1-a, 2-c, 3-d, 4-b, 5-f

Index